THE
HUDSON VALLEY
BOOK

A Complete Guide

View of the Hudson River from Montgomery Place, Annandale-on-Hudson.

THE
HUDSON VALLEY
BOOK

A Complete Guide

Evelyn Kanter

Berkshire House Publishers
Lee, Massachusetts

On the cover and frontispiece:
Front Cover: *Kykuit, Tarrytown, New York. Built by John D. Rockefeller, Sr., in the 1880s,*
  the mansion has been a National Historic Landmark since 1976. Photo by Mick Hales,
  courtesy Historic Hudson Valley
Frontispiece: *View of the Hudson River from Montgomery Place.* Photo © Tania Barricklo.
Back cover: Photo of Evelyn Kanter by Yorghos Kontaxis

ISBN: 1-58157-065-1
ISSN: 1056-7968 (series)

Editor: Constance Lee Oxley. Managing Editor: Philip Rich. Design and page layout:
Dianne Pinkowitz. Cover design: Jane McWhorter. Maps: Maps.com, Goleta California.

Berkshire House books are available at substantial discounts for bulk purchases by
corporations and other organizations for promotions and premiums. Special
personalized editions can also be produced in large quantities. For more information,
contact:

Berkshire House Publishers
480 Pleasant St., Lee, MA 01238
800-321-8526
www.berkshirehouse.com
info@berkshirehouse.com

Manufactured in the United States of America
First printing 2003
10 9 8 7 6 5 4 3 2 1

*No complimentary meals or lodgings were accepted by the author and reviewers in
gathering information for this work.*

Berkshire House Publishers'
Great Destinations™ travel guidebook series

Recommended by NATIONAL GEOGRAPHIC TRAVELER and TRAVEL &
LEISURE magazines.

. . . a crisp and critical approach, for travelers who want to live like locals.

— USA TODAY

Great Destinations™ guidebooks are known for their comprehensive, critical coverage of regions of extraordinary cultural interest and natural beauty. The authors
in this series are professional travel writers who have lived for many years in the
regions they describe. Each title in this series is continuously updated with each
printing, in order to insure accurate and timely information. All of the books contain over 100 photographs and maps.

**Neither the publisher, the authors, the reviewers, nor other contributors accept
complimentary lodgings, meals, or any other consideration (such as advertising)
while gathering information for any book in this series.**

Current titles available:
The Adirondack Book
The Berkshire Book
The Charleston, Savannah & Coastal Islands Book
The Chesapeake Bay Book
The Coast of Maine Book
The Finger Lakes Book
The Hamptons Book
The Hudson Valley Book
The Monterey Bay, Big Sur & Gold Coast Wine Country Book
The Nantucket Book
The Napa & Sonoma Book
The Santa Fe & Taos Book
The Sarasota, Sanibel Island & Naples Book
The Shenandoah Valley Book (autumn 2003)
The Texas Hill Country Book
Touring East Coast Wine Country

If you are traveling to, moving to, residing in, or just interested in any (or all!) of
these enchanting regions, a **Great Destinations'** guidebook is a superior companion. Honest and painstakingly critical, full of information only a local can provide,
Great Destinations' guidebooks give you all the practical knowledge you need to
enjoy the best of each region. Why not own them all?

Acknowledgments

This book would not have been possible without the support of a long list of people. It was heartwarming and inspiring to soak up the interest and enthusiasm so many expressed along the research and writing trail, and that includes longtime friends, more recent acquaintances, and all the new ones made along the way.

I was delighted by the sense of cooperation and community encountered everywhere, such as when a restaurant owner or B&B owner urged me to visit and include a nearby competitor — there's a long tradition of hospitality and neighborliness in the Hudson Valley.

Many local visitors boards, tourist bureaus, and environmental groups supplied invaluable assistance, above all Nancy Arena of Dutchess County, where so many fabulous historic mansions and top restaurants are located.

Since my bathroom scale would have exploded if I had eaten multi-course meals in each of the restaurants reviewed in these pages, my waistline and I owe a debt of gratitude to the "foodies" who helped me wine and dine the eight Hudson Valley counties. Thanks to Linda and Steve Cohen, wine expert Steve Searle, Peter Marotta, Adrienne and Dan Johnston, Jose Sotolongo and Donald Schwab, and particularly to innkeepers Addison Berkey and wife Lauren of the spectacular Bullis Hall and Cynthia Korn and Jack Trowell of the equally fabulous Cromwell Manor. A special thanks to Hugh and Linda Curry of the magical Tumblin' Falls House and Beth Pagano of The Grand Dutchess and the Red Hook Inn for their kindness.

I live in Manhattan, where it is madness to own a car. So, my gratitude goes to Gina Proia and Mike Albano of General Motors and to the Ford Motor Company, for loaning the vehicles that allowed me to drive and visit the wondrous spots in these pages, heightened by the joy of motoring on so many scenic stretches of country roads.

A large debt of appreciation also goes to Allison Blake, author of *The Chesapeake Bay Book*, also published by Berkshire House, for her assistance and insight in the preparation of several chapters.

Thanks to all the wonderful staff at Berkshire House Publishers, especially editor Constance L. Oxley and editorial director Philip Rich. Their bottomless reservoir of invaluable advice and enthusiasm was, always, a beacon of light and a calming compass in a sometimes wind-blown schedule.

Last, but most certainly not least, I want to acknowledge and thank my children, Michelle and Gerry, for their love, their laughter, and their lifelong support of, and patience with, mom's career.

Contents

CHAPTER ONE
The River That Flows Both Ways
HISTORY
1

CHAPTER TWO
Ways & Means
TRANSPORTATION
21

CHAPTER THREE
To Sleep, Perchance to Dream
LODGING
30

CHAPTER FOUR
Eat, Drink & Be Merry
RESTAURANTS & FOOD PURVEYORS
64

CHAPTER FIVE
So Much to See & Do
ARTS & PLEASURES
131

CHAPTER SIX
Mind Your Manors
MANSIONS OF THE HUDSON VALLEY
179

CHAPTER SEVEN
For The Fun of It
RECREATION
207

CHAPTER EIGHT
Antiques & Boutiques
SHOPPING
242

CHAPTER NINE
Gateway to the Hudson Valley
NEW YORK CITY
266

CHAPTER TEN
Facts & Figures
INFORMATION
276

Introduction

First with my parents, then with my children, I have hiked, skied, picnicked, rafted, canoed, swam, fished, picked apples and pumpkins, dined, and otherwise enjoyed the Hudson Valley all my life. Writing this book opened a new chapter of discovery and a new appreciation for the incredible range of delights and experiences in this glorious part of the world and also allowed me to meet wonderful new people, many of whom were transplants from New York City — weekend visitors who turned their visits into living here full-time.

I'm a lifelong Manhattanite, and most of the bookmarks of my life are linked to the Hudson Valley. I grew up on Thayer Street, named for "the father of West Point," on the northern tip of the island, a short walk from where Peter Minuit reportedly purchased it for that legendary $24 in trinkets. The tulip tree donated by the citizens of Holland, which marked the supposed spot, has died since my childhood, but the plaque is still there. In between Thayer Street and Inwood Hill Park is Dyckman House, the last surviving Dutch farmhouse in Manhattan, which was captured by the British during the Revolutionary War. I occasionally did my homework in the garden. The Hudson River is one block from my apartment, visible through the trees of Riverside Park.

My high school, named for George Washington, stands incongruously atop Fort George Hill, named for the British king on the opposing side of that war for independence. My first job after college was at Rockefeller Center, built by the family instrumental in saving so many of the historic sites of the Hudson Valley, including Boscobel, which was built by relatives of "my" Dyckman family.

From the first pale buds of spring through the deep green of summer to the intense red-gold palette of autumn and the snowy wonderland of winter, the Hudson Valley is a wonderful carousel of sights, sounds, and people. No wonder its landscapes and residents have inspired so many artists and writers. Hudson Valley native Washington Irving wrote, "I thank God I was born on the banks of the Hudson River, and I fancy I can trace much of what is good and pleasant in my own heterogeneous compound to my early companionship with this glorious river."

I couldn't agree more.

Evelyn Kanter
New York, New York

THE WAY THIS BOOK WORKS

ORGANIZATION

This book covers the eight counties of the Hudson Valley and focuses on the region's small towns and rural villages. Each chapter is arranged geographically by county, south to north: Westchester, Putnam, Dutchess, and Columbia counties on the east side of the Hudson River and Rockland, Orange, Ulster, and Greene counties on the west side.

Within each county, however, cities and towns are listed alphabetically rather than geographically. Chapter Eight, *Shopping,* is additionally arranged by types of shops to help you quickly locate all the shops in a particular location. In Chapter Three, *Lodging,* and Chapter Four, *Restaurants & Food Purveyors,* where a well-regarded restaurant also offers lodging, or the other way around, that also is mentioned. The hope is that this system will make it easy for travelers to cross-reference their choices.

Every effort was made to ensure that information in these pages is correct and current, but since prices, policies, names, and menus can change overnight, it is always best to call ahead. That is especially true if you have special needs or requests, whether that is handicap access or questions about smoking or children.

PRICES

Because prices change by season, by weekend, or by weekday for lodging and dining, we provide a range of prices, rather than specific prices; these are listed at the beginning of the appropriate chapter.

Note that these pages spotlight the individually owned and unique lodging and restaurant choices in the Hudson Valley, rather than on the well-known and ubiquitous chains. Simply, much of the charm of the Hudson Valley is knowing that the owner is at the front door or in the kitchen, ensuring that you are a welcomed, well-fed, and well-rested guest.

For lodging, the high-end of the price range is high-season (generally summer, fall foliage, and festivals and fairs) for double occupancy — two-night minimums are the norm, especially on weekends, plus often there are cancellation penalties. Low-season and weekdays can be as much, or as little, as half. Do take into account that rates at B&Bs may include a multicourse gourmet breakfast, effectively lowering the price of the accommodation.

For dining, prices include the cost of a starter (appetizer, soup, or salad), entrée, and dessert, but not drinks, tax, or tip. Restaurants with prix fixe menus are noted, as are casual diners and breakfast shops.

Price Codes

	Lodging	Dining
Inexpensive	Up to $65	Up to $15
Moderate	$65–$100	$15–$25
Expensive	$100–$175	$25–$50
Very Expensive	$175 and up	$50 and up

Credit Cards

The credit cards accepted at lodging and dining establishments are coded as follows:

American Express – AE   Diner's Club – DC
Carte Blanche – CB   MasterCard – MC
Discover – D   Visa – V

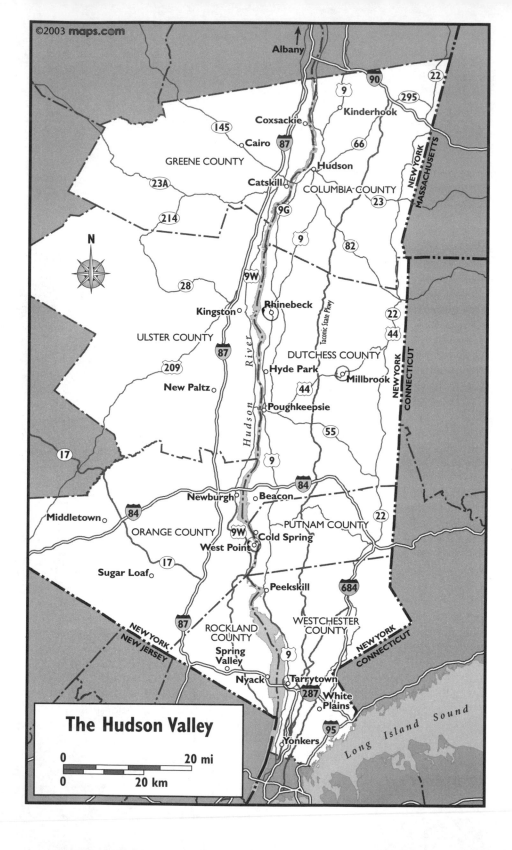

The Hudson Valley

©2003 maps.com

Albany

N

Hudson River

Taconic State Pkwy

GREENE COUNTY
COLUMBIA COUNTY
ULSTER COUNTY
DUTCHESS COUNTY
ORANGE COUNTY
PUTNAM COUNTY
ROCKLAND COUNTY
WESTCHESTER COUNTY

NEW YORK / MASSACHUSETTS
NEW YORK / CONNECTICUT
NEW YORK / NEW JERSEY

Long Island Sound

Coxsackie
Cairo
Kinderhook
Hudson
Catskill
Kingston
Rhinebeck
Hyde Park
Millbrook
New Paltz
Poughkeepsie
Newburgh
Beacon
Middletown
West Point
Cold Spring
Sugar Loaf
Peekskill
Spring Valley
Nyack
Tarrytown
White Plains
Yonkers

145
87
23A
214
28
9W
87
209
9G
9
82
66
90
9
22
295
23
22
44
44
55
9
84
17
84
17
87
9
287
95
684
22
9W

0   20 mi
0   20 km

CHAPTER ONE
The River That Flows Both Ways
HISTORY

Evelyn Kanter

The thick forests and rolling hills border the Hudson Highlands.

Drop for drop and mile for mile, the Hudson River has been home to more American history than any other stretch of river in the nation. From the beginning, the richness and diversity of the Hudson Valley's natural resources lured hard-working farmers, who may not have had time to savor the beauteous grandeur of the landscape, and enterprising entrepreneurs, who built hilltop mansions to capture the scenery into their drawing rooms.

Yes, Washington slept here and often, since this was a strategic focal point of the fight for freedom. The Hudson River was America's first highway, a water route to the interior that helped grow this great land. The Hudson Valley has a symbiotic relationship with the city at its mouth, New York City.

NATURAL HISTORY

The Hudson River begins at Lake Tear of the Clouds high in the Adirondack Mountains, on the southwest side of Mount Marcy, New York State's highest peak. A collection of snowmelt rivulets grows, deepens, and widens as it flows 315 miles to the Atlantic Ocean. Just north of Albany, New York, the Hudson is joined by the Mohawk River. The water then travels past the undulating forested foothills of the Taconic and Berkshire Mountains to the east and the Catskill and Shawangunk Mountains and the dramatic cliffs of the Palisades to the west until it reaches the man-made concrete canyons of New York City and, finally, the Atlantic Ocean.

Actually, the Hudson River isn't a river at all, but an estuary, an arm of the sea as far north as Troy, New York, and governed by the moon and tides, in which salty seawater mixes with freshwater. The tidal flow, which can be four feet in spots, prompted the local Algonquin to call it *muhheakantuk* or "river that flows both ways." The combination of salinity and tidal action fooled Henry Hudson into thinking he had found the Northwest Passage, until he sailed another 150 miles upriver from The Narrows, the entrance to New York City, and discovered the truth.

Estuaries are among the most productive ecosystems on the planet, a food chain as fertile as a tropical rain forest, and the Hudson River is rich with wetlands and tidal flats throughout its length in the many bays and coves hugging its shores. It's not unusual to see a four-foot-tall great blue heron or snowy white egret standing motionless in ankle-deep water, within sight of a river-spanning bridge, waiting for a tasty meal to swim past.

Drop by Drop

- The Hudson River and its tributaries are the watershed for more than 13,000 square miles, mostly in eastern and northern New York State, but also reaching into Vermont, Massachusetts, Connecticut, and New Jersey.
- The widest spot on the river is at Haverstraw Bay, where the Hudson River is five miles wide. The deepest spot (near West Point), measured in a 1934 survey, was 216 feet.
- The average high tide on the river is three feet higher than the average low tide.
- Starting at Troy, New York, it takes approximately 126 days for a drop of freshwater to reach the Atlantic Ocean.

The Hudson Valley was formed around 70 million years ago. There was a gradual uplift of the surface, and the ancestral river eroded the sediment, exposing the gneiss and granite core, eventually forming the Catskill and Berkshire Mountains, which border the Hudson River to the west and east. Around Bear Mountain, where the river narrows, the erosion created a deep gorge that is really a fjord.

Further south are the Palisades. This sheer rock cliff, ranging in height from 350 feet to 550 feet, is an escarpment of basalt that escaped out of the earth's crust in the Triassic period. It apparently got its name from its resemblance to a stockade or fortress wall of saplings lashed together, called a palisade.

During the last Ice Age, the Hudson Valley was covered by as much as 3,000 feet of ice. As the glaciers melted, some 18,000 years ago, the meltwater carried additional sediment and rock downriver, carving the shoreline yet deeper and leaving sediment deposits in deltalike areas of the shore, such as Croton Point, which juts into the river. In other parts of the river, shallow shoals were created, such as the extensive "meadows" around the Esopus Lighthouse.

SOCIAL HISTORY

INDIGENOUS PEOPLES

There is evidence of a Paleolithic culture as far back as 10,000 B.C. Archaeologists have found projectile points in Orange County in the same general area that mastodon skeletons have been found. Heaps of oyster shells, dating to 6,000 B.C.,have been found at Haverstraw Bay and at Croton Point.

The Iroquois had colonized the St. Lawrence Valley as far back as 2,000 B.C., gradually moving south into the upper Hudson Valley, where they began supplementing hunting and gathering with the cultivation of maize. They were fierce warriors, and internecine squabbling in the 1500s prompted them to form a confederacy of five tribes: the Seneca, Cayuga, Onondaga, Oneida, Tuscarora, and Mohawk. The tribal leader who persuaded the Iroqouis to give up their blood feuds and unite for strength and self-protection was a warrior named Hiawatha.

The Iroquois League had the political clout to negotiate with the Dutch, and they fared well in the fur trade. They allied with the British against the French during the French and Indian War, helping England gain control of Canada, and stuck with the British again in 1776. Unfortunately for the Iroquois, the British lost, and at the end of the Revolutionary War, the Native Americans were forced onto isolated reservations near the border; others fled into Canada.

The Algonquin, who dominated the lower Hudson Valley, were less organized and, perhaps, less hardy. Within a century of the white man's arrival, these tribes had been decimated by such European diseases as measles and smallpox. Although the Algonquin tribes are gone, their names survive: Manhattan, Wappinger, Tappan, Munsee, Weehauken, Ramapo, and Sinsink (Ossining and Sing Sing Prison) were the southernmost tribes, and the northernmost were the Mohican.

All the tribes traveled and traded using canoes. The Algonquin are believed to have developed the technique of stretching sheets of birch or elm bark over sapling frames lashed with root fibers; the bark was then made watertight with

pitch or tar. These woodland Indians also are believed to have invented moc-
casins, which cushioned and protected the feet against broken branches and
thorns during hunting forays and wilderness treks.

In addition to harvesting wild berries, fruits, and corn, they cleared the land
and cultivated beans, pumpkins, squash, and tobacco and took advantage of
the plentiful fish, shellfish, and game. Their settlements clustered around tributaries, which ensured easy transportation as well as abundant food, a pattern
the Europeans would duplicate. The Native American population of the
Hudson Valley numbered anywhere from six to 12 thousand and was enjoying
a period of peace and prosperity in the early 1600s. That would change.

THE DUTCH

*The land is the finest for cultivation that I ever in my life set foot upon, and it
also abounds in trees of every description. The natives are a very good people,
for when they saw that I would not remain, they supposed that I was afraid of
their bows, and taking the arrows, they broke them in pieces, and threw them in
the fire.*

Henry Hudson, *Narratives of New Netherland,* 1620s

Even though British-born navigator Henry Hudson is credited with "discov-
ering" in 1609 the river that was named for him, he was not the first
European to sight its lush and scenic shores. That man was Giovanni da
Verrazano, a Florentine who sailed up the Atlantic coast in 1524 for the French,
searching for a water route to China. Although he described it in a journal as
"the River of the Steep Hills," he did not stay long and did not stake a claim to
the land. Neither did Portuguese explorer Estevar Gomes, who sailed into
New York Bay a few years later for the Spanish flag. There also is evidence that
the Dutch prowled the American coast before 1600 without staking a claim.

Hudson had failed twice to find the Northwest Passage for a British company, both times blocked by ice packs around Greenland. His next try was for
the Dutch East India Company, and he took a more southern route in his ship
Half Moon. Although the river that Hudson explored, as far north as present-
day Albany, did not lead to the Pacific and on to India, documentation by
Hudson and members of his 13-man crew gave the Dutch their claim to what
would become history's most important colonial territory.

It took more than 400 years for Verrazano to receive credit for his efforts; the
Verrazano-Narrows Bridge, linking Brooklyn and Staten Island across New
York Bay, opened in 1952. Gomes, however, is a rarely mentioned footnote.

Hudson was fooled by the river's depth, tides, and salinity. It took two
weeks of sailing north to confirm his suspicion that this was an estuary with a
freshwater source rather than the route to the Far East. But, like any experienced traveler who makes a wrong turn and discovers something wonderful,

Hudson and his crew stopped to smell the roses — literally. The journal of one of his seamen, Robert Juet, remarks that they were intoxicated with the river's sweet perfumes of grasses, wildflowers, and trees.

The same year that Hudson arrived by sea, French explorer Samuel Champlain was traveling south from what is now eastern Canada to claim what is now the northern half of New York State, including the huge lake that was named for him, Lake Champlain.

In 1624, the first Dutch settlement was a small outpost, Fort Orange, named for the Dutch royal family, near what is now Albany. Two years later, the Dutch purchased Manhattan Island, from either the Manhattan tribe or the Canarsie tribe — historians disagree — for trinkets worth about $24, then planted their primary (second) colony of New Netherland at its southern tip. They built a series of forts along the river between the two settlements and began issuing land grants to settlers, who were both farmers and merchant traders.

The Dutch, as well as the British who followed them, granted huge tracts of land to a few, creating a small, wealthy, and powerful aristocracy, whose holdings would be tilled by poor tenant farmers and slaves; the first slaves arrived from Africa in 1626, the year that the Dutch bought Manhattan. The Dutch gave a 16-mile tract to any grantee who promised to establish a colony of 50 people.

Guides are in Dutch Colonial dress at Philipsburg Manor.

Evelyn Kanter

One of the earliest Dutch families was the Philipse family, who became one of the biggest landowners in the colonies, accumulating and farming most of what is now Westchester County. They found a ready market for Hudson Valley wheat, corn, beef, and poultry in the West Indies, and their ships returned with sugar and slaves. Another pioneer, Peter Bronck, settled in what is now Coxsackie, just south of Albany, in 1663 to trade beaver pelts with the Indians. His brother, Jonas, settled in New Amsterdam to farm a huge holding south of the Philipse farm. Jonas Bronck's farm is now The Bronx.

The river that Hudson discovered was called the Great River, the North River, the River of the Manhattans, and the River of Mountains. It was most often referred to as the North River, to distinguish it from the South River, now called the Delaware River (between New York, New Jersey, and Pennsylvania). It wasn't until the British began calling it Hudson's River in the 1700s that the name stuck.

From the beginning, the Hudson Valley attracted immigrants escaping religious persecution and entrepreneurs seeking economic opportunities. Two such entrepreneurs were the following: Louis Moses Gomez, a Jewish refugee from the Spanish Inquisition, who established a trading post north of what is now Newburgh where he bought beaver and mink pelts from the Indians to supply fur-hungry Europe; and Patrick McGregorrie from Scotland, who in 1685 opened the first trading post in what is now the Kowawesee Unique Area Riverside Park, just south of Newburgh (there's a historical marker on the spot).

All was not entirely peaceful between the settlers and the indigenous peoples. The village of Kingston was founded in 1652 along the Rondout Creek on land purchased from the Esopus tribe; it is the third oldest settlement in New York State. After some skirmishes, though, the Dutch governor of New Amsterdam, Peter Stuyvesant, ordered the settlement moved up three miles inland from the creek onto a bluff overlooking the Hudson River. A stockade was built around the area for protection. Gates in the stockade allowed farmers access to their fields. The 14-foot-high wooden fence is long gone, but many sturdy Dutch and Colonial houses of the historic Stockade area of Kingston survive.

In 1664, the British sent a fleet to New York Harbor, and Stuyvesant soon surrendered the colony, which was renamed New York, after the Duke of York. Beverwyck became Albany, Rondout became King's Town which became Kingston, but other places kept their Dutch names, including Harlem, Peekskill, Kinderhook, Catskill, Watervliet, Yonkers, and Fishkill.

The next significant wave of settlers were the Huguenot Protestants, fleeing the religious persecution of the Protestant Reformation in Catholic France. A group of 12 families settled on a fertile plain along the Walkill River just north of Kingston in the 1690s, naming their community for their original home area along the Rhine, die Pfalz. Their sturdy stone homes still stand today on Huguenot Street in New Paltz as windows to the past. The families formed a ruling council, called a duzine, a unique form of government at the time, which continued operating until after the Revolutionary War.

They were followed by the Palantine Germans in 1710, fleeing economic depression. The Palatines bought land in Ulster and Dutchess Counties from Robert Livingston, whose politically active family held the second largest private landholding in colonial New York; a Livingston family member is one of the signers of the Declaration of Independence. Other Germans settled in Rhinebeck; other British made homes in Cornwall and Highland Falls.

From the very beginning, the Hudson River and the Hudson Valley became a focus of commerce and trade, anchored by New York City, the foremost seaport of the colonies. The river was a strategic highway, and as upriver towns, such as Peekskill, Newburgh, Poughkeepsie, Kingston, and Albany grew and prospered, they threw off east-west tentacles, spreading the population and commerce inland. Consequently, hanging on to the Hudson was a top priority for British forces when the dispute between patriots and loyalists escalated into the Revolutionary War.

GOING TO WAR

By the mid-1700s, the Hudson Valley was becoming prosperous, thanks to its fertile land and industrious farmers who supplied corn and wheat to much of the northern colonies and also brought in the all-important cash crop, beaver pelts. Migration and trade was facilitated by the highway of trade, the Hudson River, as well as the Mohawk, Esopus, and Wallkill rivers and the broad, riverlike Rondout Creek. There was also a developing road system. The well-worn path from New York City through Westchester into Connecticut became known as the Boston Post Road, and the path heading west to Albany became the Albany Post Road. Another road, known as Kings Highway, ran east-west through Rockland and Orange Counties.

The diversity of the population — Dutch, German, French, British, Irish, and Scottish immigrants, plus slaves from Africa and the Caribbean, whose religions included among many Dutch Reformed, Lutheran, English Congregationalist, Quaker, and Jewish — produced a similar diversity of political views. New York had an Assembly, a popularly elected provincial government, established in 1691 and controlled by the wealthier families. Adolphe Philipse was speaker of the Assembly for much of the early 1700s.

The Hudson Valley was deeply divided between patriots and loyalists. Not surprisingly, the loyalists tended to be the baronial landowners reluctant to change the status quo, and their tenants took the opposing view. But not always. The influence of the loyalist Frederick Philipse (Adolphe's son) was counterbalanced by the patriotic Van Cortlandts. Philipse chose badly — he signed the little-known Declaration of Dependence. After the war, he fled to England to avoid being hanged. New York State confiscated his property, what is now most of Westchester County. Stephanus Van Cortlandt became the first native-born mayor of New York City.

Further upstate, Robert Livingston, a fourth generation Lord of the Manor (some 160,000 acres granted by Queen Anne in 1686), was a member of the committee that helped draft the Declaration of Independence. Because of the family's prominent role in support of independence, the family seat, Clermont, was burned by British troops in 1777. Livingston's wife, Margaret Beekman, whose family was one of the founders of Rhinebeck and had extensive land-holdings in Dutchess and Ulster counties, petitioned New York's governor to help expedite its repair. Livingston also served as the first Minister of Foreign Affairs (Secretary of State), and as Chancellor of the State of New York gave the oath of office to George Washington as the first President of the United States, in New York City.

Robert Livingston is barely known outside the circle of American history buffs, but he played a pivotal role in the development of the United States. Sent to France by President Thomas Jefferson, Livingston helped negotiate the Louisiana Purchase in 1803. Its two million acres doubled the size of the U.S., extending the new republic west from Mississippi to the Rocky Mountains and north to Canada. While in France, Livingston met a young artist and inventor named Robert Fulton and funded — today it would be called venture capital — his efforts to build a steamship. Fulton's first Hudson River steamship became known as the *Clermont*, named for the Livingston family home in Columbia County.

Other members of this prominent social and political clan of overachievers included Philip, a merchant and politician who signed the Declaration of Independence; William, the first governor of New Jersey; Henry, a Revolutionary War officer; and Edward, a congressman, mayor of New York City, and the attorney who drafted the first law code in the U.S.

Another member of the group which drafted the Declaration of Independence was John Jay, president of the Continental Congress, born and raised in Bedford Village. Jay became the first Chief Justice of the Supreme Court and also served as minister to Spain. Jay was one of the staunchest antislavery advocates in pre-Revolutionary New York, but it was not until 1799 that slavery began to be abolished in the state.

Tensions between British soldiers and civilians were mounting, and on July 9, 1776, delegates of the Fourth Provincial Congress, which convened in White Plains, endorsed independence from Britain. As the colonists began to act upon their dissatisfaction with King George III, Kingston became a center of rebel activity. As "government on the run," being chased north from New York City by the British Army, the state government moved to Kingston in February 1777, where they created a formal state constitution. It mandated a strong governor and Senate and may have served as a model for the U.S. Constitution.

While the Supreme Court remained in the courthouse and the Assembly met in a local tavern, the Senate convened its first session in the old stone home of Abraham Van Gaasbeck, which had been built a century earlier in 1676. After meeting in the Senate House for only a month, the newly formed state government hastily fled Kingston ahead of a British force sent north from New York City.

In October, British forces under the command of General William Clinton swarmed through and set fire to every house in town as punishment for Kingston's role in supporting the Revolution. The sturdy stone house of Van Gaasbeck survived, as did the stone Senate House; today, they are both museums. Kingston became the state's first capital. George Clinton, the state's first Governor, later served as Thomas Jefferson's Vice-President; he is buried in the graveyard of the Old Dutch Church in Kingston's historic Stockade district.

One-third of the Revolutionary War battles were in the Hudson Valley, and reenactments are held regularly.

Tania Barricklo

New York became the eleventh of the original 13 states to ratify the new constitution in 1788. Hudson Valley native John Jay and New York City resident Alexander Hamilton were the staunchest supporters for ratification.

REVOLUTIONARY WAR

A bout one-third of all the military engagements of the Revolutionary War took place in New York State, much of them in the Hudson Valley. Simply, the war's outcome hinged on military control of the river. Both sides realized it was a wedge that would effectively split and isolate New England from the rest of the colonies. Thus, the Hudson River became the strategic fault line. Under the British war plan, General William Howe would capture New York City and move north to meet with the army of General John Burgoyne, moving south from the British stronghold in Canada.

General George Washington tried unsuccessfully in 1776 to defend New York City against a superior force of 30,000 British troops and thousands of German mercenaries called Hessians. By 1777, Fort Washington, in upper Manhattan, and Fort Lee, on the New Jersey side (today, the anchor spots of the George Washington Bridge), had fallen to the British, as had Fort Montgomery and Fort Clinton near Bear Mountain.

Only West Point remained impregnable. New York City became British headquarters, with the Royal Navy controlling the harbor and the lower Hudson River and the patriots holding the Hudson Highlands from West Point north. For several years, there was a stalemate.

Washington considered West Point one of the most strategic positions in the Colonies and selected military engineer Thaddeus Kosciuszko to design its fortifications; the Polish officer sympathized with the American cause, joined the Continental Army, was one of the heroes of the Battle of Saratoga, and when he returned home in 1794, he led Polish troops in a similar revolt against Russia. Washington spent much of the war headquartered in the area, finally making West Point his headquarters in 1779.

One of the many weapons on display at Trophy Point at West Point.

Evelyn Kanter

West Point sits high on a rocky outcropping, where the river narrows noticeably, deepens, and curves west — a gorge, really — providing an unobstructed view north and south. The river is further narrowed by an island, Constitution Island, which also was fortified with cannon batteries and redoubts. To prevent British warships from passing, the patriots literally chained the river, building an enormous wrought iron chain across the river in 1778. The 600-yard chain weighed 150 tons; each three-foot oval weighed more than 100 pounds and was the thickness of a man's forearm. The chain, affectionately called "General Washington's Watch Chain," was floated on logs and removed for winter ice for five years. The British would not put their warships at risk and never attacked the West Point chain, so it was never tested. Links of the great chain are on display at West Point at the panoramic Trophy Point.

In May 1779, the British appeared to attack Peekskill. It was a diversionary move, and while the patriot army was occupied, the redcoats captured the peninsula of Stony Point and began to fortify it. That July, General "Mad" Anthony Wayne staged a midnight raid with a group of elite hand-picked Continental troops — 18th-century versions of the Green Berets or Special Forces — recapturing the site. Even though Washington abandoned the location three months later, it was a much-needed morale booster for the beleaguered and underequipped Continental Army. More importantly, though, the battle prevented the British troops from rescuing General Burgoyne, who was stranded in Saratoga. His defeat there was an important turning point in the war, since it ended the plan to attack the patriots from the north, as well as from the south.

A year later, the British devised a simple, bold plan to capture West Point and control of the Hudson River and Valley — they would pay the disgruntled commanding officer, General Benedict Arnold, $50,000 in gold (quite a sizable sum in those days) to betray the fortress some called the "Gibraltar of the Hudson." The plot was foiled when his co-conspirator, Major John André, was captured in Tarrytown, carrying papers detailing the betrayal plans. Arnold fled and escaped, catching up with the British ship H.M.S. *Vulture,* waiting nearby.

In one of history's little ironies, Washington's headquarters were in the DeWint House in Tappan when he gave Benedict Arnold command of West Point, and it was there Washington stayed again during André's trial, where he declined to commute the spy's death sentence. When André was hanged, it balanced the execution in 1776 of Washington's spy, Nathan Hale. Benedict Arnold had become a hero early in the brewing conflict, when he and Ethan Allen led Vermont's Green Mountain Boys to take Fort Ticonderoga, north of Albany, from the British in 1775.

In April 1782, Washington came to Newburgh to what would be his final headquarters, encamping on a slope above the Hudson River at the home of the Hasbrouck family. With the British Army still in New York City, he wanted the Northern Army close by in case hostilities erupted again, so he billeted 6,000–8,000 men, women, and children a few miles away in New Windsor. Washington ordered that their barracks should be built with "regularity, convenience, and even some degree of elegance." More than 700 buildings, including stables, kitchens, blacksmith shops, and a hospital, were constructed in six months. It was to be the last encampment of the Continental Army.

The following spring, Washington ordered a "cessation of hostilities," bringing a close to eight years of fighting. He stayed in Newburgh for six months after the British conceded defeat and evacuated New York City at the end of 1783. While in Newburgh, Washington morphed from general to statesman, rejecting a suggestion of an American monarchy. He recognized the heroism of enlisted men by creating the Badge of Military Merit, the forerunner of the Purple Heart, and advised members of Congress on the future of the new republic.

WEST POINT

The new republic's leaders, led by Washington, Knox, Hamilton, and John Adams realized the growing nation needed to be independent of foreign military help, such as from French generals Rochambeau and Lafayette (French forces led by Rochambeau defeated the British at Yorktown, effectively ending the war) and Poland's General Casimir Pulaski, who organized the first cavalry unit. In 1802, Congress established the United States Military Academy at West Point; the U.S. Naval Academy at Annapolis followed in 1845, and the U.S. Air Force Academy in Colorado Springs was established in 1954.

One of West Point's first graduates, Colonel Sylvanus Thayer, was appointed superintendent in 1817 with the mandate to make West Point "the leading institution of military education" in the world. During the first half of the 19th century, West Point emphasized civil engineering — the Army Corps of Engineers — and was for several decades the best engineering school in the country. West Point graduates were largely responsible for construction of the bulk of the nation's initial railway lines, bridges, harbors, and roads; math and engineering continue to be required and prominent in the curriculum. Thayer is revered as the "Father of West Point" for introducing uniform discipline and educational standards.

The first West Point graduating class in 1802 contained just two cadets. Currently, 1,200 new cadets enter the United States Military Academy at West Point each year. Among its more than 60,000 graduates were two men who became U.S. presidents: Dwight D. Eisenhower and Civil War General Ulysses S. Grant. Also included in the list of illustrious graduates were Confederate President Jefferson Davis, Civil War Generals Robert E. Lee, William Tecumseh Sherman, and Thomas "Stonewall" Jackson; WWI hero John J. Pershing; WWII Generals Douglas MacArthur and George S. Patton; Vietnam's General Alexander Haig, astronaut "Buzz" Aldrin, and Desert Storm commander Norman Schwarzkopf.

When West Point opened in 1802, it had 260 male students; today, there are some 4,400 cadets; women have been admitted since 1976. West Point is not just a military academy, it is the nation's oldest continuously occupied military post. Ever since the Battle of Saratoga in 1777, captured military weapons have been displayed at Trophy Point, north of The Plain (the parade ground). Also displayed here are pieces of the 150-ton wrought iron chain that the patriots stretched across the Hudson River to thwart British warships. Captured flags include the British colors surrendered by General Cornwallis at Yorktown in 1781. West Point has one of the world's largest collections of military artifacts, much of which is displayed at the museum just outside the main entrance, Thayer Gate.

The Cadet Chapel at West Point contains the world's largest church organ.

Just across the river at Cold Spring, another "West Point" also would play a key role in U.S. history. After the War of 1812, President James Madison vowed that the U.S. would end its dependence on foreign cannons and ordered four gun foundries to be built. In 1828, New York City entrepreneur Gouverneur Kemble established the West Point Foundry. The location provided easy access to iron ore, waterpower, a river link to the sea, and protection of the other West Point across the river. Since there were no skilled metalworkers in the U.S. when the foundry opened, they were imported from England and Ireland.

West Point Foundry became the most prominent heavy weapons producer in the U.S. during the Civil War, supplying the famous Parrott gun, developed by Cold Spring resident Robert Parrott. The rifled cannon, which used a bullet-shaped shell rather than a round cannon ball, was able to breach the masonry walls of southern forts and is credited with being one of the most important advantages the North had over the South.

The foundry produced the first public water pipes for New York City, Boston, and Washington, D.C., as well as the armor for the metal ship U.S.S. *Monitor* from the Civil War. Later, it produced plowshares used by farmers throughout the country, metal ships, and railroad locomotives. The foundry closed in 1911.

STEAMSHIPS & RAILROADS

More than anything else, transportation changed the Hudson Valley. Robert Fulton was a struggling young artist, studying first in London, then in Paris. By the 1790s, his interests shifted to science and engineering, and he received a British patent for a device to raise and lower canal boats from one level to another. In Paris, he designed an experimental submarine, *Nautilus*, which caught the eye of Robert Livingston, then negotiating with Napoléon Bonaparte to purchase the Louisiana Territory for the United States.

Livingston convinced Fulton to switch his efforts to a more viable steamboat design and to build it in New York; wealthy Livingston bankrolled the project. Fulton combined a German steam engine with an ocean-going ship design, and the rest, as they say, is history. It was 1807. Fulton's *North River* steamboat, eventually called the *Clermont*, after the Livingston family estate north of Red Hook, chugged along against the current and prevailing winds at five mph, traveling between Brooklyn and Albany in an astounding 32 hours, instead of several days. It was a major milestone in U.S. maritime history, and it did not take long for steam power to replace sails on the Hudson River for transporting both goods and passengers. Fulton did not invent the steamship any more than Hudson discovered the river. Fulton, however, was the first to prove that steamships could be commercially practical.

By the mid-1800s, there were more than 100 elegant steamships that carried as many as one million passengers, including sight-seers on day and weekend excursions from New York City to the fresh air and scenery of the Hudson Valley — a Victorian version of the minivacation. The grandest of these carried 4,000 passengers on three decks, with an orchestra to keep them entertained while they dined in the dining room and strolled the decks. A network of ferries also crisscrossed the river every few miles until they were replaced by bridges and automobiles.

Steamships regularly raced one another to see who was the fastest on the river; they even threw wooden furniture into the fire to produce more steam. In July 1852, a race between the *Armenia* and the *Henry Clay* ended in the *Clay* in flames, with dozens of passengers dead. One of the victims was Andrew Jackson Downing, America's first major landscape designer, who had just been commissioned to landscape the Capitol Mall in Washington, D.C. As editor of *The Horticulturalist*, Downing initiated the campaign to create New York City's Central Park. His designs influenced Frederick Law Olmsted, who eventually landscaped both Central Park and Brooklyn's Prospect Park.

Until Fulton's steamship, Hudson River traffic had been dominated for two centuries by the single-mast Dutch sloop, whose maneuverability and shallow draft allowed it to navigate the river and its tributaries. Dutch dominance of the river was such that Dutch remained the language of sloop captains well into the 1800s.

The next major change was the Delaware & Hudson Canal, one of the great examples of American ingenuity and enterprise. Recognizing the need of a growing New York City for cheap and efficient energy, two Philadelphia coal merchants, the Wurts brothers, conceived a plan to carry coal 108 miles from mines near Carbondale, Pennsylvania, to Kingston, New York, from where it would be barged down the Hudson River to New York City.

They sold stock in the company on Wall Street, raising $1 million — the nation's first million-dollar deal. The circuitous canal route wrapped around, rather than over, mountains and utilized streams and creeks. A young engineer was hired to help with the design and construction — John Roebling. The D&H Canal, which took three years to build and contained 108 locks, operated from 1828 to 1898, when it was replaced by the growing railroad system.

Roebling discovered the hydraulic properties of the limestone in nearby Rosendale, which was then used to create a cement industry in the area. The combination of coal and cement changed Kingston, New York, into a thriving and bustling river port, luring laborers from the overcrowded neighborhoods of New York City into the Hudson Valley. Between 1844 and 1900, the population of Rosendale, however, exploded from a mere 400 to more than 8,000, when there were more than one dozen cement factories in the area. Quarry-men earned about $1.50 per day.

Rosendale cement had the virtue of strengthening underwater, and Roebling later used it to build the Brooklyn Bridge. Rosendale cement also was used to construct the base of the Statue of Liberty, the wings of the U.S. Capitol, the Washington Monument, and many of the skyscrapers sprouting in New York City.

By the 1830s, New York City's rapidly expanding population was faced with a water shortage. The Croton Aqueduct Water System was constructed — of course, with Rosendale cement — to deliver fresh water 40 miles from the Hudson Valley's Croton River to the city. The $12-million project was another marvel of engineering; it also contributed to the health of the city by reducing cholera and other diseases. Parts of the old aqueduct are now used as walking and biking paths.

When the Erie Canal opened in 1825, linking the Hudson River with Lake

Erie and the other Great Lakes, it cemented the strategic value of the Hudson Valley as a valuable corridor for trade and industry. The canal helped open much of the north central U.S. to settlement, and agricultural products and manufactured goods moved in both directions along the Hudson River.

ARTISTS

Nature has spread for us a rich and delightful banquet. Shall we turn from it? We are still in Eden; the wall that shuts us out of the garden is our own ignorance and folly. May we at times turn away from the ordinary pursuits of life to the pure enjoyment of rural nature; which is the soul like a fountain of cool water to the way-torn traveler.

Thomas Cole, 1835

America's vision of itself as a wild, untamed wilderness can be traced to a group of artists and writers who were born, or chose to live, in the Hudson Valley. Their depictions of the landscape, in words and on canvas, helped shape the American attitude toward nature and mold a national identity. Nearly 200 years later, their images still resonate with tranquility, romance, and mystery.

Pride in the natural beauty of the land became a rallying point for Americans after emerging free and independent from the Revolutionary War and then defending that freedom in the War of 1812. The Hudson River became the place where the spiritual merged with the historical.

Washington Irving's stories of headless horsemen galloping through the majestic countryside and farmers hibernating for twenty years in the thickly wooded forest and James Fenimore Cooper's tales of heroic Mohicans romanticized the landscape and its inhabitants. It also inspired artists to come to the Hudson Valley and to see for themselves, turning the local landscape into a national icon and turning the Hudson into a national river.

Lush landscape by Thomas Cole, founder of the Hudson River School of artists.

Courtesy Metropolitan Museum of Art

From 1825 to 1875, these artists became known as the Hudson River School, devoting themselves to vistas instead of portraiture. Their paintings celebrated the beauty, purity, and moral value of nature just when industrialization and urbanization were beginning to transform the wilderness along the river.

The founding father of the Hudson River School was Thomas Cole, an English engraver who made his first visit to the Hudson Valley in 1825. His early paintings and sketches earned him a commission from a wealthy businessman near Albany, and he stayed, settling in Catskill. Not surprisingly, Cole also was an environmentalist; his series, The Course of Empire, traces his fear of the havoc civilization would wreak on the wilderness. Cole also wrote widely on the need to conserve the land for future generations.

The next generation of Hudson River School painters included Frederic Church, Jasper Cropsey, and Alfred Bierstadt (who kept the Hudson River School-style when he painted Rocky Mountain vistas). Church chose the site of his home, Olana, atop a bluff just south of the city of Hudson, for its inspiring, dramatic view downriver.

Hudson River School artists often reconfigured the landscape. Church superimposed a multicolored sunset that he observed from his studio in New York City's Greenwich Village onto a scene of a pristine mountain lake and named it *Twilight in the Wilderness*. Others simply edited out unsightly or unwanted features, such as ships, waterside factories, and people, or they added trees and flowers where there weren't any — or both.

By the 1850s, much of the Hudson Highlands had been stripped bare of trees to stoke the furnaces of the West Point Foundry and Fulton's steamships. The discovery of coal in Pennsylvania saved the Hudson Valley landscape from further logging, as did the advent of the railroads.

GILDED AGE

By the mid 1800s, the Hudson Valley was booming, sending agricultural goods, cement, and forged iron works on the water highway to New York City, which had become the nation's leading trade and industrial center. There was even a flourishing ice industry on the Hudson River, employing as many as 15,000 laborers; immense ice storehouses lined the shores around Newburgh, New York.

The first railway opened in 1831, between Albany and Schenectedy, and by the 1850s, the railroads were taking business away from the steamships, which would have a tremendous economic impact on the river port cities.

By the 1880s, New York City's newly minted millionaires sought to escape the city during the summer and began to build extravagant mansions along the Hudson, most prominently the so-called "robber baron" Jay Gould, J. D. Rockefeller, Sr., and a relative of Cornelius Vanderbilt.

Gould began buying railroad bonds in the 1850s and gained control of the Rensselaer and Saratoga Line. Through stock manipulation, he and partners

"Robber baron" Jay Gould's Gothic Lyndhurst mansion.

Evelyn Kanter

gained control of the Erie Railroad from Cornelius Vanderbilt. In 1869, Gould also schemed to corner the gold market, which resulted in a sudden drop and one of the worst panics in American financial history, but Gould and his partners walked away with about $11 million. Gould subsequently invested in western railroads, and by 1890, he controlled more than 13,000 miles of railroad, including the Missouri Pacific system. He also owned the New York City newspaper *The World* and the Western Union Telegraph Company.

J. D. Rockefeller, Sr., had cornered the oil market and had control of 90 percent of the oil refineries in the U.S. by 1878, creating The Standard Oil Company. At its peak, his personal fortune was $1 billion. He had been introduced to the Hudson Valley by brother William, the ruins of whose Tarrytown estate, Rockwell, is a few miles from J. D.'s Kykuit.

J. D. Rockefeller, Jr., played an important role in the growth of New York City and the Hudson Valley. He was responsible for the construction of an extensive complex of buildings in New York City known as Rockefeller Center and for donating land to the United Nations for the site of its international headquarters.

Rockefeller, Jr., also founded the Historic Hudson Valley organization to restore and preserve the Dutch and Colonial estates along the river, including the Van Cortlandt Manor and the Philipsburg Manor. The organization also operates Kykuit, the Rockefeller estate in Pocantico Hills. Junior's wife, Abby Aldrich, a passionate collector of American folk art, was one of the founders of NYC's Museum of Modern Art, and their son, Nelson, later served as the museum's president. Nelson Rockefeller also was a four-term Governor of New York State from 1958-1974 and served as Vice-President under Gerald Ford. Brother David was Chairman of the Chase Manhattan Bank, and brother Winthrop was Governor of Arkansas.

Cornelius Vanderbilt, who was born in Staten Island, started out with a ferry service between his home island and Manhattan. He fought the navigation monopoly New York State had granted to Fulton and Livingston on the Hudson River and eventually gained control of most of the shipping. He added railroads in the 1860s and consolidated several smaller lines into the New York Central Railroad, which controlled the lucrative route between New York City and Chicago.

Gould and Vanderbilt's rivalry was so bitter that either Vanderbilt banned Gould from traveling to his Hudson Valley estate, Lyndhurst, on Vanderbilt's rail tracks along the Hudson River, or Gould would not condescend to travel on Vanderbilt property. Gould traveled by yacht to Lyndhurst, his ornate, gilded "cottage" in Newport, Rhode Island. The Vanderbilt mansion in Hyde Park, where the Vanderbilts spent summers, was built by Cornelius's grandson, Frederick.

The Gilded Age mansions are interspersed with the old money estates of Hudson Valley pioneers, including Franklin Delano Roosevelt's family.

THE ENVIRONMENT

I cannot but express my sorrow that the beauty of such landscapes are quickly passing away, the ravages of the axe are daily increasing, the most noble scenes are made desolate, and oftentimes scarcely credible in a civilized nation. The wayside is becoming shadeless, and another generation will behold spots, now called improvements, which, as yet, generally destroy Nature's beauty.

Thomas Cole, 1835

When Henry Hudson sailed into uncharted waters in 1609, the water was teeming with dolphin, sturgeon, shad, striped bass, eel, and enormous oysters and mussels, and the banks were equally thick with deer, beaver, otter, deer, mink, and raccoon. The primeval woodlands were dense with oak, maple, ash, beech, tulip, cedar, and evergreens.

Three hundred years later, the river named for him had become dangerously polluted with PCBs and petrochemicals from shoreline factories, pesticides from the valley's farms, solid waste and sludge from shoreline municipalities, and puddles of oil slicks from passing tankers heading to the Erie Canal and from refineries at the mouth of the bay in New Jersey. It wasn't a pretty picture.

Concern for the vast Hudson watershed prompted the state legislature to set aside two vast tracts of land in 1885, creating the Adirondack and Catskill Forest Preserves, which halted logging operations. Fifteen years later, establishment of the joint New York and New Jersey Palisades Interstate Park Commission ended the rock quarrying that had pockmarked the Palisades. The Hudson River Conservation Society, founded in 1936, worked to halt quarrying further north.

The national environmental movement began in the 1960s in the Hudson Valley when a grassroots organization, which later became known as Scenic Hudson, emerged to fight plans to build a giant hydroelectric plant on the river at Storm King Mountain. It was the same time that Rachel Carson's book, *Silent*

Spring, was raising questions about the power of industry over the environment.

Con Edison, which served (and still serves) New York City and Westchester County, proposed cutting away much of the mountain for a pumped storage generating plant, "like a slice removed from a tub of cheese" wrote one local resident. The utility already was under fire for the massive numbers of fish sucked into the cooling tower intakes at the nearby Indian Point nuclear generating plant. Besides altering the landscape, there was concern the additional fish kill would destroy what remained of the Hudson's fragile life cycle, not to mention the general pique of Hudson Valley residents that their land was being pillaged to benefit New York City.

Although the utility obtained a license to build the Storm King plant, challenges led to a precedent-setting federal ruling requiring environmental impact studies on projects of this kind. The plant was never built (there are six power plants on the Hudson, including one nuclear facility), but the brouhaha revitalized interest in the health of the Hudson River and Valley. In 1965, a Pure Waters Bond Proposition set aside $1 billion to clean up the river, and in 1972, another $1 billion was approved for state and local governments to acquire wetlands, which are breeding and feeding sites for waterfowl and mammals, and other areas important for recreation and/or ecology.

In 1969, folk singer Pete Seeger launched Hudson River Sloop *Clearwater.* It was a brilliant idea — his replica of a historic ship evokes the simpler past, before modern industry begat modern pollution. The organization Seeger founded, also called Clearwater, is an important environmental force whose educational programs, on land and aboard the sloop, reach some 15,000 school children a year. Thousands more adults and children attend the annual Clearwater Revival Festival at Croton Point Park, which attracts international entertainers and features environmental exhibits at the water's edge.

Another long environmental dispute involved General Electric, one of the upper valley's largest employers; it was accused of illegally dumping more than one million pounds of PCBs into the Hudson River, between 1946 and 1977 from its factories around Albany. GE has been fined many millions of dollars, but the issue of whether to dredge and clean the river bottom is controversial both environmentally and financially.

The economic changes that caused factories to shutter all across the United States in the last quarter of the 20th century also affected industry along the Hudson River, but in bits and pieces, these unsightly derelicts are being rehabilitated. The old International Paper printing plant at Beacon, New York, is now one of the largest modern art museum spaces in the world, DIA: Beacon. The huge General Motors Tarrytown plant, which produced cars and trucks for nearly 100 years until 1996 and also produced WWII military airplane parts, is becoming a complex of housing and open public park space, due to begin construction in 2003.

In 1991, the New York State Legislature established the Hudson River Valley Greenway program to preserve open spaces in densely populated regions,

The sloop Clearwater *is a replica of Dutch merchant ships.*

Courtesy Hudson River Sloop Clearwater, Inc.

especially along the riverfront. The goal is to link those patches of green beyond the headwaters of the Hudson River all the way to the Canadian border. Today, the Hudson River Valley is one of 24 areas in the U.S. designated by Congress as a National Heritage Area, which recognizes the significance of these precious four million acres.

Dozens of other environmental, conservation, and outdoor recreation groups — large ones, such as the Rockefeller-founded Historic Hudson Valley and Hudson RiverKeeper, and smaller ones, such as the NY-NJ Trail Conference — are active participants in the on-going effort to reclaim and to protect the landscape from harm. With industry declining and tourism increasing in the Hudson Valley, that makes perfect sense.

The Valley is a place where the future must be built in harmony with the region's natural and historic heritage. We are convinced that economic development will not occur in areas that tolerate a deteriorated environment. We emphasize that there must be places for the residents of the Valley to live and to work just as there must be places for them to have access to the Hudson River and the Valley's beauty and harmony.

— Segment of 1991 Greenway Report to the NY State Legislature

CHAPTER TWO
Ways & Means
TRANSPORTATION

Explorer Henry Hudson could hardly have foreseen the dawn of the steamship era when he first sailed up his namesake-to-be river in 1609. Schooners, sloops, and other sailing vessels plied the river for the next 200 years. Then in 1807, Robert Fulton's first steamship, *Clermont,* steamed from New York to Albany and back in record-breaking time. The voyage marked a turning point in travel and the growth of the Hudson Valley — albeit one that caught on rather slowly — because steam power significantly sped up the duration of any trip.

Dare one suggest that Robert Fulton never could have foreseen the commuter train? Or rail connections? Or even a Sunday drive along a scenic parkway?

Antique carriages and cars are on display at the mansions of their owners.

Travelers to the Hudson Valley will find numerous modes of transport and necessary connections due to the region's close proximity to New York City. That said, visitors who choose to drive or who rent a car at the airport will find themselves ready to explore the wide range of attractions in this early Revolutionary-era stronghold — estates, wineries, scenic parkways, and all.

GETTING TO THE HUDSON VALLEY

A ir travelers are most likely to land in New York City or Albany and make connections from there. Smaller, regional airports in Westchester and Orange Counties, however, offer commuter service with connections to major cities. Amtrak and MetroNorth trains make stops throughout the valley.

BY AIR

I f you're arriving in the Hudson Valley area via air, most likely you'll land at one of New York City's three major airports. All are managed by the Port Authority of New York and New Jersey, whose web site (www.panynj.com) offers a wealth of information about navigating in, around, and between the airports. This includes everything from parking lot fees and construction updates to handicap access information and various modes of ground transportation.

New York City Area

John F. Kennedy International Airport (718-244-4444 gen. info.; 718-244-4080 parking info.; 718-244-4168 free emer. serv.; www.panynj.gov/aviation/jfk frame.HTM) Located in Queens, approximately 15-18 miles from Manhattan. Also can call the parking management company *Five Star Parking* (718-244-4168) for other general parking information. Parking fees are less costly at the lots run by *Avistar* (800-763-9295 gen. info.; 800-759-4241 JFK lot; www. avistarparking.com), which adjoins each of the three airports. Travelers in search of ground transportation should know that a flat $38 fee for up to four passengers (plus toll, if necessary) takes visitors into Manhattan in a licensed yellow taxi; the fee to the airport, however, is the normal metered fare. Coming soon in 2003: *AirTrain*, a light rail system looping within the central terminal area, then extending out into two legs: one to the Howard Beach terminal and one to the Jamaica Station. Travelers can catch buses or trains into Manhattan from there; those headed for Penn Station should connect from the Jamaica station.

LaGuardia Airport (718-533-3400 gen. info.; 718-533-3850 parking info.; 800-759-4144 Avistar; www.panynj.gov/aviation/lgaframe.HTM) Located in Flushing, Queens, about eight or nine miles from Manhattan. Ground transportation information is available at the airport's web site or from the many transportation kiosks located in the airport terminals. There is a Metropolitan Transportation Authority city bus into Manhattan, but it is recommended only to those traveling light.

Newark Liberty International Airport (973-961-6000 gen. info.; 888-397-4636 parking info.; 973-961-4750/4751 Five Star Parking; 800-825-3848 Avistar; www.panynj.gov/aviation/ewrframe.HTM) Located approximately 18 miles from Manhattan in Newark, NJ. Travelers also can take a New Jersey Transit train (North Jersey Coast Line or Northeast Corridor Line; 800-772-2222 within NJ; 973-762-5100 out-of-state; www.njtransit.com) into New York's Penn Station to make connections. Travelers to Manhattan should be aware that since this airport is in a different state (just across the Hudson River), taxi or limo fares between the city and the airport can be $60–$80.

Ground Transportation

Keep these telephone numbers handy for ground transportation to and from all three airports. *Port Authority* (800-AIR-RIDE ground transportation/parking lot info.). *Olympia Airport Express* (212-964-6233) operates regularly scheduled busses from two locations in midtown Manhattan, the Port Authority Bus Terminal at 42nd St. and Eighth Ave. and the Grand Central Station at 42nd St. and Park Ave., at about $10 per trip. *Super Shuttle* (800-Blue-Van; www.supershuttle .com) provides door-to-door service via a shared ride for $15–$20 depending on airport.

There are transportation desks within each airport baggage claim area, and uniformed dispatchers are outside at taxi stands for the city's licensed and metered yellow cabs. Travelers are urged to turn down offers by folks who stroll the airports offering rides into town; these are often unlicensed and uninsured drivers.

From Regional Airports

Albany International Airport (518-242-2200 gen. info.; 518-242-CARS parking info.; www.albanyairport.com; Albany) Located at I-87 and I-90. Commercial service is available from several regional and major carriers. Ground transporation includes *ShuttleFly* buses that run several times daily (518-482-8822) or *Greyhound* buses (800-229-9424).

Stewart International Airport (845-564-2100; 1035 First St., New Windsor) Commuter service is offered through several major air carriers with connections to major cities. For ground transportation: in addition to taxis, car rentals are available via *Avis Rent A Car* or *Hertz* (see "By Rented Car" below); *MetroNorth* train service is available from their stations. Bus service is available via *Coach/USA Shortline* (www.shortlinebus.com), with a terminal in Newburgh (845-561-0734; 800-631-8405).

Teterboro Airport (201-288-1775 gen. info.; www.teb.com/aviation/tetframe .htm; Teterboro, NJ) Located 12 miles from midtown Manhattan, this is one of the region's general aviation airports. Like the three big New York City–area airports, it is also operated by the Port Authority. This airport has all the services and amenities that are needed by those with their own wings. Charters and leasings are available.

Westchester County Airport (914-995-4860 gen. info.; 914-946-0843 parking info. (APCOA); www.westchestergov.com/airport; 240 Airport Rd., White Plains) Commercial service by several major air carriers to major U.S. hubs, as well as Air Canada service to Toronto. Along with Teterboro, this is New York's major general aviation airport. In addition to the usual taxis, ground transportation is available throughout Westchester County via the county's bus service, *Bee-Line System* (914-813-7777). *Limousine Service of Westchester* (914-592-8534) also provides on demand service.

Private Charters

Columbia County Airport (518-828-9461; 800-359-2299; www.richmor.com/ fbo/hudson.asp; Hudson) FBO services offered by Richmor Aviation.
Dutchess County Airport (845-463-6000; www.dutchessny.gov/airport.html; 263 New Hackensack Rd., Wappingers Falls).
Kingston-Ulster Airport (845-336-8400; 1161 Flatbush Rd., Kingston) FBO offering extensive services is River Aviation.

BY BUS

Greyhound Lines, Inc. (800-229-9424 gen. info.; www.greyhound.com) Two routes traverse the Hudson Valley. Terminals are listed on their web site; check to see if they're full-service terminals or "limited service," which can be a stop on the highway or another carrier's terminal. Adirondack Trailways (listed below) serves Greyhound connections.
Shortline/Coach USA (800-631-8405 gen. info.) Scheduled service between New York City, Newburgh, and Poughkeepsie with stops at other Hudson Valley destinations; scenic day trips from New York City. Check web site for schedules (www.shortlinebus.com).
Trailways: Adirondack, Pine Hill, New York (800-858-8555 gen. info.; 499 Hurley Ave., Hurley) This is the headquarters for the Trailways-affiliated companies that serve much of New York. Busses leave from NYC's Port Authority Bus Terminal for destinations north to New Paltz, Kingston, Albany, and Saratoga.

BY CAR

From New York City and Points South: The Hudson Valley region covered in this book isn't far from Manhattan; intrepid drivers on a relatively traffic-free day may only drive as long as 2 1/2 hours. There are two main north-south routes that are connected by a network of bridges that cross the Hudson River every few miles. To travel the west side of the Hudson River from Manhattan, take the George Washington Bridge to the scenic Palisades Interstate Parkway into the New York State Thruway (I-87N) and pick your exit — this is a toll road, as are the bridges. To travel the east side of the Hudson River from Manhattan, take the West Side Highway north, which becomes the Saw Mill

River Parkway, to the scenic Taconic Parkway; there are almost no services on this road, but there are services at the many towns and cities that intersect it.

From Boston and Points East: Head west on I-90W and keep change handy for the occasional toll. About 150 miles from Boston, you'll reach the New York State Thruway — again, with the occasional toll — in a few miles. Then head south on Thruway/I-87. Keep an eye out for your destination of choice.

From Montreal and Albany and Points North: It's a straight shot on the New York State Thruway. Travelers coming from Montreal will want to get onto the Autoroute 15S until it turns into I-87, part of the New York State Thruway.

From Pennsylvania and Points West: If you're coming from as far west as Pittsburgh, take I-76/Pennsylvania Turnpike to Rte. 11/I-81 toward Harrisonburg. When you reach I78, go east toward Allentown. Then get onto I-187 toward I-80. Take this for nearly 50 miles until you can get onto the New York State Thruway.

By Rented Car

Avis Rent A Car (800-831-2847; www.avis.com).
Budget Rent A Car (800-527-0700; www.rent.drivebudget.com/Home.jsp).
Enterprise Rent A Car (800-736-8222; www.enterprise.com/car_rental/home .do).
Hertz (800-654-3131; www.hertz.com).
National Car Rental (800-CAR-RENT; www.nationalcar.com).

BY TRAIN

The trains keep a'rolling north and south through the Hudson Valley, much of that distance on tracks built by Cornelius Vanderbilt for his New York Central Railroad, now called MetroNorth. For much of the way, the tracks are a stone's throw from the river's shores and one of the most scenic and restful ways to enjoy the river. The terminus of the MetroNorth commuter railroad is at Poughkeepsie in Dutchess County, about 90 minutes north of New York City. The off-peak (nonrush hour) round-trip fare to Cold Spring in Dutchess County, for example, is $15. Amtrak, though, runs express on the same tracks from the city to Poughkeepsie, where travelers can switch between the two lines.

Amtrak (800-USA-RAIL; www.amtrak.com) Train travel is easy through the Hudson Valley, with Amtrak (which also includes portions of old New York Central routes) offering many trains that provide daily service between Albany and New York City along the river's east bank. Stops north to south include Albany-Rensselaer, Hudson, Rhinecliff-Kingston, Poughkeepsie, Croton-Harmon, and Yonkers. Some trains are locals with more stops; other trains stop fewer times and are therefore faster. Amtrak also offers its New

The Hudson Valley is well served by the MetroNorth commuter line and by Amtrak.

Evelyn Kanter

York Unlimited Fare that allows unrestricted stopovers, including over-nights, along the Adirondack route with an advance reservation.

MetroNorth (212-532-4900; 800-638-7646; www.mta.nyc.ny.us/mnr/) New York City's Metropolitan Transportation Authority, or MTA, provides commuter service from the city's Grand Central Station to the Hudson Valley region via its Hudson and Harlem lines. Travelers to Westchester County find 40 stops; north-along-the-river stops are available at Beacon in Dutchess County and end at Poughkeepsie on the east bank and at Middletown on the west bank. Amtrak connects at Poughkeepsie to Albany and to points between.

GETTING AROUND THE HUDSON VALLEY

BY BUS

Bee-Line Bus System (914-813-7777; www.westchestergov.com; 100 East First St., Mount Vernon) Extensive commuter system from the Westchester County Dept. of Transportation throughout the county; also links to Yonkers, New Rochelle, and Croton-Harmon Amtrak stations.

Coach/USA Shortline (800-631-8405; www.shortlinebus.com) Scheduled service from New York to Newburgh and Poughkeepsie, as well as to the Bear Mountain-West Point area. Check the web site or call for additional stops and schedules.

Dutchess County Loop (845-437-4690; 14 Commerce St., Poughkeepsie) Ideal for getting around the county.

Pine Hill Trailways (800-858-8555; www.greyhound.com) Scheduled service between New York City's Port Authority Bus Terminal, 42nd St. & Eighth Ave., north to Albany and Saratoga, and local service west into the Catskills.

BY CAR

National car rental agency information is available under "By Rented Car" above.

Bridges

Five toll bridges cross the Hudson River (tolls vary from $1–$6, the higher fees on bridges closest to New York City). From south to north, the bridges are the following: George Washington Bridge, connecting northern Manhattan with Orange and Rockland Counties via New Jersey; the Tappan Zee Bridge, connecting Tarrytown and Nyack via I-287, part of the New York State Thruway system; the Bear Mountain Bridge, connecting Peekskill and the Orange/Rockland County line via Rte. 6 and Rte. 202; the Newburgh-Beacon Bridge that takes I-84 between Beacon and Newburgh; the Mid-Hudson Bridge that takes Rte. 44/55 via Highland and Poughkeepsie; the Kingston-Rhinecliff Bridge carrying Rte. 199 between the two towns; and the Rip Van Winkle Bridge about 30 miles south of Albany, connecting Catskill and Hudson via Rte. 23.

Major Roadways

North-south roads through the area are varied and well supplied, but one tip: if the weather is bad, stick to the New York State Thruway. Major roadways in the region are the following:

New York State Thruway (thruway.state.ny.us: toll, E-ZPass info., toll and distance calculator) This thruway runs through the Hudson Valley region primarily via I-87 and I-90, briefly through I-95, and nontoll sections of I-84 and I-287 (with the exception of the Tappan Zee Bridge). This toll road costs $2.25 from New York City to the Catskills exit, located at the valley's northern end. There are 24-hour gas stations and rest stops at each exit: Harriman, Newburgh, New Paltz, Kingston, Saugerties, and Catskill.

Taconic State Parkway This highway makes for a lovely drive along the east side of the Hudson Valley between Westchester and Columbia Counties, with several scenic overlook stops en route. Construction on the parkway began in the 1920s — back before driving required exit-ramp, gas-food-lodging services. Although there are some narrow spots with tight curves and no shoulders to pull off in parts of Westchester and southern Dutchess Counties, for the most part, this is a broad, scenic, and efficient route. Be aware, however, there are almost no services along this road; for that, you have to take one of the exits to a nearby town. Late at night and in poor weather, travelers should opt for the New York State Thruway or the two-lane Rte. 9, the commercial and business route just east of the Taconic State Parkway. No big commercial vehicles are allowed.

There also are several business routes running north-south through many of the towns and hamlets included in this book. These two-lane roads often are clogged during the day with commercial and local traffic. They are the following:

East of the Hudson: U.S. Rte. 9 and New York Rte. 22.
West of the Hudson: NY Rte. 9W and NY Rte. 32.

Bridges

The ferries that zigzagged across the Hudson River, transporting both goods and people, were gradually replaced by bridges, beginning in the early 20th century. The railroads first, then the bridges turned much of New York City's surrounding area from farmland into suburban bedroom communities within a 60- or 90-minute commute from downtown. From south to north, the Hudson River bridges are the following:

Verrazano-Narrows Bridge Connects Brooklyn and Staten Island at the entrance to New York Harbor. Opened in 1964, it is the longest suspension bridge in the U.S.; the bridge is 4,260 feet long and has six lanes of traffic on each of its two levels. Although the legendary Staten Island Ferry still links Staten Island with the island of Manhattan, construction of the Verrazano (nobody in New York City uses the word "Narrows") morphed Staten Island from quiet farmland into urban/suburban life. Legend has it that James Hoffa, ruler of the powerful teamsters union, who disappeared during the bridge's construction, is entombed in its concrete.

George Washington Bridge One of the longest suspension bridges in the world — 3,500 feet from the highest point in Manhattan, Washington Heights in northern Manhattan, and in Fort Lee, New Jersey. It is also the highest bridge across the Hudson (the water is 250 feet below), and its latticework metal design also makes it one of the most beautiful. The "GW" opened in 1931 and was designed to accommodate construction of a lower level, which planners did not think would be needed for some 50 years, but the growth of the metropolitan area spurred construction of the second level, affectionately called "Martha," in 1962. Original designs, which called for cladding the metal in Gothic-style brickwork, like the Brooklyn Bridge, and for adding colossus-style statuary at the cable ends, were dropped.

Tappan Zee Bridge Connecting Tarrytown to Nyack, this bridge curves and dips in the middle of the river, and its easternmost section sits low above the water on floating caissons. At its highest point, it is 157 feet above the water. This three-mile long bridge opened in 1955 and prompted Nyack, a summer colony of artists and writers, to grow into a year-round suburban community.

Bear Mountain Bridge Linking Peekskill to Bear Mountain State Park, the bridge opened in 1924. It was the first Hudson River bridge and was the longest suspension bridge in the U.S. at the time. It is 2,257 feet long, 150 feet above the water, and cost $3 million to build.

Mid-Hudson Bridge From Poughkeepsie to Highland, this 3,000-foot span was opened in 1933. It cost $6 million and is 135 feet above the water.

Newburgh-Beacon Bridge There are two bridges here, one taking traffic east, the

Evelyn Kanter

other west. The North bridge opened in 1963 at a cost of $19 million; by the time its twin was added in 1980, inflation increased the price tag to $94 million. Both bridges are 7,800 feet long and 135 feet above the water.

Kingston-Rhinecliff This bridge opened in 1957. It is 250 feet above the Hudson River and 7,800 feet long.

Rip Van Winkle The northernmost bridge of the Hudson Valley links Catskill, a town settled by the Dutch in the 17th century, with the town of Hudson. The 5,041-foot span opened in 1935. The two most prominent artists of the Hudson River School lived at opposite ends of the bridge, visible from one another's front porches — Frederic Church, whose estate Olana is in Hudson, and Thomas Cole, whose estate Cedar Grove is in Catskill.

BY TRAIN

There is excellent information about how to reach Hudson Valley's southern-most estates via train from New York City. Check the web site (www.hudson valley.org/web/plan-trai.html).

Amtrak (800-872-7245; 800-USA-RAIL; www.amtrak.com; 31 St. bet. Seventh & Eighth Aves., New York) Two stations in Westchester, one in Poughkeepsie, one near Rhinebeck, and another in Hudson. Call or check the web site for schedules.

MetroNorth Railroad (212-532-4900, 800-METRO-INFO; www.mta.nyc.ny.us/mmr; 347 Madison Ave., New York) More than 40 commuter stations throughout Westchester County, another near Coldspring. The line terminates at Poughkeepsie in Dutchess County.

CHAPTER THREE
To Sleep, Perchance to Dream
LODGING

The Hudson Valley always has been a well-trafficked area because of its prime location between New York City, Albany, and Boston, so it has more than three centuries of experience welcoming travelers passing through for business or pleasure, via horseback, stagecoaches, river steamers, and today's conveyances. Several of these oldest inns have survived, such as the **Beekman Arms** in Rhinebeck, which opened in <u>1766</u> at the intersection of two stagecoach roads and the Revolutionary-era **Bird & Bottle Inn** in Garrison on the Old Albany Post Road. Luckily, too, many historic private homes and farmhouses have been turned into charming inns, from the solid downtown Victorian

Courtesy Tarrytown Castle

A river view is a special feature of many Hudson Valley accommodations.

homes of wealthy merchants, such as **The Grand Dutchess** in Red Hook to the extravagant Gilded Age country mansions of the even wealthier, including **Tarrytown Castle** in Tarrytown and **Troutbeck Inn and Conference Center** in Amenia.

And then there are the monuments to a glorious getting away, such as the historic **Mohonk Mountain House** in New Paltz, which sprawls along the lake in the middle of a huge forest preserve, and the grand Western-style stone and log **Bear Mountain Inn & Lodges** in Bear Mountain State Park in Harriman.

In many B&Bs, breakfast has evolved from simple muffins or pancakes to extravagant multicourse offerings of gourmet cuisine. The upgraded menus are due to the proximity of these inns to the Culinary Institute of America in Hyde Park, where many inn owners have taken breakfast cooking courses, and also due to the bounty of the valley's farms and orchards. Apple fritters, pumpkin muffins, locally smoked sausage, cheeses, and maple syrup are just some of the wake-up wonders to be enjoyed at the dozens of comfortable and charming owner-operated inns.

Even historic properties have been modernized to include such required amenities as private bathrooms. And although there are TVs and telephones in each location, they are not always in the rooms, but rather in the public areas downstairs. These are the establishments where the primary entertainment is the country air, scenery, and solitude.

Other lodging options include more standard hotels and motels, which usually are clustered around the exits of the main north-south highways — the Taconic State Parkway on the eastern side of the Hudson River and NYS Thruway (I-87) on the western side.

This is a representative sampling that focuses on those establishments where the standouts are location, personal attention, architectural significance, the quality of the antiques and furnishings — or all those things wrapped up in an unforgettable experience.

Wherever you choose to stay, you'll notice a heritage of hospitality and a proud sense of the region's history.

LODGING NOTES

Rates

Rates are generally determined in the spring and may change slightly from year to year. Prices are based on a per-room rate, double-occupancy, and are often higher in the peak visiting seasons of summer and fall foliage. Be aware that at these times, especially on weekends, a minimum stay of two or three nights is usually required. Reservations are recommended, if not required.

During midweek and off-season, however, the rules are normally relaxed, and the prices are, without exception, lower. Since policies vary, it is wisest to know before you go.

Price Codes

Inexpensive	Up to $65	Expensive	$100–$175
Moderate	$65–$100	Very Expensive	$175 and up

Credit Cards

AE	American Express	DC	Diner's Club
CB	Carte Blanche	MC	MasterCard
D	Discover	V	Visa

Deposit/Cancellation

Deposits are normally required for a confirmed reservation, especially for peak summer and fall seasons, which can vary from one night of a two-night minimum or the entire stay.

Cancellations vary, including by season, and often carry, at minimum, a service charge. It is wise to ask before you book your accommodations. Also, be aware that properties near the valley's colleges fill up well in advance during graduation weeks in late May and June and at West Point during football season.

Special Features

Wherever pertinent, we mention special features of lodging, such as where pets are allowed. We also mention such restrictions as no smoking or no children under age 12. Realistically, in some smaller B&Bs and/or those filled with valuable antiques, young children (as well as their watchful parents) would not be as comfortable as they would in more standard accommodations. This is intended as a general guide, and it's always best to inquire before making a reservation.

Web Sites & Other Options

The various county visitors bureaus, usually ending in .org or .com, are excellent resources for local accommodations. Or contact 800-CALL-NYS; www.iloveny.com.

American Country Collection of Bed and Breakfasts (800-810-4948; www.band breservations.com; 1353 Union St., Schenectady, NY 12308).

Empire State B&B Association (www.esbba.com; P.O. Box 1020, Canandaigua, NY 14424).

Orange County B&B Association (800-210-5565; www.new-york-inns.com; 12 Powelton Rd., Newburgh, NY 12550).

LODGING: WESTCHESTER COUNTY

Croton-on-Hudson

ALEXANDER HAMILTON HOUSE
914-271-6737.
www.alexanderhamilton
house.com.
49 Van Wyck St., Croton-on-Hudson, NY 10520.
Price: Expensive.
Credit Cards: AE, D, DC, MC, V.
Restrictions: No smoking; no pets.
Special Features: Outdoor pool.

Two blocks from the center of charming Croton Village, this sprawling, white-porched 1889 Victorian mansion is filled with period antiques and collectibles and decorated with an abundance of flowered wallpaper and fabrics. Not a four-poster bed in sight here, only iron bed frames. There are seven rooms, several with fireplaces and sitting rooms. The Bridal Suite has a hot tub, pink marble fireplace, and lots of windows; the room called The Library is wood paneled, with book-lined shelves. The huge open lobby area contains an original walk-in fireplace and an antique baby grand piano. Breakfast is served on country-motif china in an airy, light-splashed room.

The house is atop a cliff overlooking the river, so the panoramic views are stunning and memorable, especially at sunset — sit in the backyard or hide out in the miniorchard and inhale the colors. All rooms have ceiling fans, color TVs, and telephones.

Innkeeper Barbara Notarius has written several books on owning and operating B&Bs, so expert treatment of guests is a given. She holds seminars on the subject, sometimes at the inn.

Rye Brook

DORAL ARROWWOOD
914-939-5500.00;
866-241-8752.
www.doralarrowwood.com.
Anderson Hill Rd., Rye Brook, NY 10573.
Price: Expensive.
Credit Cards: D, DC, MC, V.
Restrictions: No smoking.
Special Features: Business center; handicap access.

This is both a resort hotel, known for its nine-hole golf course and indoor and outdoor tennis facilities, and a popular conference facility. There are 374 rooms over a sprawling campus, a complete fitness center, indoor and outdoor pools, and three restaurants on the premises. Weekend rates include a full breakfast.

Tarrytown

TARRYTOWN CASTLE
914-631-1980; 800-616-4487.

Imposing on the outside, comfortably plush on the inside. Perched on one of the highest bluffs

Life-sized chess is a popular diversion at Tarrytown Castle.

Evelyn Kanter

www.castleattarrytown
.com.
400 Benedict Ave.,
Tarrytown, NY 10591.
Price: Very Expensive.
Credit Cards: AE, DC, MC,
V.
Restrictions: Children to
age 12 free.
Special Features: Pool;
tennis court; Equus
(formal French dining).

overlooking the Hudson River, this medieval-style stone castle was built by Spanish-American War General Howard Carroll for his family and took more than a decade to complete, from 1897–1910. There are 31 units. Nearly all of them are suites, and all are oversized and decorated with hand-carved canopy or four-poster beds, original European paintings, and plush uphol-stered sofas and chairs in either Empire or Queen Anne styles. All rooms have a separate bathroom vanity area. Several of the suites have wood-burning fire-places, turret alcoves, and spectacular river views of the Hudson as far south as New York City.

Public areas are lush with hand-carved wood paneling, huge marble fireplaces, and vaulted ceilings with exposed beams and stained glass windows. There are also fresh flowers and plants everywhere, including in the hallways between rooms. There is a fabulous stone-walled out-door pool that looks like a grotto, a fitness center, and state-of-the-art confer-ence facilities. The terraced gardens are lush and inviting. A popular outdoor activity is the life-sized chess board, with foam pieces that are easy to move.

Despite its imposing size, Tarrytown Castle bills itself as a bed-and-break-fast, and, certainly, the personal level of service makes it feel like a small coun-try inn. That includes the service at the restaurant, Equus, generally regarded as one of the best in the area, certainly one of the most formal and most expen-sive (see Chapter Four, *Restaurants & Food Purveyors*).

TARRYTOWN HOUSE
914-591-8200; 800-553-8118.
www.dolce.com.
E. Sunnyside Ln.,
Tarrytown, NY 10591.

This is a complex consisting of two historic man-sions, a modern low-rise hotel, and conference facilities. Try to stay in the mansions, known as the King House and the Biddle House. Thomas King was an executive with the Baltimore and Ohio Rail-

Price: Expensive.
Credit Cards: AE, CB, D,
   DC, MC, V.
Restrictions: No infants.
Special Features: Outdoor
   pool; tennis courts;
   Winter Palace (B, L, D);
   Sleepy Hollow Pub
   (tavern fare).

road; the stone Georgian-style house dates from 1840 and has been completely refurbished — the wood-paneled library is a gem. Mary Biddle was the only daughter of Benjamin Duke, partner in the Duke Tobacco Company and founder of Duke University, who staged lavish parties here for her husband, Anthony Drexel Biddle, a millionaire and diplomat. The elegant front great room is flanked by two sunrooms, whose curved bay windows have faceted crystal glass panes — this is where breakfast is served. Rooms in both mansions contain comfortable period furnishings, including four-poster beds. Rooms in the newer units are less expensive, but layout and decor are more like a large chain hotel.

The houses are set high on Pocantico Hills (the Rockefeller estate is less than three miles away), and many rooms offer sweeping panoramic views of the Hudson River. There's a new sculpture garden on the lawn between the two houses; King and Biddle were related by marriage, so the houses are a family-compound distance apart. This is also a large corporate conference facility, so you're more likely to be surrounded by professional adults than families with children, including on weekends. Washington Irving's Sunnyside House (see Chapter Six, *Mansions of the Hudson Valley*) is right down the hill.

White Plains

SOUNDVIEW MANOR
914-421-9080.
www.soundviewmanor
   .com.
283 Soundview Manor,
   White Plains, NY 10601.
Price: Moderate.
Credit Cards: Inquire when
   reserve room.
Restrictions: No smoking;
   no pets; no children
   under 12.
Special Features: TV in
   rooms; rose garden.

This elegant estate, built in the 1920s as a private home, sits on five acres landscaped with 200-year-old tulip, pine, quince, and Japanese maple trees. There are just four rooms, each one different, and all filled with a variety of antique furniture and chests, plus three of the rooms have balconies. The largest is a suite with a sun-filled corner accommodation with French doors to a balcony that overlooks a flower-filled garden. Each guest room has a private bath and color TV. The family-sized common room has a dramatic white fireplace and comfortable upholstered sofas.

There is both a grape arbor and a rose garden, with a sundial and old stone fountain.

HOTELS & MOTELS

Because of Westchester County's proximity to New York City and several corporate headquarters within the county, there also is a bounty of major chain accommodations in the area.

Hilton Rye Town (914-939-6300; 699 Westchester Ave., Rye Brook, NY 10573) 450 rooms on a 40-acre campus; indoor and outdoor pools; sauna; exercise room; tennis courts; two restaurants. AE, D, DC, MC, V.

Hilton Tarrytown (914-631-5700; 455 S. Broadway (Rte. 9), Tarrytown, NY 10591) Indoor pool; exercise facility; two restaurants. AE, CB, D, DC, MC, V.

Ramada Inn (914-592-3300) There are three Ramada Inns in Westchester County: in Elmsford, Armonk, and New Rochelle.

Renaissance Westchester (914-694-5400; 80 W. Red Oak Ln., White Plains, NY 10601) Resortlike facility on a 30-acre campus tract of land surrounded by woods; indoor pool; tennis courts; fitness room. AE, D, DC, MC, V.

Westchester Marriott (914-631-2200; 670 White Plains Rd., Tarrytown, NY 10591) 444 rooms; indoor pool; fitness center; business center; restaurants include a branch of Ruth's Chris Steakhouse. AE, CB, D, DC, MC, V.

LODGING: PUTNAM COUNTY

Cold Spring

HUDSON HOUSE INN
845-265-9355.
www.hudsonhouseinn.com.
2 Main St., Cold Spring, NY
10516.
Price: Moderate.
Credit Cards: AE, MC, V.
Restrictions: No smoking;
no pets; infants and
children welcome.
Special Features: River
Room Restaurant; Half
Moon Tavern.

This landmark three-story clapboard inn, built in 1832, is the second oldest continuously operating inn in New York State and originally hosted steamship captains and passengers. The inn is directly on the waterfront (it once was called the Hudson View Inn), alongside the town's charming little park and gazebo. The most appealing rooms are waterside, although rooms on the side of the building facing Main Street also have balconies offering broad glimpses of the water and Storm King Mountain on the western shore.

The 11 rooms and one suite are filled with period furniture, including a combination of sleigh beds and four-posters and decorated with Colonial-style striped and flowered wallpapers. Many rooms have exposed wood beams, and the original wide-plank flooring can be found throughout the building, including in the welcoming downstairs lounges. The sitting area just beyond the tiny tavern bar features deep, stuffed sofas and wingback chairs flanking a fireplace.

PIG HILL INN
845-265-9247.
www.pighillinn.com.
73 Main St., Cold Spring,
NY 10516.
Price: Moderate.

The dreadful name dates back to before this solid brick Georgian house was built in the mid-1800s, when this part of town was still farmland. Each of the nine rooms is decorated differently in an eclectic mix of Victorian, Chippendale, and chinoiserie. One room, with exposed original

Tania Barricklo/Daily Freeman

Built in 1832, the Hudson House Inn is steps from the Hudson River and the second oldest continuously operating inn in New York State.

Credit Cards: AE, MC, V.
Restrictions: No smoking;
   no pets; no TV or
   telephone in rooms.
Special Features:
   Landscaped garden.

beams, even has a western log cabin flavor. Five rooms have private baths; four share two bathrooms. Each room has a fireplace, some are original wood-burning, others have been converted to gas. Everything in the house is for sale, from little pig bric-a-brac and framed landscapes by local artists, decorating the common area downstairs to the hand-painted rocking chairs and handmade quilts upstairs.

The inn is located in the heart of downtown Cold Spring, two blocks from the Hudson River and smack in the middle of one of the most charming shopping and restaurant streets in the entire valley. The breakfast room is a Victorian-style greenhouse, all light and airy. The garden behind the inn is a three-level gem with landscaped nooks for privacy, for reading, or for eating one of the homemade breakfasts — or the innkeepers will serve you breakfast in bed. Even the sourdough breads and croissants are made on the premises, and recipes are willingly shared. There's always lemonade or hot cider available, depending on the season, and afternoon brownies.

Garrison

BIRD & BOTTLE INN
845-424-3000.
www.birdbottle.com.
1123 Old Albany Post Rd.
  (off Rte. 9), Garrison, NY
  10524.
Price: Very Expensive.
Credit Cards: AE, MC, V.
Restrictions: No smoking; no
  pets; no children under 12.
Special Features: Overnight
  guests receive a $75 credit
  per room toward dinner.

Originally known as Warren's Tavern, the inn opened in 1761 as a stagecoach stop and taproom on the Old Albany Post Road. During the Revolutionary War, the surrounding area was an important encampment and supply depot for colonial troops (hence the name, Garrison) deployed to prevent British occupation of the strategic Hudson Highlands. When the steamboat lured travelers from land to water, the inn became a family home and one of the most prosperous farms in the area. The house changed hands numerous times until 1982, when it was purchased by tourism consultant Ira Boyer, who reopened it as a restaurant and inn.

The restaurant (see Chapter Four, *Restaurants & Food Purveyors*) is one of the best in Putnam County. There are three rooms upstairs in the main building, which has been fully restored, and another room in a free-standing cottage just 100 feet from the main inn. Each room has a working fireplace, either a canopy or four-poster bed, and period antiques or reproductions. Original wide-plank flooring and exposed beams are throughout the building, and hallways are decorated with framed historical documents. The Emily Warren Room is of special significance because this offspring of the original family married Washington Roebling and helped her husband complete the construction of the Brooklyn Bridge after he was injured.

LODGING: DUTCHESS COUNTY

Named for the Dutchess of York, later crowned as Queen Mary, this verdant part of the Hudson Valley has played an important role in American history since before the Revolutionary War. The area is approximately halfway between New York City and Albany, and the Old Albany Post Road bisects the county. Luckily, many 18th-century stagecoach stops and 19th-century farm homesteads have been saved, restored, and reborn as charming, historic bed-and-breakfast inns, along with several 20th-century offspring, which are the country estates of famous personalities of their time.

Amenia

**TROUTBECK INN AND
  CONFERENCE
  CENTER**
845-373-9681.

Fronted by a row of towering sycamores planted in 1835, this English country estate on 422 acres was a gathering place for the literati and liberals of the 1920s visiting the home's owner (the NAACP was

www.troutbeck.com.
Leedsville Rd., Amenia, NY
  12501.
Price: Very Expensive.
Credit Cards: AE, CB, DC,
  MC, V.
Restrictions: Children over
  13.
Special Features: TV and
  telephone in rooms;
  indoor and outdoor
  swimming pools; tennis
  courts; pool table.

conceived here), a noted poet and naturalist whose friends included Emerson and Thoreau. During the week, Troutbeck is a corporate retreat and conference center, but on weekends it morphs back into a country inn with top-notch amenities and level of service. There are 42 rooms gloriously appointed with rich wood paneling, fabric-hung canopy beds, and well-lit nooks with wing chairs for curling up with a good book. Some have fireplaces, and most have bookcases filled with some of the inn's 12,000 volumes.

Rooms are spread over three buildings, the main house, farmhouse, and garden house, which overlooks a colorful flower garden. The walled gardens are quiet and restful; one is lined with sculptured trees and a gently babbling pond. The wood-paneled living room retains the flavor of a wealthy owner's private home, with a baby grand piano, thick carpeting, and interesting accessories. The dining room is bright and comparatively casual, with white ladder-back chairs and a picture window overlooking the landscaped grounds.

Bangall

Lavish decor and generously proportioned sitting rooms at Bullis Hall.

Evelyn Kanter

BULLIS HALL
845-868-1665.
88 Hunns Lake Rd.,
  Bangall, NY 12506.
Price: Very Expensive.
Credit Cards: AE, MC, V.
Restrictions: No smoking;
  no pets; no children.

The slightly sagging building-wide, 150-year-old second floor porch gives no hint of the luxury inside. There are just five suites in this 9,000-square-foot building, each larger and more sumptuous than the other, each filled with museum-quality Colonial, Federal, Georgian, French, and Chinese antiques, including Oriental carpets covering the

Special Features: TV, telephone, and VCR in rooms.

original wide-plank floors. Owner Addison Berkey is an art historian who used to publish art and architectural books; he and wife Lauren restored and furnished Bullis Hall with an expert's eye, from the marble-topped wood credenza in one bathroom to the 1810 pianoforte in the front parlor. Each suite has a large sitting room. A library downstairs is filled with everything from rare leather-bound editions to more modern fare, and there is a comfortable public area with fireplace upstairs. There is a separate wing with two suites, an adjoining sitting area, and a separate entrance. Wood-burning fireplaces are throughout the building. Behind the house is a large, quiet, landscaped garden.

This may be the smallest inn in the country with a full-time gourmet chef from the Culinary Institute of America, preparing both a full-course breakfast and candlelight dinners. Breakfast is served on a 1880s factory trestle table; dinner is beneath elegant crystal chandeliers in a room decorated with English floral wallpaper.

Bangall is so small it doesn't appear on many maps (it's a few miles northeast of Millbrook). There's not much more in town than Bullis Hall, a church, and the Bangall General Store, but it once was a thriving railroading community. This building has been a tavern, a speakeasy, and a theater (the stage was where the parlor is now).

Dover Plains

→ **OLD DROVERS INN**
845-832-9311.
Rte. 22, Dover Plains, NY 12522.
Price: Expensive–Very Expensive.
Credit Cards: AE, DC, MC, V.
Restrictions: No smoking; no pets; no children under 12.
Special Features: Open only Thurs.-Mon.

This historic Colonial opened in 1750 as a stopover for cowboys driving their cattle to New York City markets. You don't have to rent the entire place, as Elizabeth Taylor and Richard Burton once did, to indulge in its privacy and charm. There are just four rooms, each with a private bath; three have fireplaces. Rooms are small and well-appointed with antiques. The inn is more famous for its gourmet restaurant (see Chapter Four, *Restaurants & Food Purveyors*).

Hopewell Junction

BYKENHULLE HOUSE
845-226-3039.
www.bykenhullehouse
.com.
21 Bykenhulle Rd.,
Hopewell Junction, NY 12533.

Another landmark manor house, this Georgian-style structure was built in 1841 as a private home. The house has seven fireplaces, including in the accommodations upstairs. There are five rooms, all with queen-sized beds and private bath, decorated with four-poster beds, antique Colonial wood tables and cabinets, and chintz-covered seat-

Price: Expensive.
Credit Cards: AE, MC, V.
Restrictions: No smoking;
    no pets; no children.
Special Features: TV and
    telephone in rooms.

ing area furniture. The two rooms on the third floor have whirlpool tubs, and there are cozy window seats tucked into the semicircular Palladian windows in the front of the house. The double living rooms downstairs are adorned with sparkling crystal chandeliers.

A sunroom with wicker furniture overlooks the extensive gardens. Bykenhulle House sits on seven acres of meadows and gardens, including a stone fountain and a formal English garden with impeccably manicured hedges and trees. There also are flower gardens and paths for walking and biking, and a pool (unusual for a B&B). Breakfast is an ample, full country meal served in the semiformal dining room.

Beautifully landscaped grounds surround Le Chambord.

Tania Barricklo

LE CHAMBORD
www.lechambord.com.
2073 Rte. 52, Hopewell
    Junction, NY 12533.
Price: Expensive.
Credit Cards: Inquire when
    reserving room.
Restrictions: No smoking;
    no pets; no handicap
    access in main house;
    children welcome in Tara
    Hall.
Special Features: TV and
    telephone in rooms.

This 1863 Georgian mansion looks like it was dropped into the Hudson Valley from the set of *Gone With the Wind*, with a two-story pillared veranda dominating the front entrance. There are nine rooms in the main house. Each room has a private bath and is decorated in an eclectic mix of period styles. Owner Roy Benich is a local art dealer, so the house is filled with original paintings and mirrors in lush gilded frames, crystal chandeliers, and thick Oriental carpets. An additional 16 rooms and suites are in a separate wing, called Tara Hall. Accommodations are spacious and comfortable, with sitting areas, reproduction period furniture and accessories, and modern bathrooms. The two-story unit has a large, airy common area, with fireplace and comfortable stuffed furniture for socializing.

The nine-acre grounds are beautifully landscaped. The flagstone terrace in front features fountains and a small garden. In between Tara Hall and a small conference center and ballroom is a gazebo that is popular for weekend weddings, especially in the spring and summer.

Millbrook

COTTONWOOD MOTEL
845-677-3283.
www.cottonwoodmotel
.com.
2639 Rte. 44, Millbrook, NY 12545.
Price: Inexpensive.
Credit Cards: AE, MC, V.
Restrictions: Nonsmoking rooms; children welcome.
Special Features: TV and telephone in rooms; great view.

The design and decor of this roadside motel is standard fare: parking lot in front, vending machines in one corner of the lobby, and clean, comfortable rooms. What launches this inexpensive find into the stratosphere of interesting accommodations is what is behind the motel. Each room has French doors that open onto a little concrete patio wide enough for a few chairs — to sit and enjoy the serenity of an unobstructed view of rolling hills and meadows of some of the thousands of acres belonging to a nature preserve. Behind the otherwise ordinary Cottonwood Motel are huge cottonwood trees, a stream, and lots of local wildlife, including deer, wild turkey, quail, and pheasant that roam the grounds right up to those patio doors.

→ **MILLBROOK COUNTRY HOUSE**
845-677-9570.
www.millbrookcountry
house.com.
506 Sharon Turnpike (Rte. 44A), Millbrook, NY 12545.
Price: Very Expensive.
Credit Cards: AE, MC, V.
Restrictions: No smoking; no TV or telephone in rooms; no children.
Special Features: Extensive library; perennial garden.

Step inside this center-hall white Colonial and you are transported instantly into 17th-century Italy. That's because owners Giancarlo Grisi and his wife Lorraine Alexander Grisi brought much of the Grisi family furniture and artwork from their palazzo near Modena. There are 17th-century original oil portraits, plus more recent family portaits; marquetry tables in the parlor, and lavish silk draperies on many windows. The house — one part dates from 1750, the other part from 1810 — was refurbished by Grisi and Lorraine (a former editor for *Gourmet* magazine and a gourmet cook herself), leaving intact, however, many original details, such as windows, floors, and moldings.

Walls are painted in colors that showcase the furniture, such as the gold and pumpkin walls in a sunny, Baroque room with a gold-scrolled Venetian bed. Because the antique beds are a unique size, all the mattresses at the Millbrook Country House are custom-made and covered with Frette linens and spreads. Each of the four rooms has a private bath and a fragrant cedar-lined closet. There's also an extensive library, including the owners' collection of art books from Italy.

There's a charming bricked patio behind the house for breakfast in season and a perennial garden behind. Full breakfasts and afternoon tea are served on fine china.

PORTER HOUSE
845-677-3057.
17 Washington Ave.,
 Millbrook, NY 12545.
Price: Inexpensive.
Credit Cards: Inquire when
 reserve room.
Restrictions: No smoking;
 no TV or telephone in
 rooms; children
 welcome.
Special Features: 1890
 antiques.

Luckily, the original chestnut woodwork and wainscoting were intact when this 1920s stone house was restored and turned into a B&B in 2002. The woodwork has the same patina as the Victorian armoires, bedsteads, and chests that fill the four rooms and one suite. There are lace curtains and floral spreads upstairs and comfortable 1890s antiques downstairs in the sunny front parlor. A single telephone, downstairs, serves owner and guests, and the only TV in the Porter House is in the parlor. Breakfasts are continental-style: self-service muffins, cereals, and fresh fruit. The house is one block from Millbrook's main street.

Poughkeepsie

INN AT THE FALLS
845-462-5770.
www.innatthefalls.com.
50 Red Oaks Mill Rd.,
 Poughkeepsie, NY 12601.
Price: Expensive.
Credit Cards: AE, D, DC,
 MC, V.
Restrictions: No smoking;
 handicap accessible
 rooms.
Special Features: TV and
 telephone in rooms.

A few feet behind this red-shingled house, Wappingers Creek drops suddenly, and the constant whoosh of the water adds to the restfulness of this charming, light-filled house. This is a modern house (not a historic Colonial as are most B&Bs in the area), designed with blond woods and decorated in soft, pleasing shades of peach walls, jade and sky blue carpeting, and a pink marble fireplace in the common area. There are large windows everywhere, including a two-story atrium overlooking the creek. The 22 large rooms and 14 suites are decorated in a variety of Colonial, Country, and English styles, with rich wood furniture, canopy beds in some rooms, and comfortable stuffed sofas and wing chairs in sitting areas. Several rooms have whirlpool baths.

A full breakfast is served in an airy dining room, or a continental breakfast can be delivered to the guest's room.

Red Hook

THE GRAND DUTCHESS
845-758-5818.
www.granddutchess.com.
7571 Old Post Rd., Red
 Hook, NY 12571.

Built originally as a private home in 1874 for a tobacco merchant's family, but after he died his widow took in boarders to help pay the bills; at one time the imposing mansard-roofed building was

Price: Moderate.
Credit Cards: AE, MC, V.
Restrictions: No smoking;
no pets; no children
under 6.
Special Features: TV
and/or VCR available
upon request.

Red Hook's high school. From the horsehair furniture and marble-topped center console in the front parlor to the original dark wood door frames and wainscoting in some rooms, this is a stately and grand Victorian inn, befitting its name. Many features are original, including the carved marble fireplaces and milk glass light fixtures downstairs. Unlike many Victorian structures, this one is flooded with light from 10-foot floor-to-ceiling windows, allowing guests to see the 150-year-old patina on all the wood, including the original flooring.

Upstairs, rooms have been restored with colorful Victorian-style flowered wallpaper and decorated with a mix of antiques from the mid-1800s to the 1920s, much of it purchased from the auction house across the street (see Chapter Eight, *Shopping*). There are wood parquet floors in each room, and each is a different pattern. Four of the six rooms have private baths; the two remaining rooms share one bath. One of the baths has an exposed brick wall — unusual and utterly charming.

Breakfast is served on 100-year-old, floral-patterned china in the formal dining room. It's, however, not all serious — guests are called to breakfast by toots from the antique fireman's horn that sits on the dining room floor. The Grand Dutchess is owned by the same couple that owns the Red Hook Inn (see below), two blocks away.

RED HOOK INN
845-758-8445.
www.theredhookinn.com.
7460 S. Broadway (Rte. 9),
Red Hook, NY 12571.
Price: Moderate.
Credit Cards: AE, D, MC, V.
Restrictions: No smoking;
no pets; children
welcome.
Special Features: TV and/
or VCR available upon
request.

This white Empire-style clapboard house was built as a private home in 1842 and became an inn and restaurant a decade later. The current owners, Beth Pagano and husband Harold, ran out of space in their Brooklyn brownstone for the Victorian antiques they collected, so they moved to indulge a joint passion of antiques and entertaining. There are six rooms, including one two-room suite, each with a private bath. Two rooms have a whirlpool bath. Several rooms have exposed beams and fireplaces. Accessories include antique sideboards and chests, and the beds range from antique four posters and iron frames to one whose headboard is an Empire-style, black-and-gold swatch of fabric. All rooms have either a queen-sized bed or a king.

Breakfast is served in a sunny room with flowered wallpaper and such interesting touches as bent twigs used as curtain rods. Homemade breads, muffins, and pastries prepared by the same chef who mans the stove at the inn's restaurant (see Chapter Four, *Restaurants & Food Purveyors*). Because the owners have a young son, children are welcome here. There are no telephones in the rooms, but the upstairs hallway has a telephone, with desk and chair.

Rhinebeck

Tania Barricklo

Beekman Arms opened in 1766 at the juncture of two stagecoach roads.

BEEKMAN ARMS
845-876-7077.
www.beekmanarms.com.
Rte. 9, Rhinebeck, NY
   12572.
Price: Moderate–Expensive.
Credit Cards: Inquire when
   reserving room.
Restrictions: Pets welcome
   in motel units; handicap
   access.
Special Features: TV and
   telephone with dataport
   in rooms.

This imposing building in the heart of Rhinebeck claims to be the oldest continuously operating inn in America, opened in 1766 at the intersection of the roads to Albany and to the Hudson River. Revolutionary War volunteer soldiers trained in the field alongside the house. The downstairs is all dark, burnished wood and low lighting, almost too low to read the historic framed documents on the walls, including a page from an 1876 guest registration when the room rate was two dollars.

There are 19 rooms in the three-story house, decorated in reproduction Colonial four-poster beds, brass candlestick lamps, and floral wallpaper, curtains, and bedspreads. The antiques are in the hallways, where guests are less likely to increase wear and tear on fragile items. The wide-plank floorboards creak, the various wings of Beekman Arms connect via a puzzle of hallways, and the ceilings may be too low for a strapping six-footer, but Beekman Arms is history, pure and simple. Newspaperman Horace Greeley was a frequent guest; William Jennings Bryan orated from a second floor balcony; George Washington slept here and so did Franklin Delano Roosevelt — well worth visiting even if you stay elsewhere.

The inn also owns a complex of buildings behind the main house and a block away, with 63 rooms total, so unless you specifically request accommodations in the historic old building, at check-in you can be sent to these other units, several of which are older buildings with fireplaces in many of the rooms.

Downstairs, the Colonial Tap Room, the center of the original inn, serves pub fare, but there also is the more formal Traphagen Restaurant.

DELAMETER HOUSE AND CONFERENCE CENTER
845-876-7080.
www.delameterinn.com.
Rte. 9, Rhinebeck, NY 12572.
Price: Moderate–Expensive.
Credit Cards: AE, D, DC, MC, V.
Restrictions: Call early for reservations.
Special Features: TV and telephone with dataport in rooms.

This Gothic, gingerbread-style clapboard house was designed by Alexander Jackson Davis, the architect who also designed Lyndhurst, the Gothic stone mansion in Tarrytown (see Chapter Six, *Mansions of the Hudson Valley*). It sits well back from the street, guarded by a wrought iron gate and large shade trees. It's a tiny house, just four wonderfully decorated Victorian rooms, but it's not easy to get reservations. This is part of the Beekman Arms complex; next to the Delameter House are several Victorian homes, a carriage house, a conference center, and several other small buildings that have been turned into guest rooms.

HOTELS & MOTELS

It's not all historic B&Bs in Dutchess County. Several national chains have outposts here, mostly in the larger communities in the south part of the county and close to the Taconic State Parkway, the main north-south artery on the east side of the Hudson River.

Courtyard by Marriott (800-321-2211; www.marriott.com; 17 Westage Dr., Fishkill, NY 12524) 152 rooms; indoor pool; **Courtyard by Marriott** (800-321-2211; 1641 South Rd., Poughkeepsie, NY 12601) 149 rooms; 12 suites; indoor pool; whirlpool; exercise room. Both inns have handicap accessible rooms; both inns accept AE, D, DC, MC, V.

Hampton Inn (800-426-7866; www.hamptoninnfishkill.com; 544 Rte. 9, Fishkill, NY 12524) 99 rooms; indoor pool. AE, D, DC, MC, V.

Holiday Inn (845-896-6281; www.holidayinnfishkill.com; 542 Rte. 9, Fishkill, NY 12524) 156 rooms and suites; outdoor pool; health club privileges; handicap accessible rooms. AE, D, DC, MC, V.

Holiday Inn Express (800-465-4329; 1256 South Rd. (Rte. 9), Poughkeepsie, NY 12601) 121 rooms; outdoor pool; exercise room; handicap accessible rooms. AE, CB, D, DC, MC, V.

LODGING: COLUMBIA COUNTY

Hudson

Victorian accessories fill Hudson City Bed & Breakfast.

Tania Barricklo

HUDSON CITY BED & BREAKFAST
518-822-8044.
www.hudsoncitybnb.com.
326 Allen St., Hudson, NY 12534.
Price: Moderate–Expensive.
Credit Cards: AE, D, DC, MC, V.
Restrictions: No pets; no children under 12.
Special Features: TV, VCR, and telephone in rooms.

Peach walls in every room bring a flattering glow to every guest and a sunny open feel to this charming Victorian, which features brass "rain forest" showers and king- or queen-sized beds in each room and suite. Built originally in 1865 by a local railroad executive to house his family of 10 children, accommodations are spacious. Several rooms have old-fashioned Victorian soaking tubs, including a room where the tub is in the room, near the bed, rather than in the bathroom. The third floor suite has bowed walls from the mansard roof and windows that are more like skylights; this suite also has a whirlpool in its own stepped alcove. The second-floor sitting area is lined with a vast video library; there are TVs and VCRs in each room.

There's a homelike feel, with a happy clutter of antique and vintage bric-a-brac and accessories and an old-fashioned wooden swing on the porch for watching the occasional vehicle or pedestrian pass by. A thoroughly restful walled garden in the back is dotted with fountains, and the front parlor with its cozy fireplace is equally inviting. Innkeeper Ken Jacobs also is a hair stylist, and the back parlor serves as a minisalon, gift shop, and check-in.

ST. CHARLES HOTEL
518-822-9900.
www.stcharleshotel.com.
16-18 Park Pl., Hudson, NY 12534.
Price: Moderate.
Credit Cards: AE, D, DC, MC, V.
Restrictions: No smoking.
Special Features: TV and telephone in rooms.

It's been a local landmark for more than 100 years. The St. Charles is a solid brick building one block from the town's street of antique shops, with 34 rooms decorated modestly with conventional motel-type furnishings. The combination lounge and bar downstairs has a working fireplace and original 1868 oak and mahogany trim. There is a café on the ground floor, as well as a small park across the street.

LODGING: ROCKLAND COUNTY

Geographically, Rockland County is the smallest of the counties of the Hudson Valley and also one of the two closest to New York City. Lodging here is dominated by the major chains.

Comfort Inn Nanuet (800-221-2222; www.comfortinns.com; 425 E. Rte. 59, Nanuet, NY 10954) 102 rooms and suites; handicap access; free continental breakfast; outdoor pool; restaurant; guest laundry. Another branch of this chain is eight miles away in Mahwah, NJ. AE, Amoco, Bravo, CB, D, DC, MC, Novis, V.

Hilton Pearl River (800-445-8667; www.hilton.com; 500 Veterans Memorial Dr., Pearl River, NY 10965) 150 rooms and suites; handicap access; fitness center; indoor pool; restaurant.

Marriott Fairfield Inn Spring Valley (800-228-9290; www.marriott.com; 100 Spring Valley Marketplace, Spring Valley, NY 10977) 105 rooms and suites; outdoor pool; handicap access; complimentary breakfast. AE, D, DC, MC, V.

LODGING: ORANGE COUNTY

This area contains two of the most historic and popular spots for visitors in the Hudson Valley — Bear Mountain State Park and West Point — and there are ample lodging choices, from plain to fancy, antique to modern.

Bear Mountain

BEAR MOUNTAIN INN & LODGES
845-786-2731 reservations; 845-786-2701 park information.
www.nysparks.gov.
Bear Mountain State Park, Harriman, NY 10926.
Price: Inexpensive.
Credit Cards: AE, D, MC, V.
Restrictions: No pets; children welcome.
Special Features: TV and telephone in rooms; handicap access.

There are two types of accommodations in this huge, scenic, lake-studded state park. The Main Inn is an imposing stone structure that also houses the park's restaurants and main public areas. It becomes a private, quiet hideaway after dark, when the day visitors and dinner guests have gone home, and the hotel guests have the main log-lined lobby to themselves, with its stone walk-in fireplace, oversized leather sofas, and life-sized, wood-carved bears. There are 13 motellike rooms, most with one queen-sized bed, decorated in a comfortable but simple style.

Accommodations in the Stone Lodges and the Overlook Lodge are one mile from the Main Inn, across Hessian Lake. There are four Stone Lodges, each with six individual hotel rooms clustered around a central lobby and sitting area with a wood-burning fireplace. These contain queen-sized beds. Overlook Lodge is structured more like a motel and has two double beds in each room. Decor here is more outdoorsy and casual than in the Main Inn. All accommodations at Bear Mountain have private baths, and all are open year-round, giving guests instant access to hiking trails (the Appalachian Trail cuts through the park, see Chapter Seven, *Recreation*), boating, biking, an outdoor pool, and a new merry-go-round in warm weather, and ice-skating, cross-country skiing, and sledding in the winter. Reservations required at least one month in advance in the summer.

Cornwall

CROMWELL MANOR
845-534-7136.
www.cromwellmanor.com.
Angola Rd., Cornwall, NY 12518.
Price: Very Expensive.
Credit Cards: AE, MC, V.
Restrictions: No smoking; no pets; no TV or telephone in rooms; children welcome.
Special Features: Wireless Internet access throughout house.

Before it was a retirement home for New York City schoolteachers, this was a private home built by a descendant of Oliver Cromwell in 1820; his portrait, found by the owners in a local flea market, hangs above the front parlor fireplace. There are seven original wood-burning fireplaces in the house, all but two of them in rooms. Each of the nine rooms in the main house has a private bath; one oversized suite, with a separate entrance, has its own minigym/spa area with a Stairmaster and a large whirlpool.

This formal antebellum mansion is filled with wonderful, museum-quality Colonial antiques, thick carpeting, artwork, and Tiffany-style lamps by local artists (for sale, of course). The same front parlor where Mr. Cromwell resides also has an antique piano and a cello. Innkeepers Jack Trowell and Cynthia Korn have had guests who are professional musicians hold impromptu concerts after dinner.

The house sits on seven acres. Across the open field in front of the house, part of the Hudson Highlands Museum grounds, is Storm King Mountain. Also on the property is a 1764 wood cottage with exposed walls and beams and a casual country feel, much different from the main house a few yards away. There are four rooms in the cottage; two of them share a bath.

Montgomery

MEAD TOOKER HOUSE
845-457-5770;
  fax 845-457-4585.
www.meadtooker.com.
126 Clinton St.,
  Montgomery, NY 12549.
Price: Moderate–Expensive.
Credit Cards: AE, D, MC, V.
Restrictions: No smoking;
  no pets; no TV or
  telephone in rooms; no
  children under 12.
Special Features:
  Innkeeper-owned
  antique shop.

The house is named for two of its owners, Jacob Tooker, headmaster of the school that was across the street in the early 1800s, and W. J. Mead, who purchased it in 1868. Built in the early 1700s at the top of a hill in the middle of the village, this solid white Colonial is really two small houses that have been combined. The front door opens to a huge center hall and a magnificent carpeted staircase, or to the front parlor with its original fireplace, with an unusual carved wood mantel, flanked by cozy wingback chairs.

Innkeeper Nancy Michaels is an antiques dealer. Her shop, Olde Towne Antiques, is in the original basement kitchen, and she has filled the house with top-quality antiques from the 1700s and 1800s. Original wide-plank floors are partially covered by antique Oriental carpets throughout, including on the front hall staircase. Most of the eight rooms have working fireplaces, all have handmade antique quilts. There are four rooms with private baths; the four others share two baths. The grounds behind the house have a small pond, a waterfall, and a brick patio.

Breakfast is served on an antique drop-leaf harvest table with Windsor chairs, under a pewter chandelier, and more antique pewter on the sideboard. A full country breakfast includes quiche, apple crisp, and scones — that's one day's menu.

Salisbury Mills

THE CALDWELL HOUSE
845-496-2954.
www.caldwellhouse.com.
25 Orrs Mill Rd., Salisbury
  Mills, NY 12577.
Price: Expensive.

Innkeepers Carmela Turco and Eugene Sheridan are the third family to have owned this house since it was built in 1803, and, luckily, their predecessors took good care of the original wide-plank flooring, leaded glass windows, and woodwork

Credit Cards: AE, DC, MC, V.
Restrictions: No pets.
Special Features: TV/VCR and telephone with dataport in rooms.

detailing — it is all in pristine condition. The front of the house is dominated by a huge porch that wraps around three sides, a pleasant spot for enjoying the landscaped gardens. The inside is filled with antiques, ranging from a Sheridan sideboard to mahogany sleigh beds and four posters. The original deed for the land, dated 1603, hangs on one wall. Beds are covered in handmade quilts, no two alike. Another special touch — bath amenities are Bulgari. There are four rooms and suites, one with a whirlpool. The dormer room, although spacious, may not be comfortable for a six-footer because of its slanted ceilings. The downstairs sitting parlor is decorated in warm tones of rose and champagne.

A devoted cook, Carmela prepares and serves breakfasts to order. The menu can be lime-scented French toast one day, orange and ginger scones the next day. Unlike most B&Bs, where the kitchen is off limits to guests, she welcomes company and conversation.

West Point

The majestic two-story lobby at West Point's Hotel Thayer.

Tania Barricklo

HOTEL THAYER
845-446-4731; 800-247-5047.
www.thethayerhotel.com.
674 Thayer Rd., West Point, NY 10996.

In real estate, the saying "location is everything" may have been referring to the Hotel Thayer, the fortresslike hotel a few hundred yards inside the front gate of the U.S. Military Academy. Named for Colonel Sylvanus Thayer, superintendent from

Price: Moderate–Very
Expensive.
Credit Cards: AE, D, DC,
MC, V.
Restrictions: Reservations
necessary.
Special Features: TV and
telephone with dataport
in rooms; restaurant;
handicap access.

1817 to 1833 and regarded as the "father of West Point," the landmark hotel was built in 1926 of the same local granite as West Point, with a grand architectural style befitting its location. The crenellated rooflines and turrets outside impart a Gothic appearance. Flags fly from the second-floor balcony of the huge marble lobby, which is reminiscent of a grand hall in a medieval castle, with its larger-than-life fireplace and furniture.

Everything here is on a grand scale, especially the view. West Point was built on a promontory, where the river narrows — a strategic location to protect the Hudson Highlands from invasion by the British during the Revolutionary War. The views are captivating, especially from one of the terraced lawns overlooking the Hudson River or from the hotel's terrace restaurant, which has the same grand scale as the lobby.

There are 150 guest rooms and suites, furnished in reproduction Colonial style. Larger rooms have sitting areas. Because it is the only public lodging within West Point, the hotel can be sold out around the dates of major activity, which include Army football games, cadet family weekends, and graduation, so if you want to stay here, make reservations well ahead.

HOTELS & MOTELS

There are plenty of moderately priced chains in Orange County. The following are in Newburgh, clustered close to the Newburgh exit of I-87/New York State Thruway:

Comfort Inn (845-567-0567) 130 rooms and suites; outdoor pool; dataports in rooms. Call for credit card info.

Hampton Inn (800-HAMPTON) 116 rooms; indoor pool; exercise area; dataports in rooms. AE, CB, D, DC, MC, V.

Holiday Inn (800-HOLIDAY) 121 rooms; outdoor pool. AE, D, MC, V.

Howard Johnson (800-446-4656) 74 rooms; outdoor pool; tennis court. AE, D, DC, MC, V.

Ramada Inn (800-228-2828) 153 rooms and suites; outdoor pool; exercise area; meeting rooms; restaurant. Call for credit card info.

Two motels closest to West Point are the following:

Palisades Motel (845-446-9400; 17 Main St., Highland Falls, NY 10928) 53 rooms; 10 efficiencies with minikitchens. AE, CB, D, DC, MC, V.

West Point Motel (845-446-4180; 888-349-6788; 156 Main St., Highland Falls, NY 10928) 51 rooms, handicap access; just outside Thayer Gate in Highland Falls. AE, D, DC, MC, V.

RETREATS

Monroe

ANANDA ASHRAM
845-782-5575.
Sapphire Rd., Monroe, NY
  10950.
Price: Inexpensive.
Credit Cards: D, MC, V.
Restrictions: No telephone
  in rooms.
Special Features: Nature
  trails; lake; outdoor pool
  (in season).

There are accommodations for 40 guests on 100 wooded acres at this retreat operated by the Yoga Society of New York. Rooms are dormitory style, spare but comfortable, and there are some semiprivate rooms. Meals are vegetarian, and the ashram offers daily yoga, tai chi, meditation classes, and lectures.

LODGING: ULSTER COUNTY

Two of the largest cities in the Hudson Valley are in this county: Kingston, the first state capital, and New Paltz, one of the first settlements by French Huguenots and now home to a large branch of SUNY, the State University of New York. There are diverse populations and lifestyles here because the cities are still bordered by rich farmland, including endless acres of famous New York State apples and many more acres of environmentally protected forests and woodland. History and diversity also are reflected in the range of accommodations.

Gardiner

MINNEWASKA LODGE
845-255-1110.
www.minnewaskalodge
  .com.
Rte. 44/55, Gardiner, NY
  12525.
Price: Expensive.
Credit Cards: AE, MC, V.
Restrictions: No smoking;
  no pets; children
  welcome.
Special Features: TV and
  2-line telephone with
  dataport in rooms;
  fitness center.

The sheer cliff walls of the 450-million-year-old Shawangunk Mountains are directly outside the rooms on one side of this mountain lodge, built in 2001. The cliff is visible from just about anywhere inside the rooms, but it is so much more dramatic from the large decks outside each room, especially at dawn or dusk, when you are likely to see deer on the rock-strewn natural lawn between the lodge and the cliff face.

There is a decidedly Scandanavian-modern feel to this lodge, with light woods throughout, both in the construction and the furniture. The main room has a two-story cathedral ceiling with a glass wall facing the mountain and Mission furniture, whose clean lines don't compete with the view. There are cathedral ceilings as well in the second-floor rooms and suites, most of which have king-sized beds. Rooms are spacious, decorated with the same Mission furniture as downstairs; each room has a comfortable overstuffed chair, and the walls are decorated with paintings of local landscapes, painted and photographed by local artists. There are 26 rooms and suites, each with a private bath. It should be no surprise that the cliff-facing rooms are the most popular and get booked first.

There is a full-time chef, who prepares hearty country-style breakfasts, including homemade granolas, plus afternoon cookies and snacks. The lodge adjoins the Minnewaska State Park Preserve and is just up the road from the Mohonk Preserve, so there is 25,000 acres of environmentally protected woodland at the front door. There are two restaurants a short walk from the lodge, Mountain Brauhaus and Swiss Country Inn.

High Falls

CAPTAIN SCHOONMAKER
945-687-7946.
www.captainschoonmakers.com.
913 Rte. 213, High Falls, NY 12440.
Price: Moderate.
Credit Cards: No; traveler's checks accepted.
Restrictions: No pets; no TV or telephone in rooms; no children under 12.
Special Features: Outstanding breakfast menu.

Captain Schoonmaker was one of the wealthiest farmers in the area when he joined the Revolutionary Army and donated his land and money to build the iron chain across the Hudson River at West Point (see Chapter One, *History*) to stop advancing British ships. Some of his army pay stubs are framed in this small, homey B&B. The stone house was built in 1760 in post-and-beam fashion (no nails used), and the cow barn was built in 1810. There are rooms with private baths in both buildings, each decorated with antiques, including brass beds. The barn has steep, narrow stairs, but the exposed beams and country charm are worth the short climb. The buildings overlook Coxingkill Stream, popular with local fly-fishing fans.

A hearty, five-course country breakfast, enough to let you forego lunch, is served on a 12-foot-long antique farm table. A typical menu includes vegetable fritters, walnut coffee cake, scones with Hudson Valley peach sauce, and eggs from the flock of chickens in the backyard (magically, they produce without a rooster who would wake guests at dawn). Innkeepers Judy and Bill Klock also keep a flock of cats and dogs who roam the house freely, which can be a problem for those with pet allergies.

Highland

FOX HILL BED AND BREAKFAST
845-691-8151.
www.foxhillbnb.com.

If it weren't for the chlorine required by local health regulations for the in-ground outdoor pool and six-person outdoor hot tub, Fox Hill would be

55 S. Chokidee Lake Rd.,
  Highland, NY 12528.
Price: Inexpensive.
Credit Cards: AE.
Restrictions: No smoking;
  no pets; no children
  under 12.
Special Features: TV/VCR
  and telephone in rooms;
  outdoor pool; hot tub;
  allergy-sensitive,
  fragrance-free.

able to call itself a "chemical free" B&B. Everything from the carpeting, used sparingly, to cleaning products, is chemical or fragrance free and biodegradable. Innkeepers Jeri and Jerry Luke (Jeri has allergies) have put air filters in each of the inn's three guest suites, one room has no carpeting at all for those with serious allergies. The suites have different decor themes: one is "Heritage," with antique oak furniture and the steamer trunk that Jeri's grandmother used to come to America in the late 1800s; a "Garden" room with stenciled walls and wrought iron furniture; and a "Tropic" room with netted bed and lots of ferns. All have private baths and ceiling fans.

In addition to the solar-heated pool and hot tub, there are two gardens: a large perennial garden with a gravel path and benches for enjoying the hummingbirds and butterflies; and a small meditation garden with a pond filled with brightly colored koi and a small waterfall. There also is a small fitness center adjoining the pool. The house sits on a quiet residential street; behind it are acres of woodland. A paved rail trail, ideal for walking, jogging, and biking, is a few minutes away.

Kerhonkson

**HUDSON VALLEY
RESORT**
888-9HUDSON.
www.hudsonvalleyresort.
400 Granite Rd. (off Rte.
  44/55), Kerhonkson, NY
  12446.
Price: Moderate–Expensive.
Credit Cards: AE, D, DC,
  MC, V.
Restrictions: No pets;
  children welcome.
Special Features: TV and
  telephone with dataport
  in rooms; restaurant;
  cigar lounge with walk-
  in humidor; lounge with
  live entertainment and
  dancing; fitness center
  with spa; handicap
  accessible rooms;
  nonsmoking rooms.

A generation of guests knew this resort as the Granite, one of the legendary "borscht belt" hotels, but new owners and a $25-million renovation in 2002 morphed it into a modern facility with a new full-service, European-style spa. That's in addition to its 18-hole golf course and a full menu of recreational amentities, including tennis courts, full-court basketball, indoor and outdoor swimming pools, year-round miniature golf, and a lake for fishing and boating in the summer and ice-skating in the winter. Oh, yes, the 25,000 protected acres of the Minnewaska and Mohonk preserves is just down the road.

Rooms are spacious and decorated in reproduction Colonial style. The huge lobby avoids a cavernous feel with many small groupings of sofas, chairs, and tables for socializing. This is a great family destination, with a "Kidz Club" of daytime activities and meals. There is a complicated rate structure, depending on whether guests choose accommodations with no meals, one meal, two meals, or all three meals daily.

Kingston

Ornate entrance to The Black Lion Mansion.

Tania Barricklo

THE BLACK LION MANSION
845-338-0410.
www.theblacklionmansion
   .com.
124 W. Chestnut St.,
   Kingston, NY 12401.
Price: Very Expensive.
Credit Cards: AE, D, MC, V.
Restrictions: No smoking;
   no pets; no children.
Special Features: TV and
   telephone with dataport
   in rooms.

This house is set well back from the street on four acres. It is named for the cast-iron lion head inside the downstairs fireplace. Midway up the dramatic front staircase is a large bow window topped with a trio of stained glass panels, framing a breathtaking panorama east across the valley and the Hudson River to the Taconic Mountains. The house was built on the grounds of the studio of a landscape artist and member of the Hudson River School of artists, so such an exquisite vista would be expected. It sits high on a knoll atop the city, and the view takes in church steeples, farmland, and the Kingston-Rhinecliff Bridge.

The imposing Georgian-style house features ornate woodwork, Palladian windows, plaster detailing, fireplaces in some of the rooms, and beautiful parquet floors. The decor is impeccable. One room has a gold-stenciled ceiling, another a bookcase wall filled with books and a marble-topped console in the seating area, and another room has a two-person hot tub. All feature period-accurate striped wallpapers, king or queen sleigh beds, antique Oriental rugs, and lace curtains that don't obstruct the view. The breakfast area is a formal, Georgian-style room, and there is also a bricked patio and garden. Those with pet allergies should know there are six resident cats.

RONDOUT
845-331-8144;
    fax 845-331-9049.
www.rondoutbandb.com.
88 West Chester St.,
    Kingston, NY 12401.
Price: Inexpensive.
Credit Cards: Inquire when reserve room.
Restrictions: No TV or telephone in rooms; dogs welcome but not cats; children welcome.
Special Features: Landscaped gardens.

Built in 1906 on the highest point in Kingston, the huge downstairs parlor contains a nine-foot concert grand piano, which guests are welcomed, even encouraged, to play. There are four light-filled guest rooms, and the airiness is heightened by light-inducing, peach-colored walls and see-through curtains. Two rooms have private baths; the other two rooms share a bath. Rooms are spacious, with Oriental rugs and a mix of antique and reproduction armoires and chests and sitting areas containing a Victorian sofas. The house features large porches overlooking woodland and landscaped gardens.

Cooked-to-order breakfasts include pancakes, Belgian waffles, omelettes seasoned with herbs from the garden, and sautéed local apples. Breakfast is normally served in the dining room, but guests often choose to eat in the sunny, windowed corner porch overlooking the gardens. Innkeepers Adele and Ralph Calcavecchio have been hosting guests since 1985; three former guests have opened B&Bs of their own in the Hudson Valley, making Adele feel like "the mother of B&Bs."

Milton

EVELYN'S VIEW
845-795-2376.
www.evelynsview.com.
12 Riverknoll Rd., Milton, NY 12547.
Price: Moderate.
Credit Cards: No.
Restrictions: No smoking; no pets; no TV or telephone in rooms in main house.
Special Features: TV and telephone in rooms in Carriage House and Pond Cottage; in-ground pool; tennis court.

Named for previous owners, New York City engineer Fred Stiefel and his wife, Evelyn, the house sits on 12 acres overlooking the Hudson River, with unobstructed views from the glass-walled dining room and from the spacious back lawn, with well-placed garden benches for serene view inhaling. There's also a path leading down to the water. Built in the 1870s, the house's decor is Victorian, with floral wallpaper, marble-topped dressing tables, and crystal chandeliers in the rooms. There are four rooms in the main house: two have a woodland view; the other two have river views, including the room called the Captain's View, with a private balcony. The Carriage House, also from the 1870s, contains two additional rooms, and the more recent Pond Cottage, with a more woodsy feeling and overlooking its own pond, contains yet two more rooms.

An in-ground pool at a B&B is unusual enough, but this one is additionally unusual because it is one of those "zero horizon" designs that seems to have no border and floats right into the horizon, which happens to be the Hudson River. Sitting in this pool makes you feel as though you are sitting in the Hudson!

New Paltz

Jordan Fall, courtesy of Mohonk Mountain House

Fabled Mohonk Mountain House sits above a glacial lake, surrounded by thousands of acres of forest preserve.

MOHONK MOUNTAIN HOUSE
800-678-8946.
www.mohonk.com.
Rte. 44/55, New Paltz, NY 12561.

Perched on the shore of a 60-foot-deep glacier-carved lake, this resort sprawls over 4,500 acres of mountains, meadows, and woodlands in the Shawangunk Mountains, foothills to the Catskills further north. Built originally as a 10-room inn and

Price: Very Expensive.
Credit Cards: AE, D, DC, MC, V.
Restrictions: No smoking; no pets; children welcome.
Special Features: TV and telephone in rooms; restaurant; health club with spa services; ice-skating; lake swimming; horseback riding; valet parking.

tavern in the 1860s by twin brothers who fell in love with the site on a picnic, it was expanded to 251 rooms over 50 years by different architects, creating a hodgepodge of styles linked by red roofs, featuring turrets and gables. Then, the stagecoach journey to the lake, on a precipitous and winding mountain road from the nearest railroad stop in New Paltz, took the better part of a day; today, it's a scenic 30-minute drive.

The elegant Victorian ambiance is retained, with 19th-century decor, wood-paneled fireplaces, balconies in most rooms, and cozy nooks in rooms and in the lobby. Half the rooms (there are 251 guest rooms, including 28 tower rooms and suites) overlook the lake, the other half take in the picture-postcard mountain views. Mohonk Mountain House is surrounded by some 30 square miles of protected park and preserve land. It adjoins Minnewaska State Park and Sam's Point Park, so there's nothing to spoil the views. In the autumn, the multicolored panorama of foliage is simply spectacular, especially from one of the old-fashioned wooden rocking chairs on a lakeside porch.

There are manicured gardens, including a Victorian "show garden," wooden walkways around the lake and across some of its coves, an ice-skating rink, golf course, spa, and 35 miles of groomed hiking trails that attract cross-country skiers in the winter. There's a series of on-going theme programs, from language immersion to swing dancing.

HOTELS & MOTELS

Clustered around each exit of the north-south New York State Thruway, officially known as I-87, but which New Yorkers simply call "The Thruway," are outposts of national chains.

Econo Lodge Motel (800-424-4777; 530 Main St. New Paltz, NY 12561) 34 rooms; some kitchenettes. AE, D, DC, MC, V.

Holiday Inn Kingston (800-465-4329; 503 Washington Ave., Kingston, NY 12401) 212 rooms; handicap access; indoor pool with sauna and hot tub; full-service restaurant and bar. AE, CB, D, DC, MC, V.

Ramada Kingston (800-2RAMADA; www.ramada.com; Rte. 28, Kingston, NY 12401) 147 rooms; indoor pool; handicap access. Call for credit card info.

RETREATS

SKY LAKE LODGE
845-658-8556.

Nestled in a forest of cedar and white pine, this is a Shambhala Buddhist contemplative center

www.sky-lake.org.
Sky Lake Rd. (off Rte. 213),
    Rosendale, NY 12472.
Price: Inexpensive.
Credit Cards: Inquire when
    reserve room.
Restrictions: No smoking;
    no pets; no TV or
    telephone in rooms;
    children welcome.
Special Features: Beautiful
    grounds.

for meditation, with simply furnished rooms, vegetarian meals, and a variety of workshops in callig-
raphy, meditation, and chanting.

LODGING: GREENE COUNTY

Much of Greene County is part of the Catskill Forest Preserve, a protected area of woodland mountains. Even before the land begins to climb away from the Hudson River, there are rolling hills dotted with creeks and water-falls.

Athens

Evelyn Kanter

*Front-facing rooms at Stewart House have a view of the
historic Athens Lighthouse.*

STEWART HOUSE B&B
518-945-1357.
2 North Water St., Athens,
    NY 12015.
Price: Inexpensive.
Credit Cards: AE, MC, V.

Meryl Streep died here — the movie *Ironweed* was filmed in Stewart House — and her wrought iron bed still stands in the sunny, corner bedroom with its 12-foot ceilings, original oak floors, and panoramic views of the Hudson River

Restrictions: No smoking; no pets; no TV or telephone in rooms.
Special Features: Restaurant.

just steps from the front door. Walk to the shoreline and you'll also get a close-up view of the historic Athens Lighthouse, which also is visible from front-facing rooms.

Stewart House was built as a boardinghouse in 1883 and has been welcoming guests ever since — a small historical display at the entrance features an original ledger book. Architectural details are intact, including pressed tin ceilings, marble fireplace, oak pocket doors between the dining rooms downstairs, and embossed 1920s radiators upstairs. The six rooms are decorated sparingly, with a mix of Victorian and Art Deco furnishings, warmed by Oriental carpeting. Each room has a private bath, but no telephone. Actually, it's much more fun to use the 1940s Superman-style, folding-door telephone booth on the main floor. There's a restaurant downstairs, where a full breakfast is served, plus a riverside café with entertainment across the street.

Catskill

CALEB STREET'S INN
518-943-0246.
251 Main St., Catskill, NY 12414.
Price: Expensive.
Credit Cards: AE, MC, V.
Restrictions: No smoking; no pets; no telephone in rooms; TV/VCR in suites only; no children under 12.
Special Features: Wraparound porch with view.

This 1790s white Colonial on the town's main street has a wraparound porch overlooking both a shaded garden and the Catskill Creek, an ideal spot for morning breakfast, curling up in a wicker chair or upholstered settee for afternoon tea, or for the evening offering of canapés and cocktails. Inside, the house has many of its original features, including rare Minton tile wainscoting in the formal dining room and a hand-painted frieze in Latin around the ceiling of the front parlor.

Although the house is filled with Colonial and Victorian antiques, including curved arm sofas and Oriental carpets, innkeeper Rita Landry takes a decidedly modern and colorful approach to the walls and furniture placement. There are two rooms and two suites, each with a private bath. One suite has a blue-violet sitting room offset by pure white woodwork with "dental" molding (shaped like a row of teeth) around the ceiling, and the mahogany bed is placed catercorner in the bedroom. Another suite room is painted in various shades of orange and ocre and decorated with antique guns and military sculptures — a very masculine room, compared with the florals and lace of most Victoriana.

Breakfast is served on fine china, using the good silver and with candlelight. The menu ranges from spinach and leek quiches to bagels and lox.

Purling

BAVARIAN MANOR COUNTRY INN

518-622-3261.
www.bavarianmanor.com.
866 Mountain Rd., Purling,
NY 12470.
Price: Moderate.
Credit Cards: MC, V.
Restrictions: No smoking;
no pets; children
welcome.
Special Features: TV and
telephone in rooms;
handicap access.

This inn opened in 1865 as White Sulphur Springs House. The original guests came to enjoy the medicinal advantages of the springs. The house expanded over the years, and, sadly, the sulphur springs are no more, but the hospitality and vitality remain. The sprawling white clapboard building is now operated by the third generation of the Bauer family.

Each of the 18 rooms has a private bath, and the decor differs from room to room. Some have stenciled walls, others have the original oak wainscoting. The furniture ranges from '50s-style birch to Victorian oak. Three of the rooms have gas fireplaces; several have whirlpools; one room is in a corner turret. Walls in the rooms and in the hallways are decorated with an eclectic mix of Bavarian landscapes, from King Ludwig's fairy-tale Neueschwanstein Castle (the model for Walt Disney's Cinderella Castle) to historically significant Hudson Valley and Bavarian hunt paintings.

The inn sits on 100 landscaped and wooded acres, which include a lake that is off-limits to swimming because of the Volkswagen-sized snapping turtles that live there. But fishing and boating are encouraged. In the winter, there are cross-country ski trails through the property, and the year-round restaurant on the main floor (see Chapter Four, *Restaurants & Food Purveyors*) is a haven for homemade traditional German favorites from wursts to Black Forest cake.

TUMBLIN' FALLS HOUSE

518-622-3981; 800-473-0519.
www.tumblinfalls.com.
Mailing Address: PO Box
281, Purling, NY 12470.
Falls View Dr. (off County
Rd. 24), Purling, NY
12470.
Price: Inexpensive.
Credit Cards: Inquire when
reserve room.
Restrictions: No smoking;
no pets; no children.
Special Features: Private
swimming; herb garden.

The tumbling falls of Shinglekill Creek are directly in front of the house. The wonderful, restful sound of the waterfall is a soothing lullaby, a perfect backdrop for breakfast or for curling up later on the wicker furniture on the porch, overlooking the 30-foot waterfall. The waterfall feeds into a deep, cold, clear, and private swimming hole (private because the only access requires trespassing across private property). The creek feeds into Catskill Creek, which flows into the Hudson River.

Built in the 1880s when this area was a prosperous milling, tanning, and brick-making area, the house has been extended by a series of multilevel wooden decks, one of which holds an outdoor hot tub. Owners/innkeepers Hugh and Linda Curry (he was the tennis director at The Breakers in Palm Beach, and she is an artist) have transformed the

Breakfast is served with a serene view at the Tumblin' Falls House.

Evelyn Kanter

little wooden house into a sparkling jewel. She and her artist brother have stenciled walls, floors, and furniture — look for the fox hiding in a corner of the armoire painted to look like a chicken coop. They left untouched the now-extinct American chestnut paneling on the walls and doors upstairs.

Rooms are tiny but comfortable, with vintage oak furniture and handmade quilts. There are four rooms and suites. Falling Water Suite is the only one in the front, facing — good guess — the falling water. In addition to the downstairs parlor, the garage has been turned into a guest hangout, with a small bar and pool table. There's an herb garden and a "friend's garden," with stones engraved with the names of regular visitors — clearly, this is the kind of place to return to often.

HOTELS & MOTELS

Comfort Inn (845-246-1565; 2790 Rte. 32 (west of Saugerties exit on NYS Thruway) 65 rooms; handicap access. AE, D, DC, MC, V.

CHAPTER FOUR
Eat, Drink & Be Merry
RESTAURANTS & FOOD PURVEYORS

Tania Barricklo/Daily Freeman

Hudson Valley restaurants take pride in using the meats and produce grown by regional farms and the wines from local vineyards.

The Hudson Valley is a delicious place, polka-dotted with hundreds of family farms and orchards (some in the same family for hundreds of years) that grow much of the fresh fruits and produce, grass-fed beef, free-range poultry, and artisanal cheeses that local restaurants serve so proudly. And let's not forget the wines — this part of New York State has been producing bottled sunshine since the first European settlers first harvested wild grapes in the 17th century.

Regional cuisine runs the gamut from burger joints and historic roadside diners to world-class gourmet experiences, influenced in no small measure by the presence of the Culinary Institute of America, the world's only residential college devoted entirely to culinary education. Many of its graduates have opened impressive restaurants in the region, and many local bed-and-breakfast owners have taken courses at the CIA to improve the quality of their morning muffins and omelettes.

The combination of food and wine has prompted many to label the region as "the Napa Valley of the East." Except Napa doesn't have the bounty of restaurants with patios and picture windows overlooking the dramatic splendor of the Hudson River. Nor does it have its history — George Washington slept here, ate here, fought here, and won a war here. Many Hudson Valley restaurants are housed in Revolutinary-era homes, where the patina on the walls matches the perfection on the plates.

We could not include all the restaurants in this bounteous land — there are simply too many. Although the quality of food is most important, ambiance, service, decor, and overall value for price are integral, too, for a memorable meal. While this information is as up-to-date as we could make it, it is wise to call ahead, especially to make reservations for dinner on busy warm weather weekends.

Each restaurant is designated with a price code, representing the approximate cost of a three-course meal (starter, main course, dessert), but not including cocktails or wine, coffee or tea, tax, or tips. Restaurants with prix fixe menus are noted accordingly.

Serving Codes

B	Breakfast	HT	High Tea
BR	Brunch	D	Dinner
L	Lunch		

Price Codes

Inexpensive	Up to $15	Expensive	$25–$50
Moderate	$15–$25	Very Expensive	$50 and up

Credit Cards

AE	American Express	DC	Diner's Club
CB	Carte Blanche	MC	MasterCard
D	Discover	V	Visa

DINING: WESTCHESTER COUNTY

Briarcliff Manor

ORFINO'S
914-941-9833.
1201 Pleasantville Rd.,
 Briarcliff Manor, NY 10510.

This family-run restaurant has a friendly, familiar feel and classic Italian cuisine, plus some surprises. The extended multigeneration Orfino family knows regulars by name and are just as gra-

Open: Mon.–Sat.
Price: Inexpensive (L);
    Moderate (D).
Cuisine: Italian.
Serving: B, L Mon.–Sat.,
    D Wed.–Sat. at 6 pm.
Credit Cards: No.
Reservations:
    Recommended on
    weekends.
Handicap Access: Yes.

cious and welcoming to newcomers. There's a long list of the expected pasta, veal, and seafood dishes, including a hearty veal Parmesan, delicately wine-flavored veal Marsala, and a garlicky linguine with white clam sauce. Especially good is the vitella rustica, lightly breaded veal topped with shrimp, peas, and mushrooms and a sauce that's richer than tomato but not quite a meat stock gravy. The name may be rustic, but the blend of flavors is definitely sophisticated.

Lunch is casual and inexpensive, with paper place mats and napkins; tablecloths and candles come out for dinner. At midday, it's seat yourself; the regulars know this, newcomers don't, making it easy to spot first-timers. The varied daytime menu includes dinner-type entrées, plus burgers and sandwiches. Breads and pastries are delivered daily from a bakery on Arthur Ave., the Little Italy of NYC's Bronx. Portions are uniformly generous, and with the moderate prices and casual trattorìa atmosphere, Orfino's is a favorite for families, especially on Wed., when there are several pasta specials under $10. It can get pretty crowded, so go early or late if you don't want to wait for a table.

Chappaqua

**CRABTREE'S KITTLE
    HOUSE**
914-666-8044.
11 Kittle Rd., Chappaqua,
    NY 10514.
Open: Daily.
Price: Very Expensive.
Cuisine: Regional
    American.
Serving: L Mon.–Fri., D
    daily, BR Sat., Sun.
Credit Cards: AE, D, DC,
    MC, V.
Reservations:
    Recommended; yes, on
    weekends.
Handicap Access: Yes.

This landmark mansion was built in 1790 and has been serving guests since the early 1900s, so there's been plenty of time to get it right. Elegant, formal dining here includes an award-winning wine list, an inventive menu focusing on regional specialties, such as Hudson Valley foie gras, served with Bordeaux jelly and milk-fed, locally raised veal. Although the menu changes daily, venison and house-smoked salmon are always available, and the oxtail ravioli in chanterelle broth has become a favorite of repeat diners. Medallions of veal arrive with whipped sweet potatoes that have been seasoned with a hint of vanilla, a surprising taste jolt. Save room for dessert. Even those who aren't chocoholics will be tempted by the Valhrona chocolate pastry, served warm.

Tables are set with fancy china and crystal glassware, and the cutlery and plates are replaced effortlessly with every course. Service is as impeccable as the food and wine; waitstaff sometimes seem to dance around antique creaking floorboards. The elegant, formal decor of the dining area is further enhanced by fireplaces, and the gardens surrounding the house are idyllic in warm weather months when tables near the windows are hard to come by. Adding to both the formality and attention to detail, valet parking is mandatory; there is no self-parking. On weekends, there's live jazz in the bar area. This restaurant always tops local lists for a special dining experience. Crabtree's Kittle House is also a 12-room bed-and-breakfast for a romantic getaway.

Croton-on-Hudson

FORTUNA RISTORANTE
914-271-2600.
1 Baltic Place (off Rte, 9),
  Croton-on-Hudson, NY
  10520.
Open: Tues.–Sun.
Price: Moderate–Expensive.
Cuisine: Italian.
Serving: L, D.
Credit Cards: AE, MC, V.
Reservations:
  Recommended.
Handicap Access: Yes.

When most patrons are seen leaving a restaurant with smiles on their faces and take-home paper bags in their hands, it's a sure sign portions are generous and what couldn't be finished is too good to leave behind. The young owner is a second-generation restaurateur — his father and four uncles own five restaurants in New York City and nearby in Briarcliff Manor — and he is a gracious and attentive maître d' and host.

There are varnished wood walls interspersed with stencil-painted walls in skin-flattering peach tones, and the waitstaff wear brocade vests. It makes for a warm, slightly formal atmosphere, but not the least bit stuffy or pretentious. The menu contains traditional Italian favorites like fried calamari appetizer and veal Marsala, but the specialties are a double-thick veal chop on a bed of garlic-studded spinach, and a pan-roasted quail smothered in a homemade plum wine reduction on a bed of wild rice. Whole fish is deboned tableside by waiters with old-world style, experience, and flair.

Desserts are homemade from family recipes. The tiramisù and Italian ricotta cheesecake are four-inch-deep treats; one serving is more than enough to share. There also is an extensive wine list, more than 140 labels, with an equitable distribution of Oregon, Napa, and Italian reds and whites.

Hartsdale

**EPSTEIN'S KOSHER
  DELI**
914-428-5320.
387 Central Ave., Hartsdale,
  NY 10530.
Open: Daily.
Price: Moderate.
Cuisine: Kosher deli.
Serving: L, D.
Credit Cards: AE, DC, MC,
  V.

This is the closest thing to a real NYC deli in the Hudson Valley, and it's tucked into a strip mall on a busy commercial road. The corned beef and pastrami sandwiches on crusty rye are sufficiently overstuffed to rank as a full meal. Don't even think about asking for ketchup or mayo; anything other than deli mustard on a deli meat sandwich is heresy. While the fries are crispy enough to stand alone without that red dipping sauce, better you

Reservations: No.
Handicap Access: Yes.

should order a knish, either the giant square of seasoned mashed potato inside a delicately fried puff or the circular one filled with kasha, known outside deli doors as buckwheat.

Scrumptious and full-meal offerings include chicken fricassee, roast turkey with gravy, homemade Hungarian beef goulash, and chicken soup with a baseball-sized matzo ball. But the deli sandwiches are the lure here, a perfect match for the bowl on each table of half-sour pickles and make-your-mouth-pucker-and-eyes-tear super sours, alongside a second bowl of creamy coleslaw. You say you want a salad of mixed greens, heirloom tomatoes, and balsamic vinegar? Not a chance. For dessert, opt for a slice of seven-layer cake — layers a smidgen thicker than a computer diskette, separated by layers of buttercream and held together by a chocolate cover. Wash it all down with Dr. Brown's cream soda or the legendary Cel-Ray Tonic, a celery-flavored soda that, well, you have to taste it to believe how good it is.

Hastings-on-Hudson

HARVEST ON HUDSON
914-478-2800.
www.harvest2000.com.
1 River St. (bet. railroad
   tracks and river),
   Hastings-on-Hudson, NY
   10706.
Open: Daily.
Price: Moderate.
Cuisine: Mediterranean
   with French, Italian
   influences.
Serving: L Mon.–Fri., D
   daily.
Credit Cards: MC, V.
Reservations: Yes.
Handicap Access: Yes.

This is a former truck warehouse on the strip of land between the MetroNorth railroad tracks and the Hudson River. The wide drive-through bays are now huge picture windows opening to spectacular water views. Inside, the big open space has been warmed with a Mediterranean decor of tiles and polished wood, but it still can be noisy when crowded, and it does get crowded, thanks to the inventive menu and reasonable prices for the quality of the food and the view. In warm weather, the outdoor patio is the most popular spot to dine on metal tables with huge shading umbrellas, just a stone's throw from the river. In cooler temperatures, fireplaces in the dining area take away the river chill.

The menu is Mediterranean, heavy on the Italian. The house specialty is chiochiolli, which is a cheese-filled, tortellinilike pasta tossed with a tangy Gorgonzola sauce and served in a bowl with fresh peas and chunks of homemade sausage. When the waiter asks if you want Parmesan, it is freshly ground over your plate from a cylinder-shaped grinder. The antique snail-shaped pasta molds are from Italy, and Harvest on the Hudson claims to be the only restaurant in the U.S. with these pasta shapes. All the pastas are homemade. There is an excellent Chilean sea bass browned under a soy glaze, served with a crunchy/spicy side of bok choy and radish sprouts. The 42-ounce porterhouse for two is big enough to serve three or four.

The garden alongside the huge outdoor patio grows organic vegetables and herbs, including heirloom tomatoes, basil, and thyme for pesto and red sauces. Garden zucchini, lightly grilled until smoky, graces the seasonal seafood antipasto.

Katonah

BLUE DOLPHIN RISTORANTE
914-232-4791.
175 Katonah Ave., Katonah, NY 10536.
Open: Mon.–Sat.
Price: Moderate.
Cuisine: Italian.
Serving: L, D.
Credit Cards: AE, MC, V.
Reservations: No.
Handicap Access: No.

From the outside, the Blue Dolphin looks like a greasy spoon diner, replete with a tacky blue dolphin neon sign on the roof, easy to pass by if you don't know its reputation. Locals call it Westchester County's best kept secret, with top-quality fresh food at moderate prices and an ever-present owner who takes charge of every aspect, from checking each dish coming out of the kitchen to making sure everyone has a drink while waiting for tables. Since no reservations are accepted, you are likely to wait on busy weekends and peak weekday dinner times. Most people take their drinks outside and sit on one of the wrought iron benches in front of the restaurant. The atmosphere is casual and friendly.

The cuisine and decor celebrate Southern Italy, where the owners are from. There is nothing fussy or complicated about the food, which is uniformly delicious. Salmon Limone, salmon steak with a lemon-butter sauce, is accompanied by Swiss chard. Veal Caprese, with diced tomato and arugula, arrives with linguine with marinara sauce. Polenta is a house specialty, and one of the more interesting appetizers is flavorful frilled shrimp with polenta. The most interesting main course may be the black (squid ink) linguine puttanesca — a zingy caper-garlic-olive-anchovy tomato sauce over black pasta.

Save room for the intensely flavored homemade sorbets — the lemon sorbet is served inside a hollowed-out frozen lemon and the orange sorbet inside a frozen, hollowed orange. The wine list has a wide price range, with many affordable choices by the glass.

Ossining

DUDLEY'S
914-941-8674.
www.dineatdudleys.com.
6 Rockledge Ave., Ossining, NY 10562.
Open: Daily.
Price: Expensive.
Cuisine: American with Asian touches.
Serving: L Mon.–Fri., D daily.

It's hard to miss this purple house and awning, nestled in a residential street in an historic section of Ossining. Although the outside is painfully purple, the decor inside is quiet and calm. It's an interesting contrast.

Dudley's has been a restaurant since the Prohibition era, when liquor was smuggled from boats on the Hudson River through an underground tunnel

Credit Cards: AE, D, MC, V.
Reservations: Yes.
Handicap Access: Yes.

to a trapdoor, which still exists in the floor behind the bar. The place also was a favorite of crime reporters of major newspapers from New York City to Albany in the days when inmates at nearby Sing Sing Prison were front page news, so popular with reporters that telephones were installed at each bar stool. When the lights dimmed, the reporters knew the electric chair was being used and would call in their stories.

Dudley's doesn't rest on its history. The menu is lively and combines broiled steak house favorites with more ambitious efforts. For example, the certified Angus filet is grilled with truffle oil and a Madeira demi-glaze and is served with a large grilled portobello mushroom cap, garlic mashed potatoes, and candied carrots. One of the more interesting appetizers is smoked salmon wrapped around tangy daikon sprouts that add both zip and crunch, with a dollop of salmon caviar. Sometimes, though, the chef tries too hard, as with a salad of figs and walnuts over mixed baby greens drizzled with a honey-lemon sour cream dressing. But there is no faulting the melting chocolate cake with vanilla ice cream for dessert, except that if you linger, it turns into a brownish puddle on the plate that doesn't look nearly as good as it tastes.

Peekskill

Tania Barricklo

Enjoying High Tea at Kathleen's Tea Room.

KATHLEEN'S TEA ROOM
914-734-2520.

This is an utterly charming Victorian-style tea-room where you are served individual pots of tea from a vast collection of floral and Oriental

979 Main St., Peekskill, NY
   10566.
Open: Mon.–Sat.
   11am–5pm.
Price: Inexpensive.
Cuisine: British tea menu.
Serving: L, HT.
Credit Cards: No.
Reservations:
   Recommended.
Handicap Access: Yes.

china teapots. The teapots don't necessarily match the antique china plates, and each of the tables in this tiny tearoom is covered with a chintz tablecloth, also no two alike. There are more than two dozen teas on the menu, from hearty English breakfast to delicate fruit teas, such as apricot, "paradise peach," and an unusual lavender tea that is like drinking a summer garden. The exposed brick walls and original pressed tin ceiling in this 1850s storefront are softened by a profusion of unruly ferns on wrought iron stands between the tea tables and lace curtains on the front windows. It all adds up to a happy clutter, and owner Kathleen Chilcott is normally on hand to encourage socializing.

The menu is primarily light and traditional tea-style fare. Wonderfully flaky homemade scones are served with a huge dollop of imported Devonshire cream and berry jam, and crustless tea sandwiches arrive on a multitiered wrought iron stand. There's formal High Tea with scones, sandwiches, and petit fours. The heartiest things on the menu are the homemade savory pies and individual vegetarian dishes filled with combinations of sun-dried tomatoes, spinach, and cheeses. Smoked turkey and grilled chicken sandwiches get a tasty jolt from cranberry-studded mayonnaise; all the sandwiches are served with raw vegetables.

Tarrytown

CARAVELA
914-631-1863.
53 N. Broadway (Rte. 9),
   Tarrytown, NY 10591.
Open: Daily.
Price: Moderate.
Cuisine: Portuguese and
   Brazilian.
Serving: L, D.
Credit Cards: All major
   credit cards.
Reservations:
   Recommended on
   weekends.
Handicap Access: Yes

If you have a craving for fish or shellfish, Caravela is a must. Yes, there are hearty meat and poultry dishes on the menu, but the specialty of the house is robustly seasoned fresh fish and shellfish. Start with broiled Portuguese sardines, each a generous six-inches long, meaty and tender, or try the chewy grilled squid, served hot over a bed of greens. Everything is flavorful, from shrimp sautéed in fresh garlic and Portuguese olive oil to grilled swordfish covered with a spicy Brazilian red sauce. For those who prefer smaller fires, the traditional mariscada seafood stew, laden with scallops and clams is a good option or the heaping portion of paella, enough for two, which is available every day but Sat. For meat eaters, there is an excellent roast duckling with an unusual port wine and date sauce, plus several dishes are garnished with Portuguese sausage, similar to Spanish chorizo but less spicy and more meaty. Desserts are homemade. The fruit tarts are luscious and bursting with flavor.

Caravela is decorated with diagonal wood paneling and mirrors, giving it a larger feel than its actual space. Even though the waitstaff is uniformed in black vests and there are tablecloths and linen napkins at lunch as well as dinner, there is still a casual, neighborhood feel. There is even a separate bar area.

Dining at Equus combines elegant food, service, and decor.

Courtesy Tarrytown Castle

EQUUS
914-631-1980.
www.castleattarrytown
  .com.
400 Benedict Ave.,
  Tarrytown Castle,
  Tarrytown, NY 10591.
Open: Daily.
Price: Very Expensive.
Cuisine: American with
  fine French influences.
Serving: L, D.
Credit Cards: All major
  credit cards.
Reservations: Highly
  recommended.
Handicap Access: Yes.

Simply one of the best, most sumptuously decorated and expensive restaurants in the Hudson Valley, guaranteed to make you feel like the millionaire who built this medieval-style castle a century ago atop one of the highest points in Westchester County (Tarrytown Castle also offers superior lodging, see Chapter Three, *Lodging*).

Equus is comprised of three dining rooms. The Oak Room was transported from France, with richly carved walls, exposed beams, and a huge stone fireplace dominating one wall — very masculine and formal. The Tapestry Room is light and airy, with crystal chandeliers, high-back tapestry chairs, period oil paintings, and thick Aubusson-style carpeting — very feminine and formal. The Garden Room has window walls on three sides and breathtaking views across the Hudson River — on a clear day you can see the New York City skyline; in warm weather, there's an outdoor terrace.

The food is equal to the setting, served by a small army of waitstaff in tuxedos. Equus is one of the few restaurants that will make an appetizer portion of risotto, such as a moist heirloom tomato risotto with fava beans for added texture. An herb-crusted loin of lamb is accompanied by a black olive sauce, a tart change from the fruit or wine sauces usually served with lamb. Seared tournedos of Black Angus beef are so tender that a steak knife isn't needed. There is a prix fixe four-course dinner menu and a three-course lunch menu, both including dessert, which sounds reasonable until one adds wine, coffee, and tips. But for special occasion dining, Equus is very special indeed.

Be sure to request the dining room of your choice when you make a reservation, since the "uninformed" can wind up in an adjunct foyerlike area that is not quite the same elegant experience. And be sure to take time before or after your meal to stroll the stunning landscaped grounds and linger in the lobby, dotted with yet more vintage oil paintings.

DINING: PUTNAM COUNTY

Cold Spring

Located in a cul-de-sac behind a small garden, Cathryn's serves up Tuscan favorites.

Evelyn Kanter

**CATHRYN'S TUSCAN
GRILL**
845-265-5582.
www.tuscangrill.com.
91 Main St., Cold Spring,
NY 10516.
Open: Daily.
Price: Moderate–Expensive.
Cuisine: Northern Italian.
Serving: L, D, BR Sun.
Credit Cards: AE, DC, MC,
V.
Reservations:
  Recommended on
  weekends.
Handicap Access: Yes.

Tucked behind a vest-pocket garden in Cold Spring's main downtown shopping area, this gem is easy to miss if you don't know it's there. Two adjoining dining areas serve unpretentious Tuscan favorites in a similarly unpretentious atmosphere. The room to the right of the entrance has warm wood and tent-style fabric draped from the somewhat-low ceilings with tables close together, creating an intimate setting. Claustrophobics might prefer the pale plaster walls and 14-foot ceiling of the dining area adjoining the bar.

Food is uniformly excellent. Start with the appetizer sautéed calamari, a delicious change from the chewy, breaded kind served in most Italian restaurants. Cathryn's smokes its own tomatoes in the backyard, and the calamari is served in a fresh smoked tomato sauce topped with fresh herbs. Grilled vegetables are combined with smoked mozzarella, and the calves liver, found on few menus these days, is grilled in sage butter. Regulars rave about the rabbit in a grappa sauce that lends a bite of tartness to the sweetish meat, and the Tuscan fish stew is hearty and brimming with tender morsels. In season, the fettuccine with zucchini flowers, currants, pignoli nuts, and anchovies is a taste jolt of sweet, salty, and nutty in perfect symmetry. For dessert, skip all the tempting treats listed and opt for the tiramisù, homemade and light as a meringue. There's an extensive wine list, liberally sprinkled with Italian reds, and, in warm weather months, there are bistro tables in the garden.

A plaque alongside the Depot explains how Cold Spring was named.

Evelyn Kanter

DEPOT
845-265-5000.
www.coldspringdepot.com.
One Depot Sq., Cold Spring,
   NY 10516.
Open: Daily.
Price: Moderate.
Cuisine: American.
Serving: L Mon.–Fri., D, BR
   weekends.
Credit Cards: AE, MC, V.
Reservations: No.
Handicap Access: Yes.

The Depot was built in 1893 as a passenger and freight terminal for the New York Central, whose descendent MetroNorth, the commuter railroad, now stops a few yards away at a newer, more modern station. This was an active train station until 1954, when it became an auto dealership; it has been a restaurant since 1972. The present dining room was the old waiting room; the bar area was the ticket office. There are historic photos on the walls, which still have the original varnished wainscoting. The walls are sturdy enough that the pictures barely shake when the trains roar past, momentarily halting conversation — not because of the noise, but because it is wide-eyed wonderful to be so close.

The all-American menu includes steaks, chops, crab cakes, a thick filet mignon with garlic sauce, and the owner's mother's meat loaf recipe, as well as several inspired creations. The "upstate chicken" is a meaty breast sautéed with cider from local apples and dried fruit. They also have a surprisingly good Louisana-style shrimp étouffée. At lunch, choices range from wraps and sandwiches to good, thick burgers. The food is perfectly adequate, but the real appeal is the trains that whiz by the windows every 15 minutes or so. In warm weather months, there is patio service, and on weekends a Dixieland jazz band plays in the little patio bandstand.

The Depot also operates an old-fashioned ice-cream parlor next to the restaurant from May-Nov., with penny candy, freshly made shakes and malts, and 16 flavors of ice cream. Since it's just two blocks to the water, it's easy and pleasant to take an ice-cream cone for a afternoon walk along the Hudson River.

HUDSON HOUSE INN
845-265-9355.
www.hudsonhouseinn.com.
2 Main St., Cold Spring, NY
  10516.
Open: Wed.–Mon.
Price: Moderate–Expensive.
Cuisine: American.
Serving: L Thurs.–Mon., D,
  BR weekends.
Credit Cards: AE, DC, MC,
  V.
Reservations:
  Recommended.
Handicap Access: Yes.

The only way to be closer to the Hudson River is to be on a boat. The Hudson House Inn is just yards from the shore. This landmark inn opened in the 1830s when it offered overnight accommodations and meals to steamship passengers and crew, and has been serving guests ever since (see Chapter Three, *Lodging*). The owners take pride in featuring local produce, cheeses, and wines, such as the Coach Farm goat cheese appetizer with crunchy onion chips instead of more conventional crackers and the linguine with grilled vegetables in a light, almost smoky sauce. The sesame-crusted yellowfin arrives rare and barely warm, with wasabi whipped potatoes that add a sushilike punch to the fish. There's also a hearty breast of duck with a red wine reduction sauce. Save room for the pumpkin caramel cake, one of the house specialty desserts: an inch-high disk of dense, intensely flavored moist cake, topped with a two-inch dollop of fresh whipped cream and dusted with nutmeg.

Large windows facing west make the dining room bright and cheery, until sunset when the room turns absolutely golden. The Hudson House Inn is decorated throughout with Colonial farmhouse antiques and delicate floral wallpaper and, of course, has the original wide-plank floorboards. In addition to the main dining room, there is a pub-style Half Moon Tavern in the lounge area with a wide, warming fireplace. In warm weather, there is dining on the riverfront porch.

BRASSERIE LE
  BOUCHON
845-265-7676.
76 Main St., Cold Spring,
  NY 10516.
Open: Tues.–Sun.; winter:
  Wed.–Sun.
Price: Moderate–Expensive.

Le Bouchon is a classic French brasserie with some thoroughly modern touches, such as the classic, perfectly crisp and evenly salted pommes frites served in a proper paper cone, which is placed inside an aluminum martini shaker. It's not just for style — the metal keeps the pommes frites hot throughout the meal. Cassoulet du chef also is

Cuisine: French bistro.
Serving: L, D.
Credit Cards: All major
  credit cards.
Reservations:
  Recommended on
  weekends.
Handicap Access: Yes.

a switch from the traditional, prepared here with Hudson Valley duck and homemade sausage. This dish is surprisingly popular even in warm weather when such hearty dishes are rare on French restaurant menus. But chef/owner Pascal Graff, formerly of New York City's award-winning Les Halles, became famous for demystifying French cuisine. Other bistro favorites are moules à la marinière and an updated curried mussel dish, prepared with apples whose sweetness cuts the spicy bite; apples also accompany the homemade black blood sausage. There's an excellent steak au poivre, a New York strip encrusted with crushed pepper and served with a mellow cognac cream sauce. For dessert, the gigantic crème brûlée is too much for one person, but the trio of homemade fruit sorbets is just right.

Le Bouchon is housed in a Colonial-era brick building with original wide-plank floors, and the walls have been lacquered a burgundy red and hung with light-reflecting mirrors and bistro posters. Be sure to check out the original marble fireplace behind the bar area — it's been converted into a wine storage bin. There's both front porch and backyard garden dining in warm weather, and, of course, a fine selection of French wines.

NORTHGATE AT DOCKSIDE HARBOR
845-265-5555.
www.docksideharbor.com.
1 North St. (foot of Main
  St.), Cold Spring, NY
  10516.
Open: Daily.
Price: Moderate–Expensive.
Cuisine: American.
Serving: L, D.
Credit Cards: MC, V.
Reservations:
  Recommended.
Handicap Access: Yes.

This property began life in the 1960s as a yacht club. While there are still some docks, the old clubhouse, with its stone walls and huge picture windows, was turned into a restaurant in the 1980s. This is really three restaurants in one, with different menus, but the view is the same spectacular riverfront panorama. The clubhouse dining area is the most formal, with tablecloths, small flower vases, and candlelight in the evening. It serves such items as a tangy goat cheese ravioli appetizer, a seared sea scallops entrée, and a totally decadent caramel pecan fudge cake dessert. The same menu is offered in the tented patio area, which is open from mid-May to mid-Sept. Outdoors, tables are decorated with fanciful ceramic fish centerpieces, appropriate to the waterside location, and both indoors and on the patio that same whimsy is visible in the colorful china service. Plates are bright, colorful, and fun.

Beyond the patio, there is a casual burger and fries menu at the riverside bar, where food is served in picnic-style, paper-lined plastic bowls. There also are stone tables and wait service on the lawn, in between the bar and the water. If you get here at sunset, you'll be so mesmerized by the sun dipping behind Storm King Mountain that your food will get cold. On weekends in the summer, there's a live combo band in the tent.

Garrison

BIRD & BOTTLE INN
845-424-3000; 800-782-6837.
www.birdbottle.com.
info@birdbottle.com.
1123 Old Albany Post Rd.
 (off Rte. 9), Garrison, NY
 10524.
Open: Daily; winter:
 Thurs.–Sun.
Price: Moderate–Expensive.
Cuisine: American.
Serving: D, BR Sun.
Credit Cards: AE, D, DC,
 MC, V.
Reservations: Yes.
Handicap Access: No.

Both history buffs and those seeking a special gourmet dining experience will be happily satisfied in this Revolutionary-era inn, which started life as a stagecoach stop and taproom in 1761. The original wide-plank floorboards creak in spots. The low light and candlelight enhances the patina of the burnished wood tables and exposed beams and adds magic to the antique pewter accessories and framed prints decorating the walls and fireplace mantels. Tables are set with pewter chargers and fine crystal, and the food is equally elegant.

The portobello mushroom appetizer is smothered in Gorgonzola cheese, chopped artichokes, and spinach, an interesting blend of tastes and textures, and the crab cakes are generous with meaty seafood chunks. The New Zealand rack of lamb is crusted with a flavorful mix of panco (a chunky bread crumb) and horseradish, and the three double-thick chops arrive perfectly medium-rare with a garlic polenta that is more creamy than garlicky. There is always a fish entrée, such as pan-seared salmon with a cabernet reduction, and a game selection is usually venison or quail, plus the occasional marinated ostrich steak. Desserts are homemade. Fresh fruit cobblers are deep and flaky, but the real standout is the chocolate pâté, layers of bittersweet and white chocolate and praline for crunch. It's the kind of dessert that makes you close your eyes to memorize the taste.

There are three dining rooms here. Remember, this is a Colonial house with small rooms by today's standards — each has a working fireplace. The smallest, the Map Room, holds just four tables, the choice for quiet, romantic dinners or just private conversation. There is a patio and garden, and the Bird & Bottle is also a charming B&B (see Chapter Three, *Lodging*).

DINING: DUTCHESS COUNTY

Beacon

BROTHER'S TRATTORIA
845-838-3300.
465 Main St., Beacon, NY
 12508.
Open: Daily.
Price: Inexpensive.
Cuisine: Italian.

From the outside, this looks like a classic pizza take-out joint, and while they do serve pizza in big white cardboard boxes, Brother's Trattoria also serves up excellent and inexpensive made-to-order dishes from the open kitchen in the back of this long, narrow storefront restaurant. The baked ziti arrives

Serving: L, D.
Credit Cards: MC, V.
Reservations: Accepted.
Handicap Access: Yes.

piping hot, with a sauce so rich with cheese that it does not need additional spoons of Parmesan. The veal Marsala is tender and comes with a choice of angel hair or penne pasta. The "everything" pizza is smothered in grilled vegetables, sausage, and pepperoni and ample enough to serve six.

The decor is modern and unpretentious, an interesting juxtaposition against the exposed brick walls and old-fashioned Italian food. Banquettes are covered in dark tapestrylike fabric. There are dark wood tables and chairs, angular light fixtures, and good-quality framed artwork. Service can be slow when the place is crowded, because the small kitchen cannot keep up with the orders, but the food is so good and the prices are so reasonable, it's worth the wait.

THE PIGGY BANK
845-838-0028.
448 Main St., Beacon, NY
   12508.
Open: Tues.–Sun.
Price: Moderate.
Cuisine: Southern BBQ.
Serving: L, D.
Credit Cards: AE, DC, MC,
   V.
Reservations:
   Recommended for 5 or
   more.
Handicap Access: Yes

The first bite of the cornbread is a good clue that this is no ordinary Southern barbecue restaurant. It is moist, sweet, and cakelike, not crumbly, dry, and grainy. The Piggy Bank smokes its own meat, so the ribs, chicken, and pulled pork are as moist as the cornbread, with a good dose of smoke flavor and cooked to such tenderness that your knife is unnecessary. Ribs can be ordered Texas or Kansas City style, dripping with sauce, or dry-grilled, Memphis style. Sides are standard choices, but everything is homemade, from the thick fresh-cut fries to the creamy coleslaw and sauce-rich barbecue beans. Salads are listed on the menu as "lawn clippings." Or, get your fingers dirty on garlic-laced, peel-and-eat shrimp, served with a sinus-clearing jalapeño cocktail sauce. Don't worry about getting the tablecloths dirty — tablecloths here are really kitchen towels.

On Tues., the place is generally packed for the all-you-can-eat ribs special, but the "pig out sampler" of chicken, ribs, and pork is available every night. If you haven't completely pigged out, the key lime pie is a creamy, tangy palate cleanser.

The Piggy Bank is housed in Beacon's 1880 bank; the old bank vault is behind the bar and holds the restaurant's wine cellar. The original tin ceiling has been refurbished, and there are ceiling fans, mismatched, vintage carved oak chairs, exposed brick walls, and the original frosted glass windows. There's an old-fashioned wooden porch deck for warm weather dining, but unfortunately, it overlooks the parking area.

Dover Plains

OLD DROVERS INN
845-832-9311.
www.olddroversinn.com.
196 E. Duncan Hill Rd. (Old
  Rte. 22), Dover Plains,
  NY 12522.
Open: Thurs.–Tues.
Price: Very Expensive.
Cuisine: American.
Serving: L Fri.–Sat., D, BR
  Sun.
Credit Cards: All major
  credit cards.
Reservations:
  Recommended.
Handicap Access: Yes.

Small, intimate, and elegant, the Old Drovers Inn is a Hudson Valley classic, wrapped in the patina of a classic white Colonial building that has been welcoming guests since 1750, when cowboys who drove their cattle to market in NYC stopped here. The huge blazing fireplace and tabletop lanterns cast a warm glow against the broad exposed beams and wood paneling, setting the well-polished crystal sparkling in the firelight. This is a top choice for special occasion dining.

In addition to a basket of homemade breads and crisps, they also serve a plate of old-fashioned deviled eggs. Local and seasonal ingredients are always used in the choices on the menu. The restaurant's signature dish, a thick, hearty, and smooth cheddar cheese soup, almost a meal in itself, is served in an antique pewter bowl and has been on the menu for more than 60 years. Turkey hash, which is topped with a poached egg, and sweet corn succotash are other dishes that harken back to the inn's Colonial roots, but most choices are thoroughly modern and appealing. The three-bone rack of lamb with tomato chutney is perfectly pink and seasoned and served with a beet salad polka-dotted with local goat cheese. The artisanal cheese course for dessert is a well-selected mix of textures and tastes, but it's hard to resist the light crusty tart with raspberries and cream, the chocolate cake with a sauce sparkling with candied ginger, or the sinfully smooth crème brûlée.

Old Drovers Inn also is an elegantly appointed B&B (see Chapter Three, *Lodging*), and the wooded grounds are perfect for strolling before or after a meal.

Hyde Park

**CULINARY INSTITUTE
  OF AMERICA**
845-452-9600.
www.ciachef.edu/
  restaurants.
info@ciachef.edu.
Rte. 9, Hyde Park, NY
  12538.
Handicap Access: Yes.

Founded in 1946, this is the only residential college in the world devoted entirely to culinary education. An important part of the education is the four restaurants and a coffee shop on campus: each serving a different cuisine, each with a different level of formality, and each excellent. Student sous chefs, pastry chefs, sommeliers, and waitstaff, who all wear classic white uniforms, are supervised by experienced executive chefs and maître d's, who also are their professors. Each restaurant focuses on fresh, seasonal ingredients, so menus

Watch your meal being prepared by student chefs at the Culinary Institute of America.

Courtesy Culinary Institute of America

change seasonally, and each restaurant has a 3,000-bottle wine cellar specific to its menu. Reservations are recommended, if not required, especially for dinner.

Many of the school's chefs have remained in the Hudson Valley after graduation. Many of the dining spots in the area are popular and successful because of their creativity and expertise.

Everything is prepared to order, so do not expect to rush or be rushed in any of the following CIA restaurants: Escoffier, American Bounty, Ristorante Caterina de' Medici, and St. Andrew's Café. Also there is the Apple Pie Bakery Café, a take-out coffee shop.

ESCOFFIER
Open: Tues.–Sat.
Price: Expensive.
Cuisine: Classic French.
Serving: L, D.
Credit Cards: All major credit cards.
Reservations: Required; business dress; no jeans or sneakers.

Named for the legendary French chef Auguste Escoffier, this restaurant features elegant, formal fine French dining with a contemporary touch. The two dining areas are decorated with French country wallpaper, fresh flowers, and flowered china on the clothed tables. One room overlooks the stainless-steel open kitchen, the other has huge windows offering spectacular views across the Hudson River. This is the only restaurant at CIA with tableside preparation, for such dishes as Caesar salad, flambé desserts, and deboned fish.

A cream of watercress soup is surprisingly light and refreshing. Traditional escargots are updated with the addition of ground hazelnuts to the properly garlicky butter sauce, or choose your snails smothered in a tomato-basil sauce. A double dose salmon appetizer combines silky smooth smoked salmon with a dollop of salmon tartare. There's an excellent fish and seafood stew, studded with tender morsels, in a lightly seasoned cream sauce. Escoffier makes magic with duckling, such as the Gascony-style confit, with prunes, apples, and walnuts in an Armagnac black pepper sauce. If you have room, there are ethereal desserts, including crème brûlée and sweet fresh fruit tartins.

AMERICAN BOUNTY

Open: Tues.–Sat.
Price: Expensive.
Cuisine: American regional.
Serving: L, D.
Credit Cards: All major credit cards.
Reservations: Recommended; no jeans or sneakers.

The mission of this restaurant is to focus on the wealth and diversity of America's regional cultural cuisines, prepared with local ingredients and updated with contemporary, gourmet touches, but not always. Some things taste like Mother made, if Mother was an excellent cook, and most lunch entrées appear as well on the dinner menu. There are two dining areas: one room overlooks the glass-fronted open kitchen, where chefs wear fluted toques; the other room is long and somewhat narrow, but since one wall has 20-foot windows overlooking a garden, there's an open, airy feel.

A wonderful touch is a trio of soups sampler — tiny portions of the day's specials, served in demitasse-sized cups. One summer day, the trio was a roasted corn and tortilla soup with a dollop of bell pepper cream, a chilled, chunky gazpacho, and an Amish-style chicken and corn soup thick with hand-cut noodles. Another welcome feature is that the menu lists the recommended by-the-glass wine or microbrew beer below each entrée — only the bounty of American wines and beers is served in American Bounty. A cured pork loin is moistened by roasted garlic gravy and accompanied by tiny rice-apple pancakes and chard, and a "cowboy-style" steak is smothered in a salsa rich with cilantro and smashed potatoes redolent with garlic. There are intense fresh fruit sorbets, served with a lacey almond tuile cookie, apple or cherry pies, and multiple choices for the chocoholic on the dessert list, or, for fun, an old-fashioned banana split.

RISTORANTE CATERINA DE' MEDICI

Open: Mon.–Fri.
Price: Expensive.
Cuisine: Italian
Serving: L, D.
Credit Cards: All major credit cards.
Reservations: Recommended; no jeans or sneakers.

The Medicis would feel right at home in this opulent two-story Tuscan villa, with exposed beams, extravagant and huge colorful Murano glass chandeliers hanging from the ceiling, terra-cotta tile floors, and an enormous brass olive tree decorating the entrance, where the tuxedoed maître d' awaits to escort you to your table. Walls are decorated with Tuscan landscape paintings. There are three dining areas: the main dining room with its tablecloths and sturdy, Venetian-style carved chairs; a more casual area with an open kitchen, pizza oven, and antipasti bar; and an inti-

82 THE HUDSON VALLEY BOOK

mate and elegant room upstairs that is used for dinners and private parties. Even if you don't dine upstairs, do take the trip, just to stand on the balcony and be eye level with the chandeliers.

Pastas are homemade, of course, such as the gnocchi with a basil-flecked tomato sauce. The ricotta is simple and elegant, and the risottos change daily, with mussel and shrimp one day, veal and gremolata another. Risotto and pastas are available in appetizer or main-course sizes. Chicken cooked "under the brick" miraculously presses out the fat but not the juice, and the pan-roasted striped bass arrives with a side of sweet polenta and a confit of tomatoes and olives. A side dish of broccoli rabe with garlic gets an added kick from moist red pepper flakes. There's a selection of cheeses, and desserts range from simple biscottini to a sinfully rich chocolate-hazelnut cake topped with Frangelico whipped cream. In warmer weather, the patio doors open for outdoor seating.

ST. ANDREW'S CAFÉ
Open: Mon.–Fri.
Price: Moderate.
Cuisine: Asian-influenced.
Serving: L, D.
Credit Cards: All major
  credit cards.
Reservations:
  Recommended; jeans and
  sneakers okay.

In a gardenlike setting with white woodwork and contemporary artwork, this is the CIA's most casual restaurant. The menu is heart-healthy, and each dish lists both its calorie and fat count. The food is inventive and excellent, getting its taste and texture from fresh ingredients combined with Asian spices rather than butterfat. CIA students work here as part of their nutrition class education.

A roasted butternut squash soup is thick and zipped with flecks of ginger. An appetizer tofu dish arrives with toasted cubes surrounded by a mélange of red curry paste, peas, and scallions that makes the tofu taste meaty. Entrées at St. Andrew's are equally flavorful. The Thai chicken is served with glazed bok choy seasoned with red pepper and toasted quinoa, a Peruvian grain that is nutty and sweet and helps temper the spices elsewhere on the plate. Salmon is baked teriyaki style and served with stir-fried brown rice and vegetables. There is a remarkably rich white chocolate cheesecake with only 9 grams of fat — the same as the main dish of soba noodles. St. Andrew's also serves scones with a thick cream that is like Devonshire in taste, but not with the calories or fat.

Although reservations are recommended, this is the most likely spot for a "walk-in" guest to be accommodated, especially at lunch.

APPLE PIE BAKERY CAFÉ
Open: Mon.–Sat.
Price: Inexpensive.
Cuisine: Bakery, snacks.
Serving: B, L.
Credit Cards: All major
  credit cards.
Reservations: No.

This is the only place on campus for a quick bite. In a bistrolike setting, homemade pastries, sandwiches on homemade bread, and other snacks are prepared to eat in at one of the small bistro tables or to take out. This is the place to get a picnic lunch to take to one of the dramatic overlooks across the Hudson River.

Millbrook

ALLYN'S
845-677-5888.
www.allyns.com.
info@allyns.com.
4258 Rte. 44, Millbrook, NY
   12545.
Open: Wed.–Mon.
Price: Moderate–Expensive.
Cuisine: American.
Serving: L, D, BR
   weekends.
Credit Cards: AE, D, DC,
   MC, V.
Reservations:
   Recommended on
   weekends.
Handicap Access: Yes.

Allyn's is surrounded by a huge garden on one side and a farm with horse-jumping fences on the other. The inside of this former church is just as picturesque. There are three separate dining areas. Two of these rooms have flagstone floors, covered in part by Oriental carpets, with a combination of weathered barn siding walls and walls decorated with pastorals; both rooms have working fireplaces — the smaller of the two rooms is also the bar. The third room is a windowed and sunny patiolike area, pressed into service when the rest of the restaurant is full. There are tablecloths and fabric napkins at lunch and dinner, but formality is leveled by a collection of whimsical salt and pepper shakers, different ones at each table: frogs, NYC taxis, cowboy boots.

A basket of crusty bread and crackers is served with a chickpea spread laced with rosemary, and the menu is a similar blend of traditional and the unexpected. Double-thick lamb chops are seared to perfection, properly pink inside and served with chunky garlic mashed potatoes. The tuna is sesame crusted and matched with stir-fried vegetables one day and Cajun-spiced basmati rice another day. There's chicken pot pie, pastas, and homemade gnocchi for the less adventurous.

This is a locals favorite, and newcomers may find that they don't receive the same attention from the waitstaff as do the regulars. Sunday brunch is always crowded, and in warm weather, there is patio dining in the lush garden.

MILLBROOK CAFÉ
845-677-6956.
24 Franklin Ave., Millbrook,
   NY 12545.
Open: Tues.–Sat.
Price: Moderate.
Cuisine: American.
Serving: L, D.
Credit Cards: All major
   credit cards.
Reservations:
   Recommended on
   weekends.
Handicap Access: Limited.

The Millbrook Café describes its menu as "authentic 19th-century cooking in a wood-fired oven." Even the fresh-baked breads are prepared in the oven, which is behind the combination bar and open kitchen. The chef/owner only uses ash wood, which burns hot, fast, and smokeless, so the breads and meats are crusty outside and soft inside, and the restaurant air remains clear. A house specialty is a baked, stuffed Spanish onion, a delicious concoction of cheddar and fresh vegetables, available both at lunch and dinner. Entrées are served sizzling on oval iron platters set atop a wood board. A marinated game hen is crisp skinned and tender and served with a nutty wild rice pilaf and oven-grilled vegetables. The oven does similar magic for sirloin steaks and salmon steaks. The combination of marinades and the wood-fired oven gives everything an intense flavor, not spicy or salty, just intense. Appetizers and entrées are so well prepared, it is surprising that desserts are so disappointing-ooking and taste like defrosted commercial versions of the real thing.

The café is in a storefront on Millbrook's quiet main street and is decorated in hunting green, with tables and walls wood-trimmed in green. Millbrook, after all, is horse, hound, and hunt country, so the interior, decorated with hunting pictures, is in tune with the area, but this is a café, so the ambiance is more casual than formal.

Red Hook

JULIA & ISABELLA
845-758-4545.
www.juliaandisabella.com.
Rte. 9 (2 miles north of Rte.
    199), Red Hook, NY
    12571.
Open: Wed.–Sun.
Price: Moderate.
Cuisine: South American.
Serving: D.
Credit Cards: All major
    credit cards.
Reservations:
    Recommended on
    weekends.
Handicap Access: Yes.

The parents of Julia and Isabella operated a wildly successful shop in Rhinebeck that had fresh baked goods, special sandwiches, and cooked meals. Its popularity prompted them to think about opening a restaurant, and Julia & Isabella was born to the tune of high salsa. It serves an amazing list of South American dishes, plus some Greek and Eastern European favorites and others with Asian influences, from a nondescript location on an empty stretch of well-traveled Rte. 9, two miles north of Red Hook. Everything is a step or two above the ordinary and expected, such as the quesadilla with portobello mushrooms and roasted red pepper cream and the grilled scallops with a sesame-laced aïoli. Potato pierogis are imported from the Polish section of Brooklyn and served with a horseradish sauce that has as much bite as the homemade salsa.

Grilled steak and a succulent grilled chicken breast are accompanied by a traditional Argentinean chimichuri sauce (parsley, oregano, garlic, and chili pepper) and a tender grilled pork chop is topped with a sweet and smoky chipotle BBQ sauce; they also offer Polish sausage dishes and fish specials. The dinner-sized salad topped with grilled green and yellow squash and red and green bell peppers is one of the few things a vegetarian can find here, other than sides of beans and rice. One also can find a choice of pastas. Pink Heaven is a well-named and well-made dish of shrimp in a tomato-vodka sauce. Desserts are similarly excellent, especially the dense, sweet banana bread pudding.

There is jazz entertainment on some evenings, except on the nights it hops with the sounds of salsa music. It's wise to find out the entertainment schedule, since music nights are a sellout and reservations are a must.

Tania Barricklo

The Red Hook Diner is historic and nostalgic and serves hearty, inexpensive food.

RED HOOK DINER
845-758-6232.
www.historic-village-
　diner.com.
7550 N. Broadway (Rte. 9),
　Red Hook, NY 12571.
Open: Daily 6am–9pm.
Price: Inexpensive.
Cuisine: Traditional
　American.
Serving: B, L, D.
Credit Cards: No; cash only.
Reservations: No.
Handicap Access: No.

Before there was fast food, there were roadside diners that looked like railroad cars. The Red Hook Diner is one of the last, a 1920s architectural gem, a prefabricated diner built in New Jersey that has been at this main intersection in Red Hook longer than most residents can remember. The ambiance, menu, and prices are just as historic. Inside the silver diner, there are dated jade green and black tiles around the booths and counters, the vinyl covering the banquettes is a bit worn, the plastic covers on the menus are a bit yellowed, the neon sign blinks occasionally when it shouldn't, the fluorescent lighting is a bit harsh, and the young, energetic waitstaff wasn't even born when the jukebox played 45rpms instead of the CDs it now features. The Red Hook Diner is pure nostalgia for those who remember, and pure fun for those who don't.

Food is hearty, simple, tasty, and ridiculously inexpensive for things cooked to order — $3 for a cheeseburger or two breakfast eggs with potatoes and toast, served on thick oval-shaped plates. There's a long list of comfort foods, from Yankee pot roast to turkey with fixings, from thick, traditional club sandwiches cut into triangle shapes, BLTs, and grilled American cheese sandwiches to chunky oatmeal and fluffy pancakes. Coleslaw, macaroni salad, and potato salad are served in little fluted paper cups. When was the last time you saw homemade tapioca pudding or real cinnamon toast on a menu? The coffee starts perking at 6am daily.

RED HOOK INN
845-758-8445.
www.theredhookinn.com.
7460 S. Broadway (Rte. 9),
    Red Hook, NY 12571.
Open: Wed.–Sun.
Price: Moderate–Expensive.
Cuisine: American.
Serving: L Fri.–Sun. in
    summer, D Wed.–Sun.
Credit Cards: AE, DC, MC,
    V.
Reservations:
    Recommended.
Handicap Access: No.

The dining room of this Victorian B&B (see Chapter Three, *Lodging*) is warmly decorated in an eclectic mix of chintz curtains, flowered wallpaper, Oriental carpets, and Victorian antiques. The menu is similarly eclectic and creative, and the wine list consists of all New York State wines.

Appetizer raviolis are filled with duck confit and wild mushrooms, local goat cheese mixed with sun-dried tomatoes is an unexpected combination for an appetizer tart, and the goat cheese appears again in a baby spinach salad with a tartly sweet onion-cranberry vinaigrette. Local meats and produce are used widely, such as in the Hudson Valley osso bucco, tender shanks of veal braised with local apples and served with a mélange of root vegetables and mashed potatoes to soak up the sweet brown gravy. There's a delicate porcini mushroom pasta, made hearty with chunks of duck and hickory-smoked bacon, and a salmon fillet prepared with punchy Thai seasonings and served over warm soba buckwheat noodles studded with mushrooms and snow peas. For lunch, the menu includes hearty sandwiches garnished with homemade aïoli, chipotle mayo, and fresh-cut fries.

In addition to the Victorian dining room, where tables are covered with tablecloths and candles at dinner and service is on antique Spode china, there's a dining area in the bar. The Red Hook Inn is popular with locals, and owner Beth Pagano makes it easy for her neighbors and other guests by providing a babysitter on Thurs. evenings to occupy the kids while parents have a night out. In warm weather, the porch of this old house is a cool and shady spot to dine.

Rhinebeck

BEEKMAN ARMS –
TRAPHAGEN
RESTAURANT
845-876-1766.
www.beekmanarms.com.
4 Mill St. (Rte. 9),
    Rhinebeck, NY 12572.
Open: Daily.
Price: Moderate–Expensive.
Cuisine: American.
Serving: L, D, BR Sun.
Credit Cards: All major
    credit cards.
Reservations:
    Recommended.
Handicap Access: Yes.

Watch out for the low ceiling beams — people were not as tall in 1766 when the Beekman Arms first opened as an inn at the intersection of two main stagecoach roads. Traphagen Restaurant is named for one of Rhinebeck's founders and serves classic American cuisine in a publike atmosphere rich with history and decorated with dark burnished woods, wide-plank floorboards, exposed beams, and paneled walls. Low Colonial-style lighting makes it all intimate and elegant, but bright enough to read the historic documents on the walls, including 1800s ferry schedules and menus.

Thick juicy burgers are joined by thick house-cut fries, and old-fashioned turkey pot pie is thick with veggies in a flaky crust. Those who want something more modern can be satisfied with herb-crusted salmon or pan-seared mahimahi, served with mashed potatoes laced either with horseradish or scallion slivers. Most entrées are served both at lunch and dinner. The Sunday brunch is legendary, and service is attentive. The real star, though, is the sense of history.

40 WEST
845-876-2214.
40 W. Market St.,
  Rhinebeck, NY 12572.
Open: Thurs.–Tues.
Price: Expensive.
Cuisine: American with
  global influences.
Serving: D.
Credit Cards: MC, V.
Reservations: Yes.
Handicap Access: Yes.

Follow the small cul-de-sac to an unadorned door, which opens to a large room, the vestiges of an earlier barn that has been reconfigured to create two floors of comfortable dining. There are no tablecloths, just simple silverware and a candle to let you know that the food is the star. The menu is filled with creative dishes with influences from around the world.

An appetizer of chili and honey-glazed scallops is served on a cilantro crêpe, with grilled vegetable salsa drizzled with scallion oils — almost a meal in itself. Grilled yellowfin tuna is joined with coconut rice cakes, and a drizzle of red pepper oil adds just the right amount of spicy kick to the bok choy stir-fry. Charbroiled pork tenderloin with scallions is accompanied by whipped potatoes studded with pignola nuts and broccoli rabe sautéed with crisp pancetta.

Every dish is a complicated collection of ingredients whose tastes simply match. Even the desserts are multiple choice. The apple cake is moist and rich enough to stand alone, but it is served with fragrant vanilla bean ice cream and a warm caramel sauce. There's a wide selection of American and European wines, and some two dozen choices are offered by the glass.

GIGI TRATTORIA
845-876-1007.
www.gigitrattoria.com.
6422 Montgomery St.,
  Rhinebeck, NY 12572.
Open: Tues.–Sun.
Price: Moderate–Expensive.
Cuisine: Northern
  Italian/Mediterranean.
Serving: L Fri.–Sun., D.
Credit Cards: AE, D, MC, V.
Reservations:
  Recommended on
  weekends and for 6 or
  more.
Handicap Access: Yes.

From the moment you dip the crusty bread into the dish of red pepper-soaked olive oil, you know Gigi Trattoria is focused on the details. Housed in half of a former auto repair shop on Rhinebeck's main street, the high-ceilinged space is made intimate and cozy with acid-washed, sienna-colored walls and interesting lighting. Exposed ductwork is a reminder this is not a seriously formal place.

Pastas and gnocchi are homemade, but the specialty of the house is risotto. Chef/owner Gianni Scappin is from northern Italy where risottos, not pasta, are a staple, such as a goat cheese risotto in a tomato sauce flecked with cilantro and red pepper. Salads are towering affairs. Bambina is a large-sized portion of asparagus, beets, endive, roasted mushrooms, and greens, decorated with local goat cheese and walnuts. Scappin's wife, Laura Pensiero, is a nutritionist and chef, so dishes are balanced with more than just flavor. A house specialty is "skiza," Scappin's version of pizza with unusual ingredients: the Rustica combines sausage and garlicky broccoli rabe, another version combines Moroccan olives and chorizo, both on a crust so thin it's barely there. Side dishes are wonderful, too. Their fiachetto dish presents ordinary white beans turned extraordinary and upscale with rosemary and sage-infused olive oil. There is an extensive wine list, including some excellent by-the-glass choices. In the summer, there is a small sidewalk patio for outdoor dining.

LE PETIT BISTRO
845-876-7400.
www.lepetitbistro.com.
8 E. Market St., Rhinebeck,
    NY 12572.
Open: Thurs.–Sun.
Price: Moderate–Expensive.
Cuisine: Classic French.
Serving: D.
Credit Cards: AE, MC, V.
Reservations:
    Recommended.
Handicap Access: No.

This restaurant has a long history of authentic French fare. When the original French owners retired in the 1990s, they left the restaurant in the hands of two of their most trusted, longtime employees, who have continued the tradition of old-world cooking, serving skills, and charm. First-timers receive the same gracious welcome and attentive service as regulars whose names, favorite tables, and preferred wines the owners know. The small restaurant is decorated with warm wood paneling, mirrors, and local artwork, creating an ambiance between country French and formal.

The kitchen has a way with birds. Both the roast chicken and the roast duckling have crackling crisp skins and are moist and fork-tender beneath; the poulet is accompanied by a simple au jus, firmly cooked haricots vert, and roasted fingerling potatoes. Entrées come with a fresh mesclun salad and a classic mustard-based vinai-grette dressing. There is a fresh Hudson Valley foie gras drizzled with a reduc-tion of veal stock and sweet liquor, and the classic frogs legs Provençale. Crusty rolls are served hot and are dense enough to hold up to dishes that are sometimes redolent with garlic. Nightly specials are listed on an old-fashioned blackboard, and, of course, classic French escargots and rabbit are almost always on the menu. Desserts include classic crème brûlée and updated clas-sics, such as chocolate ice cream served in a meringue shell and New York–style cheesecake, an homage to another cuisine.

SCHEMMY'S
    RESTAURANT & ICE
    CREAM PARLOUR
845-876-6215.
www.schemmysrhinebeck
    .com.
19 E. Market St., Rhinebeck,
    NY 12572.

Sit at the old-fashioned ice-cream counter, watch your shake, malted, or ice-cream soda being made and handed to you in a tall, thick, footed, and ribbed glass. Schemmy's is a downtown Rhinebeck institution, part soda fountain, part restaurant.

Although the restaurant is popular with local families because of its large portions and reason-

Open: Thurs.–Mon.
Price: Moderate.
Cuisine: American.
Serving: B, L, D.
Credit Cards: All major
    credit cards.
Reservations: No.
Handicap Access: Yes.

able prices, there are more tempting choices nearby for dinner. It's an excellent spot, however, for ample and traditional eggs, pancakes, and French toast for breakfast and thick sandwiches for lunch. The real appeal here is the soda fountain favorites, including hot fudge sundaes and banana splits, so Schemmy's is busy throughout the day.

Originally this was a pharmacy, and vintage wood medicine cabinets line the wall between the entrance and the soda fountain. Above the cabinets are glass shelves holding antique glass bottles and collectibles. Banquettes and tables are on the other side of the room, and the walls on this side are papered with scenes from Rhinebeck's history.

Rhinecliff

CHINA ROSE
845-876-7442.
One Schatzell Ave.,
    Rhinecliff, NY 12574.
Open: Wed.–Mon.
Price: Moderate.
Cuisine: Chinese.
Serving: D.
Credit Cards: All major
    credit cards.
Reservations: No.
Handicap Access: Yes.

Because of the quality of the food, the ambiance, and the location, this is one of the best Chinese restaurants in the Hudson Valley. China Rose is in a Victorian brick building at the bottom of a winding road lined with similar 18th- and 19th-century homes. It is the last house before the MetroNorth and Amtrak railroad tracks and the river. The outdoor terrace, hung with colorful red paper lanterns, is always crowded during the summer, because of the incredible sunsets and of the energy of the trains when they rush past or stop at the station. Inside, a rose motif dominates, from the antique-framed rose prints on the walls to rose-colored chopsticks on the tables.

Chinese restaurant favorites are excellently prepared, and the service is friendly and professional. Hot and sour soup is fiery and filling, and the wontons, both in the wonton soup and as dumpling appetizers, are meaty and plump, as are the barbecue ribs. Moo Shu pork, shredded pork, and stir-fry vegetables are served with homemade floury pancakes for wrapping. While the rest of the menu may be traditional, desserts are not. There are excellent fruit sorbets, served in their original "homes" — lemon sorbet served in a hollowed-out lemon and coconut sorbet in a coconut shell; there also are almond pastries from New York City's Chinatown. This popular place does not take reservations, and it is open until 11pm on weekends. Nevertheless, there can be a lengthy wait on peak weekend nights.

Salt Point

QUAIL HOLLOW
845-266-8622.
360 Hibernia Rd., Salt
   Point, NY 12578.
Open: Wed.–Sun.
Price: Moderate.
Cuisine: American.
Serving: D.
Credit Cards: AE, MC, V.
Reservations:
   Recommended.
Handicap Access: Yes.

It's easy to pass by this restaurant, since it is packaged in a simple old farmhouse adjacent to the Taconic Parkway. Just beyond the entrance and the fireplace is a well-designed interior filled with art and antiques, more like a home than a restaurant. There's no pretense, either, in the menu. Everything is well prepared with fresh ingredients and attractively served. The roasted chicken is moist with a crisp skin, the sweetness of Maryland-style crab cakes is offset by a Dijon-laced sauce, and there's just enough cracked black pepper crusting the seared tuna. Entrées are served with a mixed green salad, topped with a light ginger dressing, plus there is an extensive wine list by the glass.

The house favorite dessert is a chocolate lava cake, well named because it erupts into a flow of molten chocolate that melts the accompanying vanilla ice cream into a delicious swirl of brown and white. There's also an excellent carrot cake. One of the two owners is always on hand to greet guests and to offer a choice of dining downstairs or upstairs in the bar area, where a vocalist plays '40s and '50s piano favorites on weekends.

Tivoli

OSAKA
845-757-5055.
74 Broadway, Tivoli, NY
   12583.
Open: Wed.–Mon.
Price: Moderate.
Cuisine: Japanese.
Serving: L, D.
Credit Cards: All major
   credit cards.
Reservations:
   Recommended.
Handicap Access: Yes.

Osaka is widely regarded as having the best sushi in the Hudson Valley. The restaurant in Rhinebeck became so popular and crowded that a second Osaka was opened a few miles north in the tiny village of Tivoli. It's easy to spot among the row of Victorian clapboard houses — there's a small Japanese stone temple in the postage-stamp front yard garden leading to the porch. Inside, the second floor of the two-story house has been removed, creating a light and airy space that's filled with bright red paper lanterns and kitelike paper hangings. There's a large sushi bar and tables, all in light wood, and the sushi chef is in traditional Japanese garb.

In addition to shrimp and vegetable tempura, there's a calamari tempura, a soft-textured surprise from the crunchy Italian-style that we're used to. The spicy shrimp and asparagus roll has the right amount of spice to not overpower the asparagus, and the Tokyo roll, tuna and avocado, is a silky sweet mix tempered by the jolt of scallions. The "love roll," tuna, yellowtail, and avocado, is a palette of colors an artist would love. Salmon teriyaki is properly browned and tender and served sizzling on an iron platter. The sushi is top-quality, fresh, and well presented.

SANTA FE
845-757-4100.
52 Broadway, Tivoli, NY
    12583.
Open: Tues.–Sun.
Price: Moderate.
Cuisine: Mexican.
Serving: D.
Credit Cards: MC, V.
Reservations: Accepted.
Handicap Access: Yes.

Even before you open the front door, you know this will be a lively, memorable experience. The tone is set on the outside of the building, which is a vintage clapboard that's been painted lemon yellow with periwinkle blue trim on doors and windows. Inside, the colors are just as bright, full of turquoise, fiery oranges, and desert buffs — colors of the real Santa Fe in bright sunlight and its memorable sunset. To add to the atmosphere, there's a huge pterodactyl-looking bird watching over diners from the ceiling. The crowd can be just as lively, fueled by large and festive margaritas in a variety of colors and flavors.

The food is seriously good and that is the real reason Santa Fe has been one of the more popular restaurants in the area for more than a decade. Quesadillas are filled either with spicy shrimp and spinach or with local goat cheese and sun-dried tomatoes, and the guacamole is fresh and chunky. In addition to the conventional Mexican fare of tacos, burritos, and enchiladas, Santa Fe features dishes from other parts of Mexico, including Pibil, a spicy Yucatan-style barbecued pork and an Oaxaca-style chicken with a smoky mole sauce. Some dishes from other countries sneak onto the menu, too, including a Jamaican-style curry dish and an Indonesian shrimp satay. After all that seasoning, a tartly smooth key lime pie or a delicately smooth crème brûlée will settle the taste buds.

DINING: COLUMBIA COUNTY

Hudson

THE CASCADES
518-822-9146.
407 Warren St., Hudson, NY
    12534.
Open: Mon.–Sat.
Price: Inexpensive.
Cuisine: American.
Serving: Coffee, sandwiches,
    pastries, snacks.
Credit Cards: AE, MC, V.
Reservations: No.
Handicap Access: Yes.

This is the type of place Starbucks modeled itself on — a comfortable spot to relax with coffee, fresh breakfast pastries, a sandwich, and a newspaper or magazine, or just grab something to go. Cascades has an old-fashioned hexagonal tile floor, bistrolike tables, and a neighborly feel. Go early, since they open at 7am and close at 3pm.

*Presentation is as important
as taste in Hudson Valley
restaurants.*

Tania Barricklo

CHARLESTON
518-828-4990.
517 Warren St., Hudson, NY
 12534.
Open: Thurs.–Mon.
Price: Moderate–Expensive.
Cuisine: Regional American.
Serving: L Thurs.–Sun., D.
Credit Cards: AE, MC, V.
Reservations: Yes.
Handicap Access: Yes.

Charleston is located in an early 1900's build-ing on the town's main street. The pressed tin ceiling is original, as is the carved mahogany bar and booths along one wall. There are antique pho-tographs for you to compare with when the own-ers lived behind the "store," and now. The cuisine is contemporary and eclectic and changes season-ally, with occasional theme meals that have included venison or game birds. Presentation is simple, matching the pristine white walls and tablecloths. Carol Clarke, the owner/chef, varies the menu to take advantage of local produce and usually comes out from the kitchen at least once an evening to say hello to guests.

A large pan fritter made from fresh local corn flavored with cumin is paired with a lime-honey dipping sauce — not your average fritter. Saganaki is a Greek kasseri cheese flamed with brandy and butter, so the outside is crusty and the inside is barely melted. The kitchen also has an inventive way with fish. Pan-seared red snapper is topped with pineapple-jalapeño pepper sauce, rice is flavored with saffron and lemon, and spaghetti squash in the rind has a caramelized shell. Most interesting, though, is grilled diver scallops tossed with prosciutto, capers, tomato, Swiss chard, and fusilli in a lemon-garlic sauce. Homemade desserts are excellent. When blueberries are in season, opt for the fresh pie, baked in a light tart shell and topped with freshly whipped cream. Or choose the caramel walnut pie, halfway between a conventional pecan pie and a crème brûlée, baked in a tart shell and served warm with freshly whipped cream.

PARAMOUNT GRILL
518-828-4548.
225 Warren St., Hudson,
    NY 12534.
Open: Thurs.–Mon.
Price: Moderate.
Cuisine: American with
    international influences.
Serving: D.
Credit Cards: AE, MC, V.
Reservations:
    Recommended on
    weekends.
Handicap Access: Limited.

The menu is updated American, infused with tastes of Cajun, Southwest, and Caribbean, with subtle use of seasoning and flavors to create a fresh light taste. Family-owned Paramount Grill has been a local favorite because of its neighborly atmosphere and moderate prices since before the antique stores and weekend shoppers on this main street reached critical mass. The restaurant is housed in a Victorian building with lots of antique details, including the vintage pressed tin ceiling. Weekends tend to be crowded, so reservations are recommended.

Grilled shrimp is served on a bed of mesclun and watercress and topped with an orange juice, cilantro, and lime vinaigrette for an appetizer that doubles as a salad. There's a wonderful homemade corn soup dotted with smoked shrimp and an appetizer of black mussels, steamed in a broth of wine, crushed tomato, and garlic. An ample portion of filet mignon is slathered with a blue cheese and sweet butter garnish and served with red pearl potatoes and sautéed fresh vegetables. Baby rack of lamb is rubbed with Moroccan spices, whose cumin bite is tempered by apricot chutney. Godiva chocolate cheesecake — nothing else needs to be added to those three little words.

RED DOT
518-828-3657.
321 Warren St., Hudson,
    NY 12534.
Open: Wed.–Sun.
Price: Moderate.
Cuisine: American/Belgian
    /Asian.
Serving: D, BR Sun.
Credit Cards: All major
    credit cards.
Reservations:
    Recommended on
    weekends.
Handicap Access: Yes.

There are two red doors to this charming modern bistro in another of Hudson's vintage buildings. If you want to avoid being welcomed by a wall of smoke, ignore the door on the left, which opens into the long, popular bar, in favor of the door on the right, opening into the restaurant. Be prepared for a vision of red and black. There is black wainscoting six feet high, and the rest of the 10-foot wall height and the ceiling is dark crimson red. Tables and chairs are black lacquer, and the floor is the original wood, stained and polished to a sheen. The interior is stark and striking, yet surprisingly comfortable.

Red Dot describes itself as a Belgian bistro with Asian influences. The Belgian part is well represented by classic moules and frites, a mound of meaty mussels flecked with slivers of onion and garlic and thin-cut fries in a proper paper cone set in an Art Deco holder. The Asian part of the menu includes a salad of cellophane noodles dotted with orange slices, nuts, and Thai spiced vegetables, chicken, or shrimp. There's also something called "angry fish," likely made so by being steamed in lemongrass, cilantro, and ginger. The most popular menu items are the fish and chips, another huge mound of flaky tempuralike fried fish and the same thin-cut fries that come with the mussels, plus a homemade chicken pot pie, which is a deeply browned ramekin loaded with chunks of chicken and fresh vegetables. For dessert, the crème caramel arrives surrounded by a swirl of nutty sauce and fresh berries.

There is also a huge walled garden in the back, thick with trellised vines and flowers, an inviting spot for a warm evening.

DINING: ROCKLAND COUNTY

Nyack

HEATHER'S OPEN CUCINA
845-358-8686.
www.heathersopencucina
.com.
12 N. Broadway, Nyack, NY 10960.
Open: Mon.–Sat.
Price: Moderate.
Cuisine: Contemporary Italian.
Serving: L, D, (Sat. D only).
Credit Cards: AE, MC, V.
Reservations: Recommended on weekends.
Handicap Access: No.

In this 19-century building, there are exposed brick walls, the original tin ceiling, and whirring ceiling fans in warm weather, creating a casual atmosphere that can be noisy when the place is packed, as it generally is on weekend evenings. They also offer sidewalk seating. Heather's is named for the restaurant's open kitchen and the daughter of chef/owner Henry Hovorka.

A chunk of aged Parmesan, cut from the huge wheel of cheese at the entrance, is served along with the bread basket, then followed by a moist, chunky, and garlicky tomato bruschetta to take the edge off your hunger while you look at the menu. The food is primarily contemporary Italian, with some interesting spins on classic dishes, such as king crab risotto and salmon fillet in a pesto crust. There is almost always a game dish on the menu, sometimes rack of boar, sometimes wine-marinated venison. The quartered lobster in garlic sauce will take your breath away, not a dish to order if you intend to have an intimate conversation after dinner. Classic dishes include saltimbocca and pasta specials that change daily. Save room for the dense, made-to-order, flourless chocolate mousse cake dessert. A truly sweet feature is the chef's pairing of a dessert with wine, such as crème brûlée with a Moculan Torocato. Also there's an excellent offering of wines by the glass.

LANTERNA TUSCAN BISTRO

845-353-8361.
www.lanternausa.com.
mrglanterna@aol.com.
3 S. Broadway, Nyack, NY 10960.
Open: Daily.
Price: Moderate.
Cuisine: Northern Italian.
Serving: L, D, BR Sun.
Credit Cards: AE, DC, MC, V.
Reservations: Recommended.
Handicap Access: Yes.

Housed in an 1863 storefront on the town's main street, this Tuscan-style bistro is decorated with small lantern-style candles on the white tablecloths and a collection of interesting framed Tuscan countryside photographs on the exposed brick walls. It is one of those casually elegant mixes that almost defy description — tasteful, upscale decor in a friendly neighborhood location, with lots of locals dining here regularly. Chef/owner Rossano Giannini, from Lucca in Tuscany, is currently the president of the Federation of Italian Chefs in America, and the cookbook that he co-authored with other Italian chefs is displayed prominently at the entrance.

The most popular dish is the grilled calamari appetizer, wonderfully soft and briny, unlike the normally breaded and fried kind. The cestino di Parmigiano is an edible basket made of Parmesan cheese and filled with greens, prosciutto, and goat cheese. It's enough by itself for lunch or to share at dinner. A fish soup is studded with fresh vegetables and laced with saffron. There's homemade ravioli stuffed with porcini mushrooms and covered with a truffle cream sauce, and a different daily risotto. Other excellent entrées are the rack of lamb in mustard sauce and a surprising snapper with an orange-lemon sauce that tastes better than it sounds. Desserts include tiramisù, of course.

LuSHANE'S

845-358-5556.
www.lushanes.com.
8 N. Broadway, Nyack, NY 10960.
Open: Tues.–Sun.
Price: Moderate.
Cuisine: French/Asian.
Serving: L, D Tues.–Sat., D Sun.
Credit Cards: AE, MC, V.
Reservations: Recommended on weekends.
Handicap Access: Yes.

This restaurant has the same chef and owner as Heather's a few doors away (LuShane's is named for his sons, Luke and Shane), but it is totally different in ambiance and menu. Instead of a bread basket, diners receive an architectural stack of thick homemade potato chips. An antique copper-clad raw bar in front is piled high with a variety of shellfish, including several types of oysters and mussels. The original hexagonal floor tiles and tin ceiling take the edge off the otherwise lean modern decor, allowing diners to focus on the food presentation, which leans to carefully constructed towers on unusual, colorful square plates.

The menu ranges from dim sum to traditional Swiss fondue, from French bouillabaise, thick with fish chunks, to horseradish-crusted striped bass. Selections of farm-raised game, such as kangaroo medallions wrapped in bacon, or ostrich, are also on the menu. The chili-garlic-tuna appetizer is strips of sashimi, arranged in a star pattern with grapefruit slices and drizzled with a potent dressing. The seafood parfait appetizer is multicolored layers of crabmeat, shrimp, avocado, and tomato topped with a lobster claw. The rack of lamb, crusted with a honey-herb coating, is served quite rare, as is the duck breast. The most spectacular dessert is a vision of red, white, and blue — the mixed berry, caramel cream napoleon layers phyllo pastry with cream, topped with a dollop of vanilla ice cream and surrounded with bright strawberries and blueberries on a cobalt blue plate.

RIVER CLUB AT NYACK MARINA
845-358-0220.
www.nyackriverclub.
11 Burd St., Nyack, NY
  10960.
Open: Daily.
Price: Moderate.
Cuisine: Seafood/Steak.
Serving: L, D.
Credit Cards: AE, D, DC,
  MC, V.
Reservations:
  Recommended on
  weekends.
Handicap Access: Yes.

Even though Nyack is a historic river town, this is the only restaurant directly on the water. The restaurant's logo is *Clermont,* Robert Fulton's steamship, the first successful Hudson River steamer. These side-wheelers transported passengers and cargo past Nyack between NYC and Albany for the first half of the 1800s, until they were replaced by railroads. The restaurant is decorated with paintings and prints of many historic vessels. The River Club is really two restaurants in one — one half is a casual, wrought iron and Formica café, and the other half is a more formal tablecloth dining area, each with a marina view out the huge glass windows and an identical menu of steaks, ribs, seafood, and fish. There's also a wood-lined bar area with a fireplace that becomes the favorite dining area in cold weather, and the outdoor dockside deck is a warm weather favorite.

Menu standouts are the homemade Maryland crab cakes, served with an unusual chunky sweet potato hash, and the salmon Wellington, a flaky filling of fish surrounded by a flaky pastry crust, but no Yorkshire pudding, as is the accompaniment for traditional beef Wellington. Swordfish is on the menu several ways — seasoned with southwestern-style spices and served with a colorful corn relish or in a salad resembling a salad Niçoise, with chunks of swordfish mixed with olives and hearts of palm. Beef lovers will find hefty steaks — the porterhouse is a giant 20 ounces — all hand-cut Black Angus. For those who can't choose between surf and turf, there's a filet mignon and lobster tail combo, too. Prices are quite reasonable since each grill entrée includes a salad and two sides, which include corn bread and sweet potato hash.

Pearl River

LOUIE'S ON THE AVENUE
845-735-4344.
www.louiesontheavenue
  .com.
160 East Central Ave., Pearl
  River, NY 10965.

Large portions presented artfully on the plate define this low-key restaurant on Pearl River's main street. The mozzarella roasted pepper and portobello mushroom napoleon is a tall, colorful layer made more colorful by the pesto sauce decorating one-half of the plate and a red pepper vinaigrette on

Open: Daily.
Price: Moderate–Expensive.
Cuisine: American.
Serving: L Mon.–Fri., D.
Credit Cards: AE, MC, V.
Reservations:
 Recommended for 5 or
 more; no reservations
 taken Sat.
Handicap Access: Yes.

the other half; and never mind that the construction slides into chaos after the second or third bite. This appetizer is on both the lunch and dinner menu, as is the seafood teriyaki, lightly battered pieces of shrimp, salmon, and scallops, topped with a tangle of surprisingly tasty, crunchy fried shoestring leeks. The leeks also accompany a brook trout; this fish is grilled rather than sautéed, giving it a slightly smoky flavor. For lunch, a filet mignon is served in a roll-up wrap also filled with black beans and roasted corn; on the dinner menu this is an appetizer.

Louie's On The Avenue is housed in a lemon yellow Victorian home, with several intimate dining areas in the original downstairs rooms. The owners' collection of old musical instruments, including a banjo, trumpet, and an accordian, decorate one room; another room is dominated by a wall of paved river rocks that includes a huge fireplace. There's also a glass-enclosed greenhouse patio, a wonderfully sunny choice for lunch, plus outdoor patio dining in back of the house in warm weather. Old-fashioned wrought iron chairs and tables on the front porch are a pleasant spot for a premeal drink. There are tablecloths at lunch and dinner, and the waitstaff wear white shirts and ties. Save room for the signature dessert — a homemade deep-dish pecan pie that is studded with chocolate chips, as well as pecans, and served warm enough to make the chocolate soft but not gooey.

Piermont

FLYWHEEL CREAMERY
845-398-2433.
210 Ash St., Piermont, NY
 10968.
Open: Daily.
Price: Inexpensive.
Cuisine: Ice-cream parlor.
Serving: Dessert.
Credit Cards: No.
Reservations: No.
Handicap Access: Yes.

Flywheel Creamery is an old-fashioned ice-cream parlor, with hand-dipped ice creams and sorbets, curlicue metal bistro chairs and tables, and fountain service for hand-mixed ice-cream sodas and malteds. There are modern flavored coffees and lattes, too, and some pastries, but that's not the real reason to hang out here. Savor bygone flavors while you tune in to the classic Wurlitzer jukebox from the '50s playing original 45rpm platters. Definitely a happy time warp. Don't tell the nearby restaurant where you just had lunch or dinner that you are skipping dessert because you'd rather finish your meal here, with a pistachio or black raspberry cone with sprinkles or a coffee malted. Enjoy your treat while walking around the park or sitting on the outdoor patio.

FREELANCE CAFÉ &
 WINE BAR
845-365-3250.

This is Xaviar's (see below) less expensive, less formal sibling, sharing the same building,

www.freelancecafe.com.
506 Piermont Ave.,
  Piermont, NY 10968.
Open: Tues.-Sun.
Price: Moderate–Expensive.
Cuisine: American.
Serving: L, D.
Credit Cards: No.
Reservations: No.
Handicap Access: Limited.

kitchen, and impressive wine cellar, but not the same menu. While owner Peter X. Kelly is the chef next door and created this menu, Freelance Café & Wine Bar has its own chef. The sleek, modern decor is mostly black — on the marble counter and table-tops, even the serving dishes — making a dramatic frame for the food. There are small bistrolike tables and seating along the long bar. The menu is divided into "small plates" and "large plates." The small plates are what in other restaurants are appetizers, salads, and pasta dishes; the large plates are entrées. Any of the generously sized small plates is enough for lunch or as a starter for dinner.

Small choices include hand-chopped salmon tartare over crispy rice noodles. There's also a chicken liver mousse, served with a tangy red onion compote, and a lemongrass-laced Thai coconut soup, with enough shrimp to be a filling light meal. Norwegian salmon is grilled to perfection and served with orzo; the plate is decorated with tiny mussellike cockles. It's becoming increasingly rare to find calves liver on a restaurant menu. Here, a melt-in-your-mouth version is glorified with shallots, bacon pieces, and creamy homemade mashed potatoes. The menu includes lighter entrées like steamed trout seasoned with lime and cilantro and a heftier, tender osso bucco, served with a memorable wild mushroom risotto.

There is an extensive selection of wines by the glass. No reservations are accepted, so get here early or late to avoid lines.

PASTA AMORE
845-365-1911.
www.pasta-amore.com.
200 Ash St., Piermont, NY
  10968.
Open: Daily.
Price: Moderate.
Cuisine: Italian.
Serving: L, D.
Credit Cards: AE, DC, MC,
  V.
Reservations:
  Recommended.
Handicap Access: Yes.

Huge, ceiling-high glass windows overlook Piermont's picturesque downtown waterfront park with its cupola and busy marina, making this an open, airy dining choice, especially in warm weather when the outdoor patio is set with tables. The picture windows, mirrors, and faux arches inside make the space feel much larger than it is.

Everything is homemade, including the pasta, and many items are family recipes, such as Pollo Grandma, with mushrooms and black truffles in a Madeira reduction sauce. Risotto rarely is offered in appetizer portions, but at Pasta Amore, there's a porcini-flecked version on the regular menu. A Gorgonzola dressing adds punch to the mesclun salad with wild French mushrooms. There's a long list of pasta dishes. Some of the more interesting are angel hair with crabmeat, shrimp, mushrooms, and arugula in a delicate tomato sauce, and a saffron-flavored fettuccine with zucchini and shrimp in another tomato sauce. Seafood dishes include a properly spicy seafood fra diàvolo and a grilled swordfish steak grilled with garlic-infused olive oil. The wine list not surprisingly leans toward Italian wines.

XAVIAR'S
845-359-7007.
www.xaviars.com.
506 Piermont Ave.,
   Piermont, NY 10968.
Open: Wed.–Sun.
Price: Very Expensive.
Cuisine: American.
Serving: L Fri., Sun., D.
Credit Cards: No.
Reservations: Required;
   business dress.
Handicap Access: Limited.

Xaviar's reputation for exquisite food and superior service in elegant surroundings is more impressive than its tiny dining area, which holds no more than 40 diners at a time. Tables are set with intricately detailed and colorful Rosenthal Versace pattern china, Riedel wine goblets, Baccarat crystal table accessories, and true silverware; walls are a complexion-flattering sunny gold, and Waterford crystal chandeliers hang from the ceiling. This is, most definitely, a special occasion spot. Tables are spaced far enough apart to ensure private conversation without the built-in noise level of so many restaurants. Surprisingly, all this formal elegance is inside a ramshackle, vintage clapboard building on the town's main street. Generally regarded as the premiere dining spot for miles around, chef/owner Peter X. Kelly cooks up a single dinner seating daily — there are two seatings on Sat. — and a prix fixe menu that changes daily depending on availability and season. Menu favorites include a double dose of foie gras, both hot and cold, served with a fruit compote that can be fig one night and plum the next night. Local free-range chicken is almost always on the menu, but the accompaniments change — a morel mushroom-scallion risotto today, a chanterelle and fiddlehead fern ragout tomorrow. There is often a game dish, such as grilled saddle of venison with mashed sweet potatoes laced with a kick of ginger.

Xaviar's has an extensive wine cellar, including dessert wines, and there is also a tasting menu pairing a chef-selected wine with each course. Since there is just the one seating weeknights, diners never feel rushed, and the meal can stretch over several hours. Reservations are essential since Xaviar's can be booked three to four weeks ahead.

DINING: ORANGE COUNTY

Cornwall

**CANTERBURY BROOK
   INN**
845-534-9658.
www.canterburybrookinn
   .com.
331 Main St., Cornwall, NY
   12518.

Most restaurants housed in a clapboard building more than 200 years old charge prices as large as their history, but not Canterbury Brook Inn, named for the brook it borders. The well-prepared food also happens to be very moderately priced, making it a locals' favorite. The menu is Continental,

Open: Tues.–Sat.
Price: Moderate.
Cuisine: Continental.
Serving: L Tues.–Fri. in
  Apr.–Dec., D.
Credit Cards: AE, MC, V.
Reservations:
  Recommended.
Handicap Access: Limited.

with selections from just about everywhere on the continent. That includes an excellent roast duck, crispy, well-seasoned skin covering tender meat and a traditional beef Wellington. Sauerbraten is properly briny and served with homemade spaetzle, or little dumplings. The spaetzle also are a choice, instead of mashed or roast potatoes, with other entrées and are recommended, since not many restaurants make homemade spaetzle, a traditional German-Austrian side dish. Starter salads include a German-influenced mélange of shredded beets and greens in a mild vinaigrette. For dessert, a menu favorite is the apple fritters, slices cooked in a light batter and served with a warm vanilla sauce. There's also an extensive wine list.

There are several wood-burning fireplaces, and the decor is historic without being stuffy. While male diners occasionally arrive wearing jackets and ties, such formal dress is not the rule. There are tablecloths at lunch and dinner, and in warm weather, there is outdoor creekside dining on a large, sunny deck.

Cornwall-on-Hudson

PAINTER'S TAVERN
845-534-2109.
www.painters-
  restaurant.com.
266 Hudson St., Cornwall-
on-Hudson, NY 12520.
Open: Daily.
Price: Moderate.
Cuisine: American.
Serving: L Mon.–Sat., D, BR
  Sun.
Credit Cards: D, DC, MC, V.
Reservations:
  Recommended on Fri.,
  Sat.
Handicap Access: Yes.

Painter's Tavern could be described as a restaurant with an art gallery, or an art gallery inside a restaurant. It is both — hence the name — and housed in a historic Revolutionary-era tavern, with some hotel rooms upstairs. The artwork, which includes photography, adorns most of the available wall space and represents a mix of new and established artists, most of them local. It's very popular with locals for its friendly, casual ambiance and moderate prices, so it's a great place for families. There are bare wood tables, linen napkins at lunch and dinner, and a garden for outdoor dining in warm weather, plus live music on weekends.

The menu is a mix of popular classics and some trendier choices. Appetizers include an ample quesadilla and a large portion of garlicky focàccia. The tart tang of local goat cheese is softened by a splash of balsamic vinegar. The chicken has influences from around the world: chicken Parmesan is prepared without breading; chicken with chipotle sauce and Thai chicken in peanut sauce are both mild enough for those with an aversion to serious kicks. There are vegetarian dishes, plus a selection of more than 60 beers from around the world. There is live music on most weekend evenings in the summer.

Monroe

RAINBOW
845-783-2670.
16 Rte. 17M, Monroe, NY
  10950.
Open: Daily.
Price: Moderate.
Cuisine: Northern Italian.
Serving: D.
Credit Cards: AE, MC, V.
Reservations:
  Recommended.
Handicap Access: Limited.

Everything here is homemade, including the pasta, which sometimes includes a basil fettuccine. There are six different pastas that can be heaped with a range of sauces, including fresh pomodoro, a tender ocean-fresh clam sauce, and an amatriciana studded with panchetta and onions. Poultry lovers will enjoy the chicken breasts sautéed with Gorgonzola and artichoke hearts, served atop a bed of fresh, slightly cooked spinach. Rack of lamb arrives with a side of freshly made polenta and a fragrant rosemary sauce. The pasta e fagioli is almost a meal in itself, thick with white beans and bacon bits in a garlicky broth. Fried calamari arrives, wonder of wonders, crisp outside and tender, not chewy, inside. Save room for dessert. The sampler is a perfect choice for sweets lovers who can't decide among tiramisù, chocolate soufflé cake, spumoni ice cream, or Italian ricotta cheesecake.

Don't be put off by the billiard green exterior. Rainbow used to be a billiard parlor. The color is just part of the charm, but is softened by the white table linens and comfortable upholstered dining chairs. The waitstaff is experienced and efficient. They offer an extensive wine list with a good selection of Chiantis. Portions are generous, and it's not unusual for patrons to leave with their unfinished meals wrapped for home.

Newburgh

CAFÉ PITTI
845-565-1444.
40 Front St., Newburgh, NY
  12550.
Open: Daily.
Price: Moderate.
Cuisine: Italian.
Serving: Desserts,
  sandwiches, pizza.
Credit Cards: AE.
Reservations: Yes.
Handicap Access: Yes.

This delightful little café feels like it was wrapped up and shipped intact from near the Pitti Palace in Venice. The glass showcase just inside the entrance features six shelves of legendary, sinfully rich, homemade Italian pastries: thick éclairs covered with chocolate shavings, called a toscarella; little tarts filled with berries over lemony cream filling; nut-dotted biscotti, some with their ends dipped in bittersweet chocolate, others not; sweet cheesecake; fluffy tiramisù; and tart fruit sorbets and super creamy gelatos, served in a wineglass. But it's not all dessert. A wood-fired oven prepares individual thin-crust pizzas, such as scarmoza, with sun-dried tomatoes and smoked mozzarella. And there are pannini, the toasted sandwich, filled with a variety of cheeses, meats, and grilled vegetables.

There are acid-washed sienna walls, decorative Venetian columns, and bistro café tables the size of an overgrown postage stamp. But you can linger comfortably over a cappuccino and something chocolate and enjoy the very Venetian atmosphere, including the outdoor patio fronting the river. Café Pitti's owners also own Cene 2000, the Italian restaurant a few doors away, and Il Cena' Colo, nearby, regarded as one of the best Italian restaurants in the Hudson Valley (see below).

IL CENA' COLO
845-564-4494.
www.neateateries.com.
I228 Plank Rd., Newburgh, NY 12550.
Open: Wed.–Mon.
Price: Expensive–Very Expensive.
Cuisine: Northern Italian.
Serving: L Mon.–Fri., D.
Credit Cards: AE, DC, MC, V.
Reservations: Recommended.
Handicap Access: Yes.

This Tuscan treasure is widely regarded as the best restaurant in the area. The menu is almost superfluous, since there are at least two dozen specials every evening, varying with season and availability. Start with the fresh figs and prosciutto — paper-thin slices of rosy pink ham cover the plate, and the figs are sliced and fanned into the shape of a star. In autumn, try an appetizer portion of pasta with black-and-white Italian truffle shavings; expensive, but memorable. Osso bucco, or braised veal shank, is fork tender and served with mashed potatoes scented with truffle oil. Fish dishes include a whole turbot, grilled with lemon and garlic and deboned tableside, or wild Mediterranean sea bass whose sweet, delicate meat is enhanced by minimal seasonings. Sweetbreads, served by a diminishing number of restaurants, are thickly sliced and sautéed in a brown butter, leaving them dark and moist and dusted with sage for color. And there's always a risotto on the menu, such as the Florentina, with fresh spinach and a zip of mint.

Il Cena' Colo has a full-time pastry chef, so everything is homemade, fresh, and spectacular. Most popular are the traditional ricotta cheesecake and tiramisù, both airy and smooth. Chef/owner Sali Hadzi is back and forth all evening, splitting his time and attention between the kitchen and mingling with diners; the waitstaff is equally attentive.

The restaurant is decorated like a Tuscan villa, with 200-year-old wood beams, a copper ceiling, terra-cotta tiles, and white-washed walls. A huge wooden wine rack lines much of one wall, and the restaurant's wine list is as impressive as its menu. This is romantic, special occasion dining and worth the extra effort to find the restaurant, since first-timers can miss the poorly marked turn from a well-traveled local business route. The same family owns and operates (and supplies pastries for) Cene 2000 and Café Pitti on Newburgh's riverfront.

RIVER GRILL
845-561-9444.
40 Front St., Newburgh, NY 12550.

Resist the temptation to polish off the crusty bread that arrives with a tub of butter flecked with bits of sun-dried tomatoes, peppers, and olives,

Waterside dining at the River Grill in Newburgh.

Tania Barricklo

Open: Daily.
Price: Moderate.
Cuisine: American.
Serving: L, D.
Credit Cards: AE, MC, V.
Reservations:
  Recommended.
Handicap Access: Yes.

because there is a menu full of inventive, tasty choices to come. Hickory shrimp gets a double dose of smoky flavor from being wrapped in bacon and grilled on hickory wood. A perfectly chargrilled sirloin is tender and juicy enough that it can hold its own without a slathering of horseradish butter, ditto the Delmonico steak with a peppercorn-brandy cream. The combination of shrimp, scallops, mussels, and clams can be ordered as paella, or as fra diàvolo, laced with tomatoes and spices over linguine. Grilled swordfish is a meaty center cut, one-inch thick, arriving moist, tender, and brushed with a tarragon-flavored butter and a side dish of peppery mashed potatoes. For dessert, opt for the homemade marble cheesecake, dense, creamy, and garnished with chocolate-dipped strawberries, or choose a deep-dish classic tiramisù, with liquor-soaked ladyfingers.

The owner's family used to own a restaurant in High Falls, New York, and there's a 1920s menu on the wall with 30-cent entrées. Other walls are hung with historic photos of Newburgh and High Falls, and there are contemporary tables with white linens. It makes for a casually elegant ambiance. River Grill is one of the cluster of restaurants and shops in former warehouse buildings in the revitalized downtown riverfront area. Its outdoor patio borders the riverfront promenade.

Sugar Loaf

BARNSIDER TAVERN
845-469-9810.
1372 Kings Hwy., Sugar
   Loaf, NY 10981.
Open: Tues.–Sun.
Price: Inexpensive–
   Moderate.
Cuisine: American.
Serving: L, D.
Credit Cards: MC, V.
Reservations: No.
Handicap Access: Yes.

You can tell from the motorcycles parked out front on weekends and the weathered wood both outside and inside that this is not a formal place with haute cuisine. Actually, it's a wonderfully friendly, cozy pub and restaurant, family owned and operated, and a favorite of local residents. Visitors are also attracted to Barnsider and to Sugar Loaf's many crafts shops and its rolling country roads that are ideal for cyclists, both motorized and not.

The Barnsider was a general store, built along a dirt path used by the original inhabitants and later by settlers in the 1760s. Just inside the entrance, glass cabinets display a collection of historic local artifacts, including farm implements and clothing. Be sure to look behind the bar at the massive brass cash register, which dates from the early 1900s, and to look above and around you at the vintage beams and barn siding that give this eatery its name.

The menu is several notches up from traditional pub food, with items like herbed chicken breast broiled in spinach butter and pecan-crusted mashed potatoes. Generously sized burgers and steak sandwiches, a selection of pastas, and a heap of buffalo wings are sure to add some spice to your life.

Warwick

EL BALLROOM
845-986-1801.
www.neateateries.com.
22B Railroad Ave.,
   Warwick, NY 10990.
Open: Tues.–Sun.
Price: Moderate.
Cuisine: South
   American/Mexican.
Serving: D, BR Sun.
Credit Cards: MC, V.
Reservations:
   Recommended Fri., Sat.
Handicap Access: Yes.

Before this was a restaurant, it was a ballroom in a Victorian hotel (now apartments), housed across from Warwick's railroad station; then, for a while, it was a roller-skating rink. So, this is a large space with an amazing hardwood floor that El Ballroom's owners wisely refinished and left uncovered. The decor is a bit difficult to describe — the ductwork is exposed and painted and parts of the walls are down to their original brick, while other parts of the same wall have unrestored old plaster and paint. The edgy, trendy architectural effect is softened by familiar bentwood chairs, colorful china on the slate tables, and some large, colorful art on the walls.

The menu is South American and Mexican, including a selection of tapas. Start with an excellent seviche, a mélange of seafood pieces marinated in lime juice, which helps retain their briny bite, with chopped onions and sweet red and green peppers; it is served in a diamond-shaped glass bowl. Or opt for the Mexican elote, an ear of corn that has been rolled in cayenne and grated cheese before the husk is pulled back over, and the whole thing is fire-roasted. Argentine steak is served sliced and seasoned with a traditional green chimichurri sauce, and there's a free-range chicken with a traditional mole sauce with its hint of chocolate. Shrimp is grilled in a salty calamata olive sauce, and a dish of homemade seasoned olives is part of the welcome bread basket.

West Point

HOTEL THAYER
845-446-4731.
www.hotelthayer.com.
U.S. Military Academy,
West Point, NY 10996.
Open: Daily.
Price: Moderate.
Cuisine: American.
Serving: B, L, D, BR Sun.
Credit Cards: AE, MC, V.
Reservations:
Recommended.
Handicap Access: Yes.

On a bluff high above the river, the setting is grand. There are two halves to the dining room: the inside room is elegant and is decorated with military memorabilia; the terrace area has huge limestone façade stones on one side and floor-to-ceiling windows overlooking the Hudson on the other. In warm weather, a covered outdoor patio gets you even closer to the view. There are two reasons to eat here — the view and this is the only place to eat without leaving the military base.

Meals are consistent in their inconsistency. An appetizer of vine-ripened tomato slices layered with similarly thick and flavorful, smoky fresh mozzarella drizzled with balsamic vinegar is marred by a garnish of dead lettuce. A roasted duck entrée with apple brandy glaze was perfectly crispy outside and moist and tender inside, but without a steak knife, cutting crisp duck skin with regular silverware is no easy task. The house pasta, a well-seasoned fettuccine with a fresh tomato-basil sauce and artichoke hearts, is marred by a lack of grated cheese. And the dessert trolley, as luscious as it looks at a distance, is laden with creamy tortes and pies that are commercially made and defrosted, not homemade. The welcome basket of breads, however, is delivered steaming hot and includes a dark raisin-studded pumpernickel and a baseball-sized helping of butter. As for the breakfast, the less said, the better. Avoid the hot buffet of cafeteria-quality, oversteamed bacon and eggs; instead opt for the continental buffet or à la carte pancakes. Or walk a few blocks past the West Point sentry gate to one of the fast-food places clustered there.

DINING: ULSTER COUNTY

High Falls

CHEFS ON FIRE
845-687-7778.
www.depuycanalhouse.net.
Rte. 213, High Falls, NY
  12440.
Open: Wed.–Sun.
Price: Moderate.
Cuisine: American.
Serving: B Sat., Sun., L, D.
Credit Cards: All major
  credit cards.
Reservations: No.
Handicap Access: No.

Tucked in the basement of the Depuy Canal House, Chefs On Fire is a breakfast place and bistro. The wood-fired oven bakes breads for both restaurants, plus croissants, breakfast pastries, and individual pizzas. Some items are made upstairs and eaten here, such as the local goat cheese tart laced with fennel. There are omelettes and frittatas for breakfast and quesadillas for lunch. A breakfast plate of fresh fruit arrives with a wedge of creamy flan, under a paper-thin crust of caramelized sugar, and a large, flaky croissant.

Tables are wobbly because of the uneven, original stone floor, easy to overlook considering the building's history. There's a steep and narrow 1797 staircase leading downstairs, and the bistro's stone walls are lined with a combination of local artwork, historic photographs, and a small collection of similarly historic farm implements.

Memorable meals are served at the 1797 Depuy Canal House in High Falls.

Tania Barricklo

→ **DEPUY CANAL HOUSE**
845-687-7700.
www.depuycanalhouse.net.
Rte. 213, High Falls, NY
  12440.
Open: Thurs.–Sun.
Price: Expensive–Very
  Expensive.

When chef/owner John Novi bought and restored this historic 1797 stone house in the 1970s, it was the first serious gourmet experience in the Hudson Valley. He built it, and they are still coming for inventive and excellent food; prix fixe menus are made more memorable by the historic

Cuisine: American.
Serving: D, BR Sun.
Credit Cards: AE, DC, MC, V.
Reservations:
  Recommended.
Handicap Access: Limited.

surroundings. Plan to spend an entire evening here, not because the service is slow, but because there are so many courses, especially if you opt for the 10-course tasting menu. In between courses, many diners leave their tables and walk to the second-floor balcony, overlooking the large, modern kitchen, to watch food being prepared.

The signature soup is a caramelized puree of leek and mushoom, served with triangles of thinly fried eggplant for crunch. Scallops are wrapped in a pistachio-studded dough. A slice of Hudson Valley foie gras simply dissolves in your mouth like butter, no chewing necessary; it is served atop a caramel-colored square of duck gelatin. There's an appetizer sampler of petit four-sized offerings, including a spinach mousse that is intense both in flavor and color. The signature entrée is a lobster tail, removed from the shell, pounded flat into a scallopine and barely breaded; it is remarkably tender. Carrot pasta panels are layered with ricotta, but unlike lasagna, the pasta is rolled and sliced like a jelly roll. In between courses, there is a tiny palate-cleansing serving of fennel sorbet. Try to save room for dessert, which includes a light marscapone cheesecake covered with a caramel sauce and a truly moist flourless chocolate cake.

There are several small dining areas in this old house. All feature original creaking wide-plank floorboards, stone fireplaces, steep staircases, and the patina of 200+ years. The Depuy Canal House was built by Simon Depuy and later used by the lock master of the D&H Canal, which runs behind the house (see D&H Canal Museum, Chapter Five, *Arts & Pleasures).*

Highland

THE WOULD
845-691-9883.
www.thewould.com.
120 North Rd., Highland, NY 12528.
Open: Daily.
Price: Moderate–Expensive.
Cuisine: American.
Serving: L in Dec., D.
Credit Cards: AE, MC, V.
Reservations: Yes.
Handicap Access: Limited.

The Would's owners are Claire Winslow, the chef, and Debra Dooley. The restaurant sits alongside the best bocci court in the Hudson Valley. The menu features seasonal and local foods, such as Coach Farm goat cheese, which decorates a salad of baby arugula, asparagus, and roasted beets in an anise vinaigrette; another salad pairs the bite of arugula with the sweetness of cubed mango. There is the seductive richness of pan-seared Hudson Valley foie gras over a local apple confit, and a pan-seared local organic chicken is paired with a golf ball-sized fritter flecked with tiny pieces of spicy poblano pepper. Every weekend the special is a house-aged Angus, thick and tender and brushed with cracked pepper butter; the mixed grill entrée combines steak, fresh sausage, and grilled shrimp. There are at least two vegetarian dishes on the menu each evening, such as crispy tofu wedges over Asian noodles and seasoned with a spicy-sweet lemongrass-coconut sauce. The fresh vegetables that accompany most entrées are cut so small and placed so decoratively on the plate they resemble confetti. Desserts range from homemade sorbets in such flavors as watermelon and pear to a super-rich truffle cake adorned with a spun sugar froufrou.

This used to be Hotel Di Prima, an Italian summer resort, hence the bocci court, and the restaurant hosts a bocci league. Diners can watch games from the back of the two dining rooms. Outside, the brick building is nondescript and ordinary. The interior has been transformed into a casually elegant space with fresh flowers and pots of ferns everywhere, and white tablecloths and china brighten the green carpeting and dark wood chairs. Artwork on the walls is by the restaurant's waitstaff. There is an excellent wine list, including dessert wines.

Kingston

DOWNTOWN CAFÉ
845-331-5904.
One West Strand, Kingston, NY 12401.
Open: Daily.
Price: Moderate.
Cuisine: Northern Italian.
Serving: B, L, D, BR Sun.
Credit Cards: AE, MC, V.
Reservations:
    Recommended.
Handicap Access: Yes.

Downtown Café believes in attention to detail, like the splash of truffle oil that turns a 14k risotto with seared scallops into 24k. The grana padano cheese for your pasta or salad is grated on an antique Italian cheese grater, there's a carafe of water on the table so you don't have to catch the waiter's attention for a refill, and a jar of figs is always poaching in brandy for dessert. The Venetian-born chef/owner has assembled a selection of creative menu items. Dishes that aren't Italian get a continental touch, such as the sushi-grade tuna tartare with a pignoli vinaigrette, and Italian favorites get an international touch, like gnocchi with gingered mussels. The salad of pears, Gorgonzola, and walnuts on watercress is refreshing and delicate. The rack of lamb gets a double dose of zip from a cumin crust and a shallot-peppercorn glaze. The chops are presented standing up, bones intertwined and cradling blanched asparagus. The bread basket is accompanied by a tub of garlic butter. There are always fruit and berry tarts on the menu, and a favorite is the super-rich chocolate truffle cake, made with heavy cream — best to share to protect your arteries.

Housed in a vintage storefront in Kingston's Strand area, this is an open dining area with cinnamon walls. Oriental rugs under groups of tables soak up the noise level, and there is some interesting artwork on the walls. There's also an extensive wine list. In the summer, bistro-sized tables are lined up on the sidewalk.

GOLDEN GINZA
845-339-8132.
www.goldenginza.com.

The red-toqued chef flips raw eggs into a pocket or catches them inside the tall fluted cap before scrambling them on the hibachi grill. The hibachi

24-28 Broadway, Kingston,
    NY 12401.
Open: Daily.
Price: Moderate.
Cuisine: Japanese.
Serving: L Mon.–Fri., D.
Credit Cards: AE, D, MC, V.
Reservations:
    Recommended; required
    for hibachi tables.
Handicap Access: No.

dinner consists of a monumental multicourse meal in between rounds of chef showmanship, starting with rice and noodles, a fast sliced mélange of browned onions, zucchini, bok choi, and broccoli, followed by a one-inch-thick slab of sirloin that's cubed and browned rare, and fast-cooked shrimp caramelized brown in a spritz of soy sauce, but still almost sushi. There are six hibachi tables, each holding eight to 10 diners. They fill up fast with groups of families and friends; reservations are required. There also are regular tables and a sushi bar.

Golden Ginza is all blond woods, with traditional red flags hanging from the ceiling, and a sushi chef as creative as the hibachi chef. The California roll is a colorful combo of pink-orange salmon, creamy white yellow yellowtail, and avocado. Maki roll and sushi are served on a huge wooden boat, with ginger and wasabi tucked into carrot flower "bowls" and a dish of octopus salad in the bow. Sukiyaki is flavorful and thick with paper-thin beef and sliced veggies. There's also a calamari tempura that is tender, not chewy, and an interesting change from Italian-style fried calamari. Fried ice cream is a dessert that pleases kids of all ages — tempura batter and quick frying create a warm, crunchy coating over still-frozen ice cream.

Le Canard Enchaîne is a traditional French bistro in Kingston.

Tania Barricklo

LE CANARD ENCHAÎNE
845-339-2003.
276 Fair St., Kingston, NY
    12401.
Open: Daily.
Price: Moderate–Expensive.
Cuisine: French.
Serving: L, D, BR Sun.

This French bistro sprawls across three storefronts in one of the vintage buildings on Kingston's main street. Ceiling fans turn slowly below the original pressed tin ceiling, walls are either exposed brick or a deep burgundy, and both are decorated with posters, paintings, and photographs of Paris and ducks. More ducks march atop the shelves high on

Credit Cards: All major
  credit cards.
Reservations: Required on
  Sat.
Handicap Access: Yes.

several walls, and, of course, duck is on the menu. The signature dish here is duckling with raspberry sauce, not the traditional à l'orange, which arrives perfectly tender below the crispy skin. There's also a wonderfully chunky, homemade country-style duck pâté appetizer, served on a bed of haricots vert. Pork chops are glazed with a delicious cranberry sauce.

Traditional moules à la marinière get an untraditional kick from Thai lemongrass; you can finish the excellent sauce with the accompanying, crisp French bread. The sweetness of Chilean sea bass is tempered by garlic-laced potatoes. Salad Niçoise is a bowl of unusual greens, including radicchio, lambs tongue, and bibb lettuce, topped with sashimi-grade, barely grilled tuna slices — generous enough to be a full lunch or to share as a combination appetizer and salad at dinner.

The chef/owner and much of the staff are French, and the staff wears traditional long white aprons. One of the waitstaff serves dishes with a pepper mill tucked under his arm — very French. There is no dessert menu; the waitstaff recite the daily specials. Chocolate mousse cake is served on a gigantic plate decorated with squiggles of raspberry puree, the homemade lemon tart atop a very thin crust has microscopic slivers of lemon zest that give it an intense citrus flavor. One of the storefronts is an intimate *boîte de nuit*, a bar with a baby grand piano, with live music entertainment on weekends. There is an "early bird" three-course prix fixe menu and a long list of French wines, including several by the glass.

Marlboro

RACCOON SALOON
845-236-7872.
1330 Rte. 9W, Marlboro, NY
  12542.
Open: Daily.
Price: Moderate.
Cuisine: American.
Serving: L, D.
Credit Cards: AE, D, MC, V.
Reservations:
  Recommended.
Handicap Access: Yes.

The Raccoon Saloon is famous for two things — its balcony dining area 150 feet above a water-filled ravine and waterfall and its homemade ice cream. The view is precipitous enough to induce vertigo, and the ice cream will induce instant incredulity. The light green basil ice cream is closer to mint than pesto, and the lavender ice cream smells as good as it tastes. Both are served straight up in martini glasses, and there are more happy surprises on the menu. Calamari is fried in a zippy red pepper flour and served over curried greens, a combination appetizer and salad. Fillet of skate, a delicate white fish with a texture similar to lobster, is covered with an interesting sweet-sour sauce of brown sugar and vinegary capers. Thick, juicy, huge burgers arrive with a tangle of wonderful moist sweet potato fries (skins left on) and a dish of homemade ketchup that bears no resemblance to the bottled kind; this ketchup is chunky and full of tomato flavor. There also are sandwiches and quesadillas for lunch.

The restaurant — the food is too good for a saloon — is housed in a pre-Revolutionary stagecoach stop. Don't be put off by the slightly sagging second-floor front porch or the purplish blue exterior paint. During Prohibition, this became the Pleasant View Hotel and was granted New York State's first liquor license after Prohibition. It is named for a family of raccoons that lived in the ravine below and had a habit of visiting the restaurant for a free meal. There are pictures from the 1940s of the raccoons being hand-fed by the restaurant's then-owner.

New Paltz

GADALETO'S SEAFOOD MARKET & RESTAURANT
845-255-1717.
246 Main St. (Rte. 299), Cherry Hill Center, New Paltz, NY 12561.
Open: Daily.
Price: Moderate.
Cuisine: Fish, seafood.
Serving: L, D.
Credit Cards: AE, MC, V.
Reservations: Recommended for 5 or more.
Handicap Access: Yes.

You could say Gadaleto's has cornered the fish business in town. Their wholesale operation supplies most of the restaurants in the area, the retail store supplies the do-it-yourselfer, and the restaurant adjoining the retail store feeds the rest. Diners can choose their fillet or steak, and the chef will broil, grill, sauté, or fry it. Portions are substantial, starting with a welcome basket of crispy breads and spiced olives. Dishes are named for their hometowns. New Orleans is a sinus-clearing bowl of gumbo, bursting with mussels, tiny briny crawfish, okra, and celery, and four golf ball-sized hush puppies. Baltimore is a serving of crab cakes, and Cape Cod is beer batter-fried cod, both served with a side of thick hand-cut fries and coleslaw. There are traditional Maine lobster bakes and excellent homemade chowders and oyster stews, with French sea salt on the tables. For lunch, there are salmon burgers and lots of fried things put into sandwiches. The most lethal dessert is the key lime pie on a crust of crushed Oreo cookies.

Nobody comes here for the decor, which is nautical ropes, nets dangling around the walls, and seafaring statues. This is a popular place for crowds and families. One menu item is a shrimp feast for four, which includes two pounds each of fried scrod, peel-and-eat, grilled, and popcorn shrimp. The generous portions and moderate prices mean it can get quite crowded, so go early or late to avoid waiting for a table, especially on weekends when there is a local folk singer. Gadaleto's is located in a strip shopping center.

GILDED OTTER BREWING COMPANY
845-256-1700.
www.gildedotter.com.
3 Main St. (Rte. 299), New Paltz, NY 12561.

This brewpub-restaurant is named for the ship *Gilded Otter*, which left Europe in 1660, carrying the French Huguenots, who were fleeing religious persecution and who founded New Paltz. Their surviving stone houses are a few blocks away

Open: Daily.
Price: Moderate.
Cuisine: American.
Serving: L, D.
Credit Cards: D, DC, MC, V.
Reservations: Accepted.
Handicap Access: Yes.

(see Chapter Five, *Arts & Pleasures*). In 1785, this land was owned by George Wurts, the town's first doctor. He would likely be pleased that the lagers and ales brewed in this microbrewery are in accordance with Germany's strict Purity Laws governing brewing. There are always eight to 10 varieties on tap, pulled from handles that are pieces of birch tree branches. The menu is predictable pub food — heavy on burgers, properly spicy chili, and quesadillas. There's also a selection of well-prepared schnitzels and wursts, including bratwurst braised in the brewpub's own lager.

Gilded Otter Brewing Company is in a modern stone building with huge floor-to-ceiling windows, making for an open, sunny, friendly space.

Tania Barricklo/Daily Freeman

Napping at Lake Minnewaska after a big meal.

LA STAZIONE
845-256-9447.
5 Main St. (Rte. 299), New Paltz, NY 12561.
Open: Daily.
Price: Moderate.
Cuisine: Italian.

This is the old New Paltz railroad station, completely modernized inside with a cathedral ceiling, dark wood wainscoting and window frames, and wood tables and chairs in the same dark wood. Everything is homemade — even the clams for clam sauce are shucked to order — and

Serving: L, D.
Credit Cards: AE, MC, V.
Reservations:
  Recommended for 8 or
  more.
Handicap Access: Yes.

portions are generous. Calamari is fried in a light batter and served with pasta as an entrée or with a thick, chunky tomato sauce, as an appetizer. Pasta dishes are served with the chef's own blend of freshly grated Romano and Parmesan, served in a generous bowl to laden on at your heart's content. There's always a veal, chicken, and pasta special along with traditional Italian favorites, including lasagna — a tall construction smothered under a thick layer of melted mozzarella. For lunch, the rib eye Marsala open-faced sandwich is popular (a sliced steak atop a thick slice of Italian bread, smothered in mushrooms. A selection of thick crust individual pizzas includes the La Stazione, piled with ham, olives, artichokes, and onions.

Desserts include traditional ricotta cheesecake, sometimes an untraditional chocolate version, and an excellent two-inch-deep tiramisù, cut fresh from a huge oblong baking pan. Mon. and Tues. are the busiest, with some two dozen pasta dishes offered as a dinner special, and it can be quite crowded with bargain-minded families and the students of SUNY New Paltz.

RISTORANTE LOCUST TREE
845-255-7888.
www.ristorantelocusttree
  .com.
215 Huguenot St., New
  Paltz, NY 12561.
Open: Tues.–Sun.;
  Feb.–Mar.: closed Tues.
Price: Expensive.
Cuisine: Northern Italian.
Serving: D.
Credit Cards: AE, DC, MC,
  V.
Reservations:
  Recommended,
  especially on weekends.
Handicap Access: No.

This 1759 house on the edge of the New Paltz public golf course is surrounded by towering locust trees nearly as old as the house. Inside is one of the best restaurants in the Hudson Valley. Chef Alberto Vanoli from Bergamo, Italy, and wife Amy, from upstate New York, use only local organic produce, free-range meats and game, and the freshest fish. There's a new menu nightly, according to what's available that day. In the summer, the menu is full of fresh fruits and vegetables; root vegetables and sturdier game and meats are offered in the winter.

Appetizers include a chioggia beet salad, wafer-thin slices of yellow and red beets in a light olive oil, garnished with scallops and bacon. Hudson Valley foie gras is seared and served with figs in a port wine reduction that complements the richness of the liver. The roasted quail has a perfectly golden, crisp skin, surrounded by a salad of sweetbreads and faro. Even rich and complex sauces allow the flavor of handmade semolina pasta to shine through, such as papardelle in a rabbit and black trumpet mushroom ragu and a risotto with a silky lobster reduction. The roasted, local grass-fed veal is not the pale meat one is accustomed to, but darker, more flavorful and fork tender, served with a light Fontina sauce. Desserts range from a light raspberry semifreddo with white chocolate sauce to an unusual sweet tomato tarte (yes, tomato). There's an extensive cheese tray selection and an equally impressive wine list with several well-priced Italian varietals.

The decor is simple but elegant, with bold, hand-carved moldings over the doors, high ceilings, and a large stone hearth. In the summer, there is a small outdoor patio. Tables are set with fine glassware and fresh flowers. The reasonably priced four-course tasting menu is recommended, plus there is a prix fixe menu.

Saugerties

CAFÉ TAMAYO
845-246-9371.
89 Partition St., Saugerties,
    NY 12477.
Open: Wed.–Sun.
Price: Expensive.
Cuisine: American.
Serving: D, BR Sun.
Credit Cards: DC, MC, V.
Reservations:
    Recommended.
Handicap Access: Yes.

The house specialty at Café Tamayo is the confit of duck, crisp skinned but with meat so tender it falls off the bone with a bit of prodding from the fork, no knife necessary. You are served two legs, not the half-duck with one leg, breast, and wing that most restaurants offer. The confit arrives with a wonderful, nutty wild rice, made moist and sweet with the addition of seedless white raisins and a sweet-sour red onion marmalade that tastes remarkably like German red cabbage. Traditional steak au poivre arrives with cracked peppercorns studding a juicy steak, and calves liver is perfectly medium rare and tender. An appetizer mushroom bruschetta is enough for two; the thick bread slices are grilled in olive oil and smothered in fresh mushrooms that have been grilled in dill-flavored butter. There always are pastas on the menu, in appetizer or entrée portions, such as a delicate veal Bolognese. Desserts also are homemade. Fruit sorbets range in flavor from a sweetly tart pink-orange passion fruit to a pale yellow pineapple. The molten chocolate cake is baked to order; one stab of the brownielike exterior releases a lava flow.

The restaurant is in a renovated brick building that has always housed a hotel and restaurant since it opened in 1864; there are now four rooms and suites upstairs, plus an enclosed outdoor patio. There are four small dining areas separated by pocket doors. The interior decoration includes wood wainscoting, ornately framed paintings, and white walls stenciled with leaves around the green-painted window frames. It adds up to a slightly Tuscan-villa feel. There are tablecloths and candlelight at dinner, and Forties Big Band music plays softly enough in the background to complement, rather than interfere with conversation. Be sure to stop and admire the 40-foot-long, antique-carved mahogany bar in the front dining area.

CHOWHOUND CAFÉ
845-246-5158.
112 Partition St., Saugerties,
    NY 12477.
Open: Daily.

Candida Ellis ran a successful corporate catering business in NYC, with most of her clients housed in and around the World Trade Center. After the Sept. 11 attack, she came home to Saugerties to heal and figure out what to do next.

Price: Inexpensive–
   Moderate.
Cuisine: Italian/American.
Serving: L, D, BR Sat., Sun.
Credit Cards: AE, D, MC, V.
Reservations:
   Recommended.
Handicap Access: Yes.

Chowhound Café is a labor of love — her love of creating recipes and cooking them. Everything is homemade. The linguine Francesca, available at lunch and dinner, is thick with artichoke hearts and calamata olives. Its tart bite tempered by sweet fresh basil, and there's enough thick sauce left after the linguine to finish with a spoon. Thick sandwiches are on focàccia or toasted pannini style. That includes the Reuben, a meal of maple ham, smoked turkey, swiss, and sauerkraut, but skip the Russian dressing in favor of a nutty grain mustard. A Latin-spiced chopped steak, pastel de chocio, is covered in a corn dough, baked and sliced like lasagna, juicy and moist. Side dishes are usually grilled seasonal vegetables or plantains. A dessert choice is a generous slab of chocolate cake, laced with rum, studded with chunks, not bits, of chocolate, and served in a puddle of crème anglaise.

The decor is casual. This is a vintage storefront on Saugerties' main street, with the original tin ceilings and exposed brick walls. The tall space is made more intimate with leafy six-foot-tall ferns in planters, decorative antique mirrors, and floral prints on the walls. Tables are bare for lunch, but dressed with linen and candles for dinner and weekend brunch. There's also room for a few bistro tables on the sidewalk in warm weather, and on weekends there's often live music.

DINING: GREENE COUNTY

Athens

STEWART HOUSE
518-945-1357.
2 N. Water St., Athens, NY
   12015.
Open: Tues.–Sun.; winter:
   Wed.–Sun.
Price: Moderate.
Cuisine: American.
Serving: L, D.
Credit Cards: AE, MC, V.
Reservations:
   Recommended.
Handicap Access: Limited.

The signature dish at this historic Victorian inn (see Chapter Three, *Lodging*) is cedar-planked seafood, which is how the area's Native Americans cooked the fish and shellfish that they caught in the Hudson River, just a few feet from the front door of this restaurant, but the porous cedar planks that they used were not marinated in wine and spices for several days first. The smoke from the cedar permeates the salmon, shrimp, scallops, clams, and scrod, imparting a wonderfully smoky taste. They also offer hefty nine-ounce Angus burgers, so big it's easier to cut like an entrée than try to eat with your hands, and an unusual pork Havana, a marinated and sliced tenderloin in an eyebrow-raising chili sauce, served as a sandwich at lunch or as an entrée with beans and rice at dinner. The menu is primarily seafood, and there's a raw bar.

There are two halves to the Stewart House restaurant. On the right side of the building's entrance and center staircase is the bar-bistro, with a more casual ambiance and a higher noise level than the dining room across the way. Both rooms have retained the original tin ceilings, but the dining room features an ornate, inlaid marble fireplace, oak wainscoting, and original cast-iron tables with embossed pedestals. There's an outdoor Victorian-style pavilion on the water for warm weather dining.

Catskill

SOLSTICE
518-943-1443.
www.solsticerestaurant
    .com.
162 West Main St., Catskill,
    NY 12414.
Open: Fall/winter:
    Thurs.–Sun.
Price: Moderate.
Cuisine: American.
Serving: L, D.
Credit Cards: All major
    credit cards.
Reservations:
    Recommended for
    dinner.
Handicap Access: Yes.

This bright and airy restaurant is tucked inside the Hop-O-Nose Marina, with nonstop windows overlooking the river-wide Catskill Creek. The decor is as delightful as the food, and despite its location, there is no nautical theme. There is a huge galvanized steel bar in the front dining area and galvanized steel sculptures, both made by an artist friend of the owners. There are photographs on other walls, and the high-ceilinged, large inner dining area is softened by white fabric draped tent style. Tabletops are painted with interesting designs, including celestial shapes to honor the solstice, whimsical fish (owners Mark Decker, the chef, and wife Lara, the host, are both astrological Pisces), dragonflies, and fanciful flowers. White linen napkins and dishes don't compete with the tables or the food.

Homemade crab cakes are chunky with corn kernels, and somehow they hold their shape without the breading that normally holds them together. There's a daily pasta specialty, usually homemade ravioli and usually filled with lobster, mushrooms, or duck, rarely cheese; these are generously plump, three-inch pasta envelopes. Salmon is grilled with pepper and lemon and served with a dill sauce that can be shared with the paper-thin, spiral-cut cucumbers that accompany the fish. Another section of the menu, for lunch or dinner, is "lite bites," including flaky fish and chips and burgers. There's warm weather, waterside dining on the outdoor patio.

Purling

BAVARIAN MANOR
518-622-3261.
www.bavarianmanor.com.
866 Mountain Rd., Purling,
    NY 12470.
Open: Thurs.–Sun.

This restaurant has been in continuous operation since the 1860s and in the same family for three generations, long enough to get it right (see Chapter Three, *Lodging*). Although the menu is predominantly traditional German and Austrian fare,

Price: Moderate.
Cuisine: German/Austrian.
Serving: L Sun., D.
Credit Cards: MC, V.
Reservations:
  Recommended.
Handicap Access: Yes.

there also are butter-sautéed fish dishes, including trout and fillet of sole, thick and juicy flame-broiled steaks, and even a chicken Marsala. But it is the homemade German dishes that are the real stand-outs. The schnitzels, or veal cutlets, are so large they all but hang over the plate. Wiener Schnitzel is lightly breaded, crisp outside, tender inside, jaeger schnitzel is served hunter-style with a rich brown gravy, and paprika schnitzel has a creamy, spicy pink sauce. These are served with red cabbage, cooked soft but still crunchy with the proper vinegar tang, and homemade spaetzle, the tiny dumplinglike side dish that is a staple in German-speaking Europe. There also are wurst platters. Weisswurst is the Bavarian national wurst, a delicate veal wurst served with a spicy-sweet mustard. Wurst dishes come with potatoes unless you ask for spaetzle. Do ask. Save room for dessert. Nobody should leave a Bavarian restaurant without sampling the Black Forest cake, chocolate layers separated by whipped cream and topped with candied cherries; this cake is made by Hartmann's, the Viennese bakery in nearby Round Top, New York.

The interior is as Bavarian as the menu, with lace curtains, a collection of beer steins marching across shelves near the ceiling, several huge fireplaces, historic bric-a-brac from the inn's operation, and waitresses wear traditional dirndl dresses. Often on weekends, there's live music by the band Schwarzenegger Connection. Yes, *that* Schwarzenegger. Some people in the band are Arnold's cousins.

FOOD PURVEYORS

FARM MARKETS

The fertile land that first attracted Dutch settlers nearly four centuries ago continues to produce an abundance of fruits and vegetables from apples to zucchini on family-owned farms whose silos and barns polka dot nearly every country road.

Starting in the spring with asparagus, strawberries, peaches, and melons and continuing on to summer's crisp sweet corn, fat cucumbers, and juicy scarlet tomatoes, through autumn with orchards heavy with apples, pears, and vines choked with bright orange pumpkins, no visit to the Hudson Valley is complete without a stop at one of the many roadside farm stands for freshly picked produce, flowers, and herbs. Even the area's dominant highway, the NYS Thruway (I-87), has farmers' markets at rest stops in the Hudson Valley during the prime growing season. Or, grab a basket and head into the fields yourself at one of the many pick-your-own farms and orchards.

Tania Barricklo/Daily Freeman

First you pick, then you pull.

The Hudson Valley is prime apple country, growing a range of varieties from the best known, such as the all-purpose crisp and tart McIntosh, Red Delicious, and Granny Smith to the delicate Fugi, Empire, and Macoun. Many orchards press a portion of their harvest into cider. Some use century-old presses that wheeze and grumble as they funnel golden apple cider into plastic jugs, spitting out the pits and cores to be recycled as compost or cattle feed. And let's not forget grapes — there are more than two dozen wineries in the Hudson Valley (see Wineries below).

WESTCHESTER COUNTY

Outhouse Orchards (914-277-3188; Hardscrabble Rd., Croton Falls) This is one of the largest pumpkin patches in the county, filled with giggling children and camera-toting parents each Oct. There's a farm market open year-round, with fruits, vegetables, jams, and jellies. Open daily 10am–6pm, and pick-your-own apples in autumn.

Wilkins Fruit and Fir Farm (1335 White Hill Rd. (Rte. 202), Yorktown) There is produce from several nearby farms and seasonal pick-your-own fruits and vegetables (berries, apples, peaches, tomatoes) weekends only, plus freshly cut Christmas trees Nov.–Dec. 15. Open daily.

PUTNAM COUNTY

Brewster Farmers' Market (845-279-5778; Village Hall (intersection Rte. 22 and Rte. 6), Brewster) Open year-round: Sun.; mid-June–Oct. 30: Sat., Sun.

DUTCHESS COUNTY

Barton Orchards (845-227-2306; www.bartonorchards.com; Poughquag Rd. (Rte. 7), Poughquag) Offers everything for visitors, from pick-your-own fruits to hayrides, special events, and a Christmas tree farm in season. Open May–Dec.

Green Horizons Organic Farm (845-855-5555; S. Dingle Rd., Pawling) Pick-your-own fruits and vegetables. Open Apr.–Sept.

Greig Farm & Farm Market (845-758-1234; www.greigfarm.com; Pitcher Ln., Red Hook) Huge, bustling farm just north of picturesque Red Hook, where tourists and tractors seem to be in equal numbers. Pick-your-own apples, berries, and vegetables, plus there's a tree farm, gift shop, and hayrides. Also on the premises is Alison Vineyards, a small, boutique winery. Open mid-Apr. Dec.: daily.

Tania Barricklo

Fresh fruits and vegetables bursting with flavor at Rhinebeck Farmers' Market.

Rhinebeck Farmers' Market (Rhinebeck Muncipal Parking Lot, E. Market St., Rhinebeck) Fruits, vegetables, wine, cider, fruit juice, local cheeses, free-range poultry, smokehouse products, and cut flowers are available. Open May–Nov.: Sun.

COLUMBIA COUNTY

The Berry Farm (518-392-4609; Rte. 203, Kinderhook) Pick-your-own fruits and vegetables, plus locally made maple syrup, cheeses, and honey. Open daily in season.
Hudson Farmers' Market (518-828-7217; N. Sixth and Columbia Sts., Hudson) Open June–late Oct.: Sat.

Farm stands, farmers' markets, and pick-your-own farms are plentiful.

Tania Barricklo

ROCKLAND COUNTY

Dr. Davies Farm (845-268-7020; www.drdaviesfarm.com; Rte. 304, Congers) Founded in 1881 and still in the same family, this historic farm has pick-your-own apples. Open July–Nov.: daily.
Orchards of Concklin (845-354-0369; www.the orchardsofconcklin.com; 2 S. Mountain Rd. (Rte. 45), Pomona) The Concklin family has farmed these 100 acres since the early 1700s, producing apples, pears, and other seasonal fruits. Pick-your-own apples and pears in Sept. Open Sept.–Oct.: weekends 10am–5pm.

ORANGE COUNTY

Blooming Hill Farm (845-782-7310; Rte. 208, Blooming Grove) A working organic fruit, herb, and vegetable farm. The farm store sells free-range eggs, local goat cheese, and organic baked breads. Open May–Oct.: daily.

Jones Farm & Country Store (845-534-4445; 190 Angola Rd., Cornwall, NY) In addition to fresh produce grown on the farm behind the store, this two-floor shop in an old farmhouse also has homemade jams and jellies, cookies, and fruit pies, plus imported floral-scented bath products and candles, children's toys, stuffed animals, jewelry, and kitchen accessories. Open daily.

Swissette Herb Farm (845-496-7841; Clove Rd., Salisbury Mills) Here is the largest selection of organically grown herbs in the Hudson Valley. They specialize in European herbals, homeopathic products, and tinctures. The farm store sells herbal plants and products, books, organic teas, and dried flowers. Open May–Labor Day: daily; weekends only to Oct. 31.

ULSTER COUNTY

Clarke's Westervelt Fruit Farm (845-795-2270; 38 #2 Clarke's Ln. (off Rte. 9W), Milton) It's a half-mile on a dirt road to this working farm and orchard, one of the oldest and largest in the area. You pick cherries (sweet and sour), peaches, pears, and apples, and the orchard owners will take you to the best picking trees by farm tractor. Open mid-June–Oct. 31: daily.

Hurd's Family Farm (845-883-7364; www.hurdsharvest.com; Rte. 32, Modena) Welcoming visitors has become a bigger business than growing apples and other produce, but the Hurd family does both right, with a four-acre corn maze, a huge farm store that sells fresh fruits, veggies, and homemade baked goods, plus tractor rides and hayrides for the kids. Open Sept.–Oct.: weekends.

Jenkins and Lueken Orchards (845-255-0999; www.geocities.com/Eureka/Office/2857; Rte. 299W (before juncture of Rte. 44/55), New Paltz) Offers a dozen varieties of apples, pears, and peaches, plus tomatoes and other vegetables in season, including pick-your-own apples and pumpkins. The orchard store sells farm-grown produce, honey, and cider made from one of those prehistoric, cranky apple presses. Open Aug.–May: daily.

Mr. Apples (845-687-0005; Rte. 213W, High Falls) You pick apples and pears in an orchard tucked on the side of a hill, guided by owner Philip Apple (seriously, that's his name). Open Aug.–Nov.

Prospect Hill Orchards (845-795-2383; www.prospecthillorchards.com; 40 Clarke's Ln. (off Rte. 9W), Milton) You pick cherries in June, peaches in Aug., and apples and pears in Sept. Open June, Aug., Sept.

Weed Orchards (845-236-0237; www.weedorchards.com; 43 Mt. Zion Rd. (off Lattintown Rd. from Rte. 9W), Marlboro) An unfortunate name for a fourth-generation, family-owned orchard that offers lakeside picnics, hayrides, petting zoo of smaller farm animals, and pick-your-own apples and peaches. Plus, of course, the farm store has fresh produce, homemade apple pies, caramel apples, jams, jellies, and gift items. Open Aug. 20–Oct. 31: daily.

GOURMET FOODS

WESTCHESTER COUNTY

E. B.'s Golden Harvest (914-962-5666; www.ebsgoldenharvest.com; 229 Cordial Rd., Yorktown) Only raw, unheated honey from Hudson Valley bees is sold here, including the most popular clover and wildflower honey and specialty fruit-scented raspberry and blueberry honey. Also, honey spreads are made from fresh fruits blended with the honey to use on breads or crackers or as a meat glaze, plus beeswax candles and beeswax and herbal beauty creams. Open May–Dec.

Hemlock Hill Farm (914-737-2810; 500 Croton Ave., Cortlandt Manor) All-natural poultry, meat, and game, farm fresh eggs, honey, fruits, and vegetables. Open year-round.

DUTCHESS COUNTY

Anna Marie's Organic Olive Oil (845-868-7107; oliveoil686@aol.com; 5335 Rte. 82, Clinton Corners) The farm in Portugal has been owned and operated by Anna Marie Cordero's family for five generations, in the same region that produces Portugal's port wines. Sheep graze on the farm to ensure crops are free of weeds and pests without need of chemicals. The oil is cold-pressed there and bottled in the Hudson Valley on her farm adjoining the Clinton Vineyards. The extra-virgin oil is wonderfully fruity — ideal for dipping. Call for hours.

Sprout Creek Farm (845-485-9885; www.sproutcreekfarm.org; 34 Lauer Rd., Poughkeepsie) Choose from artisanal cheeses made from the farm's own grass-fed Jersey, Guernsey, Shorthorn, and Brown Swiss cows. Cheeses include fresh Tuscan-style ricotta and mold-ripened varieties. Call for hours.

Stone walls from the 18th and 19th centuries checker the landscape.

Tania Barricklo

Uphill Farm (845-266-5005; www.beltie.com; 2947 Salt Point Turnpike, Clinton Corners) All natural (no steroids, hormones, or antibiotics) registered Galloway beef products. Call for hours.

COLUMBIA COUNTY

Highland Premium Farm Raised Venison (518-537-6397; Highland Farm, 183 County Rte. 6, Germantown) These deer are raised on pasture and fed locally grown hay, grain, and produce — no hormones or steroids — for a nongamy, delicate, low-cholesterol meat. The venison is available fresh, frozen, and smoked, in chops, roasts, medallions, and ground meat. Call for hours.

SULLIVAN COUNTY

Hudson Valley Foie Gras (845-292-2500; 877-BUY-FOIE; www.hudsonvalley foiegras.com; 80 Brooks Rd. (off Rte. 17W), Ferndale) The sinfully rich duck livers from this purveyor are featured on the menus of many of the Hudson Valley's top restaurants, and it is the choice of gourmet restaurant chefs from New York City to Saratoga and beyond. Visitors are welcome at the farm near Monticello, just west of the Hudson Valley in the Catskill Mountains. Come and visit or order by telephone or on the Web. Open daily.

ULSTER COUNTY

New York Store (845-687-7779; Rte. 213, High Falls) John Novi, chef/owner of the highly regarded Depuy Canal House (see above) opened a gourmet store in the adjoining building, dating from the 1860s. Only New York State products are sold here, including mustards and marinades, jellies (look for the wine-based jellies), fresh pastas, and maple syrup. There also are some ready-to-cook items from the Canal House menu, plus fresh breads and pastries. Open Wed.–Sun.

GREENE COUNTY

Family Alpine Pork Store (518-622-3056; Rte. 23B, South Cairo) This is an old-fashioned butcher shop, where everything is cut to order on well-worn wooden chopping blocks and wrapped in traditional butcher paper. In addition to fresh meats, there is a tempting array of homemade German wursts, from delicate veal-based weisswurst to hearty salamis and smoked pork products. Open Mon.–Sat.

MAPLE SYRUP PRODUCERS

It's a spring thing — the sap begins to flow just after the snow melts. The Hudson Valley's maple syrup producers must meet exacting standards: all natural ingredients and no less than 66 percent sugar. Some producers offer tours of the collecting and evaporation process. Since these are all working farms (mostly dairy farms), it is best to call ahead.

ULSTER COUNTY

Arrowhead Farm (845-626-7983; 5941 Rte. 209, Kerhonkson) Tours Mar.–Apr.; syrup available year-round.

Lyonsville Sugarhouse (845-626-2518; 591 County Rte. 2, Accord) Syrup and maple cream available year-round.

Mountain Dew Maple Products (845-626-3466; mountaindewmaple@aol.com; 351 Samsonville Rd., Kerhonkson) Tours Mar.–Apr.; syrup, maple sugar treats, and maple cream available year-round.

SUNDRY CONFECTIONS

DUTCHESS COUNTY

Holy Cow (845-758-5959; 7270 S. Broadway (Rte. 9), Red Hook) Simply, this is the best ice cream for miles around, and on a summer evening, the line is often out the door despite a team of six servers working fast and furious. The ice cream is homemade, butterfat thick, and in a mind-numbing choice of flavors and toppings. Purists can indulge in black raisin, pistachio, or double chocolate, while the more adventurous can experiment with a "razzle" or "flavor burst," ice cream shot through with candy pieces. And everything, of course, is in your choice of cone or cup. Sprinkles are 15 cents extra. There's also soft-serve yogurt and made-to-order shakes and malts. Unfortunately, Holy Cow is situated in a strip mall, and other than the parking lot, there's no place to stroll and enjoy your cone. Open daily.

ROCKLAND COUNTY

Krum's Chocolatiers (845-735-5100; fax 845-735-6434; 4 Dexter Plaza, Pearl River) Sadly, the strip mall location does not have the history or ambiance of the original Krum's, a combination chocolate and candy shop and soda fountain, which opened in 1933 on the then-grand Grand Concourse in The Bronx, next to the equally fabled Loew's Paradise movie palace. The heady chocolate fragrance and delicious bon bons survived the move to suburbia; the soda fountain didn't. There's also a pastry shop. Tours of the production lines are available by appt.

ULSTER COUNTY

Krause's Homemade Candy (845-246-8377; fax 845-247-0981; www.krauses chocolates.com; 41 S. Partition St., Saugerties) The third generation now runs

Chocolate at Krause's Homemade Candy is made the old-fashioned way.

Tania Barricklo

this chocolate and candy business, started in 1929, and the bon bons are still hand dipped or hand molded. Old-fashioned glass showcases are laden with similarly old-fashioned nonpareils, chocolate-covered orange peels, truffles, and nuts in bittersweet and milk chocolate varieties, and nonsugar items for diabetics. The store is at the end of the street, almost at the Hudson River. Call to arrange tours. Open Tues.-Sun.

GREENE COUNTY

Hartman's Kaffeehaus (518-622-3820; 1507 Hearts Content Rd. (County Rte. 24), Round Top) The Viennese pastries in the old-fashioned slant-front glass showcases are guaranteed to make you forget your diet. Everything is baked in the modern kitchen in the back of this 100-year-old house, from the wedge-shaped *nussecken* (nut corner), a triangle of ground nuts and honey dipped in chocolate, to berry-rich pies, multilayer cakes in chocolate and nut, and raisin-studded holiday Stollen. There's a Viennese-style café that serves breakfast, lunch, and afternoon *kaffee mit schlag* (coffee with real whipped cream). Open Easter–Christmas; call for hours.

<u>WINERIES</u>

The winemaking tradition in the Hudson Valley began in the 17th century when the Huguenots discovered that the unique combination of the limestone-based soil and a long summer with cool nights were ideal for growing grapes, and there have been vineyards in the region ever since. Nearly three dozen operating wineries produce a medley of award-winning varietals, ranging from dry and semidry to berry-sweet dessert wines and bottle-fermented sparkling wines. All but the smallest wineries offer tours and tastings.

Add these wineries to the proliferation of inventive and talented chefs trained at the Culinary Institute of America in Hyde Park (who are now working in area restaurants and even opening their own restaurants), and the combination can easily prompt comparisons to California's wine and food mecca. The Hudson Valley is being called the "Napa of the East," but unlike Napa, where vineyards tend to be huge commercial ventures, vineyards here are mostly small, family operations. You are likely to run into the vineyard owner, the cellar master, or both, hosting a tour or uncorking a taste sampling.

Most wineries are members of the **Hudson River Region Wine Council,** whose parent group, the **New York Wine & Grape Foundation,** has a comprehensive web site (www.newyorkwines.org). Also, **Vintage Hudson Valley** (914-591-4503; www.vintagehudsonvalley.com) organizes weekend winemaker dinners and cooking classes that include pairing foods with wines; these activities are held at several of the more upscale B&Bs in the valley.

WESTCHESTER COUNTY

North Salem Vineyard (914-669-5518; www.northsalemwine.com; 441 Hardscrabble Rd. (off Rte. 684), North Salem) This winery was founded in 1965 by a physician who is still passionate about the health benefits of moderate wine consumption. The 18-acre winery is adjacent to a large working orchard farm in an area close enough to New York City that many local residents commute daily. The winery is housed in a rustic, beamed barn with an unpretentious, modern glass and tile tasting room with a seating area that invites lingering and socializing. Free tours, free tastings. Open June–Oct.: daily 1pm–5pm; Nov.–Mar.: Sat.–Sun. 1pm–5pm; and by appt.

DUTCHESS COUNTY

There are three wineries that make up the **Dutchess County Wine Trail** (845-266-5372; www.dutchesswinetrail.com) Look for the green signs with grape cluster icons that lead you to the wineries.

Cascade Mountain Winery and Restaurant (914-373-9021; www.cascademt.com; 835 Cascade Mountain Rd., Amenia) Established in 1977, this 10-acre winery has bested California wines in blind-taste tests. It is more famous locally for its winery restaurant, which serves creative regional cuisine paired with Cascade's wines. Restaurant open Apr.–Nov.: Thurs.–Sun., serving lunch and dinner on Sat. Tasting room open year-round: daily 10am–5pm.

Clinton Vineyards (845-266-5372; www.clintonvineyards.com; 212 Schultzville Rd. (off Taconic State Pkwy.), Clinton Corners) This winery produces primarily fruit-based dessert and sparkling wines; Clinton wines have been served in the White House. Grand Pere is a pear wine, Rhapsody is made from wild blueberries, and Duet combines strawberries and rhubarb. Clinton also is the only vineyard in New York State that produces cassis, which is made

There have been vineyards in the Hudson Valley since the 1700s.

Dutchess County Tourism

from black currants. The winery is housed in a wonderful weathered barn that dates from the early 1800s and is across from the owners' white clapboard home. There's a small gift shop. Tasting room open Fri.–Sun. 11am–5pm; and by appt.

Millbrook Vineyards and Winery (845-677-8383; 800-662-9463; www.mill brookwine.com; Wing Rd., Millbrook) Millbrook Vineyards and Winery is the area's dominant producer, with more than 130 acres of rolling hillsides that grow grapes for Chardonnay, Gamay Noir, Pinot Noir, cabernet franc, and Tocai Fruilano, a light-bodied, Tuscan-style white wine. Millbrook wines regularly win awards and appear on many wine lists in the region's better restaurants. The vineyard is owned by John Dyson, a former commissioner of the NYS Dept. of Commerce, who helped coin the slogan, "I Love New York." He also owns vineyards in California and Tuscany. The winery is housed in a huge, six-sided antique barn, which has been modernized with massive windows to enjoy the impressive view across the valley; the land was the Wing family farm (see Chapter Five, *Arts & Pleasures*). The tasting area is in the old hayloft. In addition to tours and tastings, there are weekend concerts in the summer in front of the barn, overlooking the valley. Open daily 12noon–5pm; Mem. Day–Labor Day: daily 12noon–7pm.

COLUMBIA COUNTY

Alison Vineyards (845-758-6335; www.alisonwines.com; 231 Pitcher Ln. (off Rte. 9), Red Hook) Alison Vineyards is one of the newest in the Hudson Valley and produces French-style reds and whites in a converted dairy barn, parts of which date from the 19th century. The vineyards are adjacent to one of the largest working farms in the area. Open mid-Apr.–Dec.: daily 11am–5pm.

ORANGE COUNTY

There are three wineries in Orange County at the southern edge of the **Shawangunk Wine Trail,** where wines are more likely to be made of apples than grapes.

Applewood Winery (845-988-9292; www.applewoodorchardsandwinery.com; Kings Hwy. (bet. Rtes. 17 and 17A), Warwick) Applewood was settled by a Dutch family in 1700 and is one of the oldest working farms on the west side of the Hudson River Valley. There is a huge apple orchard on the property and some of the winery's top sellers are Stone Fence Hard Cider, named for the ubiquitous stone fences in the Hudson Valley, and three apple wines, two of which are semidry and Autumn Mist, a golden sweet dessert wine. This is also a pick-your-own farm for pumpkins, apples, and other orchard fruits, with hayrides for the kids. Located at the end of a long, rutted dirt road that may not be suitable for low-slung vehicles. Open Apr.–June: daily 12noon–5pm; July–Oct.: Fri.–Sun. 12noon–5pm.; Nov.–Dec.: Sat.–Sun. 12noon–5pm.

Brotherhood Winery (845-496-3661; www.brotherhoodnywines.com; 100 Brotherhood Plaza Dr. (off Rte. 17W and Rte. 28N), Washingtonville) Brotherhood claims to be the oldest winery in the U.S. in continuous operation since it produced its first vintage in 1839; it also claims to have the largest underground wine cellars in the country. The winery survived Prohibition by the sale of sacramental wines. Brotherhood bottles more than a dozen varietals, mostly from grapes grown elsewhere. The winery has been best known for its blended wines, including a May wine, with strawberry juice and woodruff, a spiced Holiday wine that is ideal hot as a winter "gluhwein," and wines flavored with ginseng root. The new owners, however, are moving the winery away from the mediocre to include some well-regarded varietals. The largest and certainly the most commercial winery in the area — one of the few to charge for a tasting — has a regular schedule of special events almost every weekend from June–Christmas, including grape-stomping contests every weekend in Sept.–Oct. There is an extensive gift shop and a European-style café. Open daily 11am–5pm.

Warwick Valley Winery (845-258-4858; www.wvwinery.com; 114 Little York Rd. (Rte. 94S to County Rd. 1A), Warwick) This 65-acre apple and pear orchard and winery primarily produce a European-style hard cider with a 4.5 percent kick called Doc's Draft, plus a port wine and several reds and whites, including Riesling, Chardonnay, and cabernet franc. Warwick also produces New York State's first brandy out of a fermented mash of apples, pears, or raspberries, or a combination, in a handcrafted copper still from Germany. The Grizzanti family boasts a Culinary Institute of America-trained chef who bakes for the on-premise bakery. Pick-your-own apples and pears from more than 30 varieties. Open Sept.–Dec. 31: daily 11am–6pm; Jan.–Aug.: Thurs.–Sun. 11am–6pm.

ULSTER COUNTY

The wineries clustered in the fertile crescent between the Shawangunk Mountains and the Hudson River have grouped to form the **Shawangunk Wine Trail.**

Adair Vineyards (845-255-1377; 52 Allhusen Rd. (off Rte. 32), New Paltz) Adair is housed in a landmark 200-year-old barn alongside a picturesque stream, with 10 acres under cultivation. The winery entrance is dominated by a huge solitary oak almost as old as the barn. The vineyard owners have incorporated the tree into their label, via an 1840 painting, *The Solitary Oak,* by Hudson River School artist Asher Durand. Open June–Oct.: daily; May: Fri.–Sun.; Nov.–Dec.: Sat.–Sun.

Baldwin Vineyards (914-744-2226; 176 Hardenburgh Rd. (off Rte. 52), Pine Bush) Baldwin bottles 15 different wines, including a German-style Riesling and a late-harvest golden Vignole rich enough to replace dessert, as well as luscious dessertlike strawberry and raspberry wines. Free tours, free tastings. Open July–Oct.: daily 11am–5:30pm; Apr.–June, Nov.–Dec.: Fri.–Mon. 11:30am–5pm; rest of year: weekends only 11:30am–4:30pm.

Benmarl Wine Company (845-236-4265; www.benmarl.com; 165 Highland Ave. (off Rte. 9W), Marlboro) This is the oldest vineyard in America, first planted with wild grapes in the 1700s by French Huguenots who had settled in the area. Vineyard owner Mark Miller was a Hollywood costume designer and magazine illustrator working in Europe, who claims to have brought the first French Chardonnay and German Riesling grapes to the U.S. in the 1950s. The winery includes a rather extensive art gallery, filled with Miller's and regional artists' landscapes and portraits. Benmarl's cellar is designed with a theatrical touch to resemble an antique European castle, and if Miller is on hand (as he usually is), be sure to ask for a peek at his properly dusty collection of rare, vintage bottles. From the lawn in front of the tasting house, the view opens wide across the Hudson River to the Taconic Range and Berkshire Hills in Massachussetts. The winery is about half a mile from the paved road on a bumpy, rocky dirt stretch that borders the grape vines; this road may not be suitable for low-slung vehicles. Open Apr.–Dec.: daily 12noon–5pm; Jan.–Mar.: Wed.–Sun. 12noon–4pm.

Brimstone Hill Vineyard (845-744-2231; www.brimstonehillwine.com; 61 Brimstone Hill Rd. (off Conway Rd. and Rte. 52), Pine Bush) This winery produces French-style reds and whites, as well as semisweet whites made from New York's own Cayuga grapes. There are 12 acres planted. Open July–Oct.: daily; Nov.–Dec., May–June: Fri.–Mon.; Jan.–Apr.: Sat.–Sun.

El Paso Winery (845-331-8642; 742 Broadway (Rte. 9W), Ulster Park) This is a postage-stamp-sized winery that produces inexpensive, hearty table wines that pair better with barbecue sauce than béchamel. Open Apr.–Dec.: daily.

Rivendell Winery (845-255-2494; www.rivendellwine.com; www.vintagenew

york.com; 714 Albany Post Rd. (off Rte. 44/55), New Paltz) Rivendell crafts its wines from grapes grown by small, family farms in the Hudson Valley, the Finger Lakes Region, and Long Island. Established in 1987, Rivendell has won more than its share of awards for its varietals, including the rich, dark Vampire's Blood label released in Oct. This is a large, modern winery with a large snack area set against a glass wall that faces a huge open meadow to the Shawangunk Mountains. It's not just Rivendell's wines that are stand-outs. The winery's proprietors, Robert Ransom and Susan Wine (what a wonderful name for a vintner!), have a generous attitude about their competitors — their wineshop, Vintage New York, sells wines from most of New York State's 160 wine producers, plus gourmet food products made in The Empire State. The wine tastings after the winery tour include some of these other competitor labels. There also are two Vintage New York stores in New York City. Free tours, free tastings. Open year-round: daily.

Royal Kedem Winery (845-236-4000; www.kedem.com; 1519 Rte. 9W, Marlboro) Royal Kedem only produces kosher wines; the wines contain no non-wine yeast or animal-based acidifying agents or gelatin. Kedem's parent, Royal Winery, produces Kedem label wines from New York State grapes and Baron Herzog wines from California grapes. The Herzog family was the exclusive wine supplier to Franz Joseph, emperor of the Austro-Hungarian Empire, who granted one of the early Herzog winemakers the royal title of Baron; the Hudson Valley winery was established 100 years later in 1948. Currently, the eighth generation is making wines, cordials, and sparkling wines. Open Sun.–Thurs. 10:30am–4:30pm.

Whitecliff Vineyard (845-255-4613; www.whitecliffwine.com; 331 McKinstry Rd. (off Rte. 52 and County Rd. 14), Gardiner) This vineyard is pioneering the use of the Gamay Noir grape in the Hudson Valley for French-style Beaujolais. This is a relatively new and small winery with a lovely art gallery and gift shop. Open Mem. Day–Oct. 31: Thurs., Fri., Sun. 12noon–5pm, Sat. 11:30am–6pm; Nov.–Dec., Apr.–Mem. Day: weekends; and by appt.

CHAPTER FIVE
So Much to See & Do
ARTS & PLEASURES

Fairs, festivals, and museums showcase Colonial activities.

Evelyn Kanter

There may be no other region that has had as significant an impact on American art as the Hudson Valley. In the late 1800s, the very lushness of this landscape inspired an entire generation of painters, who became known as the Hudson River School. The romantic vision of the undulating hills, craggy rock outcroppings, bountiful fields, and broad expanses of sun-sparkled water of the artists, including Thomas Cole, Frederic Church, and Albert Bierstadt (who took his Hudson Valley sensibilities to Yellowstone and the Rockies), did more than immortalize the scenery on canvas. They created a worldwide appreciation for the beauty, mystery, and spirit of this historic stretch of land.

And who among us did not as a child experience a combination of awe and fear when reading Washington Irving's legends of headless horsemen and somnolent farmers and James Fenimore Cooper's tales of heroic Mohicans.

There is an abundant cultural heritage here, nurtured in no small measure by the wealthy and well-traveled industrialists, entrepreneurs, and financiers of the Gilded Age who built their magnificent mansions along the shores of the Hudson River. The Vanderbilts, Rockefellers, Dukes, Biddles, and their compatriots surrounded themselves with now-priceless art and furnishings and invited classical musicians and other performers to entertain their guests in the days before PBS and VH1.

The Rockefellers had a profound impact on the cultural life of the Hudson Valley. Their estate, Kykuit, in Tarrytown (see Chapter Six, *Mansions of the Hudson Valley*), is really an art museum lived in by several generations. Former New York State Governor and Vice-President Nelson Rockefeller was an avid collector of modern art and sculpture, much of which is displayed at the house and grounds; his mother, Abby, was a founder of New York City's Museum of Modern Art. The Rockefellers also created Historic Hudson Valley to preserve the historic estates of their neighbors.

From a collection of community and summer stock theater groups to the grand scale of the dramatic new Bard Performing Arts Center at Bard College; from storefront art galleries to the expansive new contemporary art museum DIA: Beacon; from a funky '50s drive-in in Coxsackie to a state-of-the-art Imax in West Nyack; from a local high school marching band to the U.S. Army Band at West Point; from a window into the American past at Washington's Revolutionary War Headquarters in Newburgh to a glimpse into the galactic future at Hudson River Museum's Andros Planetarium in Yonkers; from year-round exhibits at the Harness Racing Museum & Hall of Fame in Goshen to the livestock competitions at the annual Dutchess County Fair, there is something to appreciate, educate, motivate, and just plain enjoy.

MUSEUMS & OTHER ATTRACTIONS

WESTCHESTER COUNTY — MUSEUMS

North Salem

HAMMOND MUSEUM AND JAPANESE STROLL GARDEN
914-669-5033.
www.hammondmuseum.org.
Deveau Rd. (off I-84, Hardscrabble Rd. exit), North Salem, NY 10560.
Open: Apr.–Oct.: Wed.–Sat. 12noon–4pm.

This is a little gem, a little known spot guaranteed to calm and nourish the soul. It was founded in 1957 by Natalie Hays Hammond, whose father John Hammond was a mining engineer and diplomat who discovered and developed the long-lost King Solomon's Mines in South Africa. The small museum has an interesting collection of antique fans and prints and changing contemporary exhibits, but it is the gardens that captivate most visitors. The "stroll garden" is an ancient concept designed so that complete vignettes reveal themselves with each few steps. It is no accident that Natalie Hammond was a Broadway set and costume designer.

Ossining

OSSINING HISTORICAL SOCIETY MUSEUM
914-941-0001.
196 Croton Ave., Ossining, NY 10562.
Open: Year-round:
Sun.–Thurs. 1pm–4pm.

Housed in a former private home built in 1872, the museum contains collections and exhibits that focus on local history dating from 1785, including photographs, military artifacts, and items from Sing Sing Prison.

OSSINING URBAN CULTURAL PARK MUSEUM
914-941-3189.
95 Broadway (Rte. 9), Ossining, NY 10562.
Open: Year-round:
Mon.–Sat. 10am–4pm.

The most prominent thing in this historic community is Sing Sing Prison, so it's not surprising that this display focuses on penology here and elsewhere in the United States. Exhibits include a replica of its famous electric chair and prison cells from 1825. Visitors also may enter a scaled-down version of a weir chamber of the Old Croton Aqueduct, which carried water 40 miles from near Ossining to New York City in the 1800s.

Purchase

NEUBERGER MUSEUM OF ART
914-251-6100; 914-253-2082.
www.neuberger.org.
735 Anderson Hill Rd., Purchase, NY 10577.
Open: Tues.–Fri.
10am–4pm; weekends 11am–5pm.

An impressive collection of modern, contemporary, and African art is housed in a dramatic, modern, and well-lit space — one of the largest museums in New York State. The permanent collection includes works by Georgia O'Keefe, Jackson Pollock, and Edward Hopper (who grew up in the Hudson Valley and painted many local scenes), plus examples from Nelson Rockefeller's collection of ancient art. There also is an outdoor sculpture garden with works by Henry Moore and Alexander Liberman, a museum store, and a café. The museum is on the campus of Purchase College, one of the branches of SUNY, the State University of New York, so it is an art history teaching museum, as well as an exhibit space.

Rye

SQUARE HOUSE MUSEUM
914-967-7588.

Headquarters of the Rye Historical Society, this museum is housed in a former tavern built in 1730. Yes, George Washington did sleep here once.

www.ryehistoricalsociety
.org.
One Purchase St., Rye, NY
10580.
Open: Tues.–Fri. 1pm–4pm;
and by appt.

There are five period rooms, including a ballroom
and a warming kitchen, plus rotating exhibits
reflecting local history.

Somers

**MUSEUM OF THE EARLY
AMERICAN CIRCUS**
914-277-4977.
Intersection Rtes. 100 and
202, Somers, NY 10589.
Open: Year-round: Fri.
2pm–4pm; and by appt.

Hachaliah Bailey made his fortune in the early
1800s by bringing elephants and other exotic
animals to the United States, then traveling around
and showing them to awed audiences. One of
Bailey's relatives later joined with a fellow show-
man named Barnum to create the Barnum & Bailey
Circus. This museum is housed in the former
Elephant Hotel and features early American circus
posters, costumes, and other memorabilia, plus a statue of Old Bet, Bailey's
first elephant.

↝ **WESTCHESTER
MILITARY HISTORY
MUSEUM**
914-682-4949.
www.westchestergov.com/
parks.
Lasdon Park, Somers, NY
10589.
Open: Weekends, holidays,
12noon–4pm.
Admission: None.

Housed on the grounds of a sprawling park and
arboretum with landscaped gardens, this
museum contains paintings, diaries, and other artifacts from the Revolutionary War to recent conflicts, in which Westchester residents served in the
military. The museum grounds also contain a
Veterans Memorial.

Yonkers

⇀ **HUDSON RIVER
MUSEUM**
914-963-4550.
www.hrm.org.
511 Warburton Ave. (off
Rte. 9), Yonkers, NY
10701.
Open: Wed.–Sun.
12noon–5pm, Fri.
12noon–9pm.

The name hardly describes the treasures here.
First, this is a historic, landmark Victorian
house, the Glenview Mansion, built by a wealthy
financier. Several rooms have been restored to their
original splendor. Beneath the 20-foot ceilings,
some of which are stenciled, are ornate English tile
floors, rich woodwork, and lavish original furnishings, including life-sized sculptures in the alcove of
the dining room, and magnificent views of the
Hudson River just beyond the floor-to-ceiling windows. The architecturally educated will recognize
it as a rare example of Westlake Victorian. But this core mansion is just one
facet of the multifaceted museum.
  Visitors are met with the recorded sounds of train whistles and horses,

which follow you through the exhibit, tracing the history of New York City, Westchester County, and the Hudson Valley from the 1880s, when the house was built, to today. Upstairs is an art gallery of Hudson River Valley landscapes, both of the river and the farmland by its shores. The most modern part of the museum is the Andros Planetarium, a wondrous look at the heavens via a Zeiss star machine. There are weekend shows only, including matinees designed to interest and educate kids. The bookstore/gift shop was designed by pop artist Red Grooms.

WESTCHESTER COUNTY – OTHER ATTRACTIONS

Pocantico Hills

UNION CHURCH
914-631-8200.
www.hudsonvalley.org.
Bedford Rd. Rte. 448 (off
Rte. 9), Pocantico Hills,
NY 10591.
Open: Tours Apr.–Dec.:
Wed.–Fri. 11am–5pm,
Sat. 10am–5pm, Sun.
2pm–5pm, when no
conflict with scheduled
events.
Admission: Tour $3.

On a sunny day, this is one of the most spectacular spots in the Hudson Valley, as light sparkles and dances through the stunning stained glass windows of this phenomenal church. The windows were commissioned by members of the Rockefeller family, who worshipped here, and whose grand estate, Kykuit, is just down the road (see Chapter Six, *Mansions of the Hudson Valley*). There are 10 windows by Marc Chagall, all depicting Biblical scenes — the only complete set of Chagall windows in the United States. They depict stories from both the Old and New Testaments, including the parable of the Good Samaritan, which represents the Rockefeller family's vision of their dedication to philanthropy.

Additionally, there is a floral swirl window by Henri Matisse, completed just two days before his death. The Matisse window is in honor of the wife of John D. Rockerfeller, Jr., Abby Aldrich Rockefeller, an active collector of folk art and one of the founders of the Museum of Modern Art in NYC. The church has regular Sunday services, plus an ongoing schedule of concerts and recitals.

Purchase

**DONALD M. KENDALL
  SCULPTURE GARDEN**
914-253-2082.
Anderson Rd., Purchase,
NY 10577.
Open: Daily 9am–dusk.
Admission: None.

Directly across the street from the Neuberger Museum of Art, these 20th-century sculptures are displayed in a beautifully manicured setting on the grounds of PepsiCo World Headquarters. This first-rate collection includes works by Henry Moore, Louise Nevelson, and Rodin.

Tarrytown

**OLD DUTCH CHURCH &
SLEEPY HOLLOW
CEMETERY**
914-631-1123.
Broadway (Rte. 9) at Pierson
St., Tarrytown, NY 10591.
Open: Church by appt.;
cemetery daily 9am–5pm.
Admission: None.

This church was erected by Frederick Philipse in 1697 across the street from his Philipsburg Manor (see Chapter Six, *Mansions of the Hudson Valley*) for the family, overseers, tenant farmers, and, perhaps, even the manor's slaves. If there's any doubt that Philipse was "Lord of the Manor," a historic plaque at the church describes him in those words.

The small church is plain, although historic, since it is believed to be the oldest continuous-working church in the Hudson Valley. Much more fascinating is the cemetery that wraps around three sides of the church; it represents every facet and nuance of American history, not just that of the Hudson Valley. Even if wandering about cemeteries is not your idea of a travel excursion, make an exception for this one.

Washington Irving lived in Tarrytown, worshipped at the Old Dutch Church, and is buried in Sleepy Hollow Cemetery, named for one of his stories.

Graves in the oldest part of the burying ground, as it was called originally, nearest the church, date back to pre-Revolutionary Dutch tenant farmers and their *huisevrows*. Directly behind the arched stone entrance to the cemetery is buried Frederick Law Olmsted, who designed and landscaped so many world famous U.S. landmarks, including New York City's Central Park. Washington Irving lived nearby (see Chapter Six, *Mansions of the Hudson Valley*), worshipped here, and is buried here. Irving's tale of the Headless Horseman was inspired by local Dutch stories of a headless ghost, and he named the section founded in 1864 as the Sleepy Hollow Cemetery.

Other famous names buried here include 19th-century labor leader Samuel Gompers and 20th-century theatrical producer Mark Helinger, whose mausoleum reprises the domed auditorium of a theater. Walter Chrysler is buried here, too, and he must have been turning over in his grave, as the saying goes, when General Motors built its huge Tarrytown manufacturing plant a few miles away (see Chapter One, *History*) alongside the Hudson River.

William Rockefeller, brother of John D. Rockefeller, Sr., is buried in a grand mausoleum, with multiple columns that give it the appearance of a miniature Greek temple. Much simpler — so unobtrusive that it is easy to miss, even with the detailed map available from the church office — is the grave of millionaire industrialist Andrew Carnegie and his wife. His Scottish frugality prompted only a stone cross, with traditional Celtic braid carving.

WARNER LIBRARY
914-631-7734.
121 N. Broadway (Rte. 9), Tarrytown, NY 10591.
Open: Mon., Thurs. 1pm–9pm, Tues.–Wed. 10am–6pm, Fri.–Sat. 10am–5pm, Sun. 1pm–5pm.
Admission: None.

Tarrytown resident Worcester Warner was a designer and builder of astronomical telescopes. In 1920, he endowed construction of this public library, whose classical, columned design is a true temple to knowledge and learning. The front reading room contains soaring, 30-foot ceilings and huge windows that invite long respites in the comfortable wing chairs. But the real "must see" attraction of this library may be its front door. Warner used his engineering skills to crate and ship a 1,000-pound, ornately sculptured bronze door, purchased from a mansion in Florence, Italy, and to mount it on hinges so well balanced that the door can be moved by the pressure of a single finger. It's so easy, a child can do it, and it's easy to find the right spot — look for the part of the front handle that is several shades lighter than the surrounding bronze (from decades of fingers pushing the door). When the library is closed, spotlights inside the security glass door allow visitors to see the amazing bronze door.

Yorktown

FIRST PRESBYTERIAN CHURCH
914-245-2186.
www.fpcyork.com.
2880 Crompond Rd. (Rte. 202), Yorktown, NY 10598.
Open: Church by appt.; cemetery daily dawn to dusk.
Admission: None.

Founded in 1730, when the area was part of the Van Cortlandt Manor estate (see Chapter Six, *Mansions of the Hudson Valley*), the church became the meeting place for patriots before and during the Revolutionary War when it became an arsenal and storehouse. British troops burned it to the ground in 1779, but it was rebuilt shortly after the war. In 1982, the Afro-American Cultural Organization of Westchester County erected a stone monument in front of the church honoring black Americans who died in the Revolutionary War, including during the decisive Battle of Yorktown. Behind the church is a cemetery that contains headstones dating from 1772, and inside the church is one of the largest carillons in the county. Try to be in the area at 12noon or

6pm, when a miniconcert reverberates for miles, even into the Franklin D. Roosevelt State Park across the road.

PUTNAM COUNTY — MUSEUMS

Cold Spring

FOUNDRY SCHOOL MUSEUM
845-265-4010.
63 Chestnut St., Cold Spring, NY 10516.
Open: Mar.–Dec.:
Tues.–Wed. 10am–4pm,
Thurs. 1pm–4pm,
Sat.–Sun. 2pm–5pm.
Admission: Adult $5; senior, student $3.

The West Point Foundry was one of the most important ironworks in American history. One of its craftsman, Robert Parrot, designed the most-used weapon in the Civil War, named after him and manufactured here. The Parrot Rifle was able to breach the masonry walls of southern forts and is credited with helping the North win the war. Before it closed in 1911, the foundry also crafted the municipal water pipes for New York City and the iron ships that sailed the Hudson River and the Atlantic Ocean.

The Foundry School was built in 1820 to teach the children of migrant Irish and British ironworkers, and later it became a private home. Since 1959, it has been the home of the Putnam Historical Society and contains historic photographs and a rich exhibit of rifle and cannon shells, farm implements, and other iron objects produced at the foundry. The re-created one-room schoolhouse includes a report card from 1887 on the wall above the lift-top desks. There's also a re-creation of a Colonial kitchen and an early 1800s general store. Perhaps the museum's proudest possession, though, is the painting *The Gun Foundry* — so real you can feel the heat of the foundry fire — by John Weir, one of the famous Hudson River School of artists; a duplicate of the painting is in NYC's Metropolitan Museum of Art.

PUTNAM COUNTY — OTHER ATTRACTIONS

Kent

CHUANG YEN MONASTERY
845-225-1819.
Rte. 301, Kent, NY 10512.
Open: Daily.
Admission: Donations accepted.

This is the largest Buddhist monastery in the eastern United States and contains the only library in the U.S. specializing in the Buddhist religion, some 70,000 volumes. Chuang Yen also is home to the largest indoor statue of Buddha in the Western Hemisphere, plus statues dating from the Ming Dynasty. Operated by the Buddhist Association of the United States, visitors are welcome to view the statuary or to join in morning meditation or the afternoon meal.

DUTCHESS COUNTY — MUSEUMS

Beacon

DIA CENTER FOR THE ARTS
845-440-0100.
www.diacenter.org.
3 Beekman Place, Beacon, NY 12508.
Open: Mid-May–mid-Oct.: Thurs.–Mon. 11am–6pm; Mid-Oct.–mid-May: Fri.–Sun. 11am–4pm.
Admission: Adult $10; senior, student $7; ages under 12 free.

The museum does not open until May 2003, but this is, simply, the largest museum for contemporary art in the Northeast, housed in a 300,000-square-foot factory building that was home first to Nabisco and then to International Paper. The massive space allows the display of artwork that had been rarely exhibited because of its large scale, such as Andy Warhol's 1978 work *Shadows*, comprising 102 paintings. There also are monumental sculptures by Richard Serra and Walter de Maria, numerous mixed-medium displays, and a 20-foot-deep geometric steel construction by Michael Heizer.

The 31-acre site is on the banks of the Hudson River. There are dramatic views of the museum from the surrounding riverside parkland. DIA: Beacon is a branch of the DIA Art Foundation Museum (212-989-5566 information) in NYC. There is a café, bookstore, and a lecture and seminar program.

Poughkeepsie

The Frances Lehman Loeb Art Center at Vassar College houses more than 12,000 works of art.

Courtesy Vassar College

FRANCES LEHMAN LOEB ART CENTER
845-437-LOEB.
www.vassar.edu.
124 Raymond Ave. (off Rte. 9), Poughkeepsie, NY 12601.

Vassar College is known for its fine buildings, and just inside the massive, slightly Gothic main stone gate, visitors get their first glimpse of an ethereal, glass hexagon. It is the entrance to the Frances Lehman Loeb Art Center, a first-rate collection of more than 12,000 works. The modern, spa-

Open: Tues.–Sat.
  10am–5pm, Sun.
  1pm–5pm.

cious building was designed by noted architect Cesar Pelli and is connected to the college's art library. The art center is a noted teaching collection, as well as a public art museum.

The collection ranges from ancient Egyptian masks and an astounding, Chinese glazed pottery tower from the Han Dynasty to contemporary artists. In between are such gems as Albrecht Dürer's famous 1504 engraving of *Adam and Eve* and *Autumn in America* by Frederic Church, a relative unknown at the time; it was after this painting that Church gained renown for his panorama painting *Niagara*. Church's home, Olana (see Chapter Six, *Mansions of the Hudson Valley)* is about a one-hour drive north of Vassar. Many of the docents here are Vassar students, but not necessarily art students.

DUTCHESS COUNTY – OTHER ATTRACTIONS

Beacon

TALIX ART FOUNDRY
845-838-1111.
www.tallix.com.
310 Fishkill Ave., Beacon,
  NY 12508.
Open: By appt. only.

This is the foundry that created the Franklin D. Roosevelt Memorial, the Korean War Memorial, and the curving red Alexander Calder sculpture at Storm King Art Center across the Hudson River. The most dramatic sculpture on display is the 24-foot bronze horse that dwarfs visitors, a re-creation of Leonardo da Vinci's prancing *Cavallo*. The foundry is open by appointment only for tours of the lox-wax process of casting large sculptures.

Hyde Park

→ **CULINARY INSTITUTE
     OF AMERICA**
845-451-9600.
Rte. 9, Hyde Park, NY
  12538.
Open: Daily 9am–9pm.
Admission: None.

For anyone interested in any aspect of food, this is Mecca, Harvard, and grandma's kitchen rolled together. More than 2,100 students attend this college, and graduates are in top kitchens all over the U.S. and overseas. Students roam the halls often wearing white aprons and chef's fluted toque hats. The halls are wide and lined with huge picture windows that allow visitors to watch students slicing, dicing, filleting, stuffing, layering, and frosting.

There are one-day and multiday intensive-cooking programs for those wishing to improve their culinary expertise (many of the B&B owners whose inns are included in this book have attended CIA courses for breakfast training) and a bookstore that sells top-quality knives, cookbooks, and hard-to-find kitchen gadgets. There's also an extensive food library, containing, among other things, comedian Danny Kaye's large collection of gourmet Chinese cookbooks. And what would a cooking college be without restaurants. There are five award-winning restaurants, staffed by the students (see Chapter Four, *Restaurants & Food Purveyors*).

Millbrook

INNISFREE GARDENS
845-677-8000.
Tyrrel Rd. (1 mile west of
   Rte. 44), Millbrook, NY
   12545.
Open: May–Oct.: Wed.–Fri.
   10am–4pm, Sat.–Sun.
   11am–5pm.
Admission: Adult $2
   weekends.

This is actually a series of little gardens, called "cup gardens," which were inspired by ancient Chinese principles. Each minigarden is cupped within some kind of landscaped frame, either a stand of trees, a grouping of rocks, or a tiny waterfall, so that each vignette can be enjoyed without distraction. There are 200 acres of rolling meadows and woodland, with hundreds of garden vignettes to linger over and enjoy, plus a 40-acre glacial lake.

The mapped walking path takes visitors around the lotus-filled pond, past a rock garden, and up to the foundations of what was the country mansion of artist Martin Beck and his wife Marion. Around and behind the house are water sculptures whose frames move, some like pendulums, from the weight of streams of water within the sculptures. Their babbling sounds are as mesmerizing as their movement. Weathered 2 x 4 planks of wood have been fashioned into recliner chairs, placed strategically for a perfect view, such as a view of the grove of young willow trees at the edge of the lotus pond or a view of the swans floating so serenely. There also are picnic tables overlooking the pond.

**INSTITUTE OF
   ECOSYSTEM STUDIES:
   MARY FLAGLER CARY
   ARBORETUM**
845-677-5339.
www.ecostudies.org.
181 Sharon Turnpike, Rte.
   44A (off Rte. 44),
   Millbrook, NY 12545.
Open: Apr.–Sept.:
   Mon.–Sat. 9am–6pm,
   Sun. 1pm–6pm;
   Oct.–Mar.: Mon.–Sat.
   9am–4pm, Sun.
   1pm–4pm; greenhouse
   closes at 3:30 year-round.
Admission: None.

The arboretum contains a huge tropical greenhouse with exotic foilage, a perennial garden with more than 1,000 variety of plants, a butterfly garden filled with plantings designed to attract butterflies, and a fern glen with native ferns and wildflowers, overlooking a pond and a stream. There also are miles of self-guided nature trails across meadows and through thick woodland, plus spots for picnicking.

The arboretum takes up only a small portion of this 1,900-acre preserve. The rest is dedicated to private ecological and botanical research in association with the New York Botanical Garden. Visitors must check in at the Gifford House Visitor and Education Center across the road for a free permit and maps. There is a small ecology exhibit in the Visitor Center, as well as a plant shop.

Tania Barricklo

Wing Castle in Millbrook is built entirely from recycled objects.

WING CASTLE
845-677-9085.
Bangall Rd. (off Rte. 57),
  Millbrook, NY 12545.
Open: Mem. Day–Labor
  Day: Wed.–Sun.
  12noon–5pm.
Admission: Adult $7.

When Peter Wing returned from service in the Vietnam War, he was newly married, broke, and needing a roof over his head. He started building a house on a hillside corner of the family farm, using what then were called discarded objects. Today, it's called recycling. Nearly 35 years later, the house is still a work in progress, in part because Wing, a self-taught architect, keeps changing and expanding ideas for his grand design.

The house defies description. From a distance, the façade is reminiscent of medieval English, German, and Scottish castles, with towers and turrets, gargoyles, and a moat, but close-up, there are Asian motifs, such as mosaic tile dragons imbedded into walkways, stairs, and niches, which hold Tibetan sculptures. Much of the weathered stone is from an urban renewal project in Poughkeepsie, the old water tower from nearby Pleasant Valley was turned into a dome, and so on, and that's just the exterior. Inside is a happy clutter of mannequins in Civil War uniforms, a ship's prow hanging from a balcony made of old barn beams, a WWI saddle, antique carousel horses, and a bathtub that is — or was — a giant copper planter. Peter's wife Toni is an artist, and her Native American heritage is visible in her beading and other crafts.

Wing knows the history of each "found" or recycled piece used in the house and is a charming and witty tour guide of his castle on the hill. Adults and children will be equally fascinated.

Polepell Island

The ruins of Bannerman Castle, on a rocky island in the Hudson River.

Evelyn Kanter

BANNERMAN CASTLE
845-831-6346.
www.bannermancastle.org.
Mailing Address:
  Bannerman Castle Trust,
  P.O. Box 843, Glenham,
  NY 12527.
Open: May–Oct.: via tour
  group only.
Admission: $80, includes
  kayak rental and guide.

Frank Bannerman VI was born in Dundee, Scotland, and came to the United States with his family in 1854 when he was three years old. The family settled in Brooklyn, where his father established a business of selling military articles acquired at auction. After the Civil War, young Frank expanded the business to include munitions and scrap metal, and, Bannerman's Brooklyn neighbors soon became fearful that the growing arsenal in their backyard might one day explode.

Bannerman found a safe location for his army-navy surplus goods in the middle of the Hudson River, just north of West Point, which is visible from the clifflike south side of the island. Polepell Island is a six-acre rock that Native Americans believed was haunted, possibly because of the humanlike sounds of the wind whistling through the narrows between island and shore.

From his purchase of the island in 1904 until his death in 1918, Bannerman continued to build a Scottish-style castle, with endless turrets and crenellated towers, plus a separate arsenal, from his own design. Part of the design included a huge "billboard," advertising the company name, still visible from the railroad trains that pass the castle and the Bannerman Land Arsenal on both sides of the Hudson River. The buildings were constructed totally from military surplus and civilian scrap materials, which were purchased at auction and barged up the river; the barges were sunk to create breakwaters. Fiercely proud of his Scottish heritage, Bannerman had Biblical and Scottish quotations and mottos carved into the façade and many of the rooms in the house.

Then one hot day in August 1920 — as Bannerman's Brooklyn neighbors had feared 20 years before — the powder house blew up, throwing shells all over the island and surrounding water. Bannerman Castle and Bannerman Land Arsenal still stand, looking like medieval ruins very much out of place in the middle of the Hudson River — a curious and mysterious relic visible from either shore, and even more fascinating from a pleasure boat or kayak. Although the island is now part of New York's Hudson Highlands State Park, it is closed to the public because of the danger of further structural collapse and dangerously corroding breakwaters surrounding the island.

Not totally off-limits, though — Bannerman Castle Trust is working actively to stabilize and preserve the ruins, working with scouting groups and other volunteers. A sight-seeing boat *Pride of the Hudson* (845-782-0645; www.prideofthehudson.com) circles the island from Newburgh. Even better, **Hudson Valley Pack & Paddle** (845-896-3829; www.hvpackandpaddle.com) will guide you, via kayak, one mile across the Hudson River for a "hard hat" tour of the island (visitors trade paddles for hard hats), guided by one of the trust's two historians. Both tours provide part of the fee to the trust.

From the moatlike entry under a carved stone arch to walking along the deteriorated stone paths of what is now known as Bannerman Island and to viewing the remains of Mrs. Bannerman's garden and other landscaping, everything is a grand scale. Most impressive, though, is the uneven design visible on close inspection — there are no right angles here; that is a distance-related illusion. And then, there's the breathtaking, commanding view south from the remains of the castle's front porch at the highest point of the island to past West Point and practically to New York City.

Rhinebeck

Waiting for their turn to fly at the Old Rhinebeck Aerodrome.

Tania Barricklo/Daily Freeman

**OLD RHINEBECK
AERODROME MUSEUM**
845-752-3200.
www.oldrhinebeck.org.
Stone Church Rd.,
Rhinebeck, NY 12572.
Open: May 15-Oct. 31: daily
10am–5pm; mid-
June–mid-Oct.: weekend
air shows 2pm.
Admission: Air show: adult
$12; senior $10; ages 6–10
$5; Museum: adult $6;
senior $5; ages 6–10 $2.

There are hundreds of antique aircraft on display, including original and lovingly restored Fokker tri-planes and Sopwith Camels, plus antique autos, including a Model T Ford. On weekends, air shows recreate aerial dogfights from WWI, complete with fighter pilots outfitted in leather helmets. There's also the opportunity to take scenic flights in one of the historic aircraft after the air show, weather permitting; rides are $40 per person and you must sign up in person, no reservations over the telephone.

COLUMBIA COUNTY — MUSEUMS

Hudson

**AMERICAN MUSEUM
OF FIRE FIGHTING**
845-828-7695.
117 Harry Howard Ave. (off
Rte. 23), Hudson, NY
12534.
Open: Year-round: daily
9am–4:30pm.
Admission: None;
handicap access.

It's a toss-up whether kids or grown-ups will enjoy this museum more. Tucked inside the grounds of the retirement home of New York State's Volunteer Firemen's Home, this is a little-known gem well worth visiting. The museum was founded in 1925 to preserve engines and other fire-fighting memorabilia and has expanded over the years from 3,900–21,000 square feet. It takes that much space to display the wealth of equipment, badges, hats, paintings, and more.

There's a leather helmet bearing the initials "E. K." and "engineer," which belonged to Elisha Kingsland, chief of the first paid fire department in New York State in 1865. There's a horse-drawn 1840 bucket carrier from Brooklyn, with leather hoses and buckets, and a Jefferson engine from the same period that is hand-painted with portraits of George Washington and Thomas Jefferson, plus examples of early motorized fire trucks from the 1920s. One entire wall is filled with firemen's badges, and other walls are hung with portraits of volunteer firemen in uniforms, mostly from the 1800s, before photography replaced portraiture. They stand stiffly and proudly, some wearing their helmets, others cradling them inside a bent elbow.

The museum is free, and your docent is one of the retired firemen living at the retirement home. It doesn't take much prodding to hear stories about fires he or his brother firefighters battled and about the pride in doing a job that many of us regard much differently since September 11, 2001. Follow well-marked sign; the museum is somewhat outside of town.

Old Chatham

**SHAKER MUSEUM &
LIBRARY**
518-794-9011.
www.shakermuseumand
library.org.
88 Shaker Museum Rd. (off
Rte. 295 and County Rte.
13), Old Chatham, NY
12136.
Open: May–Oct.:
Wed.–Mon. 10am–5pm.
Admission: Adult $8; senior
$6; ages 8–17 $4.

This is one of the largest collections of Shaker artifacts in the world, set amid rolling farmland in eastern Columbia County, where the Hudson Valley morphs into the Berkshire Hills of Massachusetts. The museum collection includes boxes and baskets, farm tools, machinery, and furniture; the library collection contains journals, drawings, and, of course, books.

The Shaker religious movement began in England in the mid-1750s, and its early proponents were ordered to leave for "The Colonies." By 1800, there were numerous Shaker settlements in New York and New England. They were known for their communal sharing of goods, thrift, and pacifism, plus for the clean, simple lines and craftsmanship of their architecture and furniture, which has inspired architects and designers ever since.

ROCKLAND COUNTY — MUSEUMS

Harriman

**BEAR MOUNTAIN
TRAILSIDE MUSEUM**
www.nysparks.gov.
Bear Mountain State Park,
Harriman, NY 10926.
Open: Daily 9am–4pm.
Admission: Weekends and
holidays $1; handicap
access.

Black bear, beaver, coyote, and birds of prey are some of the animals indigenous to the Hudson Valley and are on display at this small museum within one of the New York State's largest parks. The museum also has educational displays of insects and reptiles, as well as exhibits on the Native Americans who lived in the area and the Revolutionary War. The museum is on the site of Fort Clinton, which was taken by the British in 1877.

New City

**HISTORICAL SOCIETY
OF ROCKLAND
COUNTY**
845-634-9629.
20 Zukor Rd., New City,
NY 10956.
Open: Tues.–Fri.
9:30am–5pm, Sat.–Sun.
1pm–5pm.

Housed in the 1832 Jacob Blauvelt farmhouse, an interesting mix of Flemish architecture with Greek Revival ornamentation, the society has period rooms that illustrate the lifestyle of local farm families during the early 1800s, plus an art gallery with rotating exhibits, often featuring local artists. Occasional special events, such as candlelight tours, demonstrations of 19th-century country dancing, and open-hearth cooking are also available.

**LAW ENFORCEMENT
MUSEUM**
845-638-5585.
55 New Hempstead Rd.,
New City, NY 10956.
Open: Weekdays by appt.
Admission: None;
handicap access.

This is the headquarters of the Rockland County Sheriffs Department. There is a small exhibit of photos and other memorabilia relating to local law enforcement.

Orangeburg

**CAMP SHANKS WORLD
WAR II MUSEUM**
845-638-5419.
S. Greenbush Rd.,
Orangeburg, NY 10962.
Open: Weekends only
10am–3pm.
Admission: None;
handicap access.

More than one million soldiers shipped out from here, via the nearby Piermont Pier, on their way to the Normandy invasion and other battles. It was one of the two busiest embarkation points on the east coast. The small museum has an exhibit on military life at the camp, and visitors can tour a barracks.

Spring Valley

**THE HOLOCAUST
MUSEUM AND STUDY
CENTER**
845-268-2503.
www.holocauststudies.org.
17 S. Madison Ave. (off Rte.
59), Spring Valley, NY
10977.
Open: Sun.–Thurs.
12noon–4pm; closed on
major Jewish holidays.

The museum is organized chronologically, from pre-War European Jewish culture through the horrors of the ghettos and death camps to the survivors' new lives in new countries. There are sobering video interviews with survivors, many of whom live near the museum, which is in an unassuming former private home on a residential street off a main thoroughfare. It has a collection of silver ceremonial objects from the 17th and 18th centuries, a gallery of Holocaust-related art, and a "children's wall," commemorating the 1.5 million children lost.

An exhibit on the "hidden children" tells the story of youngsters, in their own words, who were taken in by non-Jewish families in Europe and in England, with photographs of them as children and as they are today. The exhibit is semipermanent, traveling part of the year to other museums. A study center upstairs includes a library and a research facility, with additional historic and first-person audiotapes and videotapes.

Stony Point

**STONY POINT
BATTLEFIELD STATE
HISTORIC SITE**
845-786-2521.

The battlefield is the location of a successful midnight assault, commanded by Brigadier General "Mad Anthony" Wayne, against a British

www.nysparks.gov.
Park Rd. (off Rte. 9W),
  Stony Point, NY 10980.
Open: Apr. 15–Oct. 31:
  Wed.–Sat. 10am–5pm,
  Sun. 1pm–5pm.
Admission: None;
  handicap access.

garrison in July 1779. The British had captured the Stony Point peninsula and were fortifying the position. Since they had just captured the fort directly across the river, the British were in position to control the Hudson River. Wayne's Light Infantry Corps, a select force that was a precursor to today's Special Forces, attacked in two columns from the north and south as a third column created a diversion. The battle helped destroy the invincible reputation of the British forces, while boosting the morale of the beleaguered Americans.

The battlefield museum features exhibits of Revolutionary War artifacts. Staff members are in period costumes and demonstrate muskets, artillery, cooking, and camp life. There also are regularly scheduled re-creations of the battle. The battlefield site is a large park with picnic areas and self-guided nature trails, a commanding view of the Hudson River, and the Stony Point Lighthouse (see Chapter Six, *Mansions of the Hudson Valley*).

ROCKLAND COUNTY – OTHER ATTRACTIONS

Haverstraw

**CENTRAL
  PRESBYTERIAN
  CHURCH**
845-429-1111.
64 New Main St.,
  Haverstraw, NY 10927.
Open: By appt. only.
Admission: None.

This church was built in the mid-1800s, and its stand-out feature is the 13 full-sized Tiffany windows that sparkle in the sunlight. Windows shown by appt. only, so call ahead.

New Hempstead

THE BRICK CHURCH
845-354-6131.
220 Brick Church Rd., New
  Hempstead, NY 10977.
Open: Year-round.
Admission: None.

So named because it is one of the few worship sites of the period that was constructed with brick instead of the standard wood clapboard or stone; it dates from 1774. The churchyard contains graves of Revolutionary solders and some original settlers.

Piermont

PIERMONT PIER
No telephone.
End of Piermont Ave.,
  (follow signs), Piermont,
  NY 10968.

The pier juts out nearly a full mile into the Hudson River from the town of Piermont, a sleepy village lined with solid Federal buildings. Today, the pier has a paved road bordered by a strip of parkland on either side, and the shallow

Open: Year-round.
Admission: None.

water along the pier is dotted with marsh grass and bobbing ducks; the pier is used by fishermen, joggers, bicyclists, and families enjoying a sunny outing. Back in the early 1940s, there were railroad tracks here, not a road, and U.S. warships lined the pier where the marsh grass now grows. A memorial plaque at the end of the pier attests to its role as a major embarkation point for troops headed to the war in Europe.

There are some benches along the pier for enjoying the views. At the end of the pier, visitors are face-to-face with the Tappan Zee Bridge, less than one mile up river, and the New York City skyline is visible in the other direction. The pier also cradles the Piermont Marsh, a 950-acre wetland and wildlife sanctuary.

West Nyack

CLARKSTOWN REFORMED CHURCH
845-358-4320.
107 Strawtown Rd., West Nyack, NY 10994.
Open: Year-round.
Admission: None.

This church was built in 1750; it contains the graves of Revolutionary soldiers and some original settlers.

ORANGE COUNTY — MUSEUMS

Cornwall-on-Hudson

MUSEUM OF THE HUDSON HIGHLANDS
845-534-7781.
www.museumhudsonhigh lands.org.
Rte. 9W, Cornwall-on-Hudson, NY 12520.
Open: Boulevard location: Fri.–Sat. 10am–5pm, Sun. 1pm–5pm; Kenridge Farm location: Sat.–Sun. 12noon–4pm; trails daily dawn to dusk.

This is a museum dedicated to the environment — experiencing it and learning about it — and most of the exhibits are outdoors. Since this is an area of dramatic natural beauty, it makes perfect sense. Guides use the outdoor classroom of forests, wetlands, steams, fields, and meadows via self-guided nature trails to watch for birds and other wildlife and to identify trees, marshes, and wildflowers. But it's not all outdoors. Indoors are re-created habitats of local and regional animals, including exhibits of live owls, snakes, turtles, frogs, and flying squirrels.

The museum has two locations, a mile and a half apart. The Boulevard location is at Kowawese on the Hudson, where there are regular lecture programs, live animal exhibits, and a nature shop. In 1993, the museum acquired historic Kenridge Farm, effectively saving its 177 acres from becoming a tract of town houses. The elegant, old, shingled farmhouse is now a gallery, featuring artwork and artists of the Hudson Valley.

Goshen

HARNESS RACING MUSEUM & HALL OF FAME
845-294-6330.
240 Main St. (off Rte. 207), Goshen, NY 10924.
Open: Year-round: daily 10am–6pm.
Admission: Adult $7.50; ages 6–15 $3.50.

Find out everything you ever wanted to know about harness racing straight from the horse's mouth. No kidding, there's a talking horse here. The horse is plastic, and the patter is prerecorded, but it sets the tone for this mostly serious look at harness racing. The serious part is an original stable that memorializes the sport's great drivers, horses, races, and tracks and the history of the sport from its beginnings on country roads.

The most popular exhibits are the interactive ones, such as the "broadcast booth" where visitors can learn the techniques used by track announcers and can even call a race. By far the most popular is a 3-D simulation of an actual race, with wind blowing through your hair, the clip-clop of racing hooves, and the roar of the crowd. Behind the museum is Goshen Historic Track, dating from the 1830s and one of the oldest in the world, now used for training.

A few miles away in Chester is the grave of Hambletonian, the legendary horse who sired more than 1,300 foals, many of them champion trotters. The museum will give you directions, or just look for the signs on Hambletonian Ave. off Rte. 94.

Monroe

MUSEUM VILLAGE
845-782-8247.
www.museumvillage.org.
1010 Rte. 17M, Monroe, NY 10950.
Open: May–June:
Tues.–Fri. 10am–2pm, Sat.–Sun. 10am–5pm;
July–Aug.: Tues.–Sun. 10am–4pm;
Sept.–Dec.: Tues.–Fri. 10am–2pm, Sat.–Sun. 10am–4pm.
Admission: Adult $8; senior $6; ages 6-15 $5; under age 6 free.

This is a re-created village of 19th-century rural life, comprising some three dozen historic buildings moved here from other locations. Wander through a fire station with hand pumpers, a print shop with a working printer, a broom maker's shop. Chat with "interpreters" in period costumes who describe in period language (our manner of speaking has changed along with our clothing) about the tasks they are performing, from spinning and weaving on antique looms to blacksmithing and candle making.

This is another one of those attractions where it is difficult to decide whether the children or the adults are enjoying it more, especially at the exhibit of an intact mastodon, excavated right here in Orange County, its huge curving tusks big enough to cradle an upside-down Volkswagon Beetle. There are also museumlike displays, farm tools, and other historical objects. Museum Village also has regular special events, including a Native American Festival and a Civil War Weekend.

Mountainville

Tania Barricklo

Storm King is the largest outdoor sculpture park/museum in the U.S.

STORM KING
845-534-3115.
www.stormking.org.
Old Pleasant Hill Rd. (off
Orrs Mills Rd. and Rte.
17K), Mountainville, NY
10953.
Open: Apr.–Oct.: Mon.–Fri.
11am–5:30pm; Nov.:
Mon.–Fri. 11am–5pm;
June–July: also open
weekends 11am–8pm.
Admission: Adult $9; senior
$7; student and over age
5 $5; free 5pm–closing in
June, July.

This is the largest sculpture park in the United States, a remarkable outdoor art museum with more than 100 monumentally sized, contemporary sculptures dotting the landscape, a combination of open meadows to gently rolling hills and woodlands. Some vistas take in several sculptures at once, and in other spots, the artwork is all but hidden from view in a cluster of trees until the visitor is almost directly upon it. The sculptures alternately mimic the lines of the surrounding landscape, including the giant oaks and hemlocks that pepper the 500-acre park or that jolt the eye with their jarring nonconformity, such as the brilliant red, curved Alexander Calder piece in a green meadow.

There are masterworks, mostly bronze and iron, by Louise Nevelson, David Smith, Richard Serra, Isamo Noguchi, and others. Some artists, like Calder, are represented by more than one piece. The first sculpture, a giant treelike construction, is visible even before you drive through the front gate from the country road leading to the park. It is an astonishing first glimpse of sights yet unseen.

Free docent-guided tours are at 2pm daily, and visitors are invited to picnic in designated areas. Wear comfortable shoes, since there's a good bit of walking, even if you take the shuttle bus tour; there is also an indoor gallery with smaller pieces. No pets are permitted.

Newburgh

**WASHINGTON'S
HEADQUARTERS
STATE HISTORIC SITE**
845-562-1195.
84 Liberty St., Newburgh,
NY 12550.
Open: Apr.–Oct.: Wed.–Sat.
10am–5pm, Sun.
1pm–5pm.
Admission: Adult $5; NYS
resident, senior $2; ages
5–12 $1.

Of the many places that claim "Washington slept here," it is certain that he did sleep here. He spent the last six months of the Revolutionary War in the Hasbrouck family farmhouse, on a bluff overlooking the Hudson River, and remained for several months after what he called the "cessation of hostilities," until the British finally evacuated New York City. In 1850, this site became the first National Historic Landmark, via an act of Congress.

Hasbrouck House is a typical, steep-roofed Dutch farmhouse, furnished to reflect Washington's stay, with papers on the desk that he used, a bedroll, and other personal artifacts. There is also a Colonial-style brick museum with an extensive display on the Revolutionary War. The house and museum sit on a large sloping lawn; close to the river is a 50-foot Tower of Victory, added on the 100th anniversary of the war's end.

Situated on the appropriately named Liberty St., the city of Newburgh has grown around the historic site. Across the street is a several block stretch of Federal houses from the 1850s, some gloriously restored and others shamefully in need of restoration.

ORANGE COUNTY – OTHER ATTRACTIONS

Fort Montgomery

**FORT MONTGOMERY
STATE HISTORIC SITE**
845-786-2701.
Rte. 9W (1 mile north of
Bear Mountain), Fort
Montgomery, NY 10922.
Open: Daily dawn to dusk;
park guides available
Apr.–Oct.: Wed.–Sun.
10am–4pm.
Admission: None.

Fort Montgomery reopened to the public on October 6, 2002, the 225th anniversary of a battle many experts believe was a turning point in the Revolutionary War. British General Sir Henry Clinton was rushing north to help General John Burgoyne, who was trapped at Saratoga. Although Clinton's soldiers won the battle, it delayed the mission to rescue Burgoyne, who surrendered one week later, ending British efforts to divide the colonies.

Visitors to the 14-acre site can follow an interpretive trail around the remains of the fort leading to features such as the Powder Magazine, blown up by the British after the battle; the Grand Battery, where massive cannons guarded the Hudson River; and the North Redoubt, where the final British assault drove the Americans from the fort.

Vails Gate

KNOX'S HEADQUARTERS STATE HISTORIC SITE
845-561-5498.
Forge Hill Rd. (Rte. 94),
Vails Gate, NY 12584.
Open: Mem. Day–Labor
Day: Wed., Sun.,
1pm–5pm; and by appt.

General Henry Knox and officers of the Continental Army camped here. Nearby were both General Washington's headquarters in nearby Newburgh and the catonement of 7,500 soldiers. In addition to the 18th-century John Ellison fieldstone house that Knox made his headquarters, the surrounding grounds contain a native plant sanctuary, nature trails, and gristmill ruins.

THE NEW WINDSOR CATONEMENT
845-561-1765.
Freedom Rd. (Rte. 300),
Vails Gate, NY 12584.
Open: Mid-Apr.–Oct.:
Wed.–Sat. 10am–5pm,
Sun. 1pm–5pm.

This was the last winter encampment of the fledgling northern army, just a few miles west from General Washington's headquarters in Newburgh and beyond the reach of 12,000 British soldiers stationed in New York City. After spending much of autumn building two-room huts that would shelter them against the harsh weather to come, 7,500 soldiers and 500 of their wives and children camped here during the winter of 1782–1783, while awaiting news from Paris of a peace treaty that would end the fighting with the British. Many of the troops had not been paid in several years, and it was here, in an emotional address to his officers, that Washington convinced the army not to rebel and quit over pay issues.

After the cease-fire in April 1783, most of the troops went home, the army auctioned off the buildings and equipment, and the grounds turned into farmland. In 1891, local citizens erected a monument recognizing the site's importance. In 1932, some of the first Purple Heart awards to WWI veterans were presented here. A year later, volunteers located a log building believed to have been one of the original huts auctioned in 1783. That hut is now on exhibit at the catonement, a state historic site, which features re-creations of Revolutionary-era life during the summer.

West Point

UNITED STATES MILITARY ACADEMY
845-938-2638.
www.usma.edu/museum.
Main St. at USMA Visitor
Center, West Point, NY
10996.
Open: Daily 10:30am–4:15pm.
Admission: None; no ID
required for entry;
handicap access.

To most of us, including many of its illustrious graduates and current cadets and in much of the academy's own literature, the United States Military Academy is known simply as West Point, the name of the promontory above the Hudson River. West Point played a critical role during the Revolutionary War because of its strategic location at a narrowing and distinct bend in the direction of the river, midway between New York City and

Cadets at West Point parade on the same ground where Revolutionary War soldiers trained.

Courtesy U.S. Military Academy

Albany. The academy was established in 1802 at the old Fort Putnam. One of its first graduates, Sylvanus Thayer, was appointed superintendent in 1817 with the mandate to make West Point "the leading institution of military education." He is known as "the Father of West Point"; the Hotel Thayer (see Chapter Three, *Lodging*), just inside the entry Thayer Gate, is named for him. Some 4,400 cadets now attend the academy, which is steeped in both history and tradition.

The campus is an architectural gem, full of imposing Gothic-style stone buildings and wide-open fields, including the Plain, where General George Washington drilled the American forces and where today's cadets parade in full dress on Sat. There are memorials and monuments throughout West Point, but the most famous is Battle Monument, a soaring obelisk designed by architect Stanford White and dedicated to the 2,240 officers and men of the Union Army who died in the Civil War. The monument stands on Trophy Point, where captured weapons have been displayed since the 1898 Spanish-American War. The Cadet Chapel, built in 1910, contains the largest church organ in the world; both it and the Jewish Cadet Chapel and Museum are open to the public when services are not being held.

The **West Point Museum** contains one of the world's largest collections of weapons, flags, uniforms, and other military artifacts. Exhibits represent more than three thousand years of warfare, from the ancient Romans and Egyptians to modern conflicts, including medieval lances and Native American tomahawks. One of the six galleries is dedicated to this historical overview, and the other five concentrate on two centuries of U.S. military history, from Revolutionary War flintlocks, the last dispatch of General George Custer to his aide, a 1916 Dodge Brothers car used by officers in World War I to artifacts from the NASA space program and current campaigns. Look for items from well-known West Point graduates, who include the Generals Dwight David Eisenhower, George S. Patton, Robert E. Lee, and William Tecumseh Sherman.

Based upon captured British materials brought to West Point after the British defeat at Saratoga in 1777, the museum predates the founding of the U.S. Military Academy in 1802. The first West Point Museum opened in 1854 and moved into the Gothic-towered facility in Pershing Center in 1989. Exhibits also are peppered with quotes on warfare, such as Plato's prescient observation that, "Only the dead have seen the end of war." Even though the museum includes cannons and cannonballs, it is only a tiny fraction of the collection; additional cannons are displayed at Trophy Point.

The museum is outside the academy's gates and adjoins a Visitor Center with additional exhibits and a gift shop. Sadly, much of the merchandise imprinted with images of the United States Military Academy is not made in the United States.

Security changes since the events of September 11, 2001, now prevent visitors from driving onto campus for self-guided tours. Visitors are now required to park at the Visitor Center and be part of a guided motorized coach tour.

West Point Tours (845-446-4724; www.westpointtours.com) Tickets must be purchased at the Visitor Center, and a photo ID is required for anyone over age 18. Price: adult $7; ages 11 and under $4. Daily tours, hourly in the summer and twice a day rest of year. No tours Graduation Week (last week in May) or on Sat. during home football games.

ULSTER COUNTY — MUSEUMS

High Falls

D&H CANAL MUSEUM
845-687-9311.
www.canalmuseum.org.
23 Mohonk Rd. (off Rte. 213),
  High Falls, NY 12440.
Open: May–Oct.: Sat.–Sun.
  1pm–5pm, Thurs., Fri.,
  Mon. 11am–5pm.
Admission: Adult $3;
  children $1; family $7.

In the 1820s, two coal merchants, brothers from Pennsylvania, concocted a plan to build a waterway from the mines in Carbondale to Kingston, where the canal barges would be off-loaded for shipment down the Hudson River to New York City. The D&H Canal (Delaware and Hudson), which runs 108 circuitous miles around nearly as many mountains, also contains 108 locks and is regarded as one of the greatest feats of American industrial ingenuity and enterprise. The canal operated from 1828 to 1898, when it was replaced by the growing railroad system.

The D&H Canal Museum is housed in an 1885 brown-shingled church and contains examples of the rock hard anthracite coal that passed through here, a working miniature model of a canal lock, chairs made out of old railroad ties, shovels and other equipment used on the canal, and paintings and watercolors depicting the canal and life around it, including one by Hudson River School painter William Rickarby Miller.

The canal passes right alongside the museum, and there is a short walking trail, less than one mile, that passes five locks. The metal bolts for the locks are still visible in some places, and the stone block walls of the canal are reminiscent of a medieval fortress.

Kingston

The heart of historic Kingston is the area known as The Stockade, named for the wooden fence, which Governor Peter Stuyvesant ordered built around the homes of the earliest settlers as protection against the local Esopus tribe. The city's finest Colonial and Victorian buildings are located in this area, as well as trendy shops and restaurants.

HUDSON RIVER MARITIME MUSEUM
845-338-0071.
One Rondout Landing,
Kingston, NY 12401.

Until the railroads usurped the Hudson River as the main transportation route for freight and passengers between New York City and Albany, Kingston was a busy port city. The Maritime Museum is located alongside Rondout Creek, which is wide and deep, a few hundred yards from where it merges into the Hudson.

The museum celebrates 350 years of New York's water highway, via photographs, line drawings and paintings, maps, and a first-class collection of miniature replicas. One exhibit traces how the square-rigged Dutch ships, like the one that brought Henry Hudson to these shores, morphed into the sleek, wide-bottomed, wide-sail sloops that plied the river until Robert Fulton's steamboat generation. There are numerous photographs of the U.S. Navy reserve "Liberty warships" that berthed in the Hudson during WWII and of the many ferries that went back and forth across the river before the George Washington, Tappan Zee, Bear Mountain, Newburgh-Beacon, and Rip Van Winkle bridges were built. Outside, sitting on railroad ties is the *Mathilda*, an 1898 steam–powered tugboat.

The museum dock also welcomes visiting vessels, including the sailing ships *Clearwater*, the replica of Hudson's *Half Moon*, and U.S. Coast Guard training ships. The dock also is the departure point for 15-minute boat rides to the historic Kingston-Rondout Lighthouse (see Chapter Six, *Mansions of the Hudson Valley*).

OLD DUTCH CHURCH
845-338-6759.
272 Wall St., Kingston, NY
  12401.
Open: Self-guided tours
  weekdays 10am–2pm;
  graveyard daily dawn to
  dusk.
Admission: None.

The original church, founded in 1659, was burned by the British in 1777. This solid brick version is the third church and dates from the early 1800s. The church is surrounded by a graveyard of note. In addition to pre-Revolutionary graves of original settlers, this is the burial spot of New York State's first governor, George Clinton, who left that office to become Thomas Jefferson's Vice-President.

SENATE HOUSE & MUSEUM STATE HISTORIC SITE
845-338-2786.
296 Fair St., Kingston, NY
  12401.
Open: Apr.–Oct.: Wed.–Sun.
  10am–5pm; and by appt.
Admission: Adult $3; NYS
  resident, senior $2; ages
  5–12 $1.

Amid the turmoil of a British invasion in the fall of 1777, a group of rebellious patriots met in Kingston to form a new state government. The system they adopted — a senate, assembly, governor, and judiciary — still exists, and after the Revolutionary War, Kingston was briefly the first New York State capital, before the capital was moved to Albany.

The British burned the city as punishment for the rebellion, but the solid stone Gaasbeek house survived, and the first Senate after the signing of the U.S. Constitution met here in the simple stone house of Abraham Van Gaasbeek, a prosperous merchant-trader. The house had been built a century before in 1676 by his wife's grandfather, Wessel Ten Broeck, a relative of the Broecks whose farm in New Netherland, now called New York City, is known now as Brooklyn.

The house, with its wide-plank floorboards, low ceilings, and sparse Colonial furniture, is lightened by colorful painted tiles of birds around the fireplace. Clay pipes, quill pens, and wartime manifests are scattered atop a desk in what was the senator's meeting room. The site also contains a separate museum, featuring Hudson Valley landscapes and portraits of local Revolutionary-era residents. Among the museum's treasures are works by John Vanderlyn and other artist members of his family, from the 1720s through the 1870s. Upstairs are examples of fine Colonial- and Federal-era furniture, furnishings, and documents.

TROLLEY MUSEUM
845-331-3599.
www.mhrcc.org/tmny.
89 E. Strand, Rondout
  Landing, Kingston, NY
  12401.
Open: Mem. Day–
  Columbus Day: only
  weekends and holidays
  12noon–5pm; last ride
  4:30pm.

Just across the Landing from the Hudson River Maritime Museum is the Trolley Museum, in the original trolley shed. There are opportunities to hear the clang, clang, clang of the trolley bell and take a short ride on the original tracks leading from the shed.

New Paltz

The Huguenot Street stone houses were built between 1692 and 1799.

Tania Barricklo

HUGUENOT STREET STONE HOUSES
845-255-1889; 845-255-1660. www.hhs-newpaltz.org. Huguenot St., New Paltz, NY 12561.
Open: First weekend in May–Oct.: Tues.–Sun. 10am–5:30pm; (Huguenot St. is a public thoroughfare and open 24 hours.) Tours are 90 minutes and start at 10am every hour on weekends; every 30 minutes on weekdays.
Admission: Adult $8; senior $7; student $5; ages 5–11 $3.

It's like stepping through an invisible curtain, or a time machine, and finding yourself three centuries back. Known as "the oldest street in Amerca with its original houses," the stone houses of Huguenot Street were built between 1692 and 1799 on a quiet tree-lined street just two blocks from the town's bustling main, traffic-choked thoroughfare. There are six neat houses, plus a church, a graveyard, and a fort, all in their original locations. The Huguenots fled France because of religious persecution, and 12 families settled here along the Walkill River, naming their community after die Pfalz, an area along the Rhine in Germany.

Each house is architecturally distinctive. The 1694 Abraham Hasbrouck House served as the community center — it is larger than the other homes. The 1698 Bevier-Elting House has an unusual extended roofline, creating a covered area where farm work could be done in bad weather. The 1694 Jean Hasbrouck House contains an unusual jamless fireplace. The 1694 Hugo Freer House is the only one with a second-floor window, through which grain supplies and hay could be hoisted in and out from storage upstairs. The 1692 Deyo House was remodeled in 1894 into a grand Victorian. The DuBois House was built with gun ports, so it could serve as a place of protection in case of attack by local tribes, and thus became known as the "Fort." All the houses have a wealth of original furnishings, including family quilts and fine delft china.

The Stone Houses of Huguenot Street are operated by the Huguenot Society, which includes descendants of the original settlers. There is also a research library and genealogical archives, open by appointment. Tours leave from the DuBois Fort, which serves as a visitor center and contains a small gift shop. Tour guides are dressed in period costume.

Rosendale

THE SNYDER ESTATE/CENTURY HOUSE HISTORICAL SOCIETY
845-658-9900.
www.centuryhouse.org.
Rte. 213, Rosendale, NY 12472.
Open: May–Oct.: Wed., Sat., Sun. 1pm–4pm.

At one time, this little town 10 minutes from New Paltz produced half of the cement used in the U.S. A young architect named John A. Roebling had discovered the cement and its durability in the 1820s when he was staying nearby helping to construct the D&H Canal (see above). Roebling later used Rosendale limestone cement to construct the Brooklyn Bridge, and it also forms the pedestal of the Statue of Liberty.

The Snyder Estate contains an exhibit of industrial items made in the Hudson Valley, from bottles and stoneware to the bridges and tunnels manufactured from Rosendale cement. There's also a museum-quality collection of buggies, horse-drawn sleighs, phaetons, and buggies from the 1980s and early 1900s.

Be sure to visit the vast Widow Jane Mine behind the Snyder house and adjoining carriage house. This is a walk-in mine with broad 20-foot-high pillars holding up the vaulted ceilings of the mine "rooms." It is acoustically superb and used for local concerts and theater productions, even weddings. The estate also contains kilns where the rock was crushed for shipment.

Saugerties

KIERSTED HOUSE
845-246-9529.
119 Main St., Saugerties, NY 12477.
Open: Sat.–Sun. 2pm–4pm.
Admission: Donations accepted.

Built in 1727, this whitewashed house is set back from the street behind a broad lawn dotted with enormous and leafy locust trees that date from the 1750s. It was the home of the first doctor in Saugerties, Dr. Christopher Kiersted, who volunteered his services to the Continental Army. Well before he became a traitor, Colonel Benedict Arnold met his wife at a dinner party here. The house was expanded in the 1870s by a descendant, the contractor who built the foundations for the railroad in the area. In the 1950s, the A&P tried to buy the property and raze the house for a supermarket, but lost the bid to a local WWII veteran determined to save the historic house.

Now operated by the Saugerties Historical Society, the house is unfurnished, but contains changing exhibits of local and regional history. A permanent exhibit is the cabinet in the front parlor, containing 8,000 years of archaeological finds from the property, from Stone Age flint stones, Colonial pottery shards, to errant golf balls from today's backyard duffers.

ULSTER COUNTY – OTHER ATTRACTIONS

Kingston

→ **FOUR CORNERS**

This is the only spot left in the United States with pre-Revolutionary houses on each of four corners. It is the intersection of John and Crown Streets in The Stockade area. The stone houses, which date from the early 1700s, have been restored and are private. They are the Jansen House, the Persen House, the Roggin House, and First Academy, which was a school.

Mount Tremper

KAATSKILL KALEIDOSCOPE
800-303-3936.
www.catskillcorners.com.
Rte. 28 at Mt. Pleasant Rd., Mount Tremper, NY 12457.
Open: May–Oct.: Fri.–Sat. 10am–7pm, Mon., Wed., Thurs., Sun. 10am–5pm.
Admission: Adult $9; senior and ages 4–6 $7 for kaleidoscope and film; kaleidoscope only $5.

This is the world's largest kaleidoscope, housed inside a converted barn silo at the foot of Mount Tremper, one of the higher peaks in the Catskill Mountains, just beyond the "official" border of the Hudson Valley. Visitors step inside the kaleidoscope, a series of reflecting and refracting mirrors and lights, actually becoming part of the pattern. There is also a multimedia program, which changes seasonally, including a history of America and a look at the changing seasons.

The Kaleidoscope is part of a complex called Catskill Corners, which includes a gallery of sculptures using neon and other light, a lodge, and shops. Of course, there is a shop selling kaleidoscopes, and not just the souvenir kind, but handmade art versions and antique kaleidoscopes.

Rifton

PERRINE'S BRIDGE
845-338-8109; 845-338-7659 (historical info.).
Rte. 213 (follow signs to Rifton-Tilson), Rifton, NY 12471.

This is a picture-postcard perfect covered bridge, an increasingly rare sight. It spans the Walkill River between Rifton and Tilson, both rural farming communities just minutes from the state university campus at New Paltz. The bridge is the last surviv-

Open: Year-round.
Admission: None.

ing example in New York State of an arch-truss design. It is open to pedestrian traffic only. Bring a camera and a picnic lunch.

Saugerties

OPUS 40
845-246-3400.
50 Fite Rd. (off Rte. 9W and Glasco Turnpike), Saugerties, NY 12477.
Open: Mem. Day weekend– Columbus Day weekend: Fri.–Sun. 12noon–5pm.
Admission: Adult, student, senior $5; school-aged children $4.

Saugerties bluestone was an important construction material a century ago, and this was an important rock quarry, which was abandoned when bluestone was replaced by less expensive architectural materials. Sculptor Harvey Fite took over the site in the 1940s as a setting for his large stone carvings, which dot the six acres of lawns, woods, and pools.

The dominant piece of artwork, though, is a massive bluestone obelisk soaring into the air, framed against the Catskill Mountains to the west and the multilevel sculptured patio at its base. The entire construction is made of hundreds of thousands of finely fitted bluestone pieces. Fite worked alone for some 40 years to create Opus 40, using hand tools and a hand-powered boom to break and move the rocks. He also built, also alone, a small museum to showcase quarryman's tools and artifacts.

GREENE COUNTY — MUSEUMS

East Durham

IRISH HERITAGE CENTER
845-634-2286.
Rte. 145, East Durham, NY 12423.
Open: Mem. Day–Labor Day: Wed.–Sat. 11am–4pm, Sun. 12noon–4pm; Labor Day–Columbus Day: Sat.–Sun. 12noon–4pm; also by appt.
Admission: Adult $3.50; senior, children $2.

Housed in an 1850s farmhouse, the Center is a small but compelling museum in the heart of the so-called "Irish Alps" in a border area between the Hudson Valley and the foothills of the Catskill Mountains. One permanent exhibit is dedicated to Irish-American presidents. John F. Kennedy and Ronald Reagan are included, of course, but also those with a more distant Irish lineage, such as Ulysses S. Grant, one of whose ancestors in the 1600s was from Devon. There's also an excellent geneology library.

Behind the Gaelic football field behind the museum is a growing Irish Village that details life in 19th-century Ireland. The village includes an authentic Irish cottage from County Donegal. The village is still under construction, with some pieces already open. It is scheduled for completion the summer 2003; no hours for the village yet.

GREENE COUNTY – OTHER ATTRACTIONS

South Cairo

Mahayana Temple and Monastery surround a peaceful lake.

Evelyn Kanter

MAHAYANA TEMPLE AND MONASTERY
518-622-3619.
700 Ira Vail Rd. (follow signs about 2 miles from Rte. 23W), South Cairo, NY 12482.
Open: Daily 7am–7pm.
Admission: Donations accepted.

All the buildings here are a deep red cinnabar and an ocre-tinged yellow, including the multitiered pagoda just beyond the curved metal gates. The Pagoda of Jade Buddha sits on the far side of the Lake of Letting Go. The vision from one of the benches that perfectly frames the small lake and the pagoda is soothing and peaceful enough to prompt the viewer to, truly, let go of momentary stress. The complex includes a main temple with three huge smiling golden Buddha figures and the 500 Arhats Hall, lined with triple rows of golden Buddha figures in various poses, ranging from serious to comical, and lit only with spotlights and candles.

The temple is the retreat of the Eastern States Buddhist Temple of America, based in New York City's Chinatown. It welcomes visitors, whether it is just to enjoy the architecture and the peaceful wooded setting or to participate in meditation every Sun. at 10am, followed by a communal lunch of rice and steamed vegetables.

Woodstock

WOODSTOCK

This legendary arts colony is just a few miles beyond the Hudson Valley, within the Catskill Mountains. Although it is still home to painters, potters, jewelers, and writers, some of whom are unrepentant 1950s-style beatniks who still favor tie-dyed clothing and unkempt beards, visitors are more likely to find upscale restaurants, art and craft galleries, and typical tourist-town souvenir shops. It's worth a side trip.

THEATER & CINEMAS

WESTCHESTER COUNTY

Elmsford

WESTCHESTER BROADWAY THEATRE
914-592-2222.
www.broadwaytheatre.com.
One Broadway Plaza (off Rte. 100C), Elmsford, NY 10523.
Open: Year-round.
Admission: Changes, depending on performance.

This is one of the first, and still is one of the biggest and busiest dinner theaters in the eastern half of the country. Popular Broadway musicals live on here after they close on Broadway. Recent performances have included Cole Porter's *Kiss Me Kate* and Bob Fosse's *Chicago*. The price for a meal and a song and dance is less than for just the show, downtown, but you have to contend with the occasional clinking of table items during performances.

Katonah

Enjoying classical performances at the annual Caramoor International Music Festival.

Courtesy Caramoor Center for Music and the Arts

CARAMOOR CENTER FOR MUSIC AND THE ARTS
914-232-1252.
www.caramoor.org.

The annual Caramoor International Music Festival is one of the best-known and most prestigious in the United States, attracting world-class classical, operatic, and jazz artists and dance

149 Girdle Ridge Rd.,
   Katonah, NY 10536.
Open: May–Oct.:
   Wed.–Sun. 1pm–4pm;
   and by appt.
Admission: Changes,
   depending on
   performance; mansion
   tour: adult $7; ages to 17
   free.

Peekskill

PARAMOUNT CENTER FOR THE ARTS
914-739-2333.
www.paramountcenter.org.
1008 Brown St., Peekskill,
   NY 10566.
Open: Year-round.
Admission: Changes,
   depending on
   performance.

Pleasantville

JACOB BURNS FILM CENTER
914-747-5555.
www.burnsfilmcenter.org.
364 Manville Rd.,
   Pleasantville, NY 10570.
Open: Year-round.
Admission: Changes,
   depending on
   performance.

Purchase

PERFORMING ARTS CENTER, PURCHASE COLLEGE
914-251-6200.
www.artscenter.org.
Anderson Hill Rd.,
   Purchase, NY 10577.
Open: Year-round.

groups. Although the festival is just for eight weeks each summer, Caramoor hosts concerts year-round in its outdoor and indoor stages and theaters, including one that is an actual 18th-century Venetian theater. There are weekend performances for children, as well. The setting is magical — a Mediterranean-style mansion built to house the owner's outstanding art collection. The mansion is open for tours (see Chapter Six, *Mansions of the Hudson Valley*).

When this theater was built in the 1930s, movie theaters were really movie palaces, with lush architectural details inside and out to rival the drama on screen. Luckily, the 1,000-seat Paramount retains its Art Deco drama, including the original 2,000 bulb façade and marquee with running chase lights. There are movies during the week and concert performances on weekends, with such recent names as Branford Marsalis, the Duke Ellington Orchestra, and Blood, Sweat, and Tears.

Since it opened in 2001, this has become the area's center for alternative cinema, exhibiting the foreign films and documentaries, independent films, classics, and retrospectives shunned by the multiplexes that feature only the latest Hollywood megareleases. There are three theaters and an intimate screening room. There also are regular lectures by filmmakers and actors. Jacob Burns has an alliance with NYC's Lincoln Center Film Festival and with Human Rights Watch.

This is the largest regional performing arts center in the Hudson Valley, with five theaters, including an experimental "black box" theater, on the campus of one of the branches of SUNY, the State University of New York. There are year-round dance, classical music, jazz, and drama performances by world-class artists and groups. In recent

Admission: Changes, depending on performance.

seasons, these have included cellist YoYo Ma, violinist Itzhak Perlman, the Harlem Dance Theater, Pilobolus modern dance group, and jazz artists Pat Metheny and Ashford & Simpson.

Tarrytown

THE TARRYTOWN MUSIC HALL
914-631-3390.
www.tarrytownmusichall.org.
13 Main St. (Rte. 9), Tarrytown, NY 10591.
Open: Year-round.
Admission: Changes, depending on performance.

This landmark theater, built in 1885 by a local chocolate manufacturer, has Queen Anne, Victorian, and Art Deco architectural elements inside and out. It was turned into a movie house in the 1920s, and the Art Deco marquee that was added at that time was restored recently to its original megawatt brilliance. The theater is reputed to have acoustics the equal of Carnegie Hall in New York City and the Mozartsaal in Vienna. A variety of performances and concerts are held year-round, including jazz, folk, blues, classical, and musical theater. Recent artists have included Lyle Lovett, Wynton Marsalis, The Preservation Hall Jazz Band, and The Paper Bag Players for children.

WESTCHESTER COUNTY CINEMAS

All Westchester Saw Mill (914-747-2333; 151 Saw Mill River Rd., Hawthorne).
Cinema 100 (914-946-4680; 93 Knollwood Rd., White Plains).
Clearview Cinema (914-793-3292; 2630 Central Park Ave., Yonkers).
Greenburg Multiplex (914-592-1500; 320 Saw Mill River Rd., Elmsford).
Jefferson Valley Mall (914-245-4688; www.shopsimon.com; Yorktown Heights)
   More than 100 shops and an eight-screen cinema complex.
Movieland 1234 (914-793-0002; 2500 Central Park Ave., Yonkers).

PUTNAM COUNTY

Garrison

HUDSON VALLEY SHAKESPEARE FESTIVAL
845-265-9575.
www.hvshakespeare.org.
Rte. 9D, Garrison, NY 10524.
Open: June–Aug.
Admission: None.

For 12 weeks each summer, the timeless words of Shakespeare ring forth under a giant outdoor tent on the grounds of Boscobel Restoration (see Chapter Six, *Mansions of the Hudson Valley*). This is grand theater in a memorable setting, and the region's only resident professional Shakespeare company, performing since the mid-1980s. There are pretheater tours of the mansion, and theatergoers are welcome to picnic on the lawn overlooking the Hudson River and to stroll the 30 acres of landscaped gardens and woodland.

DUTCHESS COUNTY

Annandale-on-Hudson

BARD PERFORMING ARTS CENTER
845-758-6822.
www.bard.edu/pac.
Rte. 9G at Annandale Rd.,
  Annandale-on-Hudson,
  NY 12504.
Open: Year-round.
Admission: Changes,
  depending on
  performance; handicap
  access.

Architect Frank Gehry has designed a stunning building that literally shimmers in the sunlight under its undulating stainless steel canopy. The roof does more than just catch the sunlight and make it dance, not unlike the performers inside the building. The building overlooks the Hudson River on the bucolic Bard College campus, and the shape of the roof mimics the shapes of the Catskill Mountains west of the river.

This $25-million arts center opened in 2003 with two performance venues. It is, quite simply, a magical theater setting. The main theater is an acoustically superb 900-seat space that hosts the annual summer Bard Music Festival, with the American Symphony Orchestra in residence, and other concerts and theater performances by students of the liberal arts-oriented college. A second, 300-seat "black box" theater is for smaller and more experimental productions.

Poughkeepsie

BARDAVON OPERA HOUSE
845-473-2072.
www.bardavon.org.
35 Market St.,
  Poughkeepsie, NY 12601.
Open: Year-round.
Admission: Changes,
  depending on
  performance.

No, it's not just opera. This is the oldest operating theater in New York State and the twelfth oldest in the U.S. and presents a range of live performances that includes classical ballet and symphony, bluegrass, jazz artists, and rock. Recent performers at the landmark 1869 theater have included Dave Brubeck, doo-wop icons The Persuasions, Jefferson Starship, the Ballet Gran Folklórico de México, and the American Ballet Theater studio company. Bardavon is also home to the Hudson Valley Philharmonic orchestra, and there are also showings of classic Hollywood movies and children's performances on weekends.

The 944-seat theater is classically designed, with an ornate proscenium arch and rich detailing, including graceful columns that draw the eye to the dome, 40 feet in diameter. It was one of the first theaters to be built at street level; it was normal at the time for theaters to be on the second floor, above stores or businesses, so that incomes would help support the theater. Poughkeepsie is midway between New York City and Albany and became a natural venue for traveling artists, such as the Barrymores, Mark Twain, John Philip Sousa, and Sarah Bernhardt. The theater was almost torn down during urban renewal several decades back, but was saved and restored to its original splendor.

VASSAR & NEW YORK STAGE AND FILM
845-437-5599.
www.vassar.edu/power house.
124 Raymond Ave., Poughkeepsie, NY 12601.
Open: Summer.
Admission: Changes, depending on performance; handicap access.

For eight weeks each summer, the college's main Powerhouse Theater hosts shows headed for Broadway and Off Broadway, with the original cast members. Inevitably, some of these dramas and musicals close on the road before they open in NYC, but the summerlong festival is theater enchantment. The festival includes smaller performances in the Susan Stein Shiva Theater, readings, lectures, and films. There also is a free outdoor series of abbreviated versions of classic plays, performed by students on the Rockefeller Lawn.

Tivoli

KAATSBAAN INTERNATIONAL DANCE CENTER
845-757-5106.
www.kaatsbaan.org.
PO Box 482, Tivoli, NY 12583.
Open: Year-round.
Admission: Changes, depending on performance.

Housed on a grand 150-acre estate, overlooking the Hudson River, this is a professional residence/performance center for all forms of dance, from classical to avant-garde and folk. Kaatsbaan is Dutch for "playing field," but the dancers here are serious, dedicated students and performers. The center regularly hosts guest performers from the American Ballet Theater and international dance troupes.

DUTCHESS COUNTY CINEMAS

Luckily not all the movie theaters here are super-sized, multiplex extravaganzas. There are still some old-fashioned, single-screen gems with somewhat worn-out seats. They are a haven for fans of classic, film noire, and foreign films.

Lyceum Cinema (845-758-3311; S. Broadway, Red Hook) This is an old-fashioned movie house, similar to Upstate Films.

Upstate Films (866-FILMNUT; 845-876-2515; www.upstatefilms.org; 6415 Montgomery St. (Rte. 9), Rhinebeck) Another such theater, and its toll-free telephone number describes its dedication to off-beat cinema. The theater is set back from the street, and the tiny plaza in front of the entrance has benches where film nuts can wait comfortably for the movie to start.

COLUMBIA COUNTY

Hudson

HUDSON OPERA HOUSE
518-822-1438.
www.hudsonoperahouse
.org.
327 Warren St., Hudson, NY
12534.
Open: Year-round.
Admission: Changes,
   depending on
   performance; handicap
   access.

In this multiarts center in the former Hudson City Hall on the town's main shopping street, there are multimedia exhibitions, often showcasing local artists and Hudson River School landscape artists of the late 1800s, plus concerts, readings, and lectures. This Greek Revival structure, designed by a local architect, opened in 1865. The auditorium upstairs was used for lectures, and when opera and other theater performances were staged there, Hudson residents began referring to it as the Opera House, and the name stuck.

STAGEWORKS
518-828-7843.
www.stageworkstheater.org.
133 Warren St., Hudson, NY
12534.
Open: Year-round.
Admission: Changes,
   depending on
   performance.

This bistro-style theater, on the second floor above a row of antique stores on Hudson's main street, offers mostly one-act and one-person comedies and dramas. Stageworks also stages full-scale performances at their Mainstage in Kinderhook and also on the grounds of nearby mansions, including Olana (see Chapter Six, *Mansions of the Hudson Valley*).

Spencertown

**SPENCERTOWN
   ACADEMY**
845-392-3693.
www.spencertown.org.
790 Rte. 203, Spencertown,
NY 12165.
Open: Year-round.
Admission: Changes,
   depending on
   performance.

Since it opened in 1847, this has been a teacher's training school and a private school. Now, it is a performing arts center with an art gallery. Or, perhaps, the other way around, since there are both. There are year-round performances, mostly in the summer, of folk, jazz, and classical music, plus readings by works of well-known poets and authors. There's also a full schedule of performances for children on weekends, such as a shadow puppet show of *Aesop's Fables*.

COLUMBIA COUNTY CINEMAS

The next city of significant size north of Hudson is Albany, close to one hour away, so it's not surprising that there are multiplex theaters in Hudson.

Fairview Cinema III (518-828-1900; Fairview Ave., Hudson) Located in Fairview Plaza.

Hudson Movieplex 8 (518-822-1049; 350 Fairview Ave., Hudson) Located adjacent to Fairview Plaza.

ROCKLAND COUNTY

Nyack

The Last Night at Ballyhoo *at the Helen Hayes Performing Arts Center in Nyack, hometown of "The First Lady of American Theater."*

Bob Vergara/Helen Hayes Performing Arts Center

HELEN HAYES PERFORMING ARTS CENTER
845-358-6333.
www.hhtco.org.
123 Main St., Nyack, NY 10960.
Open: Year-round.
Admission: Changes, depending on performance; handicap access.

The much beloved actress lived in Nyack most of her adult life. Her husband, playwright Charles MacArthur, was born here, and the couple moved here, 40 minutes from Broadway, to raise their family. Helen Hayes was called "The First Lady of American Theater," so it is appropriate that the theater that bears her name is housed in a purpose-built center in the heart of downtown Nyack. Surrounded by restaurants, shops, and art galleries, this center is similar, on a smaller scale, to NYC's Broadway theater district. Since it moved to the large, modern facility in the mid-1990s, the resident Helen Hayes Theatre Company, a nonprofit arts organization, has staged year-round performances, ranging from Broadway-bound musicals and revivals, such as *The Sound of Music* and *Evita*, to dramas and cabaret-type single-performance shows.

ROCKLAND COUNTY CINEMAS

Palisades Center (845-353-5555; Rte. 59, West Nyack) In this megamall, there's a 21-screen multiplex, including an IMAX Theatre.

ORANGE COUNTY

Chester

**BOODLES OPERA
    HOUSE**
845-469-4595.
39 Main St., Chester, NY
    10918.
Open: Wed.–Sun.

It may have been an opera house when it took over an old carriage factory built in 1855, but now it is a rollicking, sometimes hokey, place with singing waitstaff, as well as professional performers, including jazz, blues, and comedy acts.

Sugar Loaf

LYCIAN CENTER
845-489-ACTS.
Kings Hwy., Sugar Loaf,
    NY 10981.
Open: May–Sept.
Admission: Changes,
    depending on
    performance.

Lycian refers to the home of the god of light in Greek mythology, and the two theaters that make up this complex contain more than 400 theatrical lights, made by local craftspeople. The main stage theater contains 684 seats, but despite its size, seats are no more than 100 feet from the stage. A variety of musicals, dramas, and dance is performed here, including by national touring companies. There's also a 300-seat pavilion, used for smaller performances, including children's theater. An outdoor amphitheater overlooks the surrounding farmland and is used for concerts in warm weather months.

West Point

**EISENHOWER HALL
    THEATER**
845-938-4159.
www.eisenhowerhall.org.
USMC, West Point, NY
    10996.
Open: Year-round.
Admission: Changes,
    depending on
    performance; photo ID
    required to purchase
    tickets and to attend.

Housed inside a massive, modern red brick building within the grounds of the United States Military Academy, this is New York State's second largest theater (after Radio City Music Hall in NYC). It has state-of-the-art production capabilities and a huge backstage area that allow the theater to stage full-scale Broadway musicals, ballets, and concerts. Recent productions have included *Cats, My Fair Lady,* and *Cabaret,* the New York Pops, and concerts by Ray Charles and Arlo Guthrie. In addition to the 4,400-seat theater, Eisenhower Hall houses the 1929 Gallery, with changing exhibits of artwork by Hudson Valley artists.

**UNITED STATES
    MILITARY ACADEMY
    BAND**
845-938-2617.

The band performs year-round a mix of classical, jazz, and popular tunes, and some performances are accompanied by members of local

www.usma.army.mil/band.
USMA, West Point, NY
 10996.
Open: Year-round.
Admission: None; photo ID
 required to attend
 performances.

ULSTER COUNTY

Highland

**VILLA BAGLIERI
 DINNER THEATER**
845-7395; 800-84-VILLA.
www.villabaglieri.com.
200 Foster Rd. (off Rte. 9W)
 Highland, NY 12528.
Open: Year-round.
Admission: $30-$35,
 depending on date.

Kingston

BACKSTAGE STUDIOS
845-338-8700.
www.backstagestudios.net.
323 Wall St., Kingston, NY
 12401.
Open: Year-round.
Admission: Changes,
 depending on
 performance.

**BROADWAY THEATER
 AT UPAC**
845-339-6088.
www.upac.org.
601 Broadway, Kingston,
 NY 12401.
Open: Mar.–Dec.
Admission: Changes,
 depending on
 performance; handicap
 access.

ballet and modern dance troupes. In the summer, there are weekly concerts outdoors in a natural amphitheater at Trophy Point. The band is showcased in front of a semicircular see-through acoustical shell and behind them is a majestic panorama north up the Hudson River.

You have to love a small town dinner theater that stages performances like *Joe and Mary's Irish-Italian Wedding* and *Disorganized Crime*. Villa Baglieri must be doing something right, because the takeoffs of popular Broadway and television shows have been happening here since the 1950s. This is a catering company, so they are used to throwing parties for large audiences.

This is a performing arts complex built around a former vaudeville theater, where visiting stars like Al Jolson and Eddie Cantor once performed, before the space was turned into a movie house. It was totally renovated again in 2001 into a live performance theater for touring companies of Broadway shows. The complex also contains an art gallery on the main floor for exhibits of local artists, plus a dance studio, rehearsal space, and a recording studio upstairs.

An Art Deco gem that used to be a vaudeville theater, the Broadway Theater was renovated recently to its original 1927 splendor, except for the huge, original Venetian-inspired chandelier that was suspended from the center of the auditorium. The chandelier was removed in 1954 when the theater was converted into a movie house, and it has vanished. The theater now features Broadway musicals, concerts, and children's theater performances. Recent offerings have included the Red Army Chorus and Dance Ensemble and the national touring company of *Ain't Misbehavin.*

The theater is located in the so-called "uptown" section of Kingston, a some-what seedy area between two high-rent districts of historic houses, upscale restaurants, The Stockade, and the Rondout areas. Behind the theater is a newly illuminated parking area.

New Paltz

PARKER THEATRE
845-257-3872.
S. Manheim Blvd. (Rte. 32S), New Paltz, NY 12561.
Open: Summer: Thurs.–Sun.; call for schedule for other times.
Admission: Tickets $12; handicap access; visitors use parking lot #32.

During the academic year, but especially during the summer, there are regular concerts and theatre performances by students and visiting pro-fessionals. The New Paltz Summer Repertory Theater began in the 1970s when professors of the-ater converted an empty dining hall into a theater. Since then, the program has been moved into Parker Theatre, a modern full-facility building. The summer program also includes Shakespeare Under the Stars and the PianoSummer Concert Series.

ULSTER COUNTY CINEMAS

Cinema 6 (845-336-4188; 1300 Ulster Ave., Kingston).
New Paltz Cinema (845-255-0420; New Paltz Plaza, Rte. 32, New Paltz) A mul-tiplex.

Drive-Ins

When was the last time you were at an old-fashioned drive-in theater? You remember — the kind that you sit in your car and hook up the speaker from the pole next to your parking space. Drive-ins are becoming as rare as the proverbial hen's teeth and are being replaced by multiplexes.

The Hudson Valley holds tight to tradition and history, so it should be no surprise that these '50s-style gems are still here.

DUTCHESS COUNTY

Hyde Park Drive-In Theater (845-229-2000; 510 Albany Post Rd. (Rte. 9), Hyde Park) Across the road from the FDR Library, this theater shows first-run films.
The Overlook Drive-In Theater (845-452-3445; Overlook Rd., Poughkeepsie).

ORANGE COUNTY

Middlehope Drive-In Theatre (845-568-5840; 5258 Rte.9W, Newburgh).

GREENE COUNTY

Hi-Way Drive-In (845-731-8672; Rte. 9W, Coxsackie) Just south of Bronck Mansion. Open year-round.

FAMILY FUN

It's fun to be a kid in the Hudson Valley. In addition to several children's museums, many others places have special children's programs, as do a number of the Revolutionary and Colonial sites. In the winter, snow-tubing and ice-skating are designed for families to do together, and the rest of the year, there are fairs and festivals guaranteed to keep a kid fascinated and giggling. Or, just grab a picnic basket and head for the riverfront and let the kids run loose.

WESTCHESTER COUNTY

Somers

MUSCOOT FARM
914-864-7282.
Rte. 100 (follow signs),
  Somers, NY 10589.
Open: May–Oct.: daily
  10am–6pm until Labor
  Day; rest of year
  10am–4pm.
Admission: None.

An interpretive 777-acre farm that recreates farm life in the late 1800s and early 1900s. A variety of farm animals and displays of vintage equipment appeals to young children, as well as to their parents and grandparents. The horses, cows, sheep, and ducks are tame enough for young children to get close to, and there are demonstrations of cooking and other farm chores, hayrides, and nature trails.

The farm was built in 1885 — Muscoot means "something swampy" in the local Native American language — and was a model of innovation, with natural insulation and chutes from the hayloft to feed the cattle. Now owned by the county, it is still a working farm, growing herbs and heirloom fruits and vegetables.

DUTCHESS COUNTY

Poughkeepsie

**MID-HUDSON
  CHILDREN'S
  MUSEUM**
845-471-0589.
www.mhcm.org.
75 N. Water St.,
  Poughkeepsie, NY 12601.
Open: Tues.–Sun.,
  11am–5pm.
Admission: Adult, child $5.

Youngsters can climb through a heart the size of a small truck, travel the pathway of a red blood cell, build a replica of Robert Fulton's Hudson River steamboat and simulate its journey up and down the waterway, or try to clamber to the top of a rock-climbing wall. The museum moved in 2002 from a cramped space in a shopping mall to a bright, airy, and well-designed facility overlooking the river. There's also an educational play space for toddlers.

Stanfordville

Owls are among the residents at the Hudson Valley Raptor Center.

Tania Barricklo/Daily Freeman

**HUDSON VALLEY
RAPTOR CENTER**
845-758-6957.
South Rd. (off Rte. 199),
Stanfordville, NY 12581.
Open: Sat.–Sun. 1pm–4pm;
2pm falconry demonstra-
tions.
Admission: Adult $7; senior,
student $5; ages under 12
$2.50.

Besides flying demonstrations and educational exhibits about these fearsome, awesome birds of prey, this center also provides rescue and reha-bilitation for raptors, so there is a rotating guest list, including bald eagles, snowy owls, and pere-grine falcons. The small, backyard feel of this cen-ter is a comfortable, nonthreatening place to intro-duce young children to these beautiful creatures.

Wappingers Falls

**STONY KILL FARM
ENVIRONMENTAL
EDUCATION CENTER**
845-831-8780.
Rte. 9D, Wappingers Falls,
NY 12590.
Open: Year-round: weekdays
8:30am–4:45pm, Sun.
1pm–4pm.
Admission: None; handicap
access.

A working farm with programs on natural his-tory, ecology, and, of course, farming, this cen-ter has hiking trails and small lakes for fishing. The farm is open in the winter for snowshoeing.

GREENE COUNTY

Catskill

CATSKILL GAME FARM
518-678-9595.
www.catskillgamefarm
.com.
Game Farm Rd. (off Rte.
32), Catskill, NY 12414.
Open: May 1–Oct. 31: daily
9am–5pm; July–Aug.:
daily 9am–6pm.
Admission: Adult $16.95;
ages 4-11 $12.95; ages 3
and under free.

Lions and tigers and bears, oh my, and ducks, giraffes, even a rhino or two!The petting zoo is one of the most popular places in this sprawling (more than 2,000 animals) and crawling (with kids) spot. Regularly scheduled shows make the furry and feathered creatures less threatening to the wide-eyed, sneaker-clad ones. There's a tram to transport the weary, and a picnic area. This is one of the oldest game farms in the country.

HUDSON VALLEY FAIRS & FESTIVALS

SPRING

WESTCHESTER COUNTY

Crafts at Lyndhurst (914-631-0046; Lyndhurst, Tarrytown) 300 artisans show their handicrafts on the lawn. May, Oct.

International Music Festival (914-232-1252; www.caramoor.org; Caramoor, Purchase) Annual eight-week event of classical, opera, jazz, cabaret, and chamber music concerts, plus international folk dance performances. Mid-June–mid-Aug.

Pinkster Festival (914-631-3992; Philipsburg Manor, Tarrytown) Celebrates the region's 18th-century African and Dutch heritages, with authentic music, dance, and games. May.

Westchester County Fair (914-968-4200; Yonkers Raceway, Yonkers) Rides, shows, games, food, and performances. Mid-May–mid-June.

ORANGE COUNTY

International Week (845-938-8797; U.S. Military Academy, West Point) West Point celebrates its past and future relationships with the international community. Apr.

ULSTER COUNTY

New Paltz Art & Crafts Fair (845-679-8087; www.quailhollow.com; Ulster County Fairgrounds, New Paltz) Juried fair, featuring 300 artists and artisans from throughout the U.S., plus entertainment and demonstrations. Memorial Day and Labor Day weekends.

SUMMER

The **Hudson River Valley Ramble** (845-334-9574; 800-453-6665; www.hudsonvalleyramble.com; www.hudsonvalleyheritage.com) This is a festival of more than 100 activities and events from New York City to Albany, including guided walks and hikes, river paddling, equestrian events, and historical and ecological lectures. Held annually on the last full weekend of summer.

WESTCHESTER COUNTY

Blue crabs from the Hudson River at one of the many riverside festivals.

Tania Barricklo/Daily Freeman

Great Hudson Revival Festival (845-454-7673; www.clearwater.org; Croton Point Park, Croton-on-Hudson) Extravaganza benefiting the *Clearwater* sloop and the environmentally conscious Clearwater Organization founded by folk singer Pete Seeger. Concerts, dance bands, dance tents, activities, storytelling and performances for the kids, food and crafts displays, and exhibits on everything from solar energy to endangered species. June.

Wine and Food Festival (914-669-5518; North Salem Vineyard, North Salem) A dozen Hudson Valley vineyards, several dozen restaurants, gourmet food producers, and farm stands gather for samplings and tastings. Aug.

PUTNAM COUNTY

4-H Fair (845-278-6738; Putnam Veteran's Memorial Park, Carmel) Real country atmosphere with a horse show, fishing, and livestock-judging contests, plus food. July.

DUTCHESS COUNTY

The annual Dutchess County Fair is one of the largest in New York State.

Dutchess County Tourism

Dutchess County Fair (845-876-4001; www.dutchessfair.com; Rhinebeck) Second largest agricultural event in the state. More than 1,500 farm animals judged for excellence, agricultural and flower-arranging competitions, demonstrations and contests of farm activities, including hay baling and horseshoeing. Aug.

COLUMBIA COUNTY

Columbia County Fair (518-392-2121; www.columbiafair.com; Chatham) Rides, exhibits, livestock competitions, children's petting zoo, concerts, horse shows, and a microbrewery. Labor Day weekend.

ORANGE COUNTY

Orange County Fair (845-343-4826; www.orangecountryfair.com; Middletown Fairgrounds, Middletown) Concerts, rides, games, food, demonstrations. July.

ULSTER COUNTY

Ulster County Fair (845-255-1380; www.ulstercounty-fair.com; Ulster County Fairgrounds, New Paltz) Competitive exhibits in such areas as horticulture, arts and crafts, cooking, livestock and agricultural shows, truck and tractor pulls, horse shows. July–Aug.

AUTUMN

WESTCHESTER COUNTY

Battle of Pells Point Encampment (914-667-4116; St. Paul's National Historic Site, Mount Vernon) Reenactment of Revolutionary War battle, plus lectures and performances. Mid-Oct.

Crafts at Lyndhurst (914-631-0046; Lyndhurst, Tarrytown) 300 artisans show their handicrafts on the lawn. May, Oct.

→ **Fright-Fest** (914-631-8200; www.hudsonvalley.org; Sunnyside, Tarrytown) "The Legend of Sleepy Hollow" comes alive for kids (and adults, too) as the Headless Horseman and other ghouls celebrate Halloween with parades and activities.

Heritage Crafts Weekend (914-271-8981; www.hudsonvalley.org; Van Cortlandt Manor, Croton-on-Hudson) Demonstrations and hands-on activities of Colonial crafts, including cheese making, soap making, quilting, spinning and weaving, coopering, basketry, candle making, cider making, hearth cooking. Mid-Oct.

Jazz Festival (914-631-1000; www.jazzforumarts.org; Sunnyside, Tarrytown) Open-air performances by international jazz artists. Sept.

ULSTER COUNTY

Hudson Valley Garlic Festival (845-246-3642; www.hopefarm.com/garlic; Cantine Field, Saugerties) Weekend event with garlic foods, lectures, crafts, and music. Sept.

New Paltz Art & Crafts Fair (845-679-8087; www.quailhollow.com; Ulster County Fairgrounds, New Paltz) Juried fair, featuring 300 artists and artisans from throughout the U.S., plus entertainment and demonstrations. Mem. Day and Labor Day weekends.

WINTER

WESTCHESTER COUNTY

→ **Candlelight Tours** (914-631-8200; www.hudsonvalley.org) Annual tradition of tours of decorated historic homes, including Philipsburg Manor and Sunnyside in Tarrytown and Van Cortlandt Manor in Croton-on-Hudson.

ULSTER COUNTY

International Pickle Festival (845-658-9649; www.picklefest.com; Rosendale Recreation Center, Rosendale) Barrels of mouth-puckering choices from around the world, including fruits, vegetables, meats, and fish. Pickle-drawing contests for the kids, plus music. Nov.

CHAPTER SIX
Mind Your Manors
MANSIONS OF THE HUDSON VALLEY

"All that is within me cries out to go back to my home on the Hudson River."
— Franklin Delano Roosevelt, 1944

FDR's family settled in the Hudson Valley in the 17th century.

These homes pepper the shores of the Hudson River starting about 30 miles north of New York City in Westchester County and continue northward another 90 miles, almost to Saratoga. More than 300 years of political, social, and economic history of this nation are rooted in these structures of wood, stone, and marble.

The river was one of America's first major thoroughfares. Beginning in the 1620s, Dutch settlers — farmers and fur traders — sailed north from New Netherland, and by the time the English took over and renamed the colony New York, travel was continuous. The early pioneers planted crops and built cottages, gristmills, trading posts, and manor homes along the water's edge.

They were followed two centuries later by millionaire industrialists and entrepreneurs who built castlelike mansions, with commanding panoramic

on the hillsides, and then came the artists, writers, and inven-
inspiration from the pastoral views. In some places, the old
der are within a few moments walk or drive, as with Colonial
Пил, nor and the Rockefeller family's art-filled Kykuit estate, both in
Tarrytown.

Like other chapters in this book this one is organized by county, south to
north from New York City, and cities within each county are listed alphabetically rather than geographically. Naturally, if you were to drive north with an
eye to seeing everything (a trip only for the hardy), your stops would be in a
different order. In Westchester, for example, the sequence of mansions would
be: Philipse Manor, Sunnyside, Lyndhurst, Phillipsburg Manor, Kykuit, and
Van Cortland Manor.

MANSIONS

EAST SIDE OF THE HUDSON

WESTCHESTER COUNTY

Croton-on-Hudson

**VAN CORTLANDT
MANOR**
914-271-8981.
www.hudsonvalley.org.
Rte. 9, Croton-on-Hudson,
NY 10591.
Open: Apr.–Oct.: daily,
except Tues.; Nov.–Dec.:
weekends only; closed
Jan.–Mar.
Admission: Adult $9; senior
$8; ages 5–17 $5; under 5
free; grounds only $4.

The first Van Cortlandt was a soldier employed
by the Dutch West India Company, who arrived
in what is now New York City in 1638. Oloff
Stevense became prosperous as a brewer, involved
himself in local politics, adding the aristocratic suf-
fix. Son Stephanus became the first native-born
mayor of New York City and aquired 85,000 acres of
what is now Westchester County under a Royal
Charter.

The manor house dates from 1748 and remained
in the family for 200 years, so artifacts reflect the
history and wealth of the family, from Colonial-era
delft tiles around the fireplace to 19th-century
French credenzas; much of the furnishings are original (fabrics in some rooms
were reproduced from scraps of the originals). The estate's mills supplied the
Revolutionary Army with wheat, George Washington is said to have slept here,
and Stephanus's son Pierre, an active patriot, fled north to Rhinebeck when the
British approached (there is Revolutionary War–era graffiti carved into one of
the fireplace mantels). At war's end, only the shell of the house remained, but
Pierre rebuilt it with bricks made on the premises by the estate's slaves.

The house and land passed to Van Cortlandt descendants until the title was
transferred to Historic Hudson Valley in 1959. Guides are in Colonial dress.

There are gardens planted with 18th-century produce, including tobacco, flax, mustard, and gourds, and demonstrations of spinning, weaving, and black-smithing.

Tarrytown

The grand entrance to the dramatic and opulent Kykuit, the Rockefeller estate.

Evelyn Kanter

→ **KYKUIT**
914-631-9491.
www.hudsonvalley.org.
Rte. 9, Tarrytown, NY 10591.
Open: Apr. 27–Nov.3: daily,
  except Tues.; closed
  Jan.–Mar.
Admission: Adult $20;
  senior $19; ages to 17 $17;
  not appropriate for
  children under 10. Tickets
  for tours of Kykuit must
  be purchased at
  Philipsburg Manor;
  visitors are transported
  from there to Rockefeller
  estate.

One of the finest and best preserved Beaux Arts houses in the nation, this was the home to four generations of Rockefellers and reflects their different personalities and interests. Kykuit was built by John D. Rockefeller, Sr., founder of Standard Oil Company. In 1884, he moved his company and his family from Cleveland to New York City, and in 1893, he purchased 400 acres at Pocantico Hills, with a commanding view of the Hudson River. Kykuit is the local Native American tribe's word for "look-out."

Design and construction was supervised by John D. Rockefeller, Jr., who grew up with wealth and had a better sense of art and architecture than his self-made father, who was known both for his personal frugality and his generous philanthropy. The son made sure the house and grounds featured lush details, reflecting the family's prominent position, and he filled it with lavish furnishings, including museum-quality folk art collected by his wife Abby Aldrich Rockefeller. The experience seemed to have a profound effect on him: JDR, Jr., built Rockefeller Center in midtown Manhattan, was the force behind the creation of Colonial Williamsburg, and founded Sleepy Hollow Restorations, now called Historic Hudson Valley, to preserve Hudson Valley historic sites nearby. Kykuit's architects, Delano and Aldrich, were relatives of President Franklin Delano Roosevelt, Jr., and Abby Aldrich Rockefeller.

Perhaps the most impressive additions were made by one of Junior's and Abby's sons, Nelson, the four-term governor of New York, vice-president under Gerald Ford, and an avid collector of both modern and ancient Oriental art. Nelson filled the house, a specially built basement gallery, and gardens with paintings, tapestries, and sculpture by Picasso, Alexander Calder, Juan Miró, Henry Moore, and others.

Nelson lived here until his death in 1979 and entertained many heads of state here, including President Ford, who dedicated Kykuit as a National Historic Landmark in 1976. Nelson willed the house and 86 acres to the National Trust for Historic Preservation; Historic Hudson Valley operates the visitor services.

There are separate tours of the house and the sculpture gardens, but the playhouse with its pools, tennis courts, and bowling alley is off limits, since it is still used by family members.

LYNDHURST
914-631-4481.
www.lyndhurst.org.
Rte. 9, Tarrytown, NY
  10591.
Open: Tues.–Sun.

Regarded as the best example of Gothic Revival design in the U.S., this mansion was built originally as a retirement home for former New York City mayor and U.S. Congressman William Paulding in 1838. Architect Alexander Jackson Davis designed much of the interior and the furnishings, so there is an integrated look inside and out, such as chair backs carved with the same detailing as the roof. The house also is unusual because virtually all the furnishings are original, not reproductions.

In 1858, the house was sold to industrialist George Merritt (among other things, he invented the shock absorber for railroad cars), who rehired Davis to expand the house. By now, Sing Sing Prison had been built in nearby Ossining, and the limestone for the façade was cut by its prisoners. Much inside is not what it seems — "faux" was chic in the 1860s, and many walls and ceilings are plaster or wood painted to look like marble and brickwork; the real marble around the fireplaces was copied for the faux marble elsewhere.

Twenty years later, the house was bought by Jay Gould, whose business practices had earned him the name "robber baron." At various times, he owned the Erie and Missouri Pacific railroads, Western Union, and the *New York World* newspaper. Gould first arrived at Lyndhurst (named for the linden trees that blanket the property) by yacht, which he moored at the foot of the lawn. Although traveling by railroad would have been faster, his bitter enemy, Cornelius Vanderbilt owned and operated the New York Central Railroad and its tracks at the water's edge — and either Gould would not set foot upon them, or Vanderbilt wouldn't allow him to do so.

Jay Gould's impressive Renaissance art collection reaches the 20-foot ceilings of the cathedral-shaped, wood-paneled upstairs manor room. There are stained glass windows throughout the house, including an unu medallion-shaped window above his ornately carved bed, and ri   ..cing windows feature magnifying glass to bring the view closer. Three generations of Goulds lived here until 1961, when a granddaughter turned it over to the National Trust for Historic Preservation.

PHILIPSBURG MANOR
914-631-3992.
www.hudsonvalley.org.
Rte. 9, Tarrytown, NY 10591.
Open: Mar.: weekends only;
  Apr.–Dec.: daily, except
  Tues.; closed Jan.–Feb.
Admission: Adult $9; senior
  $8; ages 5–17 $5; under 5
  free.

The Philipse family was one of the wealthiest and most politically active in Colonial America, accumulating over three generations more than 50,000 acres spread along 22 miles of the Hudson River in what is now Westchester County. The family ran its shipping and trading business from their homes in Manhattan and Yonkers. This farming and milling complex was managed by an overseer in charge of dozens of slaves and tenant farmers.

Philipse family members visited regularly to check the books and wanted the same comforts here as in their other homes. Inside the plain, whitewashed house is a treasure of 17th-century furnishings from the Netherlands, England, and the Orient, much of it brought back by their own ships. There also are many historic documents, including a bill of sale of some of the family's slaves.

This is now a living history farm, with livestock that have been back-bred to 17th-century authenticity. Sheep and chickens roam about, and there are demonstrations of weaving and other farm activities by guides in Colonial costumes. The property sustained extensive damage by Hurricane Floyd in 1999, and the restoration, including the picturesque gristmill and bridge, took three years.

SUNNYSIDE HOUSE
914-631-8200.
www.hudsonvalley.org.
Rte. 9, Tarrytown, NY
  10591.
Open: Mar.: weekends only
  10am–4pm; Apr.–Oct.:
  Wed.–Mon. 10am–5pm;
  Nov.–Dec.: Wed.–Mon.
  10am–4pm; closed
  Jan.–Feb.
Admission: Adult $9; senior
  $8; ages 5–17 $5; under 5
  free.

Washington Irving grew up in New York City, near what is now 14th St. and Irving Pl., son of a wealthy merchant family that went bankrupt following the War of 1812. By then, the young lawyer had begun making a name for himself as a satirist, as in his 1809 *Knickerbocker's History of New York*, a lampoon of the city's Dutch period. His short stories "Rip Van Winkle," "The Legend of Sleepy Hollow," also gentle lampoons, and other books made him rich and famous.

Many of his most famous stories were written during a 17-year sojourn in Europe, when he was the U.S. Minister to Spain from 1842–1846. When he returned home, he purchased a two-room cottage and farm, once part of Philipsburg Manor, on the banks of the Hudson River in Tarrytown. Irving expanded the cottage, incorporating architectural ideas from his European travels, including walk-in closets, skylights, and gravity-fed "run-

Washington Irvings's desk was a gift from his publisher, G. P. Putnam, in 1856.

Courtesy Historic Hudson Valley

ning" water. Styles include a Moorish tower, a Venetian veranda, and stepped gables mimicking a 17th-century English country cottage. The original rooms became his book-filled study and dining room. His international fame kept the house bustling with literary guests, and Irving's two nieces served as his hostesses (he never married after the death of his childhood sweetheart).

The house is airy and unpretentious, unlike his next door neighbor, the dark, gothic Lyndhurst, half a mile up the road. Irving may have been introduced to the area by a writer friend whose brother built the original house there. Sunnyside sits about one hundred yards from the water. Because of the noise of the steam engines when the railroad went in along the water's edge in the 1850s, Irving moved his riverside bedroom to the other side of the house. Irving died here in 1859 just four months after the publication of the final volume of his five-volume biography of the man for whom he was named, George Washington.

Tour guides are dressed in period costumes. There is a small garden café.

Yonkers

PHILIPSE MANOR HALL STATE HISTORIC SITE
914-965-4027.
www.philipsemanorfriends.org.
29 Warburton Ave. and Dock St., Yonkers, NY 10701.
Open: Apr.–Oct.: Wed.–Sun.

This high-style Georgian mansion was built between 1680 and 1775 by wealthy Dutch merchant, gentleman farmer, and slave trader Frederick Philipse; Philipse owned thousands of acres several miles north in what is now Tarrytown. The family's trading and shipping business was based in New York City, so the Yonkers manor home was a midway location for "watching the store." The house has an original 1750s papier-mâché ceiling and selections from the Collection of American Portraiture.

PUTNAM COUNTY

Garrison

**BOSCOBEL
RESTORATION**
914-265-3638; 845-265-3638.
www.boscobel.org.
Rte. 9D, Garrison, NY
10524.
Open: Daily, except Tues.,
Thanksgiving,
Christmas; closed Jan.,
Feb., Mar.
Admission: Adult $8; senior
$7; ages 6–14 $5; under
age 6 free.

One of the nation's best examples of neoclassical Federalist architecture and furnishings, this bright yellow symmetrical house sits atop a knoll overlooking the Hudson at the river's deepest and narrowest point, directly across the river from the U.S. Military Academy at West Point. It features an important collection of furniture by Duncan Phyfe and other New York State cabinetmakers of the period, plus reproduction carpeting, wallpaper, fabrics, and elegant architectural details, including a grand staircase and arched doorways. The mansion was built in 1805 by States Morris Dyckman, a Loyalist of Dutch ancestry, who died before the house was completed. Much of the family's English porcelain and china, silver, and leather-bound books also are on view.

The Dyckman family lived here until 1888, then the house belonged to different owners until 1955 when the federal government sold it to a contractor for $35, who promptly dismantled the house. That raised such a furor that local history buffs tracked down the missing parts, and with the financial backing of Lila Acheson Wallace, co-founder of the *Reader's Digest*, Boscobel was fully restored to its original elegance. The house and extensive grounds were opened to the public in 1961.

A brick walkway leads through an apple orchard to the formal rose garden, which contains more than 100 rose varieties. A one-mile Woodland Trail starts at the south side of the property and winds through 29 acres of wooded landscape. When the trees part, there are spectacular river views, enjoyable from the benches and shaded gazebo along the path. In the summer, the property hosts the Hudson Valley Shakespeare Festival under a huge tent on the lawn (see Chapter Five, *Arts & Pleasures*).

DUTCHESS COUNTY

Annandale-on-Hudson

MONTGOMERY PLACE
845-758-5461.
www.hudsonvalley.org.

One of the most significant and meticulously preserved country estates in America, this Federal-style mansion was the home of Janet

Tania Barricklo

Montgomery Place contains original furnishings from the 18th century.

River Rd. (Rte. 103), Annandale-on-Hudson, NY 12504.
Open: Apr.–Oct.: Wed.–Mon. 10am–5pm; Nov.: weekends only 10am–4:30pm; Dec.: first 2 weekends 12noon–5pm; closed Jan.–Mar.
Admission: Adult $7; senior $6; ages 5–17 $4; under 5 free; grounds only $4.

Livingston Montgomery, born into one of the most prominent Revolutionary and 19th-century political families (see Clermont below) and widow of Revolutionary War General Richard Montgomery, killed in battle when she was 32 years old.

Built in 1802 and remodeled and expanded to 23 rooms over succeeding generations, it was the family home until the 1980s when it was purchased and restored by Historic Hudson Valley. Furnishings reflect the range of family history rather than one period or style. The drawing room, focal point of family gatherings for two centuries, contains the original wallpaper from the mid-19th century and a huge French crystal chandelier from the 1870s. The dining room contains family portraits believed to have been painted by Gilbert Stuart, the famous George Washington portraitist. In the 1860s, architect Alexander Jackson Davis (Lyndhurst, Locust Grove) added a columned curved portico on the west entry side of the house and a porticoed porch on the east side, with its dramatic views of the Hudson River.

The house sits amid 434 acres of landscaped grounds, which include formal gardens, a nature trail through the woods to a waterfall where the Sawkill meets the Hudson, and extensive apple orchards.

Hyde Park

FRANKLIN DELANO ROOSEVELT HOME, LIBRARY, AND MUSEUM
845-229-9115.

The Roosevelts had ties to the Hudson River Valley dating back to the 17th century. FDR's forbears moved to the Hyde Park area in 1818, and Franklin's father James bought a large farmhouse in

FDR's bedroom at Hyde Park is unchanged since his last visit.

Courtesy National Park Service

www.nps.gov/hofr.
Rte. 9G, Hyde Park, NY
   12538.
Open: Year-round:
   9am–5pm; library and
   museum: Apr.–Oct.
   9am–6pm; Nov.–Mar.
   9am–5pm.
Admission: Adult $10;
   children $5.

1867, fifteen years before FDR was born. After his father's death in 1900, Franklin and his mother Sara transformed it into a grand three-story red brick Colonial called Springwood. FDR grew up here and returned at every opportunity, including for respite from Albany when he was governor and for more than 200 stays throughout his presidency. He jokingly referred to it as the Summer White House.

The house contains many mementoes, including his boyhood collection of stuffed birds, his stamp collection, and the bed in which he was born. The living room is a comfortable wood-paneled room with overstuffed furniture, and the bedroom he used as President remains as it was during his last visit, weeks before his death in 1945.

Franklin and Eleanor Roosevelt are buried in the Rose Garden, between the house and the FDR Library. There also are extensive landscaped walkways to enjoy.

FDR designed the library, which became the first presidential library (until then, presidents had just taken their papers with them or deposited them in an existing library). It was completed before his death, and he used the study to deliver his famous wartime fireside chats. The library contains more than 40,000 books and additional manuscripts and photographs. The museum has an extensive display on the war effort.

VAL-KILL COTTAGE
845-229-9422.
www.nps.gov/hofr.
Rte. 9G, Hyde Park, NY
   12538.
Open: May–Oct.: daily;
   Nov.–Dec., Mar.–Apr.:

The only National Historic Site dedicated to the memory of a First Lady, this charming Dutch Colonial cottage was constructed alongside a stream that was a favorite Roosevelt family picnic spot. It became a retreat for Eleanor Roosevelt from her husband's strong-willed mother, his political weekends only; closed Jan.–Feb. Admission: $5.

cronies, and the Secret Service. After his death in 1945, it became her permanent residence. It was here that the "First Lady of the World" entertained both foreign dignitaries and American politicians, including a young John F. Kennedy, who sought her blessings for his 1960 presidential campaign.

The house is filled with mementoes from her days as the wife of New York State's governor, then President, and her humanitarian career. After her death in 1962, the house was sold to private developers, but concerned citizens sparked interest in establishing it as a national historic memorial site.

Mrs. Vanderbilt's gilt and brocade bedroom overlooks the Hudson River.

W. D. Urban, Courtesy National Park Service

VANDERBILT MANSION NATIONAL HISTORIC SITE
845-229-9115; 800-967-2283.
www.nps.gov/vama.
Rte. 9, Hyde Park, NY 12538.
Open: Daily 9am–5pm; grounds open until dusk.
Admission: $8; grounds free.

This imposing Beaux Arts mansion was Frederick and Louise Vanderbilt's hot weather escape from their mansion on New York City's Fifth Avenue, much like grandfather Commodore Cornelius Vanderbilt used his "cottage," the fabulous Breakers, in Newport, Rhode Island. Frederick was one of the heirs to the Vanderbilt fortune, which included the New York Central Railroad (now MetroNorth) that runs along tracks at the water's edge down the hill from the mansion.

McKim, Mead, and White designed, constructed, and decorated the home starting in 1895, an ornate example of the "Gilded Age," before the days of federal income tax. The formal Renaissance dining room is paneled in carved walnut with gilt borders, a floor-to-ceiling carved marble fireplace, and a ceiling mural. Upstairs, Mrs. Vanderbilt's bedroom and separate boudoir are reminiscent of Versailles, something Marie Antoinette would have been comfortable retiring to.

The Vanderbilts had no children, and the property passed to a niece in 1938.

The niece preferred Newport and put the property on the market, but the Depression had changed the gilded lifestyle, and there were no buyers. A next-door neighbor convinced the heiress to copy what he had just done and donate the 211-acre property to the people of the United States. The next-door neighbor, of course, was President Franklin Delano Roosevelt.

The National Parks Service operates the Vanderbilt Mansion, and for some unaccountable reason, the 45-minute tour spends the first 30 minutes outside the house, where NPS guides discuss family history. Fifteen minutes inside this magnificent mansion is an appetizer leaving many visitors hungry for more.

Poughkeepsie

Portrait of Samuel F. B. Morse and replica of his first telegraph.

Dutchess County Tourism

LOCUST GROVE
845-454-4500.
www.morsehistoricsite.org.
Rte. 9, Poughkeepsie, NY
12601.
Open: May–Thanksgiving:
daily 10am–3pm; year-round by appt.; grounds open year-round until dusk.
Admission: Adult $5; senior $4; ages 6–18 $2.

Samuel F. B. Morse was a Renaissance man, sometimes referred to as "the American Leonardo da Vinci" — professor of literature and design, portrait artist, and founder and first president of the National Academy of Design. But he is most famous, of course, for one of his inventions — the telegraph and its communications code. Morse's home, on a hillside overlooking the Hudson River, reflects all his interests.

He bought a Georgian home from the Montgomery family (see Montgomery Place above) and hired his friend and design colleague, Alexander Jackson Davis (who also designed the Gothic Revival Lyndhurst mansion in Tarrytown for industrialist Jay Gould) to expand and reconfigure the structure into a Tuscan-style villa. Original pieces are exhibited in period-room settings, including the family silver and porcelain. These are interspersed with items from the family that bought the house in 1901 (three decades after Morse's death), were aware of its historic importance, and preserved the estate. There are pristine Chippendale, Federal, and Empire furnishings, as well as a rare bound collection of *Birds of America* by J. J. Audubon. And, of course, Morse's very first working telegraph. It's a replica of the one he used to send that first, powerful message, "What hath God wrought!" from Washington, D.C. to Baltimore. One has to wonder what he would think about today's worldwide Internet. Morse designed the lush, romantic gardens, which remain as he envisioned. There are 150 acres of trees, gardens, a lake, three miles of walking trails along the river, and a waterfall. Locust Grove is named for a stand of locust trees that date to before Morse's time.

Rhinebeck

**WILDERSTEIN
   PRESERVATION**
845-876-4818;
   fax 845-876-3336.
www.wilderstein.org.
Rte. 103, Rhinebeck, NY
   12572.
Open: May–Oct.: Thurs.–
   Sun. 12noon–4pm;
   Thanksgiving–Dec.:
   weekends only; closed
   rest of year.
Admission: $5.

Wilderstein means "wild man's stone." It was named for an Indian petroglyph in a riverside cove, a reminder of the cultural heritage in the Hudson Valley for thousands of years before the European settlers arrived. This was the home of Thomas Suckley, a wealthy merchant and descendent of the Livingston and Beekman (see Beekman Arms, Chapter Three, *Lodging*) families; the home stayed in the family for 125 years and three generations.

Suckley's son, 35 years later, remodeled and enlarged the original Italianate villa built in 1852 into a fanciful Queen Anne–style building with a turret and columned porticos that frame dramatic river views. Interiors were designed by Joseph Burr Tiffany, who incorporated several exquisite stained glass windows made by his cousin, Louis Comfort Tiffany. Ground floor rooms are decorated in two contrasting styles that were popular at the time, Revival and Romantic.

The gardens, though, are pure romance, designed by Calvert Vaux, who also landscaped Central Park in New York City. There is an intricate network of carriage drives, walks and trails adorned with specimen trees and ornamental shrubs, and gazebos placed at spots that provide picture-postcard views of the Hudson River and the Catskills beyond.

The last family member to live at Wilderstein was Margaret Lynch Suckley, who lived there until her death in 1991 at the age of 100. She served as an archivist in the FDR Library and often worked with the President on his papers at nearby Hyde Park. She gave FDR the Scottie, Fala, who became his close companion. She also was FDR's distant cousin, whom he called "Daisy," and was with him when he was fatally stricken at Warm Springs, Georgia, in 1945.

Staatsburg

MILLS MANSION
845-889-8851.
Old Post Rd. (off Rte. 9),
  Staatsburg, NY 12580.
Open: Apr. 1–Labor Day:
  Wed.–Sat. 10am–5pm,
  Sun. 12noon–5pm; Labor
  Day–late Oct.: Wed.–Sun.
  12noon–5pm.; grounds
  open year-round until
  dusk.
Admission: $5.

Located on property acquired in 1792 by New York's third governor, Morgan Lewis and his wife, Gertrude Livingston (see Clermont below), this 79-room Beaux Arts mansion was the country estate of Ruth Livingston and her husband, financier and philanthropist, Ogden Mills from 1890 to 1929. Even though he was wealthy, it was "new" money. Livingston family members helped write the Declaration of Independence and accepted the sword of surrender at the Battle of Yorktown, ending the Revolutionary War. The house and its 1,400 surrounding acres remained Livingston property — hers— highly unusual in those days.

Ruth was the social doyenne of the Hudson Valley, and the house was built for grand, lavish entertaining. The 30-foot by 50-foot dining room contains a 32-foot table that seats 24, walls are covered by Belgian tapestries, and the ceiling is gilded. Dinner guests would gather in an adjoining room, and at the proper moment, a servant would pull back the pocket doors for a dramatic first look at the ornate room and the ornately set table. Even the butler's pantry was plush, with an oak-paneled Mosler safe for the family silver and oak paneling all the way to the 20-foot ceilings. Family portraits in gilded frames — her family mostly — line the entry hall, paneled in English oak with baronial-carved moldings.

Ruth's bedroom is a huge, airy corner room overlooking the Hudson River, with raspberry silk walls and Lalique chandeliers. Mills's adjoining suite, on the other side of a bathroom with a clawfoot tub, is more sedate. The rooms have been refurbished recently, guided by photographs of the house in its heyday.

Walk down the long sloping lawn to the river, for a close-up view of the Esopus Meadows Lighthouse (see "Lighthouses" below).

COLUMBIA COUNTY

Germantown

CLERMONT
518-537-4240.
www.friendsofclermont.org.
One Clermont Ave. (off
  Woods Rd.),
  Germantown, NY 12526.
Open: Apr. 1–Oct. 31:
  Tues.–Sun. 11am–5pm;
  Nov. 1–Dec. 15: weekends

This was the first of the great riverfront estates, standing on land awarded to the family in 1686. It was the family seat of seven generations of the prominent Livingston family until 1962. Actually, the word "prominent" is an understatement. The Livingstons helped draft and signed the Declaration of Independence and served as military officers, gov-

Seven generations of Livingstons lived at Clermont, on land awarded to the family in 1686.

Tania Barricklo

only; grounds open year-round until dusk.
Admission: Adult $3; senior $2; ages 5–12 $1.

ernors, and ambassadors. Patriarch Robert Livingston was minister to France and negotiated the Louisiana Purchase. He also bankrolled the young developer of the steamship, Robert Fulton, whose first working ship on the Hudson River was known as the *Clermont*.

The original house was burned by the British during the Revolutionary War, rebuilt, and expanded. Outside, it is a simple, even plain, white structure. Inside, however, is a sumptuous mix of Colonial, Federal, and Victorian furnishings and artifacts of the family's political and social activities, including framed letters from Napoleon and General Andrew Jackson. The dining room is the only room in the house that was never electrified — the family always dined by candlelight. The oak-lined library contains part of a collection of 5,000 volumes, some dating to the 1600s — at one time, only Thomas Jefferson's library at Monticello was larger. There also are sculptures by Alice Livingston and paintings by Montgomery Livingston, one of the Hudson River School of artists. Front hallways are lined with portraits of multiple generations.

The house sits amid 500 acres, including four formal gardens and walking trails, and is framed by towering locust trees that are several hundred years old.

Hudson

OLANA
518-828-0135.

Frederic Church was the most famous artist in the U.S. in his time and one of the founders of

www.olana.org.
Rte. 2, Hudson, NY 12534.
Open: Apr. 1–May 31:
Wed.–Sun. 10am–4pm;
June 1–Sept. 30:
Wed.–Sun. 10am–5pm;
Oct. 1–Nov. 1: Wed.–Sun.
10am–4pm; closed rest of
year.
Admission: Adult $5; senior
and ages 5–12 $3.

the Hudson River School of Art. Church, a ninth generation New Englander, was born into wealth. His father, a Massachusetts businessman, owned, among other things, a paper mill in Lee.

Church purchased a 126-acre farm south of Hudson directly across the river from his former art teacher, Thomas Cole (see Cedar Grove below), after his artist's eye recognized "views most beautiful and wonderful." The house is on a promontory above a bend in the river, so the view from the front porch looks directly south, straight down the Hudson. Another porch faces directly west to the green-black distant Catskills, framed by arched columns. Church planted trees and designed the five miles of carriage roads to frame the vistas.

He designed this Moorish/Persian-influenced house and grounds the same way he designed his romantic and mysterious landscapes, with pencil sketches followed by more finished color sketches. Instead of painting the final work of art, he built it, choosing and mixing on his palette the colors for every room and overseeing the placement of furnishings.

Construction and decoration took 20 years. The result is a work of art by an artist. Church collected 17th-century masters, and the Renaissance paintings cover the two-story dining room walls, making the room look like a Venetian loggia. Church also painted myriad pastoral scenes from Olana, inspired by the dark mysterious woodlands and water reflected in the sunlight beyond his studio windows.

Tours are limited to 12 persons, and tickets can sell out early in the afternoon, so get there early.

WEST SIDE OF THE HUDSON

ULSTER COUNTY

Marlboro

GOMEZ MILL HOUSE
845-236-3126.
www.gomez.org.
Mill House Rd. (off Rte.
9W), Marlboro, NY
12542.
Open: Wed.–Sun.
10am–4pm.
Admission: $4.

This is the oldest surviving Jewish homestead in the United States, and its subsequent owners — five families in all — also are historically significant. Artifacts from all these families make this an amazing look at the history of a region — indeed, a nation.

Luis Moses Gomez arrived from Europe in 1695 and 10 years later received from Queen Anne of England a certificate called an Act of Denization, giving him the right to own property and to conduct business without pledging allegiance to the

Church of England. A copy of that certificate in Latin is displayed in the house. Gomez established himself as a merchant in New York and the new-world Colonies, trading mostly with other Jewish merchants in France and the Caribbean. He was one of seven Jewish leaders who helped finance the steeple construction at Trinity Church near Wall Street and the construction of America's oldest Jewish congregation, Shearith Israel in New York.

In 1714, he moved to Marlboro, built a stone house, a sawmill, and a grist-mill, and began trading timber, milled limestone, and furs to house and clothe a growing City of New York. Gomez Mill House contains rare 17th-century Jewish artifacts, including a brass holiday menorah. After his death in 1748, the house and its 800 acres were sold to Dutch patriot Wolvert Acker; local revolutionaries met here regularly, and Acker served in the militia. His family bible is on display.

In 1835, wealthy and aristocratic Edward Armstrong bought much of the property and built an imposing Greek-style waterside mansion (now the site of a utility generating plant). One of his sons, Harry, preferred a simpler life and moved into the bucolic Mill House in 1862 with his bride. A tireless gentleman farmer, he raised fruit, racehorses, and purebred pointers.

The next owner, arriving in 1912, was an "escapee" from the increasingly mechanized world. Dard Hunter was a leader of the Arts and Crafts movement, which advocated handmade items in simple forms. He was a skilled cabinetmaker, papermaker, and printer; his hand-carved type is in the Smithsonian Institution, and his books on papermaking are considered classics. Hunter rebuilt the decayed gristmill into a paper mill in the style of an English cottage, with a thatched roof, and restored the original Gomez fireplaces and stained glass windows.

The last family, Jeffrey Starin and his wife Mildred, bought the house in 1948 on a GI Bill mortgage. Inside, they found chandeliers by Gustav Stickley, a 19th-century chair, and more. Realizing the historical importance, they preserved the property, creating the foundation that now runs it as a historical landmark and museum.

GREENE COUNTY

Catskill

CEDAR GROVE
518-943-7465.
www.thomascole.org.
218 Spring St., Catskill, NY 12414.
Open: Fri.–Sun. 10am–4pm; and by appt.
Admission: $4.

This was the home and studio of Thomas Cole, regarded as the founder of the Hudson River School of Art and America's most prominent landscape painter of the late 1800s. In the early 1900s, one of his students, Frederic Church, who became even more famous, built his home and studio, Olana (see above), directly across the Hudson River in Hudson.

Hudson River School of Art founder Thomas Cole painted the view from his home, Cedar Grove.

Evelyn Kanter

Their landscape paintings helped create a tourist industry, as visitors sought to see for themselves the beauty, energy, and mystery of the vistas depicted by the Hudson River artists. Cole also was an early environmentalist and wrote widely on the need to conserve the land — and its landscapes — for future generations.

Cole came to the Hudson Valley in the 1830s via a wealthy patron, a native of nearby Coxsackie, who commissioned Cole to paint a series of works for his home. Cole rented a studio on an 83-acre farm and orchard nearby, fell in love with the farmer's daughter, and moved into the farmhouse he renamed Cedar Grove for its grand stand of majestic trees. They raised five children in the house, which remained the family home until the 1960s. The allegorical series Cole painted for his patron traced the course of civilization. The first, the *Course of Empire,* was exhibited publicly and made him an instant celebrity.

The yellow clapboard, Federal-style house is simple outside and inside, the exact opposite of Cole's lush paintings. There are many family heirlooms, even Cole's most popular painting, which sits atop a steamer trunk in his bedroom. His studio contains his six-foot-tall easel for his mural-sized paintings and Greek and Roman bust sculptures that he used as models. There are two galleries: one on Cole's work, another containing the works of other Hudson River School artists.

The house was restored in 2000 and opened to the public in 2001 to focus attention on the environmental movement.

Coxsackie

BRONCK MUSEUM
518-731-6490.
www.gchistory.org.

There are 11 remaining structures on what was the Bronck family farm, built on land purchased in 1662 from the local Mohican tribe by

Rte. 9W, Coxsackie, NY 12051.
Open: Mem. Day weekend–Oct. 15: Tues.–Sat. 10am–4pm, Sun. 1pm–5pm.
Admission: Adult $4; senior $3.50; ages 12–15 $2; ages 5–11 $1.

Pieter Bronck. The original 20-foot by 20-foot portion of the main house dates from 1663 and is the oldest in Greene County and one of the oldest in New York State — the family already had lived here for 113 years when the Declaration of Independence was written.

Pieter was a cousin of Jonas Bronck, who owned a large estate in what is now New York City; the Bronck's estate has been called The Bronx for the last three centuries. Pieter, though, was a tavern owner in Albany, 20 miles away, and may have moved here to the wilderness to trade in fur pelts with the Mohicans; the Bronck house was built along a main north-south walking trail.

Eight generations of Broncks lived here, expanding the original structure into a sprawling architectural mix that traces the social and economic development of the Hudson Valley. The original single-room stone house was utilitarian — protection from the elements. In 1738, Pieter's grandson built his house a few feet from the 1663 dwelling and connected them. The addition possesses the rawboned elegance of classic Dutch Colonial dwellings, with patterned brickwork, double Dutch doors, and a steep sloping roof. Later additions reflect the growing prosperity of the family; by the early 1800s, this was the single most valuable property in the county.

Most of the furnishings in the house, such as the mahogany table and chairs in the dining room, are from the 1800s, but there are some family heirlooms from the 1700s, including a carved, gilded mirror from the 1720s in the drawing room. That room also contains a portrait of Leonard Bronck, a member of the Revolutionary War militia; he and his father supplied food to the troops and were active in politics. Leonard was the first judge in Greene County.

Other farm structures have been turned into minimuseums, focusing on a particular period. The barn exhibits clothing, silver, and a carved rosewood piano organ from the Victorian era.

HISTORIC HOMES

In addition to the magnificent estates and manor homes in the Hudson Valley, there are numerous additional historic homes worth visiting, many with Revolutionary War history. Since the earliest homes were built on main stagecoach thoroughfares that grew into main automotive routes, such as the Old Albany Post Rd., their prime locations made them targets of modern real estate developers. Several of these historically and architecturally significant houses have been saved from being razed. Some are house museums, and others have become the homes of local historical societies, which usually offer small historical exhibits.

EAST SIDE OF THE HUDSON

WESTCHESTER COUNTY

Chappaqua

HORACE GREELEY HOUSE/NEW CASTLE HISTORICAL SOCIETY
914-238-4666.
106 King St., Chappaqua, NY 10514.
Open: Tues.–Thurs. 1pm–4pm, Sat. 12noon–4pm.
Admission: Donation.

The summer home of Horace Greeley, who, as editor of the influential *New York Tribune*, crusaded against slavery and in favor of women's rights; he is credited by some for making slavery a front page, national issue. He also was a presidential candidate in 1872, but may be most famous for urging the westward expansion of the U.S. with his slogan, "Go west, young man; go west!" Exhibits in the house focus both on Greeley and local history.

Hastings-on-Hudson

JASPER F. CROPSEY HOME AND STUDIO
914-478-1372.
49 Washington Ave., Hastings-on-Hudson, NY 10706.
Open: By appt. only.
Admission: Donation.

Cropsey was a prominent member of the Hudson River School of Art, whose lush and darkly romantic landscapes defined American art in the late 1800s. Cropsey also was an architect who designed part of the New York City subway system. The house is Gothic, with Victorian furnishings, plus an enormous collection of Cropsey's paintings and sketches.

Katonah

CARAMOOR CENTER FOR MUSIC AND THE ARTS
914-232-5035.
www.caramoor.org.
149 Girdle Ridge Rd., Katonah, NY 10536.
Open: May–Oct.: Wed.–Sun. 1pm–4pm; and by appt.
Admission: Adult $7; ages to 17 free.

Caramoor is world-renowned for the annual outdoor International Music Festival held on its expansive grounds (see Chapter Five, *Arts & Pleasures*). The grounds overshadow the astonishing mansion built by financier Walter Tower Rosen to house his international art collection, which includes sculptures, tapestries, porcelain, and paintings from medieval Europe and ancient China. The house was created by taking entire rooms from European villas and palaces and placing them inside a Mediterranean-style shell. The music room is from an Italian Renaissance villa, and one bedroom is from an Alpine cottage. The Venetian Theater, where indoor concerts are held, dates from the 15th century. The 117-acre estate also contains beautiful landscaped grounds and gardens.

**THE JOHN JAY
  HOMESTEAD**
914-232-5651; 914-232-5969.
400 Jay St. (Rte. 22),
  Katonah, NY 10536.
Open: First Wed. in
  Apr.–last Sun. in Nov.:
  Mon.–Sat. 10am–4pm,
  Sun. 12noon–4pm;
  grounds open year-
  round until dusk.
Admission: Adult $3; senior
  $2; ages 5–12 $1.

This 18th-century farmhouse was the residence of the president of the Continental Congress and America's first Chief Justice, plus four generations of decendents. Jay retired here in 1801, and although there is ample memorabilia of the Republic's earliest years, furnishings and decorative items reflect more of succeeding generations. There are two formal gardens and an herb garden.

Rye

JAY HERITAGE CENTER
914-698-9275.
www.jayheritagecenter.org.
210 Boston Post Rd., Rye,
  NY 10580.
Open: House: Sun. only
  2pm–5pm; museum:
  Mon.–Fri. 10am–4pm.
Admission: House $3;
  museum free.

This is the site of John Jay's boyhood home, and he is buried on the property. The house was rebuilt in 1838 by one of his sons as a Greek Revival. The house is open for tours; the main historical exhibit is in the Carriage House.

DUTCHESS COUNTY

Beacon

Evelyn Kanter

*Woman in slave costume, Philipsburg Manor (see page 183).
Slavery was finally abolished in New York State in 1827.*

**MADAME BRETT
  HOMESTEAD**
845-831-6533.

Seven generations of the Brett family lived in this house, built by Roger and Catheryna Brett.

50 Van Nydeck Ave., Beacon, NY 12508.
Open: First Sun. each month 12noon–4pm; and by appt.
Admission: Donation.

Widowed early, Madame Brett was a fiercely independent woman who managed the 28,000-acre estate while raising three sons. She also operated a mill and formed the first producer's cooperative to bring goods to New York City. The property is believed to have been a storage center for military supplies during the Revolutionary War, and Madame Brett hosted visits from George Washington, the Marquis de Lafayette, and the Baron von Steuben.

Built originally in 1709, this is Dutchess County's oldest home; the town of Beacon grew around it. It features handmade scalloped shingles, sloped dormers, Dutch doors, and a significant amount of original furnishings, including China-trade porcelain and a rare, carved canopy bed. In 1954, the house was scheduled to be razed to make way for a supermarket, but was saved by the Daughters of the American Revolution. The property's six acres include a restored Dutch garden.

MOUNT GULIAN
845-831-8172.
145 Sterling St., Beacon, NY 12508.
Open: Apr.–Oct.: Wed.–Fri., Sun. 1pm–5pm;
Nov.–Dec.: Wed., Sun. 1pm–5pm; closed rest of year.
Admission: Adult $5; ages 6–17 $3.

Mount Gulian is historically significant because of its role during the Revolutionary War. Built between 1730 and 1740 by Gulian Verplanck, a prominent Dutch merchant, the house served as the headquarters of America's General von Steuben. It was here that our country's first veterans' organization, the Society of the Cincinnati, was formed by officers of the Continental Army. Mount Gulian is the official headquarters of the society, which is still in existence.

The house is also architecturally significant, with a gambrel roof that slopes downward and outward like a bell to form the veranda roof and double chimneys on either side of the house. There is also a formal English garden designed in 1804.

Fishkill

VAN WYCK HOMESTEAD/ FISHKILL HISTORICAL SOCIETY
845-896-9560.
www.vanwyckhomestead.com.
Rtes. 9 and I-84, Fishkill, NY 12524.
Open: Mem. Day–Oct. 31: weekends 1pm–4pm; and by appt.
Admission: Donation.

Built by Cornelius Van Wyck in 1732, this Dutch Colonial house served as General Israel Putnam's headquarters from 1776–1783 and was the main northern supply depot for Revolutionary War troops. British double agent Enoch Crosby was tried here (he was held prisoner down the road at the Dutch Reformed Church and escaped). Crosby's story and the house are believed to have been the inspiration for James Fenimore Cooper's *The Spy*.

The house features 18th-century furnishings,

portraits of prominent Hudson Valley residents, some archaeological finds, and an extensive genealogical and Revolutionary War library. Guides are sometimes in period costumes, and there are craft demonstrations.

Poughkeepsie

SPRINGSIDE LANDSCAPE RESTORATION
845-471-0183.
185 Academy St.,
  Poughkeepsie, NY 12601.
Open: Daily dawn to dusk
  self-guided tours.
Admission: Donations
  accepted.

This was the summer home of Matthew Vassar, a prosperous Poughkeepsie brewer and founder of Vassar College. At the time of his death in 1868, he had spent more than $100,000, a small fortune in those days, to turn the farm into a remarkable landscaped estate. He hired influential landscape designer Andrew Jackson Downing, who died in a Hudson River steamship fire as he was finishing Vassar's plans and was beginning the landscape design of The Mall in Washington, D.C. Springside is the only surviving Downing landscape in America (many more landscape designs by his protégé, Frederick Law Olmsted, survive) and is a rare opportunity to study and to enjoy the way Downing tempered severe rock outcroppings with round-headed trees and open meadows. Although the house is gone, the Downing-designed gatehouse survived years of vandalism and neglect, and the property was declared a National Historic Landmark in 1969.

COLUMBIA COUNTY

Kinderhook

LINDENWALD
518-758-9689.
Old Post Rd. (Rte. 9H),
  Kinderhook, NY 12106.
Open: May–Oct.:
  Wed.–Sun. 10am–4pm;
  grounds open until dusk
  year-round.
Admission: Adult $3; ages
  to 17 free.

The two-story Georgian brick house, completed in 1797, stands on land once owned by ancestors of Martin Van Buren, eighth U.S. President and the first president born under the U.S. flag. Van Buren, who was born in Kinderhook, had been a New York State senator and attorney general before becoming Andrew Jackson's Vice-President, and then President. After being defeated in 1844 for a second term, he retired here and renovated and expanded the house in a jumble of Federal, Italianate, and Victorian styles. Furnishings are Victorian, including red tufted armchairs, French wallpaper depicting hunting scenes, and a collection of personal and presidential memorabilia, including portraits of personal friends, such as Thomas Jefferson. Van Buren turned the 220 acres into a working farm and added formal gardens and wooded paths, describing himself in the 1859 census as a farmer.

Van Buren is buried nearby in Kinderhook. For the century after his death, the house served as a private residence, a nursing home, and an antiques shop. It became part of the National Park Service in the 1970s and has been restored.

LUYKAS VAN ALEN HOUSE
518-758-9256.
Broad St. (Rte. 9H),
  Kinderhook, NY 12106.
Open: Mem. Day–Labor
  Day: Thurs.–Sat.
  11am–5pm, Sun.
  1pm–5pm.

The Columbia Historical Society operates both the Luykas Van Alen House and the one-room Ichabod Crane Schoolhouse on the grounds. The Van Alen House is a Dutch farmhouse dating from 1737, with a steep-pitched roof and filled with Colonial furniture and furnishings. If you get a case of déjà vu, it's because the house was used in Martin Scorsese's film of the Edith Wharton novel, *The Age of Innocence.*

Ichabod Crane was a schoolteacher, and Washington Irving supposedly based the "Legend of Sleepy Hollow" character on Crane, or at least used the man's name. The Schoolhouse has been restored to appear as it did in the 1920s, rather than when Ichabod Crane taught there.

WEST SIDE OF THE HUDSON

ROCKLAND COUNTY

Nyack

EDWARD HOPPER HOUSE
845-358-0774.
82 N. Broadway, Nyack,
  NY 10960.
Open: Year-round:
  Thurs.–Sun. 1pm–5pm;
  and by appt.
Admission: Free; donations
  encouraged.

This is the birthplace and boyhood home of the eminent realist painter, one of the more popular American artists of the first half of the 20th century. Hopper was born in the house in 1882. Many of his paintings portray images of Nyack, and one of the rooms in the restored 1858 house, which was built by his grandfather, is devoted to materials about his life and work in the riverside town.

The house also functions as a community arts and cultural center, and concerts and theatrical performances are given in the garden in warm weather months.

Tappan

DEWINT HOUSE
845-359-1359.
www.nymasons.org.
20 Livingston Ave., Tappan,
  NY 10983.

George Washington used this house as his headquarters periodically during the Revolutionary War; he was here in 1780, during the spy trial of British spy Major John André (he conspired with Benedict Arnold and was hanged). Washington

Open: Year-round: daily 10am–4pm.
Admission: Free; donations encouraged.

stayed here at the end of the war in 1783 to meet with Sir Guy Carlton, his counterpart in the British army, to discuss evacuation of the defeated British troops.

The house was built in 1700 by one of 17 Dutch patentees for the area, who shared the land to farm in common. John DeWint is believed to have been the third owner of the house, which was purchased by the Masons in 1932 to commemorate Washington's participation in the fraternal organization. The house and adjoining carriage house are filled with authentic 18th-century furniture, including rope beds, bed warmers, spinning wheels, and an unrestored bridal chest.

A perennial garden is planted with more than 2,000 tulips in the spring to commemorate the house's Dutch heritage.

ORANGE COUNTY

Campbell Hall

BULL STONE HOUSE
845-496-2855.
183 County Rd. 51, Campbell Hall, NY 10916.
Open: Mon.–Sat. by appt.
Admission: $1.

This fieldstone homestead was built by stone-mason William Bull in 1722 and has been lived in continuously by the Bull family for eight generations. The family has annual reunions, with as many as 500 descendents gathered on the lawns and gardens. The 10-room, two-story house is filled with original furnishings from Colonial, Federal, Victorian, and more current periods.

Constitution Island

WARNER HOUSE
845-446-8676.
Constitution Is., NY 10996.
Open: Wed., Thurs.
Admission: Reservations required and can be made only by telephone; only access to island is from U.S. Military Academy at West Point.

The island, the house, and the Warner family are all historically significant. Part of a 10,000-acre grant from the British Crown to the Philipse family, which once owned nearly all of what is now Westchester County in the 17th century (see Philipsburg Manor above), it was the site where George Washington chose to defend the Hudson Highlands, which involved constructing a 40-ton iron chain across the river from West Point, just across the narrow channel, to sabotage invading British warships (see Chapter One, *History*).

In 1836, New York City attorney Henry Warner, a widower, was visiting his brother, West Point's chaplain, and decided the deserted island would be an ideal spot for a summer home for himself, his two teenaged daughters, and his sister. He bought the island and added an eight-room Victorian wing with high ceilings onto an abandoned Revolutionary War barracks. The family later moved here year-round.

As adults, the sisters commuted to West Point by boat and taught Bible classes to cadets. Both gained prominence as authors, but Anna Warner is best known for having written the lyrics to the hymn "Jesus Loves Me," and they are the only civilians buried in the West Point Cemetery; at Anna's funeral in 1909, cadets Dwight D. Eisenhower and George W. Patton would have been part of the military escort.

The house is filled with family and mementoes and West Point memorabilia, plus 6,000-year-old tools uncovered in archaeological digs on the island. Guides are dressed in 18th- and 19th-century costumes.

Newburgh

CRAWFORD HOUSE
845-561-2585.
189 Montgomery St.,
 Newburgh, NY 12550.
Open: June–Oct.: Sun.
 1pm–4pm; and by appt.
Admission: Donation.

Built in 1830 and modeled after English country houses of the Palladian tradition, this house contains the largest collection of Hudson River School paintings in the area, plus steamboat models and a spectacular view of Newburgh Bay.

ULSTER COUNTY

Kingston

**FRED J. JOHNSTON
 MUSEUM**
845-339-0720.
63 Main St., Kingston, NY
 12401.
Open: May–Oct.: Sat., Sun.
 1pm–4pm.
Admission: None;
 handicap access.

The Johnston House is a treasury of 18th- and early 19th-century furniture, porcelain, and artwork, displayed like jewels in eight elegant rooms in a sparkling 1812 Federal-style house. Fred J. Johnston was a nationally noted antiques dealer, who loved to entertain and show off his collection of antiques; the house was both his home and his showroom. At his death in 1893, Johnston left the house and its treasure trove of contents to the Friends of Historic Kingston.

Adjacent to the Johnston House is a gallery space with changing exhibits of local history, a research archives, and a museum gift shop.

LIGHTHOUSES

For nearly 200 years, until the railroads arrived in the late 1800s, the Hudson River was the main transportation route linking New York City with Albany, and via the Erie Canal, the cities of the Great Lakes and the Midwest.

Starting with the dugouts of the Mohican and Algonquin tribes through Henry Hudson's *Half Moon*, Robert Fulton's steamships, today's supertankers and barges, river traffic in the Hudson Valley has been nonstop.

During the late 1700s and early 1800s, cities along the Hudson River, upriver from New York City, were major shipping ports, including Yonkers, Kingston, Saugerties, and Albany. There were eight lighthouses, built in the 1830s, each placed to protect shipping from dangerous shoals, a major directional shift, or an unexpected narrowing of the shoreline — seven remain standing. The lighthouses were lighted by whale oil, and the keeper and his family lived in the attached dwelling section. The lighthouses have been decommissioned, and several have been turned into museums, even a bed-and-breakfast. Historic and picturesque are apt descriptions.

The ninth act of the first U.S. Congress created the United States Lighthouse Establishment, which took over jurisdiction of existing lighthouses operated by private owners and individual colonies. More recently, the lighthouses were operated by the U.S. Coast Guard and became automated in the 1950s. Now they are National Historic Landmarks, most restored and operated by local nonprofit groups. Heading north from New York City, the lighthouses are the following:

Hudson River lighthouses were in use until the early 1900s.

Tania Barricklo

THE LITTLE RED LIGHTHOUSE
No telephone.
Open: Not open to the public.

This is the southernmost lighthouse, a beacon of color directly under the George Washington Bridge linking Washington Heights of northern Manhattan across to New Jersey's Palisades. Built to guide shipping away from Jeffrey's Hook, the lighthouse was replaced in the 1920s by navigation lights on the bridge. It was due to be torn down, but was saved by the community. The Little Red Lighthouse is the star of a children's book by the same name. The lighthouse is accessible by foot or bicycle from the riverfront Greenway Trail.

THE TARRYTOWN LIGHTHOUSE
914-242-727.
Kingsland Point Park,
Palmer Ave., N.
Tarrytown, NY 10591.
Open: Call for hours.

Tarrytown Lighthouse is just north of the Tappan Zee Bridge, a white tower jutting into the Hudson River from a stone outcropping on the eastern shore. It was decommissioned in 1965, and Westchester County turned it into a museum to illustrate what life was like in a lighthouse a century ago; logbooks, photographs, and furniture are displayed. Guided tours are available.

STONY POINT BATTLEFIELD LIGHTHOUSE
845-786-2521.
Stony Point Battlefield,
Park Rd. (off Rte. 9W),
Stony Point, NY 10980.
Open: Apr. 15–Oct. 31.

This lighthouse is not on the river, but on a bluff above it, on the site of a successful 1779 midnight assault commanded by Brigadier General Anthony Wayne against a British garrison. It was built in 1826 and contains a museum.

ESOPUS MEADOWS LIGHTHOUSE
845-297-1569.

Esopus Meadows was built at the mouth of the Esopus Creek to warn mariners of the mudflats to the west of the opening. It cost $6,000 to build in 1839 at the end of a timber pier. Fifty years later, after being battered by flood tides and ice floes, it was replaced by a new structure built on a stone base and remains the only Hudson River lighthouse constructed with a wood frame, mansard roof, and clapboard exterior. It actually looks like a private home with a lighthouse tower. It was operated by the U.S. Coast Guard from 1939 until it was closed in 1965 and its light automated. It is now operated by the Save Esopus Lighthouse Commission, which is restoring the building into a bed-and-breakfast, small museum, and research library. Best viewed from the lawn of the Mills Mansion in Staatsburg (see above) or Lighthouse Park, River Rd., Port Ewen, NY.

KINGSTON-RONDOUT LIGHTHOUSE
845-338-0071.
www.hrmm.org.
One Rondout Landing,
Kingston, NY 12401.
Open: June–Sept. cruises.

At the mouth of Rondout Creek is the "twin sister" of the Esopus Meadows Lighthouse, three miles to the south. The original wooden structure, built in 1838, was so battered by the elements that it had to be replaced 30 years later. The first structure cost $5,000, and the replacement, constructed of local bluestone, cost $22,000; its six-light beam could be seen for 11 miles. In the 1870s, the Army Corps of Engineers built two dikes at the entrance of Rondout Creek, changing the direction and flow of the river, making the lighthouse unusable. It was dismantled, and the light was shipped to Bristol, Rhode Is., where it was used until 1953. That was the second Rondout Lighthouse — the third one, constructed in 1915, is the newest and largest of the Hudson River lighthouses. It has an affixed white light that flashes every six seconds and an automatic fog signal. The lighthouse is now part of the Hudson River Maritime Museum in Kingston (see Chapter Five, *Arts & Pleasures*), which operates cruises to the structure.

SAUGERTIES LIGHTHOUSE
845-247-0656 (ferry service from Waterfront Park, East Bridge, Saugerties).
www.saugertieslighthouse.com.
Open: Mem. Day–Labor Day: weekends, holidays; and by appt.

The first Saugerties Lighthouse was built in 1838 on a timber-framed pier at the mouth of the Esopus Creek, lighted by five whale oil lamps with parabolic reflectors. It was replaced in the 1860s by a sturdier structure, constructed on a stone foundation that stands today. Its huge Fresnel lens, fueled with kerosene, directed traffic when Saugerties was a busy passenger port, with daily boats to New York City and ferries across the river to Tivoli. In 1888, the harbor was enlarged by building jetties, and the island lighthouse became connected to the mainland — this is the only Hudson River lighthouse that visitors can walk to, except during high tide. The U.S. Coast Guard automated the light in 1954 and sealed the building, which deteriorated further until 1985, when the nonprofit Saugerties Lighthouse Conservancy began renovation, including restoring the light. There is a museum and two second-floor bedrooms, available for an overnight stay with advance reservation. The conservancy also maintains a nature trail around the marsh and shore meadows, which surround the property.

HUDSON-ATHENS LIGHTHOUSE
518-828-5294.
Two First St., Athens, NY 12015.
Open: Summer tours; call for reservations.

This lighthouse is a dramatic red brick structure trimmed in white, sitting on a sturdy stone island at the southern edge of dangerous shallows in the middle of the Hudson River. Built in 1874, one of the last lighthouses on the river, its design overrides the failures of its southerly sisters. The base was designed so ice floes would not damage the foundation or the structure. The U.S. Coast Guard still operates the light.

CHAPTER SEVEN
For The Fun of It
RECREATION

Cruising on the river on a sunny afternoon.

There are four distinct seasons in the Hudson Valley, each offering a different palette of colors and menu of activities.

In warmer weather, there is hiking along hundreds of acres of trails that thread through richly wooded mountains and along panoramic escarpments and biking on flat, former railroad beds and aqueducts. People who love fishing will find plenty of fight in the fish that ply the Hudson River and the hundreds of valley lakes and streams. Golfers will be challenged by the variety of terrain at various courses. There's swimming in the spring-fed lakes and off sandy beaches alongside the river.

For the serious adventurer, there is rock climbing on some of the premier rock slabs in North America, on the granite faces of "The Gunks." Or, take a kayak for a leisurely paddle and a world-class view of the scenery.

Enjoy the amazing multicolored magic of a Hudson Valley autumn, when leaves burst into red-orange glory, begging to be admired during a stress-relieving picnic lunch. In the winter, grab your cross-country skis or snow-shoes for an invigorating work-out in a picture-postcard setting.

BICYCLING

→ **BICYCLE TRAILS**

There is a regional system of 1,000 miles of multiuse pedestrian/bicycle paths and trailways and auto/bicycle roadways in the Hudson Valley. There are three signed State Bike Routes (5, 9, and 17). Look for the green oval signs featuring a bicycle. The entire 340-mile length of Rte. 9, from New York City to Montreal, is a Greenway bike route; 124 miles are within the Hudson Valley.

Bicycles are permitted on the George Washington Bridge, Bear Mountain Bridge, Newburgh-Beacon Bridge, FDR Mid-Hudson Bridge, and Rip Van Winkle Bridge. Riders are not permitted on the Tappan Zee Bridge, and restrictions apply on the Kingston-Rhinecliff Bridge. Contact the NYS Dept. of Transportation bicycle hot line, 888-NYS-BIKE.

Some especially picturesque or rugged bike areas are the following:

Hereford State Preserve (914-889-4100; access from Taconic State Pkwy., Pleasant Valley) For advanced riders only, with steep terrain and tight single tracks. No trail maps, so advisable to go with a group or another rider familiar with the landscape.

James Baird State Park (845-452-1489; 122D Freedom Rd., access from Taconic State Pkwy., Pleasant Valley) Rolling terrain, good for beginners and families. Trail maps available.

Mills-Norrie Point State Park (845-889-4646; Staatsburg) For advanced riders only, with frequent and difficult hills. Rest stops are rewarding, though, with stunning river views; some of the toughest portions are along the river. Trail maps available, helmets recommended.

Minnewaska State Park Preserve (845-255-0752; www.nysparks.com; Rte. 44/55, New Paltz) Ideal for beginner and intermediate cyclists. Dozens of miles of wide gravel and paved carriage roads, with lots of scenic overlooks, long downhills, and relatively easy uphills. Trails are well marked; trail maps are available; helmets are required.

Mohonk Preserve (845-255-0919; www.mohonkpreserve.org; Rte. 44/55, New Paltz) Adjacent to Minnewaska State Park Preserve, but with more strenuous terrain. More suitable for more experienced riders. Helmets mandatory, trail maps available.

Mount Beacon (off Rte. 9D at Howland Ave., Beacon) This abandoned skiing hill is a downhill rip in some parts, dangerous rock-strewn trail in others.

The tough part is the uphill climb, since the ski lift is gone. No telephone.

Old Croton Aqueduct Trailway State Park (914-693-5259; Croton) Level, gravel track with numerous dramatic panoramas.

Stewart International Airport Buffer Zone (914-564-2100; Newburgh) This strip of state land is designed to muffle airport noise away from surrounding residential areas. Mostly single track trails. A free permit and helmets are required; the area is patrolled by airport security personnel, and fines are issued to those without permits.

BICYCLE CLUBS & TOURS

Mid-Hudson Bicycle Club (914-229-5618; www.mhv.net/~mhbc) Club has organized rides and activities.

Orange County Bicycle Club (845-457-6027; www.sussexonline.com/ocbc) Weekend rides year-round for riders of all ages and levels. Rides combine road cycling and off-trail mountain biking.

DUTCHESS COUNTY

Bikeway (914-297-BIKE; www.bikeway.com; 1173 Rte. 9, Wappingers Falls) Shop offering occasional organized group rides.

Wheel and Heel (914-896-7561; 2275 Rte. 9, Fishkill) Shop offering occasional organized group rides.

ROCKLAND COUNTY

Bicycle Depot (845-735-8686; 9 East Central Ave., Pearl River).

Piermont Bicycle Connection (914-365-0900; 215 Ash St., Piermont).

ORANGE COUNTY

Bryan's Bikes (845-534-5230; 240 Main St., Cornwall).

Joe Fix-Its (845-294-7242; 20 West Main St., Monroe).

ULSTER COUNTY

Benson's Mountain Store (845-255-2999; intersection Rte. 44/55 and Rte. 299, Gardiner).

Bicycle Depot (845-255-3859; www.bicycledepot.com; 15 Main St., New Paltz).

Cycle Path (845-255-8723; www.cyclepathny.com; 138 Main St., New Paltz).

Table Rock Tours & Bicycle Shop (845-658-7832; www.tablerocktours.com; 292 Main St., Rosendale) Shop and organized full-day and half-day tours, mostly off-road, for all levels.

BOATING

The Hudson River was New York's original highway, a waterway busy through the ages, from the dugouts plied by native tribes to today's ferrying of huge barges and tankers between the Atlantic Ocean and the canals leading to the Great Lakes. Shipping on the Hudson is a commercial necessity; boating is simply a joy.

There are dozens of marinas and boat launches — some large enough to accommodate 1,000 pleasure boats and many rent powerboats and jet skis for an afternoon excursion. An excellent source of information on boating on the Hudson is the magazine, *Boating on the Hudson* (914-739-1338; www.boatingonthehudson.com; PO Box, 627, Verplanck, NY 10596).

WESTCHESTER COUNTY

Charles Point Marina (914-736-7370; 5 John Welsh Blvd., Peekskill).
Cortlandt Yacht Club (914-736-3011; 238 Kings Ferry Rd., Montrose).
Half Moon Bay Marina (914-271-5400; www.halfmoonbaymarina.com; Croton-on-Hudson) Located at the edge of the sprawling Croton Point Park.
Tarrytown Marina (914-631-1300; www.tarrytownmarina.com; Tarrytown) This marina is just north of the Tappan Zee Bridge, with a spectacular view and in-town access.
Viking Boatyard (914-739-5090; 50 Kings Ferry Rd., Verplanck).

There are hand-launch sites at Croton Point Park, Croton Point Ave., and Croton-on-Hudson. Trailer-launch sites are located at John F. Kennedy Memorial Park and Marina; in front of the Hudson River Museum on Warburton Ave. and JFK Blvd., Yonkers; and at Peekskill Riverfront Green Park Municipal Launch, Railroad Ave., Peekskill.

PUTNAM COUNTY

Cold Spring Boat Club (845-265-2465; Main St., Cold Spring).
Garrison Landing–Garrison Yacht Club (845-424-3440; Garrison).

DUTCHESS COUNTY

Chelsea Carthage Landing Marina (845-831-5777; Front St., Wappingers Falls).
Hyde Park Marina (845-473-8283; www.hydeparkmarina.com; 31 River Point Rd., Hyde Park) Accommodates vessels up to 200 feet.
Norrie Point Marina (845-889-4200; Mills Norrie State Park, Staatsburg).
White's Hudson River Marina (845-297-8520; New Hamburg) The area's largest marina, with 300 slips.

There is a hand-launch site at Tivoli Bays (off Rte. 9G). Trailer-launch sites are located at the Municipal Launch, Red Flynn Dr., Beacon; at Norrie Point Marina, Staatsburg; at Rhinebeck Landing on Hutton St., Rhinecliff; and at Victor Waryas Park, foot of Main St., Poughkeepsie.

COLUMBIA COUNTY

There are trailer-launch sites at the City of Hudson pier, foot of Water St.; at the end of Anchorage Rd. and at Cheviiot Landing Park (both off Rte. 9G), Germantown.

ROCKLAND COUNTY

Action Marine Services (845-358-6511; 1 Van Houten St., Nyack).
Belle Harbor Marina (845-786-5823; 66 Beach Rd., Stony Point).
Cornetta's Marina (845-359-0410; 641 Piermont Ave., Piermont).
Haverstraw Marina (845-429-2001; www.haverstrawmarina.com; 600 Beach Rd., West Haverstraw) This marina has room for 1,000 boats, has an Olympic-sized swimming pool, and is adjacent to a restaurant complex.
Nyack Boat Club (845-358-9724; Gedney St., Nyack).
Penny Bridge Marina (845-786-5100; www.pennybridgemarina.com; 21 Grassy Point Rd., Stony Point).
Stony Point Bay Marina & Yacht Club (845-786-3700; 29 Hudson Dr., Stony Point).
Tappan Zee Marina (845-359-5522; 845 Piermont Ave., Piermont) Located just south of its namesake, Tappan Zee Bridge.

There is a hand-launch site at Nyack Beach State Park, at the end of N. Broadway, Upper Nyack.

ORANGE COUNTY

Front Street Marina (www.frontstreetmarina.com; Front St., Newburgh) This marina is adjacent to the Riverwalk complex of restaurants and shops. It has the deepest dockage north of the George Washington Bridge.
Gull Harbor Marina (845-561-2637; 2 Washington St., Newburgh).
Highland Falls Marina (845-446-2402; Station Hill Rd., Highland Falls) Just south of West Point at the entrance to the Hudson Highlands.

ULSTER COUNTY

Anchorage Marina (845-338-9899; 182 Canal St., Kingston).
Hideaway Marina (845-331-4655; 170 Abeel St., Kingston).
Kingston Municipal Dock (845-331-6270; end of Broadway, Kingston).
Lynch's Marina (845-246-8290; 2 Ferry St., Saugerties).

Rondout Yacht Basin (845-331-7061; Kingston) Located on the broad and deep Rondout Creek across from downtown Kingston; it has a pool and restaurant access.

Saugerties Marina (845-246-7533; 24 Ferry St., Saugerties).

Shoreline Docking (845-236-3521; Dock Rd., Marlboro).

West Shore Marine Services (845-236-4486; Dock Rd., Marlboro).

There are hand-launch sites at the City of Kingston Docks, West Strand Park; there are trailer launch sites at Charles Ryder Park, Ulster Landing Rd.; at Ulster Park (one mile south of Kingston-Rhinecliff Bridge); and at Kingston Point Boat Launch, Delaware Ave., Kingston.

GREENE COUNTY

Catskill Marina (518-943-4170; 800-747-2720; Catskill) Next to Hop-O-Nose Marina, it has a heated indoor swimming pool.

Forlini's Marina (518-943-3321; West Main St., Catskill) Located next to a restaurant.

Hagar's Harbor (518-945-1858; Athens) This harbor overlooks the picturesque Athens Lighthouse.

Hop-O-Nose Marina (518-943-4460; Catskill) This marina is on the Catskill Creek a few minutes inland from the Hudson River. The old boathouse is now the upscale Solstice restaurant (see Chapter Four, *Restaurants & Food Purveyors*).

There is a hand-launch site at Catskill High School, West Main St., Catskill. Trailer-launch sites are located at Dutchman's Landing, foot of Main St., Catskill; and in Athens where Rte. 385 curves against the Hudson River.

CRUISES & TOURS

Within a few decades after Robert Fulton designed the first successful steamship and sailed it up the Hudson River, the waterway was polka-dotted with cargo shipping, passenger ferries, sight-seeing vessels, and more than a few millionaire's yachts, delivering their owners between homes in New York City and summertime mansions farther north. By the late 1800s, sight-seeing steamers were grand affairs, the larger ones holding as many as 1,000 passengers in their Sunday finery. Then railroads and multilane highways replaced the steamers as travelers' interests became more focused on getting to their destination quickly, rather than admiring the scenery en route.

Still, few things compare with the serenity and beauty of a scenic Hudson River cruise, from the dramatic rock cliff face of the Palisades opposite New York City to the thickly forested rolling hillsides of the Hudson Highlands, the massive fortresslike buildings of West Point, and even the silver slivers of MetroNorth commuter trains darting along the shoreline. There are many opportunities to spend a day on this magnificent river.

Hudson Highlands Cruises (914-534-SAIL; www.commanderboat.com or www.hudsonhighlandcruises.com/history; Peekskill Riverfront Green, Peekskill) On the last Sat. of every month from May–Oct., the historic *Commander* plies the Hudson River on a three-hour narrated cruise through the Hudson Highlands, past West Point, Fort Montgomery, Garrison, Constitution Island, and under the Bear Mountain Bridge. Originally a ferry between Queens and Brooklyn, the *Commander* was pressed into service by the U.S. Navy in WWI to guard the NYC coastline from German Zeppelins and has the distinction of being the last operating vessel that saw service in that war. The *Commander* has been in service as an excursion boat, first with the Rockaway Boat Line in NYC, and then, since 1981, on the Hudson River. Sailing on the *Commander* is simultaneously a historic and a scenic trip. May–Oct. Adult $15; senior, children to age 12 $13; advance reservations required.

Hudson River Adventures (845-782-0685; www.prideofthehudson.com; Newburgh Landing, Newburgh) Narrated sight-seeing tours on the modern 130-passenger *Pride of the Hudson* excursion boat, with both wraparound glass windows on the main deck and an open top deck. This is the official boat for Bannerman Island cruise tours, the historic castle ruins near West Point (see Chapter Five, *Arts & Pleasures*), with a portion of the excursion fee going to support the castle restoration. The Bannerman Island cruise includes a 45-minute historic lecture and video tour of the island; *Pride of the Hudson* passengers do not disembark to tour the island. There also is a more general Hudson River cruise that includes West Point, Storm King Mountain, and other river sites; there are special brunch cruises on holidays, such as Mother's Day. Sailings daily May–Oct. Adult $16; senior and ages 4–11 $15; reservations recommended.

The Rip Van Winkle, *named for one of the Hudson Valley's most famous residents, offers tours of the Hudson River.*

Hudson River Cruises (845-255-6515; 800-843-7472; www.hudsonrivercruises .com; Rondout Landing (end of Broadway), Kingston) The *Rip Van Winkle* is a modern 300-passenger sight-seeing boat that loops from Kingston south to Hyde Park, passing some of the most dramatic riverfront mansions, including the Mills and Vanderbilt mansions, and the Rondout and Esopus Lighthouses — a narrated two-hour tour. There are evening music and dancing cruises for passengers 21 and older (photo ID required) on weekends. May–Oct. Sight-seeing cruises: adults $13; seniors $12, ages 4–11 $6; evening music cruises $20; reservations recommended.

The Hudson River Sloop *Clearwater* (914-454-7673; www.clearwater.org; 112 Market St., Poughkeepsie) Perhaps the most famous vessel on the Hudson River, this sloop was built and is operated by the environmental education organization founded by folk singer Pete Seeger. There are both on-board and land-based educational programs for children and families, as well as sight-seeing tours of the river. The HRS *Clearwater* is a replica of the broad-beamed, shallow-draft Dutch vessels that sailed the waterway for more than a century. Passengers are encouraged to join in hoisting the sails. May–Oct. Sail times, from spots along the river: daily 11:30am, 2:30pm, 6pm; reservations recommended. Adult $25; ages 12 and under $10.

Hudson Valley Riverboat Tours (914-758-4000; www.IMCLTD.com/boat; Sixth St. dock, Verplanck) The *River Queen,* a historic and refurbished 64-foot paddlewheeler, sails from Verplanck north to West Point and south to the Tappan Zee Bridge, passing Bear Mountain and the Tarrytown Lighthouse. July–Aug. and holidays, including Mother's Day and Labor Day. Adults $20; seniors, children $15; reservations required.

New York Waterways (800-533-3779, www.nywaterway.com) This is the largest sight-seeing operator on the Hudson River, with a fleet of dayliners and a full line of cruises from New York City. In addition to harbor cruises along Manhattan Island, there are full-day excursions trips to West Point and Bear Mountain, Washington Irving's Sunnyside and railroad tycoon Jay Gould's Lyndhurst castle, or the Rockefeller family estate at Kykuit and the Phillipsburg Manor Dutch colonial farmstead, with the opportunity to spend the afternoon touring the land attractions and take the boat back to 42nd St. The boats are modern, fast, with both outside and inside seating, snack bar, and excellent historical narration from guides, who have different stories for the northbound and return trips. There's also a weekend package combining the cruise, overnight accommodations at Dolce Tarrytown House, and entry to the estates of Sunnyside, Lundhurst, Kykuit, and Phillipsburg. Or, passengers can join the dayliner at Tarrytown for a North Hudson cruise or at West Point to see the dramatic landscape of the Hudson Highlands. Hudson River cruises are May–Nov.; departure times and prices vary widely. NYC cruises depart from Pier 78 at West 38th St., Manhattan; there is a free NY Waterways bus on both 42nd St. and 34th St. between the subways and the pier. Tarrytown cruises depart from the foot of Main St., and the Highlands cruise departs from South Dock at West Point.

North River Cruises (845-246-8705; West Strand Park, Kingston).

River Rose Cruises (845-562-1067; www.riverrosecruises.com; Newburgh Landing (end of Water St.), Newburgh) A Mississippi-style paddleboat that is a popular weekend brunch activity for families; on summer weekend evenings, they offer a rollicking dance party cruise. Sight-seeing cruises: adults $15, seniors, ages 5–12 $12; dance party cruises $30. Fares range from $15–$30, depending on event.

KAYAK TOURS

Y ou can't get closer to the water unless you're swimming, but the brightly colored flat-bottomed kayaks used by river guides are so stable and easy to maneuver that you have to try really, really hard to tip them over. It's a wonderful perspective, up close and personal as the TV commentators say, and easy for any but the least coordinated to master.

Hudson River Recreation (914-524-0046; 888-321-HUDSON; 215 Palmer Ave., Sleepy Hollow) Guided summer kayak tours.

Hudson Valley Outfitters (845-265-0221; www.hudsonvalleyoutfitters.com; Cold Spring) Kayak rentals, instruction, and tours.

Evelyn Kanter

The calm Hudson River is ideal for kayaking and canoeing.

Hudson Valley Pack & Paddle (845-896-3829; www.hvpackandpaddle.com; 361 Rte. 82, Hopewell Junction; 845-265-2760; 12 Market St., Cold Spring) This organization operates out of two locations. The store, with a full line of touring, recreational, and whitewater paddling gear, is in Hopewell Junction; rental equipment is housed in a waterfront site one block from the MetroNorth train station in Cold Spring. Instruction is offered, of course, but also available are guided excursions to explore Constitution Marsh at West Point or the tidal basin at Tivoli Bays and Norrie Point. HV Pack & Paddle also has teamed with the Bannerman Castle Trust to offer the only guided walking tour of the island's ruins. It's a couple of miles across the water from Plum Point by Newburgh Bay through the breakwater to a protected cove at the island, where one of the trust's two guides dispenses safety hard hats for a one-hour walking tour. Half the $100 fee is donated to the trust for its restoration efforts. Tours and instruction May–Oct., retail store open year-round; reservations required for the Bannerman Island tour.

SAILING

Croton Sailing School (914-271-6868; Senasqua Rd., Croton-on-Hudson) Sailing lessons, rentals.
Great Hudson Sailing Center (845-429-1557; West Strand Park, Kingston) Charters, rentals, and a sailing school.
Riverview Marine Services (518-943-5311; 103 Main St., Catskill) Speedboat and jet ski rentals.

CAMPING & CAMPGROUNDS

PUBLIC PARKS

Campsites in New York State parks (www.nysparks.org) and those within the Palisades Interstate Parks Commission system and county parks tend to be basic, with picnic tables, fireplaces, rest rooms, and shower facilities, often on the edge of a lake or even directly on the Hudson River, but few offer utility hookups. Reservations are required, and they are open seasonally only.

Bear Mountain State Park (845-786-2701; Harriman, NY 10926).
Clarence Fahnestock State Park (845-225-2707; Cold Spring, NY 10516).
Croton Point Park (914-271-3293; Croton-on-Hudson, NY 10520). Cabins available
Harriman State Park, Beaver Pond Campground (845-947-2792; Harriman, NY 10926).
Harriman State Park, Lake Sebago Cabins (845-351-2360; Harriman, NY 10926).
Mills-Norrie Point State Park (845-889-4646; Staatsburg, NY 12581).
Sylvan Lake Beach (845-221-9889; Hopewell Junction, NY 12533).
Taconic State Park (518-789-3059; Millerton, NY 12546).

COMMERCIAL CAMPGROUNDS

These offer more creature comforts, including family activities, and are larger and more crowded than the more secluded park sites. Except where noted, these campgrounds are also seasonal, from Apr. or May to Sept. or Oct. A good resource for Hudson Valley campgrounds is the web address: www.go campingamerica.com.

DUTCHESS COUNTY

Interlake RV Park (845-266-5387; 428 Lake Dr., Rhinebeck, NY 12572) Electric and full hookups, fireplaces, 20-acre lake with boating and fishing, children's play area, recreation building, in-ground pool, and kiddie pool. Open Apr.–Oct.

Snow Valley Campground (845-897-5700; Rte. 9, Fishkill, NY 12524) Tent sites and full hookups, lake with beach for fishing and swimming, recreation building.

Sylvan Lake Beach Park (845-221-9889; County Rte. 10, Beekman, NY 12533) Wooded sites with full hookups, spring-fed lake with beach, swimming, fishing, and boat launch, children's play area.

ORANGE COUNTY

Black Bear Campground (845-651-7717; www.blackbearcampground.com; 197 Wheeler Rd., Florida, NY 10921) Motor home sites and pull-through sites, swimming pool, fishing pond, recreation building, miniature golf, children's playground, free showers. Open year-round.

Winding Hills Park (845-457-4818; Rte. 17K, Montgomery, NY 12549) Tents, trailer, and motor home sites, some electric hookups.

ULSTER COUNTY

Blue Mountain Campground (845-246-7564; 3783 Rte. 32, Saugerties, NY 12477) Electric and full hookups, children's activities, hiking trails, fireplaces, pets allowed. Open Apr.–Oct.

Hidden Valley Lake (845-338-4616; 280 Whiteport Rd., Kingston, NY 12401) Electric and full hookups, children's play area, fireplaces, swimming, fishing, and boating, bird and game sanctuary and hiking trails, pets allowed. Open year-round.

Newburgh KOA (914-564-2836; 800-562-7220; Freetown Hwy., Plattekill, NY 12568) Full hookups and pull-through sites, free cable TV and movies, lake for fishing and boating, swimming pools, miniature golf course.

Rip Van Winkle Campgrounds (845-246-8114; 800-246-8334; 149 Blue Mountain Rd., Saugerties, NY 12477) Electric and full hookups, fireplaces, hiking trails, pets allowed, handicap accessible. Open May–Oct.

Saugerties KOA (845-246-4089; 882 Rte. 212, Saugerties, NY 12477) Electric and full hookups, pool, children's play area, fireplaces, cabins available, pets allowed. Open Apr.–Oct.

Yogi Bear's Jellystone Park Camp-Resort at Lazy River (845-255-5183) Electric and full hookups, canoe rentals, fishing, boat launch site, pool, recreation building, children's play area, pets allowed. Open May–Oct.

FISHING

The Hudson River, environmentally much healthier than in the past, is once again a prime fishing ground. Striped bass can grow as large as three feet and put up quite a fight, and the mountain lakes and streams that feed the river boast a bounty of sport fishing for walleye pike, pickerel, trout, and perch. Yes, the Hudson River Valley is a great fishing destination for anglers.

Fishing is permitted in all state and county-owned streams and lakes, except where signs are posted against trespassing. A New York State fishing license is required for most locations for those over age 16. Call 914-864-PARK for a list of license application locations or the **NYS Dept. of Environmental Conservation** (845-256-3161; 21 S. Putt Corners Rd., New Paltz) for fishing information. For a free guide to hunting and fishing supply shops, call 800-DIAL-UCO.

Hudson Valley lakes and streams lure anglers.

Tania Barricklo/Daily Freeman

A special free permit is required to fish at any of the City of New York reservoirs in the Hudson Valley, and application requires a NYS fishing license. Call 845-657-2213 for information.

In Dutchess County, reliable sources of what is biting when and where are the **Federation of Dutchess Fish and Game Clubs** (845-635-1606) and the **Trout Unlimited Mid-Hudson Chapter** (845-868-7715).

Many bait shops provide licenses. In Orange County, the **O&H Bait Shop** (845-489-2566; 48 Main St., Chester) issues both fishing and hunting licenses. Open daily 6am–5:30pm.

In Columbia County, there is year-round fishing at **Lake Taghkanic State Park** (off Rte. 82, Taghkanic) for such sport fish as chain pickerel, rock bass, brown bullhead, and the occasional American eel has been found in the lake. At **Taconic State Park** (Rte. 344 (off Rte. 22), Copake Falls), Ore Pond is stocked with trout.

The lakes of **Bear Mountain State Park** and **Harriman State Park,** which includes Lake Tiorati, Lake Sebago, and Lake Welch, are all open for fishing. Sterling Lake in **Sterling Forest State Park** has both largemouth and smallmouth bass. The parks, part of the vast **Palisades Interstate Parks Commission,** straddle the county line of Rockland and Orange Counties.

FLY-FISHING GUIDES

Ed's Fly Fishing & Guide Services (845-657-6393; Shokan, NY 12481) Provides certified FFF instruction.

Fly Fishing with Bert & Karen (845-338-8164; 845-658-9784; 1070 Creek Locks Rd., Rosendale, NY 12472) School and guide service.

GOLF

M ost of these golf courses are open March to November, and all of those listed below are open to the public. Call ahead for tee times, of course.

Price Codes:

Inexpensive	Up to $25
Moderate	$25 to $50
Expensive	Over $50

WESTCHESTER COUNTY

Dunwoodie Golf Course (914-231-3490; Wasylenko Ln., Yonkers) 18 holes; par 70; collared shirts; restaurant; snack bar; pro shop; driving range. Moderate.
Mohansic Golf Course (914-962-4049; Baldwin Rd., Yorktown Heights) 18

holes; par 72; no tank tops or cutoffs; restaurant; snack bar; driving range; no credit cards. Moderate.

Pehquenakonck Country Club (914-669-6776; Bloomerside Rd., North Salem) 9 holes; par 35; snack bar; no credit cards. Inexpensive.

Pound Ridge Golf Club (914-764-5771; Highbridge Rd., Pound Ridge) 9 holes; par 35; collared shirts; convenience food; driving range; no credit cards. Inexpensive.

DRIVING RANGES

Fairview Golf Center (914-592-1666; www.fairview-golf.com; 300 Waterside Dr., Emsford) Two 18-hole minigolf courses; 80-stall two-tier heated practice area; pro shop; PGA teaching pros; "swing cam" video machine. Open year-round.

Family Golf Center at Yorktown (914-526-8337; 2710 Lexington Ave., Mohegan Lake) 18-hole minigolf course; 36-stall two-tier heated practice area; pro shop; PGA teaching pros; snack bar.

Sports Underdome (914-663-2323; www.sportsunderdome.com; 657 Garden Ave., Mount Vernon) Indoor, climate-controlled golf field.

Westchester Golf Range (914-592-6553; 701 Dobbs Ferry Rd., White Plains) 75 lighted tees; PGA teaching pros.

PUTNAM COUNTY

Centennial Golf Club (845-225-5700; 185 John Simpson Rd., Carmel) 27 holes; par 72; collared shirts; no denim; restaurant; driving range. Expensive.

Eagle Ridge Country Club (845-628-3451; Hill St., Mahopac) 18 holes; par 72; collared shirts; restaurant; driving range. Moderate-Expensive.

Garrison Golf Club (914-424-3605; Rte. 9, Garrison) 18 holes; par 72; no tank tops or cutoffs; restaurant; snack bar; driving range. Expensive.

Highlands Country Club (845-424-3727; Rte. 9D, Garrison) 9 holes; par 35; collared shirts; no credit cards. Inexpensive.

Sanctuary Country Club (914-962-8050; Rte. 118, Yorktown Heights) 18 holes; par 72; collared shirts; snack bar. Moderate.

DUTCHESS COUNTY

Dinsmore Golf Course (845-889-4112; Rte. 9, Staatsburg) 18 holes; par 72; no tank tops or cutoffs; restaurant; putting green. Inexpensive.

Dogwood Golf Center (845-226-7317; Rte. 376, Hopewell Junction) 9 holes; par 35; no dress code; restaurant. Inexpensive.

Dutcher Golf Course (845-855-9845; 135 E. Main St., Pawling) 9 holes; par 35; no dress code; snack bar, putting green. Inexpensive.

Fishkill Golf Course (845-896-5220; Rte. 9, Fishkill) 9 holes; par 35; soft spikes required; restaurant; snack bar; driving range. Inexpensive.

James Baird State Park Golf Course (845-452-1489; James Baird State Park, Pleasant Valley) 18 holes; par 72; restaurant; snack bar; driving range; Robert Trent Jones, Jr. architect. Inexpensive.

McCann Memorial Golf Course (845-454-1968; 155 Wilbur Blvd., Poughkeepsie) 18 holes; par 72; no tank tops or cutoffs; soft spikes required; amenities restaurant; snack bar; no credit cards. Moderate.

It's hard to concentrate on the ball when the scenery is so lush.

Dutchess County Tourism

Red Hook Golf Club (845-758-8652; RR 2, Red Hook) 18 holes; par 72; collared shirts; no denim; restaurant; practice facility. Moderate.

Vassar Golf Course (845-473-1550; Vassar Campus, Raymond Ave., Poughkeepsie) 9 holes; par 35; no tank tops or cutoffs; snack bar. Inexpensive.

Whispering Pines Golf Club (845-452-4256; Rte. 9, Poughkeepsie) 9 holes; par 35; collared shirts; no denim; restaurant; snack bar; no credit cards. Inexpensive.

ROCKLAND COUNTY

Mill Creek Golf Course (845-236-3160; 900 Rte. 9W, Marlboro; 9 holes; par 35; no tank tops or cutoffs; restaurant; snack bar; driving range; no credit cards. Inexpensive.

Ramapo Spook Rock Golf Course (845-357-6100; 199 Spook Rock Rd., Suffern) 18 holes; par 72; snack bar; restaurant; driving range; no credit cards. Inexpensive.

Rockland Lake State Park Golf Course (845-268-6260; Rte. 9W and Lake Rd., Congers) 36 holes; par 72; collared shirts; no denim; snack bar; driving range. Inexpensive.

Scott's Corners Golf Course (845-457-9141; Rte. 208, Montgomery) 9 holes; par 35; restaurant. Inexpensive.

DRIVING RANGES

9W Golf Range (845-359-1313; Rte. 9W, Palisades) 18-hole minigolf course; 24 practice tees. Open year-round.

ORANGE COUNTY

Central Valley Golf Club (845-928-6924; 206 Smith Clove Rd., Central Valley) 18 holes; par 70; soft spikes preferred; restaurant; putting green; golf shop. Inexpensive.

Golf Club at Mansion Ridge (845-782-7888; 1292 Orange Pike, Monroe) 18 holes; par 72; collared shirts; no denim; restaurant; snack bar; driving range; Jack Nicklaus architect. Expensive.

Monroe Country Club (845-783-9045; 63 Still Rd., Monroe) 9 holes; par 35; collared shirt; restaurant; no credit cards. Moderate.

West Point Golf Course (845-938-2435; Bldg. 1230, West Point Military Academy, West Point) 18 holes; par 72; collared shirts; no denim; snack bar; Robert Trent Jones, Sr., architect. Inexpensive.

Winding Hills Golf Club (845-457-3187; Rte. 17K, Montgomery) 18 holes; par 72; convenience food. Inexpensive.

ULSTER COUNTY

Alapaha Golf Links (845-331-2334; 180 Sawkill Rd., Kingston) 9 holes; par 35; no credit cards; no dress code; no spikes required. Inexpensive.

Apple Greens Golf Course (845-883-5500; 161 South St., Highland) 18 holes; par 71; collared shirt; snack bar; driving range. Moderate.

Hudson Valley Resort (845-626-2972; Granite Rd., Kerhonkson) 18 holes; par 79; collared shirt; no cutoffs; restaurant; driving range; golf school. Moderate.

Katsbaan Golf Club (845-246-8182; 1754 Old Kings Hwy., Saugerties) 9 holes; par 35; no tank tops; no credit cards. Inexpensive.

Mohonk Mountain House Golf Course (845-256-2154; Mohonk Mountain House, New Paltz) 9 holes; par 35; no tank tops or cutoffs; restaurant; snack bar. Inexpensive.

Nevele Grand Hotel (845-647-6000; Nevele Rd., Ellenville) 18 holes; par 72; collared shirts; no denim; restaurant; snack bar; driving range. Tom Fazio architect. Expensive.

New Paltz Golf Course (845-255-8282; 215 Huguenot St., New Paltz) 9 holes; par 36; no tank tops or cutoffs; restaurant; driving range. Inexpensive.

Rondout Country Club (845-626-2513; Whitfield Rd., Accord) 18 holes; par 72; no tank tops or cutoffs; restaurant; snack bar; driving range; no credit cards. Moderate.

Stone Dock Golf Club (845-687-9944; Berne Rd., High Falls) 9 holes; par 36; restaurant. Inexpensive.

Town of Wallkill Golf Club (845-361-1022; 40 Sands Rd., Middletown) 18 holes; par 71; no tank tops or cutoffs; restaurant; driving range. Moderate.

GREENE COUNTY

DRIVING RANGES

Hillsdale Driving Range (845-325-5429; Rte. 23, Hillsdale) 18-hole minigolf course; go-karts. Open daily.

HORSEBACK RIDING

DUTCHESS COUNTY

Cedar Crest Farm (518-398-1034; www.equestcenter.com; 2054 Rte. 83, Pine Plains) Lessons in show-jumping, cross-country, and dressage.
Southlands Foundation (845-876-4862; www.southlands.org; 5771 Rte. 9 South, Rhinebeck) 200 acres along the Hudson River, offering riding lessons, pony rides, and horse shows.
Western Riding Stables (518-789-4848; Sawchuck Rd., Millerton) Trail rides, lessons, overnight pack trips, hayrides, and sleigh rides.

ORANGE COUNTY

Borderland Farm (845-986-1204; 340 South Rte. 94, Warwick) 230-acre riding facility with miles of trails, indoor ring, lighted outdoor track. Reservations required.
Clove Acres Riding Academy (845-496-8655; 299 Mountain Lodge Rd., Monroe) English lessons and riding, pony rides, tack shop.
Gardnertown Farm (845-564-6658; 822 Gardnertown Farm Rd., Newburgh) English only; polo lessons and tournaments. Appt. necessary.
Juckas Stables (845-361-1429; www.juckasstables.com; Rte. 302, Bullville) English or Western; trail rides and lessons, friendly farm atmosphere.
Silent Farms Stables (845-294-0846; Axworthy Ln., Goshen) English and Western; indoor arena, trails, riding lessons. Annual Sept. rodeo.

ULSTER COUNTY

Angel View Farm (845-236-4576; 551 Lattintown Rd., Marlboro) Trail rides and lessons.
Hudson Valley Resort (888-9-HUDSON; www.hudsonvalleyresort.com; Granite Rd., Kerhonkson) Trail rides.

Mohonk Mountain House (800-772-6646; www.mohonk.com; New Paltz) Trail rides and carriage rides through 7,500 historic acres, including the Mohonk Mountain Preserve.

DUDE RANCHES

ULSTER COUNTY

Pinegrove Dude Ranch (800-346-4626; www.pinegrove-ranch.com; Kerhonkson) Family-owned and -oriented resort on 60 acres in the Shawangunk Mountains, with picturesque trails and instruction for all levels and ages. Also, water slide and climbing wall.

Rocking Horse Ranch Resort (800-647-2624; www.rhranch.com; Highland) Year-round resort rated 3 diamonds by AAA, including winter trail rides and sleigh rides on snow and on-property hill for snow-tubing. Handicap accessible.

ICE-SKATING

WESTCHESTER COUNTY

Ebersole Ice Rink (914-422-1348; Lake St., White Plains) Figure skating instruction, ice hockey clinics and leagues. Public skating sessions daily.

New Roc City (914-637-757; Le Count Pl., New Rochelle) Two large rinks, public skating sessions daily, plus figure-skating instruction and hockey clinics.

Playland Ice Casino (914-813-7059; www.ryeplayland.org; Playland Pkwy., Rye) Three temperature-controlled indoor rinks. This is the practice home of the New York Rangers hockey team, with open practice for spectators during the season. Open year-round.

Westchester Skating Academy (914-347-8232; www.skatewsa.com; 91 Fairview Park Dr., Elmsford) Two NHL-sized ice rinks in a temperature-controlled bubble; figure-skating classes and lessons. Open year-round.

DUTCHESS COUNTY

Mid-Hudson Civic Center McCann Ice Arena (845-454-5800; midhudsoncivic-center.com; 14 Civic Center Plaza, Poughkeepsie) Indoor ice-skating arena.

ROCKLAND COUNTY

Palisades Center Ice Rink (845-353-4855: Level 4, Rte. 59, Nyack) Indoor skating rink within huge shopping mall/entertainment complex. Open year-round.

ULSTER COUNTY

Kiwanis Ice Arena (845-246-2591; intersection of Small World and Washington Ave. ext., Saugerties) Indoor arena.

PARKS & NATURE PRESERVES

There are more than 50 state and county parks, wildlife preserves, and nature centers, totaling more than 20,000 acres of woodlands, wetlands, lakes, hiking and biking trails, much of it along the scenic shores of the Hudson River, plus additional parkland operated by New York State and the entities governing the historic mansions.

Some Westchester County parks or certain facilities within them, such as swimming pools or golf courses, require county residency; these are not included in this list. Except where noted, dogs are permitted, but they must be leashed. And, except where noted, parks are open year-round, daily through dusk.

WESTCHESTER COUNTY

Evelyn Kanter

Croton Falls feeds a reservoir that supplies much of New York City's water.

Croton-on-Hudson

Croton Gorge Park (914-827-9568; Rte. 129) This 97-acre park is at the base of the Croton Dam. The huge open lawn with picnic tables at the base of the spillway is a wondrously cool spot on a hot day, cooled by the microsopic waterfall spray, and the sound of the tumbling water is an equally relaxing respite. There is direct access to the Old Croton Aqueduct, for both hiking and biking, and another trail to the top of the overlook to the falls; the Croton Reservoir, south of the falls, supplies much of New York City's water. When it was built in the 1840s, this huge stone dam was considered one of the wonders of the world.

Croton Point Park (914-271-3293; Croton Point Ave.) This expansive park is on a peninsula that juts from the eastern shore of the Hudson River, at one of its widest spots. There are more than 500 acres, including lakes for swimming and boating, hiking trails, playing fields, cabins and tent sites, and children's playgrounds, along nearly four miles of picturesque shoreline, with picnic tables scattered throughout. The park also is the site of caves that are thought to be the oldest wine cellars in New York State. The Croton Point Nature Center, which offers a year-round schedule of interpretive programs and displays, including artifacts from oyster shell middens, which confirm that the peninsula was inhabited by Native Americans almost 7,000 years ago. The nature center is open Mon.–Fri. 9am–5pm.

Old Croton Aqueduct Trailway State Park (914-693-5259) This is a level, 26-mile hiking and biking trail from the Croton Dam to Van Cortlandt Park in The Bronx, passing through 11 communities and uncounted panoramas of the Hudson River. The packed dirt trail is rocky in spots and follows the route of the Old Croton Aqueduct, which carried water to New York City for more than 100 years, beginning in 1842. Most of the aqueduct is beneath the trail and has been designated a National Historic Landmark.

Montrose

George's Island Park (914-737-7530; Dutch Rd.) A 208-acre waterfront park offering magnificent views, tidal wetlands, wooded trails and boat access.

Mount Kisco

Westmoreland Sanctuary (914-666-8448; 260 Chestnut Ridge Rd. Eight miles of hiking trails on a 625-acre nature sanctuary, plus a small nature museum.

North Salem

Mountain Lakes Park (914-864-7311; Hawley Rd.) This is one of the largest parks in Westchester, covering more than 1,000 acres and includes Mt.

Bailey, the highest point in the county. There are rugged hiking trails through a native hardwood forest, plus swimming in spring-fed lakes.

North White Plains

Cranberry Lake Preserve (914-428-1005; Old Orchard St.) Wetlands, forest, and a 10-acre lake carved by glaciers thousands of years ago comprise this 165-acre nature park. Part of the trail system is a loop around the lake, which was named for a growth of wild cranberry that still grows in the lakeside bog. There are weekend nature programs during warm weather months. Open Mon.–Fri. 9am–5pm.

Peekskill

Blue Mountain Reservation (914-862-5275; Welcher Ave.) There are dozens of miles of hiking and biking trails in this 1,500-acre park, including challenging hikes to the tops of two large peaks, Mt. Spitzenberg and Blue Mountain. The park also includes the Blue Mountain Sportsman Center, a target shooting range.

Pocantico Hills

Rockefeller State Park Preserve (914-631-1470; Rte. 117) This sprawling preserve is adjacent to Kykuit, the Rockefeller estate (see Chapter Six, *Mansions of the Hudson Valley*). In addition to a variety of habitats, including wetlands, thick woodlands, meadows, fields, and a lake, there are miles of hiking and bridle trails, some of which are old carriage paths and offer spectacular river views. One section of the preserve is called Rockwood Hall; it is the former estate of William Rockefeller, brother of John D. Rockefeller, Sr. Only the stone foundation of the house still exists and still offers a spectacular view across a sloping lawn dotted with massive willows and oaks to the Hudson River and beyond. This section is tucked behind the huge Phelps Memorial Hospital off Rte. 9 and is unmarked. Drive past the hospital parking lots to a barricaded road (Rockwell Hall Rd.). After a quarter mile, the concrete path ends; take the cobblestone path to the right toward the mansion ruins (the path on the left leads to the hospital). There are no services here. A visitor center in the main preserve section hosts exhibits of local and historical interest and offers guided nature and birding hikes.

Rye

Marshlands Conservancy (914-835-4466; Rte. 1) Peter Jay, son of a French Huguenot merchant, moved his family here from New York City in 1745 to escape a typhoid outbreak and establish a farm. It was here his son, John Jay, first Chief Justice of the U.S. and New York State's second governor, grew up (see John Jay Homestead, Chapter Six, *Mansions of the Hudson Valley*). Marshlands is a 173-acre wildlife sanctuary composed of salt marsh, forest, and meadow. There is a half mile of shoreline on Long Island Sound and three miles of trails. Open Mon.–Fri. 9am–5pm.

Somers

Lasdon Park, Arboretum & War Memorial (914-864-7260; Rte. 35) This magnificent 234-acre property includes woodlands, open grass meadows, and formal gardens, which include the Chinese Friendship Pavilion, a gift from the People's Republic of China, and the Azalea Garden, which explodes in a riot of color in the spring. It had been the country estate of William and Mildred Lasdon, whose interest in horticulture prompted them to introduce trees, shrubs, dwarf shrubs, and flowers from around the world. There is an adjoining 22-acre Bird and Nature Sanctuary, where as many as 20 types of warblers have been spotted during migratory seasons. This is also a horticultural research facility and houses the Westchester Veterans Memorial and Museum (see Chapter Five, *Arts & Pleasures*).

Yonkers

Lenoir Preserve (914-968-5851; Dudley St., off Rte. 9) Densely forested, this 40-acre preserve is adjacent to the Old Croton Reservoir on a slope overlooking the Hudson River. The preserve boasts some magnificent copper beech trees, Asian gingkos, and Pacific firs, plus native sugar maples, red oaks, pines, and tulip trees. The preserve is a major hawk migratory route, and a butterfly and hummingbird garden is maintained by the Hudson River Audubon Society. The nature center building was the home of a tobacco executive, who named his estate after Lenoir, North Carolina, where he grew up. Open Mon.–Fri. 9am–5pm.

Yonkers to Valhalla

Bronx River Parkway (914-723-4058; Bronx River Pkwy.) This is a linear park, one of the first in the nation, extending some 13 miles alongside the Bronx River and the parkway that runs parallel. There are 800 acres of ponds, wooden footbridges, and both paved and dirt paths for biking and hiking. At its northern edge, it meets with the open space of the Kensico Dam across the Bronx River, where there is a 98-acre park with picnic areas and additional trails.

Yorktown Heights

Franklin D. Roosevelt State Park (914-245-4434; 2957 Crompound Rd.) Fishing (largemouth bass, perch, and pickerel) and boating on Mohansic

Lake and Crom Pond are available and an enormous swimming pool, miles of hiking trails, plus rowboat rentals. In the winter, the park provides trails for snowmobilers and cross-country skiers and a hill for sledding. The park's two lakes feed into the Croton Reservoir, which is a main water supply for New York City, and it is just across the road from the historic Yorktown Presbyterian Church (see Chapter Five, *Arts & Pleasures*), close enough that park visitors can hear the carillon bells chime at noon and 6pm. This is a carry in-carry out park. There are no garbage receptacles.

TRAILWAYS

There is an extensive system of paved bicycle and pedestrian paths in Westchester County, part of the growing network of linear parks, many former rail tracks (914-864-PARK).

South County Trailway is a five-mile path from Hastings to Elmsford. Another linear park runs 12 miles from Ossining to the Blue Mountain Reservation in Peekskill. North County Trailway is 22 miles of paths from the town of Mt. Pleasant north to the Putnam County line in Yorktown. And there is another walking path between the historic estates of Lyndhurst and Sunnyside in Tarrytown (see Chapter Six, *Mansions of the Hudson Valley*).

PUTNAM COUNTY

Cold Spring

West Point Foundry Preserve (845-265-4010; Chestnut St., behind the Foundry Cove Museum) The grounds around what was once the country's largest and most modern iron foundry (see Chapter Five, *Arts & Pleasures*) are restored wetlands and are being developed by a co-operative group of governmental agencies and environmental groups for hiking, bird-watching, canoeing and kayaking, and picnicking. There are 87 acres, including river-front and alongside a brook.

Garrison

Constitution Marsh Wildlife Sanctuary (845-265-2601; Indian Brook Rd., off Rte. 9D) A 270-acre wildlife sanctuary operated by the National Audubon Society, with a bit over a mile of hiking and birding trails for spotting marsh wrens, egrets, wood ducks, and more. There's also a visitor center with displays of local wildlife. Open year-round.

Manitou Point Preserve (845-473-4440; Mystery Point Rd.) There are four miles of lush trails along Manitou Marsh and scenic overlooks of the Hudson River in the wooded upland area. The restored historic mansion on the property (it belonged to one of the Livingston family members; see

Clermont, Chapter Six, *Mansions of the Hudson Valley*) is the national head-quarters for Outward Bound.

Kent

Clarence Fahnestock State Park (845-225-7207; Rte. 301, also an entrance from Taconic State Pkwy.) Located in thickly wooded, rolling highlands, this 10,000-acre playground has the most developed trail system in Putnam County, including a several mile stretch of the Appalachian Trail, which meanders through the park, and Canopus Beach, a lakeside complex, including a large, sandy beach and picnic groves. There also are campsites and four fishing ponds. Dogs are permitted on trails on a leash, but not in the campground, beach, or picnic areas.

DUTCHESS COUNTY

Annandale-on-Hudson

Hudson River National Estuarine Research Reserve (845-758-7010; Tivoli Bays) A 1,799-acre reserve, wildlife management area and field laboratory for research and education about the Hudson River. Canoe the marsh and wetlands or bicycle or hike along one of five marked trails that wander along the river's edge and through thick woodland.

Beacon

Beacon Landing (845-473-4440; Main St.) This urban shoreline park, opened in 2003, offers wonderful river views and passes DIA: Beacon, the huge contemporary art gallery that opened in 2003 (see Chapter Five, *Arts & Pleasures*). There is also fishing access and picnic areas.

→ **Hudson Highlands State Park** (845-225-7207; Rte. 9D) Within this undeveloped wilderness preserve of 4,000 thickly wooded acres, there are two sections with 25 miles of hiking trails, ranging from comfortable to strenuously steep. There are spectacular views west to the Hudson Highland Range from Sugarloaf, Bull Hill, and Breakneck Ridge Mountains.

Fishkill

→ **Fishkill Ridge Conservation Area** (845-473-4440; Maple Ave. from Rte. 52) Panoramic views of the Hudson River and Catskill Mountains from this 1,900-acre ridge that is home to eagles, falcons, and other rare species. There are mostly rugged hiking trails, some of which connect to Hudson Highlands State Park in Beacon, but also open areas for picnicking.

Hyde Park

→ **Historic Hyde Park Trail** (845-229-9115; access from FDR Presidential Library ticket booth) There are nearly nine miles of hiking trails connecting several historic sites, including the Franklin D. Roosevelt and Vanderbilt homes. Bicycles not permitted.

Pleasant Valley

James Baird State Park (845-452-1489; 122D Freedom Rd., access from Taconic State Pkwy.) This former farmland is now one of the most popular parks in the area, with an 18-hole public golf course designed by Robert Trent Jones, tennis courts, and miles of scenic, wooded hiking and biking trails. There is also a small nature center that loans out recreational equipment. Open year-round.

Red Hook

Tania Barricklo/Daily Freeman

The romantic vistas of Poet's Walk inspired both artists and writers.

Poet's Walk Romantic Landscape Park (845-473-4440; River Rd.) A combination of rolling open fields and lush wooded paths, opening on dramatic river views — the same panorama said to have inspired author Washington Irving and artists of the Hudson River School. The park is landscaped with walls of foliage that evoke "rooms." Go at sunset and enjoy the panorama from one of the bentwood benches or gazebos scattered throughout the 120-acre park. The path to the river can be strenuous, since it drops 200 feet in less than one mile.

Staatsburg

Mills-Norrie Point State Park (845-889-4830) This riverfront park sprawls from the Mills Mansion (see Chapter Six, *Mansions of the Hudson Valley*) to Norrie Point. It includes 10 miles of hiking and biking trails, through wooded terrain and broad open fields. The **Norrie Point Marina** is a popular spot for starting and ending river kayaking trips; the cove choked with water lilies is beautiful to paddle past or enjoy from the shore. Here also is where you'll find the **Norrie Point Environmental Center**, a small history museum with live and taxidermist displays of local wildlife, including two aquariums filled with Hudson River bass, bullhead, and catfish. There also are guided field trips with a park ranger.

COLUMBIA COUNTY

Greenport

Olana Watershed (518-828-0135; entry from Rte. 9G) This is the land and the view that attracted 19th-century artist Frederic Church to build Olana (see Chapter Six, *Mansions of the Hudson Valley*), which stirred and inspired him to paint these views. There are more than 600 acres of protected orchards, woodlands, and marshland, with trails offering magnificent vistas. Olana sits atop a bend in the river, and the view from the front porch area is directly south, framed by the Catskills and the Taconic Range. The grounds are free; there is an admission fee for the house tour.

Taghkanic

Lake Taghkanic State Park (845-851-3631; Rte. 82, access from Taconic State Pkwy.) A little bit of everything, including swimming and boat rentals, and hiking trails that become snowmobiling trails in the winter. There also are cottages and campsites.

TRAILWAYS

There are four linear parks in the county, for walking and bike riding, operated by the Harlem Valley Rail Trail (845-789-9591).

ROCKLAND COUNTY

Congers

Rockland Lake State Park (845-268-3020; access from Rte. 9W) Located on a ridge of Hook Mountain, with swimming pools, tennis courts, a golf course, and trails for walking, hiking, and biking. Handicap accessible.

Haverstraw

Emeline Park (845-473-4440; New Main St.) This is a tiny (a mere three acres) riverfront view with gigantic vistas. It sits at the widest expanse of the river, where the Hudson is five miles wide. Panoramic views, a shady gazebo, children's playground, walking paths, picnic tables, and a boat ramp.

High Tor State Park (845-634-8074; Mountain Rd.) The 1937 fight to save this picturesque peak from commercial development was the subject of Maxwell Anderson's Pulitzer Prize winning play, *High Tor*. In addition to swimming and picnicking, there are spectacular views from the higher elevations of the Hudson River and as far south as New York City — a line of sight that prompted American patriots to use the peak during the Revolutionary War to light signal fires warning of approaching British troops. The Long Path passes through the park just before the trail meanders inland and north to the Catskills. Handicap accessible.

Nyack

Nyack Beach State Park (845-268-3020; Broadway) More than 60 acres of riverfront parkland, including swimming and fishing, and trails and paths for hiking and biking.

Orangetown

Clausland Mountain Park (845-473-4440; County Rte. 28) Walking trails along a rocky ridgeline overlooking the Hudson River, with stunning views south to New York City. Also more rugged hiking trails.

Palisades

Talman Mountain State Park (845-359-0544; Rte. 9W) Wonderfully wooded grounds for walking and hiking on the Palisades uplands overlooking the Hudson River; also tennis courts, swimming pool, ball fields, and picnic areas.

ULSTER COUNTY

New Paltz

Minnewaska State Park Preserve (845-255-0752; www.nysparks.com; Rte. 44/55) Situated on the dramatic Shawangunk Mountain ridge that rises dramatically more than 2,000 feet above the Hudson River, this rugged terrain is thickly forested with hardwoods, dotted with lakes and streams, has a waterfall that empties into a deep pool for swimming, and rises and dips into cliffs and valleys. Minnewaska is adjacent to Mohonk Preserve (see below), and together they create one of the largest undeveloped, protected tracts of land in the Hudson Valley.

→ **Mohonk Preserve** (845-255-0919; www.mohonkpreserve.org; Rte. 44/55) The largest visitor-supported nature preserve in New York State, sprawling over nearly 6,500 acres of the Shawangunk Ridge, which links the northern section of the Appalachian Mountains with the southern section of the Catskills and Adirondacks. Some of the best rock climbing in the country is here, with more than 1,000 technical routes, in what locals refer to simply as "The Gunks." Any day of the week you can see climbers hanging from their carabiners on a sheer rock wall. The preserve includes a 50-mile protected greenway and contains some 100 miles of walking, jogging, and hiking paths, ranging from easy strolls on century-old horse carriage roads to rough ascents that require both fortitude and outdoor expertise. The preserve provides refuge for 29 rare plant and animal species and is one of 13 hawk sighting sites in the state. There is also a "Kids' Corner" discovery area and ruins of a 19th-century cabin on Trapps Mountain. The preserve surrounds Mohonk Mountain House (see Chapter Three, *Lodging*). Day use only, no overnight camping; number of daily visitors is limited so go early on summer weekends; admission: weekdays $5; weekends $7.

TRAILWAYS

The Hudson Valley Rail Trail (845-483-0428) This trail extends more than four miles north from the Mid-Hudson Bridge in Highland to the town of Lloyd. There is a paved portion for strollers, roller-blading, and wheelchairs, but most of the distance is packed dirt for hiking and horseback riding.

Walkill Valley Rail Trail (845-255-3842; www.gorailtrail.org) More than 12 miles of level dirt and paved paths for walking and cycling, through New Paltz and Gardiner, on the rail bed of the former Walkill Valley Railroad, which carried fresh produce and dairy products from Ulster farms to New York City for more than a half century.

THE PALISADES/INTERSTATE PARKS SYSTEM

Palisades Interstate Parks System (845-786-2701; fax 845-947-5293; www.nys-parks.com) This group of state parks totals more than 100,000 acres over five counties in two states, New York and New Jersey (hence the "interstate" part of the name) and operated by the Palisades Interstate Parks Commission, which also oversees the Palisades Interstate Pkwy., a busy north-south route that both bisects and parallels park land. The land in Rockland and Orange counties, nearest to New York City, was donated early in the 1900s by a group of wealthy businessmen, including railroad tycoon and former New York State Governor W. Averell Harriman (whose family estate, Arden House, is within park land) to stop the destruction of the Palisade cliffs from rock quarrying and to preserve the land, while providing outdoor recreation for a growing urban population nearby. The parks are among the most popular in the U.S., attracting more visitors annually than Yellowstone National Park in Wyoming and offering nearly every outdoor activity imaginable, including cross-country skiing in the winter. In addition to visitor centers within the parks, there is a building in the center island of the Palisades Interstate Pkwy., between exits 16 and 17, where park maps, hiking trail maps, and fishing and hunting licenses can be purchased (845-786-5003). For information on the sections in New Jersey, contact: 201-768-1360; www.njpalisades.org.

Bear Mountain State Park (845-786-2701; Rte. 9W or directly from Bear Mountain Bridge) This park was named because the profile of the mountain resembles a bear lying down. The park contains four trailside museums, numerous exhibits related to the local wildlife and environment, lakes for boating and fishing, an ice-skating rink, playing fields, walking and hiking trails with dramatic river views, restaurants, and lodging (see Chapter Three, *Lodging*). The Appalachian Trail cuts through the park. Perkins Memorial Dr., which leads to a fire tower overlook on the top of the mountain, is one of the prettiest, most scenic drives in the Hudson Valley, and the view from the top is a memorable 360-degree panorama. Open year-round; handicap accessible.

Harriman State Park (845-786-2701; from Palisades Interstate Pkwy. or Rte. 59) This park is so big it contains 31 lakes and reservoirs, several offering sandy beaches for swimming and picnicking, 200 miles of hiking trails through lush, rolling landscapes, camping, fishing, and boating. Larger parts of the park are known as Anthony Wayne Recreation Area (845-942-2560) with a monstrous swimming pool, open fields, and picnic areas; Lake Welch (845-947-2444) and Lake Sebago (845-351-2583), both offering sandy beaches, swimming, and picnic areas; Lake Tiorati (845-351-2568) with boating and hiking; and Beaver Pond Campground (845-947-2792) with camping. The Seven Lakes Pkwy. threads through the park.

Sterling Forest State Park (845-351-5907; from Rte. 17 at Sloatsburg) This park is more than 15,000 acres of natural terrain, including 1,400 acres set aside as the Doris Duke Wildlife Sanctuary, with several miles of trails and a small nature center.

THE CATSKILL FOREST PRESERVE

It would be shameful to ignore this bounty of forests, meadows, lakes, waterfalls, fire towers, and wildlife in the glorious Catskill Mountains west of the Hudson Valley. The preserve now totals 300,000 acres, primarily within Greene County, but extending into Ulster and beyond. The main portions include the following:

Catskill Park In this park, old-growth hemlock and northern hardwoods have survived the logging and charcoal industries of the last 300 years.

Bluestone Wild Forest This preserve is just three miles from the city of Kingston, with rolling hills and lakes for biking, fishing, and cross-country skiing. Before it was protected and reforested, the land was stripped virtually bare and quarried until the mid-to-late 1800s for its bluestone.

Sam's Point Dwarf Pine Ridge Preserve This is a 4,600-acre tract, containing rare dwarf pines. The preserve also contains the natural caverns of Ice Caves Mountain. The preserve also includes the towns of Hunter and Windham, popular destinations for downhill skiing in the winter (see the section Winter Sports & Activities) and Phoenicia, for inner-tubing on the Esopus Creek in the summer.

Slide Mountain Wilderness This is the first area to be included in the "forever wild" portion of the preserve. The terrain is rugged and mountainous, with elevations ranging from 1,100-4,180 feet.

ROCK CLIMBING

The Shawangunk Ridge, a few minutes west of New Paltz and known locally as "The Gunks," is world famous for its several hundred feet high, sheer rock cliff wall that lures a range of climbers from beginner/novice to technical expert. Even if you have no desire to climb, it's fascinating to watch. You'll know the spot on Rte. 44/45 when you see a line of cars parked alongside the road just after the 10mph hairpin turn. In the winter, it changes from rock climbing to ice climbing. With the popularity of "The Gunks," it's not sur-

Tania Barricklo/Daily Freeman

The granite walls near New Paltz attract climbers of all levels.

prising that there are a number of rock climbing instruction schools and indoor climbing walls in the area.

Diamond Sports Rock Climbing School (800-776-2577; Gardiner) Individual and group instruction.

Inner Wall (845-255-ROCK; New Paltz) Indoor climbing wall. Open year-round.

Rock and Snow (845-255-1311; www.rocksnow.com; New Paltz) One of the premier climbing stores in the Northeast (see Chapter Eight, *Shopping*). It is also the area's best resource for licensed instructors.

Squirrel Island Expeditions (203-966-2569; New Canaan, CT) Operates day and weekend climbing instruction trips (also hiking and kayaking) out of New York City, with round-trip transportation.

TENNIS

There's a combination of public and private courts throughout the Hudson Valley. The courts are a combination of clay, hard, and synthetic grass that regular players claim combines the best of all. Public courts do not take reservations and are first-come, first serve; they are open seasonally, although that may be beyond Labor Day, even Columbus Day, until the first snowfall.

DUTCHESS COUNTY

Edward R. Murrow Park (845-855-1131; Lakeside Dr. and Old Rte. 55, Pawling) Four free outdoor courts.

James Baird State Park (845-452-7207; Taconic State Pkwy. and Rte. 55, Old Grange) Four free outdoor courts.

Sports and Wellness (845-227-9231; 190 Old Sylvan Lake Rd., Hopewell Junction) This club has five indoor courts at $48 an hour to walk-ins who are not health club members, plus 10 outdoor courts.

COLUMBIA COUNTY

Columbia-Greene County Community College (Hudson) Public courts.

ROCKLAND COUNTY

Merritt Tennis Courts (845-623-0377; 390 Ehardt Rd., Pearl River) There are two indoor courts, at $14 an hour, and four outdoor courts.

Rockland Tennis Academy (845-638-2075; 18 Squadron Blvd., New City) There are both indoor and outdoor courts.

ULSTER COUNTY

Cantine Field (Saugerties) Public courts.

Hotels with outdoor tennis courts that are available to nonguests include **Mohonk Mountain House** (845-255-1000; New Paltz), **Dolce Tarrytown House** (914-591-8200; Tarrytown), **Hudson Valley Resort** (888-9HUDSON; Kerhonkson).

Total Tennis (845-247-0221; 800-221-6496; 1811 Old Kings Hwy. (off Rte. 32), Saugerties) This is an adult tennis camp, with some weekends and school holidays for families with children, in a renovated 1920s resort hotel in Ulster County. There is a variety of programs from two-day to a full week, and each day includes a combination of private and group lessons and open court time, and three full meals plus high-energy snacks (the full week program totals 34 hours of group instruction and two hours private lessons). There are 20 outdoor courts (11 red clay, seven hard, and two synthetic grass) and five indoor-cushioned courts. Open year-round.

WINTER SPORTS & ACTIVITIES

To many outdoor enthusiasts, winter is the most magical of seasons in the Hudson Valley, when a covering of snow mutes sounds as well as colors, vistas are turned into shades of black and white, and the air is crisp enough to sting the nose. The rolling landscape becomes a wonderland for sledding, and the northernmost part of the valley stays cold enough long enough for ponds and lakes to freeze smooth and solid for ice-skating. There are ample opportunities for downhill skiing and snow-boarding, or bumping down a hill on an updated version of a tire inner tube. Or, just take off for a walk in the woods on a pair of cross-country skis or snowshoes and listen to the quiet.

DOWNHILL SKIING & SNOW-BOARDING

The Hudson Valley is just that — a valley — and the ski slopes in a valley simply aren't as long or as challenging as those in the mountains beyond in the Catskills and Adirondacks northwest and the Berkshires northeast. But this is not to say that the Hudson Valley is bereft of places to schuss down a groomed ski run. There are several family-oriented ski areas ideal for beginners, who can increase their comfort and skill levels without the hustle and bustle of large, crowded slopes. The season generally runs from Thanksgiving weekend to mid-March, augmented by snowmaking, and the resorts welcome both skiers and snowboarders and offer instruction for both.

Mount Peter (845-986-4940; 845-986-4992 for conditions; www.mtpeter.com;

Rte. 17A and Old Mount Peter Rd., Warwick) It has a vertical drop of 400 feet, with eight downhill slopes and a rental shop. Open daily in season; night skiing Fri. until 9pm, Sat. until 10pm.

Sterling Forest Ski Area (845-351-2163; 800-843-4414; Sterling Forest Park, 581 Rte. 17A., Tuxedo) It has a 400-foot vertical drop, seven slopes, a NASTAR self-timed race course, and instruction. Open daily in season; night skiing Wed.–Sat. until 9pm.

Proximity makes it easy and convenient to stay overnight in the Hudson Valley and still be on a chairlift in the Catskills at "first chair" at 8:30am or 9am.

Belleayre Mountain Ski Center (845-254-5600; www.belleayre.com; Rte. 28, Highmount) It is a state-owned area, so unfortunately, it pales against the commercial competition nearby. It offers a 1,400-foot vertical drop and some great trails for practicing technique and a good choice to escape the crowds.

Hunter Mountain (518-263-4223; 800-FOR-SNOW; www.huntermtn.com; Rte. 23A, Hunter) It is the granddaddy of Catskill mountain resorts and claims to have invented, or at least perfected, the technology of snowmaking used worldwide. Hunter boasts a 1,600-foot vertical terrain, challenging enough for top expert skiers, multiple high-speed detachable chairlifts, snowboard terrain parks, and a huge lodge able to handle the crowds, which include die-hard skiers on a day trip from New York City.

Lake Placid/Whiteface Mountain (518-946-2223; 800-482-6236; www.white-face.com; Rte. 86, Wilmington) The largest ski resort in the Adirondacks, which is 2–3 hours from the Hudson Valley.

Ski Plattekill (607-326-3500; 800-NEED-2-SKI snow conditions; www.plat-tekill.com; Plattekill Mountain Rd., Roxbury) This is a family-owned mountain that bills itself as offering big mountain terrain with small mountain charm. It's true. There's a 1,000-foot vertical drop with several straight down expert chutes, modern lifts, and a friendly hometown feel.

Ski Windham (518-734-4300; 800-729-4746; www.skiwindham.com; CD Lane Rd., Windham) It also boasts a 1,600-foot vertical drop with more than 36 trails, 97 percent of which are covered by snowmaking. There are several high-speed detachable lifts, a business center with high-speed Internet access, and a range of terrain, from gentle novice runs to experts-only bumpers.

The ski and snow-boarding resorts closest to the Hudson Valley in the Berkshires of Massachusetts are the following:

Bousquet Ski Area (413-442-8316; www.bousquets.com; Dan Fox Dr., Pittsfield).

Butternut Basin (413-528-2000; www.butternutbasin.com; Rte. 23, Great Barrington).

Catamount Ski Area (313-528-1262; www.catamountski.com; Rte. 23, South Egremont).

Jiminy Peak (413-738-5500; www.jiminypeak.com; Corey Rd., Hancock).

→ **CROSS-COUNTRY SKIING**

The downhill ski/snowboard resorts also have cross-country ski trails and rental facilities, and many of the areas golf courses groom tracks for Nordic skiing. Conditions permitting, many state and local parks have groomed trails, and those that don't groom still allow X-C skiing during daylight hours. For example, the broad lawn in front of the Mills Mansion **(Mills-Norrie State Park)** slopes down to the river and is popular with both youngsters on sleds and grown-ups on skinny skis.

    Fahnestock Winter Park (845-225-3998; Rte. 301, Carmel) This park has 15km of scenic meadows and forests on a mapped trail system. There are machine-groomed trails for ski-skating and tracked trails for classic.
    Thomas Bull Memorial Park (914-457-4949; 211 Rte. 416, Montgomery) It has four miles of X-C trails over the fairways and open spaces of the Stony Ford Golf Course. Open weekends in season.

The Hudson Valley turns into a winter wonderland after a snowfall.

Tania Barricklo/Daily Freeman

    There are cross-country trails, as well, at **Mohonk Mountain House** (845-255-1000; New Paltz), **Williams Lake Hotel** (845-658-3101; www.willylake.com; Rosendale), and in the Catskill Mountains at **Mountain Trails XC Ski Center** (518-589-5361; www.mttrails.com; Rte. 23A, Tannersville).
    In Westchester County, there are groomed trails at **Blue Mountain Reservation,** Welcher Ave., Peekskill; **Lenoir Preserve,** Dudley St., Yonkers; **Mountain Lakes Park,** Hawley Rd., North Salem; and **Saxon Woods Park,** Mamaroneck Ave., White Plains.
    In Columbia County, the **Harlem Valley Rail Trail** is open for X-C skiing in the winter, call 845-789-9591 for access information.

SNOWSHOEING

If you can walk, you can snowshoe, with high-tech lightweight, aluminum-frame platters with clawlike teeth to grip the snow, strapped on to hiking boots or other waterproof footwear. Many of the same trail systems for cross-country skiers also accommodate snowshoers, or just take a walk in a snowy meadow.

Bryan's Bikes (845-534-5230; 240 Main St., Cornwall) They rent snowshoes and have information on local trails.

Hunter Mountain (518-263-4223; 800-FOR-SNOW; www.huntermtn.com; Rte. 23A, Hunter) It has trails at the summit and rents snowshoes in the base shop; a chairlift ticket is required to ride the lift.

SNOW-TUBING

The growing popularity of snow-tubing, sometimes described in a single word missing the letter W — snotubing — is because it is simple enough, safe enough, and fun enough for any age. Safer than a flat sled with stiff metal runners, snow tubes are updated tire inner tubes with handles, so the soft tubes absorb the bumps on the way downhill, and the handles allow steering. Tubing can be done on any hill that attracts sleds and giggling children, but it's a lot less exhausting to go to a special tubing hill where runs are groomed, and there's an uphill lift to save grown-up legs and lungs. Usual rates $4–$6 per hour.

Brodie Mountain (413-443-4572; www.skibrodie.com; Rte. 7, New Ashford) No longer open for downhill skiing or snow-boarding. It is now exclusively a lift-served snow-tubing park, with five tubing lanes. Open weekends until 9pm.

Hunter Mountain (518-263-4223; 800-FOR-SNOW; www.huntermtn.com; Rte. 23A, Hunter) It has the largest snow-tubing facility in New York State, with 12 chutes and three tows; $12 all-day rate weekdays; $12 for two hours on weekends and holidays. Open Fri.–Sat. until 10pm.

Ski Plattekill (607-326-3500; 800-NEED-2-SKI snow conditions; www.plat-tekill.com; Plattekill Mountain Rd., Roxbury) It calls its lift-served, snow-tubing park Tubapalooza. Open weekends.

Ski Windham (518-734-4300; 800-729-4746; www.skiwindham.com; CD Lane Rd., Windham) It has eight lanes, two tows, and a complimentary shuttle from the resort parking lot. Open weekend evenings until 10pm.

Thomas Bull Memorial Park (845-457-4949; 211 Rte. 416, Montgomery) This park has five groomed lanes, a rope tow, stadium lights for evening sessions, and a stone lodge with a restaurant and views of the Shawangunk Mountains. Adjacent facilities for cross-country skiing, sledding, and ice-skating. Open weekends in season.

CHAPTER EIGHT
Antiques & Boutiques
SHOPPING

From today's hand-made candles to yesterday's handmade Revolutionary-era candle-sticks, there is a wealth of treasures awaiting discovery in myriad shops and galleries. Whether you are a recreational browser or a die-hard bounty hunter, whether you seek hand-painted clothing or hand-sculpted pottery, the Hudson Valley is a shopper's paradise. Take a deep breath, wear comfortable shoes, and don't forget your credit cards.

Dutchess County Tourism

Handmade crafts and Colonial and Victorian antiques lure shoppers to the Hudson Valley.

All the shops and galleries included in this chapter are the kind of old-fashioned shopping where the owner or a family member is behind the counter, perhaps actually sewing, stringing, or repairing an item for the display shelves, while ready to offer knowledgeable, attentive, friendly service. Most shops are housed in historic buildings in small, quaint downtown areas that are simultaneously quiet and vital — the kind of old-fashioned towns where neighbors chat on the sidewalk and pedestrians can cross a street that doesn't have a stoplight on every corner. There's even one entire community of craft shops, Sugar Loaf, which was founded in 1749 as a hamlet for artists and artisans. The town still creates marriages between those who want to create one-of-a-kind, handcrafted items and those who want to own them.

Of course, there are several shopping malls in the Hudson Valley with outposts of major department stores and chains, including Palisades Center in West Nyack, the nation's second largest, containing designer and factory outlet stores. These tend to be in the largest suburban communities closest to New York City or adjacent to and visible from major highway exits, such as

Woodbury Commons outlet mall at the intersection of the NYS Thruway and Rte. 17, both highly traveled thoroughfares.

Hours of operation change seasonally; stores are open longer and more days in the peak summer and fall tourist season. Most shops are open weekends and closed either Mon. or Tues., or both. If in doubt, it's best to call ahead.

SHOPPING: WESTCHESTER COUNTY

Tarrytown

PHILIPSBURG MANOR VISITOR CENTER (914-631-3993, ext. 20; Rte. 9, Tarrytown) There are gift shops attached to most of the Hudson Valley's mansions and historic homes (see Chapter Six, *Mansions of the Hudson Valley*), but perhaps because it serves both Philipsburg Manor and the Rockefeller estate, Kykuit, the largest and best of these is the gift shop at the Philipsburg Manor Visitor Center. A large selection of old-fashioned wooden children's toys and unusual games, locally crafted silver and jewelry with semiprecious gems, art glass, books on gardening and local history, and the usual collection of souvenir gifts. Open daily 10am–4pm.

SHOPPING: PUTNAM COUNTY

Carmel

CRAFTS

Burchetta Glass Studio & Gallery (845-225-1430; www.burchetta.com; 1544 Rte. 6, Carmel) Brilliant colors and fluted shapes define these limited edition art glass bowls, vases, and decorative items, produced in a 100-year-old barn. Also glassblowing demonstrations on weekends. Open Wed.–Sun.

Cold Spring

The cold spring for which the town was named in the 1700s has been covered up by modern civilization. Luckily, this charming town's Colonial buildings have been restored and are filled with wonderful little shops within a few block stretch east of the MetroNorth commuter train station.

ANTIQUES

Bijou Galleries (845-265-4337; 50 Main St., Cold Spring) Thirty dealers under one roof, with everything from furniture and china to jewelry and clothing, all organized in a well-lit space. Open Thurs.–Sun.

Antique clocks are repaired and sold at Country Clocks in Cold Spring.

Evelyn Kanter

Country Clocks (845-265-3361; 142 Main St., Cold Spring) The owner restores every antique clock before selling it. There are bronze carriage clocks from the 1800s, wooden mantel clocks from the 1900s, and unusual European pendulum clocks. Repairs also. Call for hours.

Decades (845-265-9515; 131 Main St., Cold Spring) Housed in an 1870s clapboard house with creaky floorboards, this shop specializes in Bakelite jewelry and flatware from the '20s–'40s, Fiestaware from the '50s, and barkcloth upholstery fabric from the '40s. Open Fri.–Mon.

Once Upon A Time Antiques (845-265-4339; 101 Main St., Cold Spring) Hundreds of antique and vintage dolls, from the 1850s to the 1950s, many in their original lace and satin clothing, antique soldiers, a collection of vintage French and German tin chocolate molds, and barrels of penny candy in the front of the store. Open Thurs.–Mon.

Serious Toyz (845-6543; 165 Main St., Cold Spring) Vintage toys, specializing in tin windups dating as far back as the '20s, pressed tin trucks from the '30s, character toys and playing cards, including early Disneyana and Dick Tracy, plus board games and matchbox miniatures. The store is equally popular with adults revisiting the games of their youth as with kids who have never seen, much less played with these things.

Silver Lady (845-265-1014; 125 Main St., Cold Spring) Vintage Victorian silver jewelry and costume jewelry from the '40s and '50s, baskets of silk scarves and flowers, and hard-to-find circular hat boxes. Open Thurs.–Mon.

BOOKS

Salamagundi (845-265-4058; 75 Main St., Cold Spring) An eclectic mix heavy on local maps for hiking and boating, and a sunny greenhouse room in the back that is the children's book area and reading room. Open Tues.–Sun.

CLOTHING

Staley Gretzinger (845-265-4469; 800-827-1030; 75 Main St., Cold Spring) Hand-dyed and hand-printed clothing in nonwrinkling fabrics ideal for travel. Loose, comfortable shapes. This label is also sold in upscale boutiques and department stores. Open Wed.–Sun.

CRAFTS

Momminia (845-265-2260; 113 Main St., Cold Spring) One side of this shop is filled with beads and jewelry-making supplies, the other with silver and bead jewelry fashioned by one of the owners, a trained sculptor. There are antique beads from Afghanistan and Tibet, Venetian and Czech glass beads, stacks of freshwater and Tahitian pearls and gemstones, including turquoise and coral. Open daily.

OTHER SHOPS

Back in Ireland (845-265-4570; 103 Main St., Cold Spring) Everything Irish, and it's a long list — flags, heraldic plaques, Galway crystal, Nicholas Mosse pottery, packaged food, Claddagh rings and Celtic knot jewelry in silver and gold, CDs, and, of course, shelves and shelves of legendary and traditional hand-knit fisherman's sweaters in a collection of colors, including emerald green. Open daily.

SHOPPING: DUTCHESS COUNTY

Beacon

The Hudson River is the town's front porch, and Mount Beacon is its back yard. Downtown is lined with solid brick buildings from the 1920s and earlier, with a cluster of interesting shops in a few block stretch.

ANTIQUES

Beacon Hill Antiques (845-831-4577; 474 Main St., Beacon) An eclectic blend of period furniture, accessories, decorative items, and folk art. Open Thurs.–Mon.

Dickinsons (845-838-3014; 440 Main St., Beacon) Specializes in antique clocks and clock repairs, plus furniture and lamps. Open Thurs.–Mon.

GALLERIES

Beacon Camera Club/Screen 16 (845-838-9882; 432 Main St., Beacon) Gallery exhibiting vintage and contemporary fine art and photography. Also, screenings of vintage 16mm educational and animated films. Call for hours.

OTHER SHOPS

Jacqueline (845-838-1737; 478 Main St., Beacon) Handmade women's hats, from sensible to dramatic "grand entry" designs, also jewelry, handbags, and scarves. Open Thurs.–Sun.

Kringle's Christmas House (845-838-2830; 475 Main St., Beacon) European and Eastern European ornaments, nutcrackers, and other holiday decorations, plus homemade chocolate and fudge. Open daily.

Hyde Park

This village is dominated by the Culinary Institute of America (see Chapter Four, *Restaurants & Food Purveyors)* and the FDR and Eleanor Roosevelt homes and presidential library (see Chapter Six, *Mansions of the Hudson Valley)*. There's no real downtown to stroll and window-shop; for that, most visitors drive another 10 minutes north to Rhinebeck.

ANTIQUES

Hyde Park Antiques Center (845-229-8200; 4192 Albany Post Rd./Rte. 9, Hyde Park) The original part of the building dates to the late 1700s, when it was a post house on the old Albany Post Rd. Later a farmhouse, it was the headquarters for the U.S. Secret Service when FDR was in residence less than one mile down the road. More than 30 dealers are represented, and not surprisingly, there's lots of FDR and WWII memorabilia, including recruiting and War Bond posters. Also, vintage cameras, Oriental and Art Deco furniture, pocket watches, and leather-bound books from the 1800s. Open daily.

Village Antique Center (845-229-6600; 4331 Albany Post Rd./Rte. 9, Hyde Park) A jumble of 10-foot-tall Victorian and Federal armoires and credenzas, coin proof sets, inlaid mosaic boxes, porcelain figurines, all guarded by a front lawn populated by huge stone and bronze lions and fountains. Open daily.

OTHER SHOPS

Rustic Cabin (845-229-2281; www.rustic-cabin.com; 4274 Albany Post Rd./Rte. 9, Hyde Park) Rustic and log home gifts and accessories, much either in the shape of or decorated with moose, bears, wolves, or horses. Open daily.

Millbrook

This is horse country, with local polo matches and fox hunts, and a surrounding landscape dotted by jumping fences and stables. Local shops in the picturesque, old-fashioned downtown village reflect that interest.

→ ANTIQUES

Millbrook Antique Mall (845-677-9311; fax 845-677-1019; 3301 Franklin Ave., Millbrook) The largest antiques center for miles around, with more than 30 dealers. Everything from 18th-century furniture to 19th-century framed botanicals, porcelain, and delft tiles. Open daily.

OTHER SHOPS

British Sporting Ltd. (845-677-8303; fax 845-677-5756; www.bsaltd.com; 3684 Rte. 44, Millbrook) Downstairs are antique and modern long guns, some with beautifully inlaid silver stocks, also gift items related to shooting, such as hand-carved walking sticks, flasks, and bird sculptures. Upstairs is a full line of Italian, British, and Danish tweed and leather outerwear and handbags, plus woven ties with bird and dog motifs. Open Tues.–Sun.
Rare Finds (845-677-1776; fax 845-677-6399; 3286 Franklin Ave., Millbrook) Horse and dog motif ties and gift items, carved walking sticks, and Irish and English candles and bath products. Open Wed.–Mon.

Red Hook

ANTIQUES

Attic Memories (845-758-9283; 18 E. Market, Red Hook) Twenty-two dealers specializing in vintage clothing and jewelry from the '50s, antique lace tablecloths, linens, books, and magazines. Open daily.
George Cole Auctions (845-758-9114; www.georgecoleauctions.com; 7579 N. Broadway, Red Hook) Largest and most respected auction house in the area. Quality vintage and antique furniture and accessories. Call for hours.

BOOKS

Merritt Books (845-758-BOOK; fax 845-677-5894; 796 S. Broadway, Red Hook) A little bit of everything in this corner store, including a section of historic titles about local towns. Open daily.

CRAFTS

Cavallo Fine Jewelry (877-716-2511; fax 845-758-0068; 4B Tobacco Ln., Red Hook) The husband-wife owners trained as a gold and silver smith and a graphic artist, and they design and make many of the pieces in the shop. Also, a selection of handblown glass, pottery, and hand-painted silk accessories by local artisans. Open Mon.–Sat.

OTHER SHOPS

Don's Tackle Service (845-758-4211; 7376 S. Broadway, Red Hook) Antique fishing tackle, plus brand new Orvis fishing gear and clothing and a complete fly shop. Open Wed.–Sun.

Rhinebeck

Rhinebeck is a historic town is filled with historic things to buy. Most shopping is clustered around the Beekman Arms, the oldest inn in the U.S. (see Chapter Three, *Lodging*). The adjacent U.S. Post Office and parking lot behind the inn was a field where Revolutionary War troops trained. Rhinebeck is not only antique shops, it just seems that way.

→ **ANTIQUES**

Archer House Antiques (845-876-1974; fax 845-876-1796; 6380 Mill St. (Rte. 9), Rhinebeck) Museum-quality Colonial and Federal furniture, lamps, and candlesticks in an equally impeccably restored Colonial clapboard house, directly across the street from the Beekman Arms. Open Tues.–Sat.

Old Mill House Antiques (845-876-3636; 144 Rte. 9, Rhinebeck) Housed in an old mill house (hence the name) just south of town; the display is more like a private home where everything is for sale. Open daily.

CLOTHING

Winter Sun Summer Moon (845-876-3555; fax 845-876-2223; 10-14 E. Market St., Rhinebeck) Two adjoining stores with an eclectic selection of comfortable, countryish clothing and walking shoes, silk accessories from Thailand,

An antique barn filled with antiques in Rhinebeck.

Evelyn Kanter

jewelry from Tibet and India, all natural personal care products from Europe, plus stationery and gift items. Open daily.

JEWELRY

Hummingbird Jewelers (845-876-4585; fax 845-876-3177; 20 W. Market St., Rhinebeck) Top-quality imported fashion gold, silver, and diamond jewelry, many with colored gemstones, including Austrailian opal and coral, South Sea and Tahitian pearls, plus some antique items. A Tiffany-trained pearl stringer and engraver and a gemologist are on staff. Open Wed.–Mon.

Rock City

CLOTHING

Morehouse Farm Sheep's Clothing (845-758-3710; intersection of Rtes. 308 and 199, Rock City) Hand-knit hats, mittens, scarves, and sweaters in silky soft Merino wool from the Merino sheep raised on the farm. Also sheepskin clothing from the same animals and knitting yarns. Open daily.

Tivoli

This little town is located between Rhinebeck and Red Hook just south, and Bard College and Hudson just north and is a refuge for college students and others seeking relatively inexpensive rents.

BOOKS

Village Books (845-757-2665; 18 Broadway, Tivoli) Combination of new, used, and out-of-print books, specializing in social and political history, art, and local and regional titles. Across the street from the Lost Sock Launderette. Open Wed.–Sun.

GALLERIES

Artists Co-Op (845-757-2667; 60 Broadway, Tivoli) Rotating exhibits of local artists and sculptors, including John Corcoran, who has been commmissioned to create a memorial to honor murdered *Wall Street Journal* reporter Daniel Pearl. Open Fri.–Sun.

SHOPPING: COLUMBIA COUNTY

Hillsdale

BOOKS

Rodgers Book Barn (518-325-3610; 476 Rodman Rd., Hillsdale) There are some 50,000 used books in this two-floor barnlike shop. Large selection of arts and literature, including leather-bound books and children's books. Also, 33rpm records, mostly jazz and classical music and used CDs. Open Thurs.–Mon.

Hudson

This port city, founded by the Dutch, went into economic decline when the railroads arrived in the late 1800s. Now, the city and its solid downtown Victorian buildings are getting new life as an antiques center. More than 50 antiques shops line both sides of a five-block stretch of Warren St. It would be folly to list them all, so here are some standouts, and not just antiques.

→ **ANTIQUES**

Angelika Westerhoff (518-828-3606; www.angelikawesterhoffantiques.com; 606 Warren St., Hudson) Three floors of museum-quality Early American and period furniture, including rare (and costly) Stuckley, Shaker, Tiffany, and Chippendale. Also rare first edition books, especially 1880s travel and ethnology, some in foreign languages. Open Fri.–Tues.

Armory Antiques (518-822-1477; corner State & N. Fifth Sts., Hudson) This turreted red brick building, built in 1897, served as a National Guard Armory until 1967, and multiple dealers are taking advantage of the huge center hall. There are large pieces, including the occasional horse carriage and impressively sized chandeliers hung from the rafters. Also smaller items, including furniture and accessories. Open Thurs.–Mon.

K. Stair Antiques (phone/fax 518-828-3351; 621 Warren St., Hudson) Fine English and Continental furniture and accessories from the 17th, 18th, and 19th centuries. Open Thurs.–Mon.

CRAFTS

Hudson Valley Arts Center (518-828-2661; 800-456-0507; fax 518-828-3434; www.fncraft.com; 337 Warren St., Hudson) More than 100 artisans are represented here, most of them local and regional. Items include glass sculptures, carved gourds, happily decorated children-sized tables and chairs, delicately handwoven scarves, and colorful hand-knit sweaters, plus jewelry, ranging from funky costume styles to 18k gold elegant. Open Thurs.–Mon.

OTHER SHOPS

Hudson Photographic Center (518-828-2170; 623 Warren St., Hudson) The Brooklyn-born owner is a photographer and a baseball buff. In addition to current fine color photography prints, there are vintage black-and-whites of the legendary Brooklyn Dodgers and Ebbets Field and the New York Giants and Polo Grounds, plus autographed baseballs from the likes of Willy Mays and Bobby Thompson. Also vintage cameras. Open Mon.–Sat.

Lillian and Loo (518-822-9492; 345 Warren St., Hudson) Interesting, well-designed items from South Africa, including poplar branches woven into baskets and urns, bamboo place mats, and carved horn jewelry and serving pieces. Also, Asian silk pillows, Mexican wire baskets, and other gift items. Open Tues.–Sun.

SHOPPING: ROCKLAND COUNTY

Nyack

Anchoring the western edge of the Tappan Zee bridge, this river town has become the area's antiques capital, and most of the shops are clustered in a six-block area downtown, interspersed by several interesting restaurants (see Chapter Four, *Restaurants & Food Purveyors*).

ANTIQUES

Antique Masters (845-727-7700; 87 Main St., Nyack) Mostly French country furniture, including armoires and chandeliers, plus European crystal, china, and paintings. The Egyptian-born owner attends Paris auctions twice a year for the block-deep shop. Open Tues.–Sun.

Hudson Valley Emporium (845-358-7226; 37 S. Broadway, Nyack) Nine antiques dealers sharing space within the old YMCA building. Open Tues.–Sun.

BOOKS

→ **Ben Franklin Bookshop** (845-358-0440; fax 845-358-5442; 17 N. Broadway, Nyack) It's easy to get lost in the stacks here and browse everything from rare first editions to 19th-century family photographs and $5 almanacs from the 1840s, which is around when this musty, eclectic, friendly bookstore first opened. Children's books from the 1950s are joined by more recent novels and biographies. Open Tues.–Sun.

Trevian Bookshop (845-348-3474; 30 N. Broadway, Nyack) Specializes in antique architecture, decorative arts, gardening, landscaping, and cookbooks in English, as well as from French, Italian, and German publishers. Also, a collection of bound magazines from the 1800s. Open Tues.–Sun.

OTHER SHOPS

Hickory Dickory Dock (845-358-7474; fax 845-358-6519; www.hickorydock. com; 43 S. Broadway, Nyack) Hundreds of cuckoo clocks, from tiny souvenir sizes to extravagant hand-carved gems with complicated choreography. Mercifully, the clocks are set at different times so they don't all chime and cuckoo simultaneously. There's also a collection of nutcrackers and holiday decorations.

My Dollhouse (845-358-4185; 7 S. Broadway, Nyack) Old-fashioned hand-crafted wooden doll houses, both finished and in kit form, plus a vast selection of furniture and decorative details, from shingles to canned goods, to customize your dream minihouse. Even the lights will work, via a 12-volt transformer.

Pearl River

ANTIQUES

Dreams (845-735-4621; 3 W. Central Ave., Pearl River) Antique and vintage dolls, including porcelain and Raggedy Anns, doll carriages, and child-sized china tea sets. The owner also repairs handmade dolls.

Linmargo Wholesale Jewelry (845-620-1618; 39 E. Central Ave., Pearl River) Antique and vintage sterling serving pieces, estate jewelry, and porcelain, including Depression glass. Also sterling silver jewelry, including jewelry with semiprecious stones, modern marquisite selections, and some 14k gold, all at true wholesale prices.

OTHER SHOPS

Central Military Surplus (845-620-9324; fax 845-620-9335; 1 N. Main St., Pearl River) Camouflage jackets, pants and hats, metal detectors, WWII wool coats and sweaters from the U.S. and European services, scratchy Army wool blankets, combat boots, and an extensive selection of military ribbons and medals from WWII to the present. The camouflage motif extends to the plastic shopping bags in which your purchases are placed.

The Stitchery (845-735-4534; 49 E. Central Ave., Pearl River) This is an old-fashioned knitting shop, with multicolored, multitextured yarns stacked in bins to the ceiling and racks and stacks of pattern books. The store has been owned by the same family since the 1970s. Also, needlepoint canvases and a huge selection of novelty buttons to decorate those hand-knit sweaters.

Piermont

What was a cluster of abandoned, derelict mills, factories, and warehouses in this quaint and quiet riverside town has been restored and turned into a complex of art galleries and shops now called Piermont Landing.

ANTIQUES

Buttercup & Friends (845-359-1669; 535 Piermont Ave., Piermont) Take a trip back to your childhood. This cluttered shop has old-fashioned Lionel trains, hand-sewn puppets, wooden handled jump ropes, kites and such, and the owner usually is playing '40s big band music on the stereo.

GALLERIES

Bon à Trier (845-365-3333; fax 845-365-1902; 3 Round House Rd., Piermont) The specialty here is works on paper, and this gallery is the match of any you would find on New York City's Madison Ave., without the pretension of marked-up prices. There always are pen, pencil, and charcoal works by Picasso, Braque, and Winslow Homer, plus watercolors by Shawn Wyeth.

Flywheel Gallery & Piermont Fine Arts Gallery (845-365-6411; 845-398-1907; 218 Ash St., Piermont) These adjacent galleries represent some 25 local artists and offer rotating exhibits of their work, mostly painting and sculpture.

Hudson River Art Gallery (845-398-1242; fax 845-398-0367; www.the-art-site.com; 10 Round House Rd., Piermont) Predominantly paintings of water scenes, ranging from the Hudson to Venice, by both local and international artists.

Sneden's Landing

ANTIQUES

Yonderhill Antiques (phone/fax 845-398-0269; Rte. 9W, Sneden's Landing) Housed in a former church dating from the 1850s, with the original wide-plank wood floors and crammed with a collection of 19th- and 20th-century lighting, furniture, and paintings, plus a trove of Early American quilts and paintings.

SHOPPING: ORANGE COUNTY

Cornwall

CRAFTS

Cornwall Country Crafts (845-534-4317; 240 Main St., Cornwall) Hand-painted wood, jewelry, dried flower wreaths and arrangements, and gifts. Open Tues.–Sun.

GALLERIES

Gayle Clark Fedigan Gallery (845-534-3575; 240 Hudson St., Cornwall) Hudson River landscapes and still lifes by more than one dozen local artists. Open Wed.–Sun.

Highland Falls

OTHER SHOPS

Vasily's Inc. (845-446-5918; 800-238-9969; fax 845-446-2024; 427 Main St., Highland Falls) Larger selection and lower prices for West Point T-shirts and sweats, including teams and sports, than at the West Point Museum across the street. Also, military unit patches, such as the fabled 10th Mountain Division, medals, and ribbons, miniature international flags, and gift items, such as camouflage-printed lighters. Open daily.

Salisbury Mills

GALLERIES

Bethlehem Art Gallery (845-496-4785; 800-948-4248; fax 845-496-2878; 58 Orrs Mills Rd., Salisbury Mills) Artist Paul Gould is locally renowned as a landscape artist, painting teacher, and art restorer. His oil and water color scenics of the Hudson Valley, New England, and Ireland are lush and colorful. Open Wed.–Sat.

Sugar Loaf

This tiny hamlet was founded in 1749 as a community of artists and crafts-people, and the main street still is known by its original name, Kings Highway. Most of the shops are in historic houses or barns dating back to the 1700s and 1800s. Many of the craftspeople live upstairs or alongside their shops, and you are likely to find the shop owner or a relative painting, sewing, or bead string-ing while you browse. All the shops and galleries are closed Mondays, some on Tuesdays, too, and many shops are on the web site: www.sugarloafartsvillage .com.

ANTIQUES

18th Century Furniture (845-469-5159; Wood Rd. (adjacent to a municipal parking area), Sugar Loaf) As its name implies, this red farmhouse building just outside of the downtown crafts strip is filled with Colonial and later chairs, tables, cabinets, and accessories.

William J. Jenack Auctioneers (www.jenack.com; 62 Kings Hwy. Bypass, Sugar Loaf) Fine art, antique furniture and accessories, estate jewelry, col-lectibles. Monthly sales; call for dates.

CRAFTS

Hand-dipped candles hang from the ceiling at The Candle Shop in Sugar Loaf, a town founded in 1749 as an artisans colony.

Evelyn Kanter

Bostree (845-469-6113; 1361 Kings Hwy., Sugar Loaf) Nearly everything is made by the owner and local and regional artists and includes decorative pottery, stained glass, swirled glass perfume bottles, and jewelry. One popular item is a swirled glass pen that uses real old-fashioned inkwell ink.

The Candle Shop (845-469-4927; 1378 Kings Hwy., Sugar Loaf) Taper pairs in various lengths hang from pegs on the exposed ceiling beams and along the walls in a rainbow of colors, including such unusual ones for candles as lime, lavender, mulberry, and turquoise. When the shop isn't busy, the owner is busy dipping candles in the back of the shop.

Into Leather (845-469-5519; 1365 Kings Hwy., Sugar Loaf) Handcrafted leather briefcases, handbags, wallets, belts, gloves, and photo albums are made in the back of the store. There's also a selection of fringed, Western-style and motorcycle jackets, plus more city-oriented blazers and lined coats. A display case holds Native American and silver belt buckles.

Olala (845-469-1926; 1376 Kings Hwy., Sugar Loaf) The buckets of loose beads attract teenaged girls, but it is the Victorian-inspired beaded necklaces, earrings, and bracelets that appeal to grown-ups. The French owner-artist blends offbeat combinations of decorative beads, including vintage iridescent glass beads. There also are fully beaded handbags, checkbook covers, and eyeglass cases.

Quilted Corner (845-469-7119; 14 Romer's Alley, Sugar Loaf) Handmade quilts, including from nonallergenic organic cotton fabric and batting. Baby quilts come with matching bibs, and there's another collection of bibs from fabric scraps. The artist-owner also paints pet portraits from photographs. Sugar Loaf was a stop on the slave Underground Railroad, and the owner displays a collection of "code" quilts — a diamond pattern meant "meet at the crossroads," and a series of triangles was a map to head in the direction of the triangles.

Rosner Soap (845-469-5931; www.rosnersoap.com: 1373 Kings Hwy., Sugar Loaf) Traditional handmade soaps, made in the basement of this old clapboard house by a French-trained soap maker. Ingredients are olive oil, coconut oil, palm oil, and pure essential fragrance oils. And what fragrances! The heady scent fills the tiny shop, once the front parlor. Lemongrass, lavender, peppermint, cinnamon, anise, and florals, some with or without exfoliant, sold by the ounce.

Wishes & Dreams (845-469-0999; 5 Romer's Alley, Sugar Loaf) Wonderful, whimsical handmade stuffed animals with handmade clothes that can be removed, "tooth fairy" pillows in the shape of a molar, with a pocket for the secret tooth/payment exchange, plus hand-painted glassware and homemade jams and jellies. Everything is made by the owner, her sister, brother, or in-laws.

Warwick

ANTIQUES

Antiques Warwick (845-986-9919; 7 Main St., Warwick) When his long-time employer moved from New Jersey to California, Dennis Christensen opted to stay east and used his severance pay to indulge in his love of quality antiques: American and European furniture, from Colonial to French Art Deco, lighting, carpenter's wood tool chests from the 1800s. Open Wed.–Sun.

The Garage at the Eclectic Eye (845-986-5520; 16 Railroad Ave., Warwick) The carved stone doorway still says Warwick Auto Company; this building began life in 1908 as an auto dealership and garage. Now, it's filled with an eclectic mix of antique Oriental carpets, Colonial and Victorian furniture, vintage French and Italian couture clothes, shoes and accessories, including Chanel and Ungaro. There's also a custom cabinetmaker on hand to build antique-looking distressed tables and armoires. Open Wed.–Sun.

BOOKS

A. R. Backer (845-590-1873; 7 West St., Warwick) Tucked into an alley off the main street, this crowded shop specializes in used and out-of-print art books, both instructional and coffee table types, signed first editions, and leather-bound books and sets. Open Wed.–Mon.

OTHER SHOPS

Victorian Treasures (845-986-7616; 21 Main St., Warwick) China tea sets, lace curtains, place mats, and an entire back room filled with antique reproduction teddy bears and dolls. Also, imported English floral-scented bath and body products. Open daily.

Washingtonville

CRAFTS

Village Emporium (845-496-5715; 2 South St., Washingtonville) Handblown glass, handmade greeting cards, hand-painted pottery and serving pieces, silk and dried floral wreaths, and handmade holiday ornaments and gift items, many by regional craftspeople. Open daily.

SHOPPING: ULSTER COUNTY

High Falls

This historic village is small enough that shops along the main street, which is Rte. 213, do not have street addresses; location is either east or west of the bridge over the Rondout Creek.

ANTIQUES

Cat House Antiques (845-887-0790; 138 Bruceville Rd., High Falls) Specializes in kitchenware from the '30s, '40s, and '50s, including enamel kitchen tables and Hoosier cabinets, chenille spreads and tablecloths, colored glass Pyrex dishes. Open Fri.–Mon.

GALLERIES

Potter Kaete Brittin Shaw in her studio in High Falls.

Evelyn Kanter

Kaete Brittin Shaw Gallery (845-687-7828; Rte. 213 (next to Bird Watcher's Country Store), High Falls) Inlaid multicolored porcelain in glaze and matte finishes are all handmade in the studio behind the showroom gallery. Both functional vases, bowls, and mugs and stylized decorative art pieces. Potter Shaw is best known for her assymetrical stackable bowls and teapots reminiscent of Alice in Wonderland's Mad Hatter. Open weekends and by appt.

Westcote Bell Studios (845-687-7526; Rte. 213 (behind Canal House), High Falls) Pottery and paintings. Vaughn Smith decorates most of his tableware, lamps, and art pieces with animals: dogs, cats, horses, giraffes, zebras. Also earthenware and stoneware bathroom sinks to custom order. Visitors are welcome to watch the pottery making. Smith's wife, Jaqueline Cohen, is the painter, producing colorful watercolors and collages in styles reminiscent of Chagall and Klee. Open Thurs.–Mon.

OTHER SHOPS

Bird Watcher's Country Store (845-687-9410; www.birdwatcherscountrystore.com; Rte. 213 (west of bridge), High Falls) Two floors of everything to do with wild birds, from seed and feeders to gifts, including weather vanes, birdbaths, ceramics, bird-related prints, even bird-shaped letter openers. Also bird-centered children's books and toys, field guides, birdsong CDs, binoculars, and Barlow enamel jewelry. Open daily.

Hurley & West Hurley

ANTIQUES

Van Deusen House Antiques (845-331-8852; 59 Main St., Hurley) Country and formal furnishings, early porcelain, glass and tools, housed in an 18th-century landmark building. Call for hours (owner lives above store).

CRAFTS

Crafts People (845-331-3859; 262 Spillway Rd., West Hurley) More than 500 craftspeople are represented here, in a sprawling selection housed in four buildings scattered on 25 acres. Take a picnic lunch, enjoy the gardens, watch craft demonstrations, and browse for pottery, blown glass, jewelry, and clothing. Open Fri.–Mon.

Kingston

ANTIQUES

Skillypot Antique Center (845-338-6779; 41 Broadway, Kingston) More than one dozen dealers in this large corner shop, including glass bottles, Fiestaware, and a large selection of antique postcards. Open Thurs.–Tues.

BOOKS

Three Geese in Flight (845-338-2358; www.threegeeseinflight.com; 277 Fair St., Kingston) Specializes in Arthurian legend, rare Celtic and Scottish books, Revolutionary War histories, and local and regional histories, new and used, and Scottish and Celtic CDs. Open Mon., Tues., Thurs.–Sat.

Taking a break from shopping to enjoy the river view.

Evelyn Kanter

GALLERIES

Coffey Gallery (845-339-6105; 330 Wall St., Kingston) Changing exhibits by local artists: metal, sculpture, and paintings. Open Tues.–Sun.

The Gallery at Artists Studio on the Rondout (845-331-4310; 89 Broadway, Kingston) Local photographers and artists. Open Tues.–Sun.

OTHER SHOPS

Uptown Cigar Company (845-340-1142; fax 845-340-1139; 32 John St., Kingston) Fuente, Macanudo, Padson, Davidoff, and other top brands from Latin America and Europe, plus imported cigarettes, inlaid wood humidors, pipes, and loose tobacco. A separate section is a coffee shop with upholstered furniture.

Well Seasoned Nest (845-338-4639; 303 Wall St., Kingston) Country-style gifts and table accessories, plus imported jams, jellies, and candles. Housed in an 1874 bank building; check the vault for table settings. The owners also rent the vault for catered candlelight dinners for two.

New Paltz

ANTIQUES

Aphrodite's Antiques & Gifts (845-255-2769; 77 Main St., New Paltz) It's tough to turn around in this jam-packed shop, which mixes new items such as stained glass lamps with antique chandeliers and jewelry, much of it displayed in antique-carved wooden cases with curved glass. Housed in a Victorian storefront with original tin ceilings and exposed brick walls.

BOOKS

Ariel Booksellers (845-255-8041; www.arielbooksellers.com; 3 Plattekill Ave., New Paltz) Huge, chain-sized store just off Main St., with 250,000 titles in stock (this is a college town). Large selection of New York State field guides and birding books, plus a separate shop for used books and CDs. Open daily.

Esoterica (845-255-5777; 81 Main St., New Paltz) Specializing in books on yoga, healing arts, shamanism, spirituality, and meditation. Also children's books and CDs. Open daily.

CRAFTS

Handmade and More (845-255-6277; 6 N. Front St., New Paltz) Candles, pottery, art glass, jewelry, hand-painted glassware, inlaid wooden chopsticks and serving pieces, and women's clothing from artisans in the U.S., Mexico, and the Far East. Open daily.

GALLERIES

Mohonk Images (845-256-0323; 800-438-7838; www.mohonkimages.com; 5 N. Front St., New Paltz) Fine art color photography of area landscapes. Especially beautiful are the fall foliage and snow-covered scenes. Prints by gallery owner and photographer G. Steve Jordan decorate many restaurants and B&Bs in the area. Open Tues.–Sun.

OTHER SHOPS

Rock and Snow (845-255-1311; fax 845-255-2380; www.rocksnow.com; 44 Main St., New Paltz) This is the premier shop for rock climbing and ice-climbing gear in the northeast, not surprising, since the fabled "The Gunks" cliff rock-face wall is just a few miles away. Full line of climbing shoes and clothing, ropes, and harnesses, plus climbing and hiking guidebooks, and a list of certified climbing instructors and guides. Open daily.

Water St. Antique & Arts Village (Corner Main and Water Sts., New Paltz) A "village street" of individual shops and galleries offering a range of items from small furniture and gifts to handmade jewelry and pottery. Open Wed.–Mon.

Rosendale

ANTIQUES

Rural Delivery Antiques (845-658-3485; 407 Main St., Rosendale) This is the largest of three antique shops next door to one another, housed in an 1890s brick building that was a tavern when Rosendale was the cement-making capital of the U.S. Specialties are Mission oak furniture, lamps, and lighting, and the owner does rewiring.

CRAFTS

Women's Studio Workshop (845-658-9133; www.wsworkshop.org; 722 Binnewater Ln., Rosendale) Ongoing exhibitions of printmaking, papermaking, photography, and pottery. Open Tues.–Fri.

Saugerties

ANTIQUES

Central Hotel Antiques Center (845-247-8183; 83 Partition St., Saugerties) A catchall mix of Art Deco and Victorian furniture and lighting and vintage cut velvet and lace fabrics. Housed in a brick building built as a hotel in the 1840s.
Saugerties Antique Center (845-246-8234; 220 Main St., Saugerties) Multiple dealers, everything from antique postcards to five-piece 1940s bedroom sets. Open 7 days.

BOOKS

Hope Farm Press & Booktrader (845-246-3522; 800-883-5778; www.hopefarm.com; 252 Main St., Saugerties) What may be the world's largest selection of books on New York State history, archaeology, politics, and Native American history, totaling more than 2,700 current and out-of-print titles. Also specializes in military history, art, photography, and children's books. Owner Richard Frisbee is a walking encyclopedia of local and regional information. Open Tues.–Sun.
Inquiring Mind (845-246-5155; 65 Partition St., Saugerties) Eclectic mix of new and used books. Open Tues.–Sun.

OTHER SHOPS

The Arts & Clay Company and Copperworks (845-246-7741; 124 Partition St., Saugerties) Reproduction art, pottery, and copper decorative items, ranging in size from bud vases to nearly life-sized statues, also Tiffany-style lamps. Open Thurs.–Mon. and by appt.
Leonard Robbins (914-246-5331; 2891 Rte. 32, Saugerties) Vintage farm and carpentry tools and 1950s motorcycle and auto parts from when the owner had a repair shop here. Also, hundreds of shoe boxes filled with vintage baseball, basketball, football, hockey, and NASCAR trading cards. Open daily, May–Nov.

SHOPPING: GREENE COUNTY

Acra

CRAFTS

Gilded Grapes (518-622-9751; Rte. 23, Acra) The only purple house on the road is not easy to miss; even the flower boxes have purple flowers. The German-born owner and her daughter sell their hand-painted and decorated mirrors, doorstoppers, holiday ornaments, and dried flower wreaths. Also, old-fashioned handmade stuffed dolls and animals and vintage German lace and embroidered tablecloths. Open daily.

Catskill

ANTIQUES

Day & Holt Co. (518-943-2650; 349 Main St., Catskill) One side of this double storefront is the town's hardware store, and you enter through that to reach the antiques, primarily duck decoys and tools. Also glass milk bottles and their wooden crates (which milkman used to deliver them), furniture, and glassware. Open Mon.–Sat.

Townhouse Antiques (518-943-7400; 375 Main St., Catskill) Miniature toy soldiers and trains, Asian porcelain, 1880s transferware china, and Victorian pressed glass. Open Thurs.–Sat. and by appt.

GALLERIES

Greene County Arts Council (518-943-3460; 398 Main St., Catskill) Rotating exhibit of local and regional artists. Open Mon.–Sat.

OTHER SHOPS

Ann Stewart Kiltmaker (518-943-0975; 384 Main St., Catskill) Anything and everything Scottish, including bagpipe accessories, bagpipe and folk CDs, maps, heraldic shields, tartan scarves, and kid-sized kilts. The real specialty, though, is the selection of tartans and the owner's wide-flung reputation for custom-made kilts, for individuals and such marching bands as West Point and the New York City Police Department (NYPD). Open Mon.–Fri.

East Durham

Rte. 23, which runs east-west across the Hudson Valley, also is the dividing line on the west side of the river, between two culturally distinct vacation areas. South of the road lie the "German Alps" and on the northern side the "Irish Alps." The rolling landscape of East Durham and adjacent Leeds are more than one type of green.

OTHER SHOPS

Guaranteed Irish (518-634-2392; fax 518-634-7409; Rte. 145, East Durham) One of the largest selections of Irish music in the Northeast, plus Belleck and Royal Tara china, jams, jellies, teas, candies, Claddagh gold and silver jewelry, and heraldic shields. Head past the souvenir T-shirts and coffee mugs to the basement, a treasure trove of hand-knit sweaters, hats, and scarves and handwoven or loomed coats and capes, Donegal hats, and blankets. Open daily.

East Windham

Technically, this is outside the Hudson Valley, up into the foothills of the Catskill Mountains. But the 15-minute drive west on Rte. 23 from the river is spectacular, especially the lookout area that — on a clear day — offers a panorama glimpse of Massachusetts's Berkshires and Vermont's Green Mountains to the northeast and New York's Adirondacks and Catskills to the north and southwest. Even without the view, this shop is worth leaving the valley briefly to visit.

CRAFTS

Blue Pearl (518-734-6625; www.ulladarni.net; 7751 Rte. 23, East Windham) Ulla Darni is a world-class glass artisan. Her ceiling lamps are semicircular domes painted on the inside with fanciful florals and Asian-inspired patterns that shimmer three-dimensionally, softly, even mystically, when illuminated. Also, similarly made palm-sized discs catch the light in a window. A three-floor shop in a restored Victorian home also offers Indian, Tibetan, and Native American jewelry, jade sculptures, and Balinese textiles. Open daily.

SHOPPING MALLS

Millions of people live within a 50-mile circle around New York City. While local civic pride prevents these towns and villages from considering themselves "bedroom communities" for commuters, the reality is that population density and real estate values make huge suburban shopping malls the rule, rather than the exception. So it's no surprise that the biggest, most bustling malls are within 45 minutes of Times Square. Sleepy main streets lined with architecturally significant vintage buildings and family-owned businesses — where the post office is the place to pick up your mail and run into neighbors, in towns where residents often leave their doors unlocked — are farther.

WESTCHESTER COUNTY

The Galleria (914-682-0111; White Plains) Four-story mall with 140 shops and a food court.

Jefferson Valley Mall (914-245-4688; www.shopsimon.com; Yorktown Heights) More than 100 shops, including H&M and Macy's, an eight-screen cinema complex, and a food court.

Manufacturers Outlet Center (914-241-8503; Mount Kisco) Two dozen discount shops and an on-site restaurant.

The Westchester (914-683-8600; www.the-westchester-ny.com; White Plains) More than 150 upscale fashion and gourmet food shops, including Neiman Marcus and Nordstrom's. Valet parking, full-service concierge, and original artwork scattered throughout the huge complex make this a scenic attraction, as much as a shopping experience.

DUTCHESS COUNTY

Poughkeepsie Galleria (845-297-7600; www.poughkeepsiegalleriamall.com; 2001 Rte. 9, Poughkeepsie) Two-story mall anchored by Sears, Filene's, JCPenney, and Target and adjacent to smaller South Hills Mall, an enclosed shopping center.

ROCKLAND COUNTY

Nanuet Mall (845-623-9040; Rte. 59, Nanuet) Smaller and less crowded than its giant newer neighbor and anchored by Sears and Macy's.

Palisades Center (845-348-1000; Rte. 59, West Nyack) This 3.0-million-square-foot, four-level monster mall is the second largest in the U.S. In addition to department stores, including Filene's, Target, and JCPenney, there's a huge entertainment complex, including a restored antique carousel, Ferris wheel, ice-skating rink, and a 21-screen movie theater, including an Imax theater.

ORANGE COUNTY

Woodbury Commons Premium Outlets (845-928-4000; 498 Red Apple Crt. (intersection of NY State Thruway and Rtes. 32 and 17) Central Valley) Top designer shops, including Armani, Chanel, Brooks Brothers, Versace, plus store outlets, including Neiman Marcus, Off-5th-Saks Fifth Avenue, and Williams-Sonoma. There is a nonstop shopper's bus service from the Port Authority bus terminal in NYC.

CHAPTER NINE
Gateway to the Hudson Valley
NEW YORK CITY

In this short chapter we give recognition to the fact that many visitors to the Hudson Valley will have occasion to pass through New York City. The following is a highly selective compendium of attractions that have particular connection to the history, places, and pleasures of the Hudson.

Taking a bite out of the Big Apple is no easy task. New York City has more of everything than any other place in the world.

Culture? **The American Ballet Theater, New York City Ballet, New York Philharmonic,** and the **Metropolitan Opera** call the **Lincoln Center** home. In New York City, there's a museum for every taste in art and history, plus several museums showcase photography.

Entertainment? Don't miss **Broadway** and **Off-Broadway** theater and the incomparable high-kicking precision of the **Radio City Music**

NYCVisit

The watchful lady in New York Harbor.

Hall Rockettes. Uptown, it's the **Apollo Theater** in Harlem for music; downtown, it's the velvet rope scene of the clubs and discos in **Greenwich Village** and **Soho;** and midtown, it's **Swing 46** for zoot-suited live bands playing '30s and '40s music for a dancing crowd whose ages range from 20 to 80, more or less.

History? New York City was the nation's first capital, and its first president, George Washington, took his inaugural oath of office in 1789, where **Federal Hall Memorial** now stands at 26 Wall Street. The building that stood there then, English City Hall, also was where John Peter Zenger was tried and acquitted for libel in 1735 — he was defended by Alexander Hamilton in a precedent-setting decision, later reflected in the Bill of Rights guaranteeing freedom of the press.

Recreation? You could chip golf balls into the Hudson River at **Chelsea Piers,** except for the three-sided, three-story fence around this driving range. Or, grab a tennis racket and play on any of the hundreds of courts dotting the city's parks, including **Riverside Park** at the edge of the Hudson and **Central Park,** that monument to urban planning — a green escape valve for the city smack in the middle of the island. Or, borrow a kayak from the **Downtown Boathouse** (212-385-2790) at Pier 26 near Canal Street and paddle west toward the center of the Hudson River for a magnificent view. You can bicycle along the uninterrupted **Greenway,** a paved strip from one end of Manhattan to the other, alongside the Hudson River, or ice-skate under the watchful eye of a giant statue of Prometheus in **Rockefeller Center.**

Sports? Brooklyn has never forgiven the Dodgers for heading west in the 1950s, but the wound is finally healing thanks to the **Brooklyn Cyclones,** the farm team for the **New York Mets**. The minor league team plays in a brand-new stadium in Coney Island (718-449-8497). **Liberty** is the record-setting women's basketball team that plays in Madison Square Garden (877-962-2849). And, of course, the **New York Yankees,** whose stadium is in The Bronx, a part of NYC named for its original Dutch settlers, the Bronck family.

Kids? Check out the life-sized blue whale and the dinosaurs at the **Museum of Natural History,** watch the sea lions cavorting in the pond at the **Central Park Zoo,** or visit the lions, tigers, and giraffes at the **Bronx Zoo.** Kids of all ages enjoy watching the giant balloons get inflated the night before the annual **Macy's Thanksgiving Day Parade** or riding across the bay on the **Staten Island Ferry.**

Transportation? The NYC bus and subway fare is $2, and a single fare permits a transfer between two busses or between a subway and a bus. Busses do not accept bills, only coins or a Metrocard (212-METROCA; www.mta.nyc.ny.us), which can be purchased in any subway station and in many other locations, for any number of rides. There is also a Fun Pass, which provides a day of unlimited subway and bus rides for just $6.

NEW YORK CITY ATTRACTIONS

THE TIES THAT BIND

Despite occasional political rifts and rivalries that divide New York City and the Hudson Valley, the history of the two is tied, inexorably and symbiotically, via the waterway that the Native Americans called "the river that flows both ways." From Henry Hudson's days to today, commerce and wealth moves in both directions along with the tidal flow of the Hudson River. These places, more than others, have a special link.

MANHATTAN

Lower Manhattan

The original 1624 Dutch settlement of New Netherland ended at the protective stockade wall, now known as Wall Street. This part of lower Manhattan is filled with narrow streets designed for horse traffic, not SUVs, in a crazy quilt pattern that predated the grid system introduced in the 1800s.

George Washington returned from his headquarters in Newburgh to bid goodbye to his troops at **Fraunces Tavern** at the corner of Broad and Pearl Streets, where a replica built in 1907 now stands. There is evidence that the original tavern was owned by a French West Indian. The restaurant is downstairs (212-968-1776), and a small museum is upstairs (212-425-1778).

In 1792, a group of merchants gathered under a buttonwood tree on Wall Street to draw up a trading agreement. That became the **New York Stock Exchange** (212-656-5165 free tour) at 20 Broad Street. In 1860, financier Jay Gould, who spent summers at his estate Lyndhurst in Tarrytown, and his partners manipulated the market to gain control of the Erie Railroad from Cornelius Vanderbilt. A few years later, they tried and failed to corner the gold market, but only succeeded in setting off financial panic.

In the 1820s, two Pennsylvania coal merchants sold enough stock to pay for construction of a 108-mile canal to Kingston, where the coal would finish its trip to NYC on the Hudson River. One of the architects for the D&H Canal was John Roebling, who later designed and built the **Brooklyn Bridge,** a few blocks east. Walk across this Gothic confection on the pedestrian promenade and enjoy some of the most amazing vistas in town.

While working for D&H, Roebling discovered a superdurable cement made in Rosendale that he used in the bridge's construction. Rosendale cement also was used to construct the base of the **Statue of Liberty** (212-363-3200; www.nps.gov/stli), a gift of the people of France. Just north of Liberty Island is **Ellis Island** (212-363-3200; www.ellisisland.org) where, between 1892 and 1924, 12 million immigrants first set foot on the shores of freedom. After years of neglect, it reopened as a museum to immigration. Go and find your ancestors.

The original Dutch settlers played an outdoor ball game that developed into hockey, golf, or bowling, perhaps all three. Adjacent to a park called Bowling Green sits a huge 1907 Beaux Arts structure, originally the U.S. Customs House, now the **National Museum of the American Indian** (212-514-3700; www.si.edu.nmai), a branch of the Smithsonian Institution. In addition to artifacts from U.S. tribes, including the Hudson Valley's original inhabitants, there are displays of Maya and other cultures of the Americas.

Battery Park, the southernmost tip of Manhattan, once held a Colonial battery of 28 cannons to fend off British attack. The fort area is now **Castle Clinton National Monument** (212-344-7220) and contains a small museum. George Clinton was New York State's first governor and Thomas Jefferson's Vice-President; he is buried in Kingston. The park also is the departure point for ferries (212-269-5755) to the Statue of Liberty and Ellis Island. Also within the park is the **Museum of Jewish Heritage – A Living Memorial to the Holocaust** (212-968-1800; www.mjhnyc.org) — a granite hexagon — a tribute to the six-pointed Star of David and to the six million who died in WWII.

On September 11, 2001, New York City, even the entire world, was changed irrecoverably by the destruction of the **World Trade Center,** which dominated lower Manhattan and the city skyline. The twin towers were the tallest in New York and among the tallest in the world, filling 16 acres of the world's most valuable real estate. It is a sad and somber space that must be visited.

A century before it became a center for memorial services after the WTC attack, **Union Square** was the site of prolabor rallies. It is also home to the city's largest greenmarket, dominated by Hudson Valley farms. Cheeses and smoked meats, herbs and flowers, fresh produce, including apples and peaches, and baked goods — every Monday, Wednesday, Friday, and Saturday.

Midtown

The **Empire State Building** (212-736-3100; www.esbnyc.com) is once again the city's tallest. Built in an astounding 13 months in the 1920s, it attracts four million visitors a year to its famous 86th-floor observation deck. Perhaps the most famous of those visitors was King Kong. It is on 34th Street, one block from **Macy's,** whose block-square flagship store claims to be the world's largest. From the Empire State Building, you can see the **Chrysler Building** a few blocks east and north, an Art Deco gem that was the city's tallest for a few weeks until the Empire State Building climbed higher. Automobile titan Walter Chrysler is buried in Sleepy Hollow Cemetery in Tarrytown.

Theodore Roosevelt is the only U.S. president from New York City. His birthplace, at 28 East 20th Street, is now the **Theodore Roosevelt Birthplace National Historic Site** (212-260-1616; www.nps,gov/thrb) and is filled with Teddyana, including versions of the Teddy bear named for him.

DIA Center for the Arts (212-989-5566; www.diacenter.org) is a museum of contemporary art that has outgrown its space and is opening a giant facility in a former factory in Beacon.

Grand Central Station is the world's largest (76 acres) and busiest (half a million commuter railroad and subway users passing through it daily) and one of the world's most beautiful train stations. Imposing Beaux Arts on the outside and an incomparable 12-story-high main concourse inside, whose ceiling depicts the celestial heavens, complete with twinkling stars. There's also an extensive food court downstairs with outposts of some of NYC's famous restaurants. Now called MetroNorth, this railroad, built by Cornelius Vanderbilt, is the former New York Central, whose tracks run along the Hudson River past the glorious Gilded Age millionaire mansions, including the Vanderbilt Mansion in Hyde Park.

Vanderbilt, also known as "the Commodore," also had extensive shipping interests, including the Cunard Line, whose piers around 23rd Street are where the Titanic would have docked. Those original Cunard piers are now **Chelsea Piers,** a sports and recreation complex.

Intrepid-Air-Sea-Space Museum (212-245-0072; www.intrepidmuseum.org) is the city's only floating museum and is located on the Hudson River at 42nd Street. This retired aircraft carrier, as long as the Empire State Building is high, has many exhibits, including an A-12 Blackbird bomber, lunar modules, WWII and Vietnam memorabilia, and a submarine, which is docked alongside.

At the other end of 42nd Street on the East River is the **United Nations Headquarters** (212-963-7713; www.un.org), built on land donated by the Rockefeller family. There is an hour-long guided tour of the artwork and some meeting rooms; a photo ID is required for admission to the grounds, which include a lovely sculpture garden.

Patience and Fortitude are the names of the two stone lions guarding the entrance to the formidable **New York Public Library** (212-930-0800; www.nypl .org) — formidable because it contains six million books, 12 million manuscripts, and nearly three million pictures and photographs, some dating back to the Dutch and English; there also are on-going historic exhibits.

It was the Great Depression when John D. Rockefeller, Jr., conceived of an urban renewal project that would provide jobs and revitalize mid-Manhattan. **Rockefeller Center** sprawls across 22 acres, north from 47th to 50th Streets and east from Sixth to Fifth Avenues. Although the complex is home to numerous national and international corporations and a below-ground shopping arcade, it is best known for the studio where NBC broadcasts the *Today* show and for **Radio City Music Hall** (212-247-4777; www.radiocity.com), home of the Rockettes; call for backstage tours. This is where the world famous Rockefeller Center Christmas tree stands, framed by an ice-skating rink and the **Channel Gardens** pedestrian plaza.

The Rockefeller family lived at Kykuit in Tarrytown. While John D. was building Rockefeller Center, his art collector wife, Abby, was founding the **Museum of Modern Art** (212-708-9400; www.moma.org) a few blocks away on

Gilded Prometheus watches over visitors to Rockefeller Center.

the site of their original NYC home. Currently this building is undergoing an extensive renovation; until it reopens in 2005, the museum is in temporary quarters in Long Island City.

The building at 767 Fifth Avenue at 58th Street used to be the **General Motors** building, and the lobby was a showcase for its vehicles, many of which were produced at the sprawling 96-acre GM plant in Tarrytown, which closed in 1996. The factory space is being converted into housing and parks, and the lobby space now is an F. A. O. Schwarz store, selling toys for a different generation.

Industrialist Andrew Carnegie paid for the Moorish design concert hall that bears his name. Since 1891, **Carnegie Hall** (212-247-7800; www.carnegiehall .org) has hosted the world's finest and most famous musicians and singers, starting with Tchaikovksy conducting one of his own compositions on opening night, plus Toscanini, Bernstein, Ellington, even The Beatles. There's a small museum and a backstage tour. Andrew Carnegie is buried in the Sleepy Hollow Cemetery in Tarrytown.

Upper Manhattan

Carnegie's 64-room mansion, at Fifth Avenue and 91st Street, is now the **Cooper-Hewitt National Design Museum** (212-849-8400; www.si.edu/ndm), a branch of the Smithsonian Institution. Exhibits focus on a wide range of design, from jewelry to hotel rooms, showcased in rooms that have retained their ornately carved wood walls and ceilings — Carnegie built the house in the early 1900s when he was one of the world's richest men. There is also a wonderful garden. The **Cooper-Hewitt** (named for granddaughters of industrialist Peter Cooper, who assembled much of the collection) is in the middle of "Museum Mile."

This stretch of Fifth Avenue, from the mid-80s and the low-100s, includes the **Metropolitan Museum of Art,** the circular **Solomon R. Guggenheim Museum,** designed by Frank Lloyd Wright, the **Museum of the City of New York,** and the **Museo del Barrio,** which focuses on Latin American and Caribbean art. **The Jewish Museum,** the **American Irish Historical Society,** the **Neue Gallery,** a collection of early 20th-century German and Austrian furniture and art organized by cosmetics heir Leonard Lauder, and the **Frick Collection** all are housed in former mansions, albeit not as extravagant as Carnegie's.

At the northern tip of Manhattan are two spots often classified as "off the beaten path," but well worth the effort. **The Cloisters** (212-923-3700; www.met museum.org) is a jigsaw puzzle of four medieval French and Spanish monasteries, assembled in 1938 atop a rocky hill where the British defeated the rebels in 1776 and renamed the outpost Fort Tryon for the British governor. It was financed by John D. Rockefeller, Jr., as a museum to showcase the family's medieval art. Now a branch of the Metropolitan Museum of Art, The Cloisters is home to six priceless 16th-century Unicorn Tapestries. The surrounding **Fort Tryon Park** contains steep but picturesque walkways, a landscaped garden at the southern end, and spectacular views of the Hudson.

Two blocks from the northern end of Fort Tryon Park sits the **Dyckman Farmhouse Museum** (4881 Broadway at 204th St.; 212-304-9422; www.dyck-man.org). Dating from 1785, this is the last Dutch farmhouse in Manhattan. Inside the gambrel-roofed house are original furnishings and Revolutionary War uniforms and weaponry; also there is a charming garden in the back of the house. The patriot Dyckman family fled when the British approached — perhaps to their Dyckman cousins at Boscobel in Garrison — and the house was occupied by Hessian soldiers. The Dyckmans returned after the war and continued to live here for several generations.

THE BOROUGHS

Brooklyn

If it were anywhere else in the world, the **Brooklyn Museum of Art** (718-638-5000; www.brooklynart.org) would be a national treasure; unfortunately this impressive 1897 Beaux Arts building, housing a world-class collection of ancient Egyptian artifacts and contemporary artwork, is overshadowed by the even bigger "Met" in Manhattan. There's a subway stop right on the corner of the museum, which is right next door to the equally impressive **Brooklyn Botanical Garden** (718-623-7200; www.bbg.org), with one of the largest collections of bonsais outside of Japan.

Long before the Civil War, **Plymouth Church of the Pilgrims** (718-624-4743; Orange & Henry Sts.) became a center of antislavery activity, thanks in part to sermons by Henry Ward Beecher (brother of Harriet Beecher Stowe, who wrote *Uncle Tom's Cabin*). The church is famous as an important stop on the Underground Railroad and for its stained glass windows by Louis Comfort Tiffany.

Prospect Park, like its Manhattan sibling Central Park, was designed and landscaped by Frederick Law Olmsted and Calvert Vaux. At its western edge, adjoining the **Prospect Park Zoo** and the carousel is the Dutch farmhouse, the **Lefferts Children's Historic House Museum** (718-399-7339).

The Bronx

G eorge Washington stayed at the Van Cortlandt house in the northeast Bronx several times during the Revolutionary War. The Dutch family's farm is now **Van Cortlandt Park** (718-543-3344), the third largest park in NYC, and the restored 1748 **Van Cortlandt Manor** is furnished with a mix of family possessions and period antiques. There is an extensive nature trail system here and in nearby **Wave Hill Park,** and the NYC Parks Dept. Urban Rangers give free tours.

The New York Botanical Garden (718-817-8700; www.nybg.org) is one of the world's leading botany centers, with two significant ties to the Hudson Valley — one is the Institute of Ecosystem Studies: Mary Flagler Cary Arboretum, a botanical and ecological research facility in Millbrook, and the other is the Peggy Rockefeller Rose Garden, with nearly 3,000 rose bushes of more than 250 varieties. There's also a children's adventure garden and a Victorian-era glass house that contains 17,000 glass panes protecting a tropical rain forest. Adjacent to the Botanical Garden is the **Bronx Zoo** (718-367-1010; www.wcs.org), with 4,500 animals, a children's zoo, and Wild Asia, where lions and tigers roam free.

Other than the fact that Edgar Allen Poe and Washington Irving wrote wonderful, fanciful tales at around the same time, there's no real connection between Poe and the Hudson Valley, but the **Poe Cottage** (718-881-8900; E. Kingsbridge Rd. and Grand Concourse) in The Bronx is one of those wonderful little gems that is undervisited. Poe wrote several of his most famous poems here, including *Annabel Lee.*

Queens

T he largest of NYC's five boroughs, some one-third of the entire city area, Queens is home to more than 2 million people, and some world-famous businesses, including Steinway Piano and **Kaufman-Astoria Studios,** the movie and television studio that produced such hits as *The Wiz, The Cosby Show,* and the ground-breaking children's television series *Sesame Street* that made international stars of Miss Piggy and Kermit. This studio is next door to the **American Museum of the Moving Image** (718-784-0877; 36-01 35th Ave.), which pays homage to silent movies, talkies, and television.

Flushing Meadows-Corona Park is home to the **National Tennis Center,** where the U.S. Open is held every year, and **Shea Stadium,** where the **New York Mets** play baseball. The park also is the site of the 1964 World's Fair, with the 140-foot-high globe known as the Unisphere, and two museums, the **Queens Museum of Art** and the **New York Hall of Science,** housed in former World's Fair pavilions.

Staten Island

O ften called New York's forgotten borough, it is linked to the others by the legendary, picturesque, and thoroughly functional **Staten Island Ferry** and the **Verrazano-Narrows Bridge.**

Historic Richmond Town (718-351-1611), on the site of an early Dutch settlement, is a complex of 30 historic buildings, including a jail, some dating to 1685. The complex is a few minutes walk from the Jacques Marchais **Museum of Tibetan Art** (718-987-3500), with the largest collection of its kind outside Tibet.

NEW YORK CITY DINING

I f you ate in a different restaurant every day, it would take you several years to mangia, fress, and otherwise bon appétit your way through town — from the inexpensive marinated lamb kabobs of the Afghanistan restaurants on Ninth Avenue in midtown Manhattan and the dim sum palaces of **Chinatown** to the haute prices of white glove service at the **21 Club,** a former speakeasy, legendary **Lutèce,** relative newcomer **Gramercy Tavern,** or the over-the-top crystal and glass decor of **Tavern on the Green** in Central Park. Or, just drop into one of the city's ubiquitous pizza places for a wedge-shaped slice of arguably the world's best fast food, unless you make the trip to Coney Island for one of **Nathan's Famous** hot dogs, slathered with briny sauerkraut and pungent mustard. Munch it on the way to the boardwalk overlooking the Atlantic Ocean or to the subway a block away that takes you back to Manhattan.

Although the following restaurants have no direct Hudson Valley connection, there is enough history here to merit mention. Aaron Burr's former carriage house in Greenwich Village is now a romantic restaurant, **One If By Land, Two If By Sea,** named for Paul Revere's famous revolutionary ride. In the midtown theater district, **Keen's Chop House** is equally famous for its mutton chops and its ceiling hung with hundreds of clay pipes of long-ago patrons, including Teddy Roosevelt, General Douglas MacArthur, and "Buffalo Bill" Cody. O'Henry wrote *Gift of the Magi,* while sitting in a booth at **Pete's Tavern,** a few blocks from Irving Place, where Washington Irving lived before moving to Sunnyside.

NEW YORK CITY LODGING

NYC & Company (800-846-ROOM; U.S., Canada; 212-582-3352, international; www.nycvisit.com) is the city's premiere tourist bureau.

The **Waldorf Astoria Hotel,** a few blocks from Grand Central Station, is built atop giant "shock absorbers" to soak up vibrations from the railroad tracks below. The hotel is a successor to the original, further downtown, built by John Jacob Astor and named for his hometown, Waldorf, Germany.

Two other historic hotels, favored by writers and theatrical performers, are **The Algonquin,** where such literary lights as Eugene O'Neill, Dorothy Parker, and H. L. Mencken gathered weekly at The Roundtable during the 1920s and 1930s, and the **Chelsea Hotel,** where Mark Twain, Arthur Miller, and Dylan Thomas stayed.

County Name Origins

The origin of the names of Hudson Valley counties are wrapped up in the early history of the region, a combination of Dutch, English, and Revolutionary War history.

- Albany County: Named in honor of the brother of King Charles II, Duke of York and Albany, who later became James II.
- Columbia County: Named for the Latin feminine form of Columbus. At one time, Columbia was seriously considered as the name for the newly independent colonies.
- Dutchess County: Named in honor of the Dutchess of York, wife of James.
- Greene County: Named for Nathanael Greene, considered by many to be the greatest officer of the Revolutionary War after George Washington.
- New York County: Named for James, Duke of York and Albany, who became King James II after the death of brother Charles; home of New York City.
- Orange County: Named in honor of the Dutch royal family, the House of Orange.
- Putnam County: Named in honor of General Israel Putnam, a Revolutionary War hero.
- Rockland County: Named for the "rocky land" that the early settlers found in the region.
- Saratoga County: Named for how the Dutch and English pronounced the Indian word *sah-rah-kah,* said to mean "the side hill."
- Ulster County: Named for the Duke of York's earldom in Ireland.
- Westchester County: Named for Chester, England

CHAPTER TEN
Facts & Figures
INFORMATION

Tania Barricklo

View of the Hudson River from the Vanderbilt lawn in Hyde Park, New York.

This chapter is a brief compendium of information that may be useful during your trip or in an emergency. It covers the following topics:

AMBULANCE, FIRE, POLICE

Emergency **911** for fire and police operates in all the counties covered in this book: Westchester, Putnam, Dutchess, Columbia on the east side of the Hudson; Rockland, Orange, Ulster, and Greene on the west side. Should you need additional guidance, the NYS Police maintains troop headquarters and multiple stations on either side of the river:.

Troop K Headquarters (845-677-7300; 2541 Rte. 44, Salt Point, NY) Located east of the river, about 10 miles northeast of Poughkeepsie; it covers Westchester, Putnam, Dutchess, and Columbia Counties.

Troop F Headquarters (845-344-5300; 55 Crystal Run Rd., Middletown, NY) Located west of the river and slightly west of the area covered by this book, about 28 miles from Newburgh; it covers Rockland, Orange, Ulster, and Green Counties.

Poison Control: Call the National Hot Line (800-222-1222), which routes callers to their local poison control offices.

AREA CODES

Two area codes serve most of the Hudson Valley region: **914** for Westchester County and lower Rockland County and **845** for almost everywhere else in the region covered in this book. Northern and western portions of Ulster County, Greene County, and north to Albany and Saratoga, use the **518** area code.

Travelers alighting in New York City will find the **212** area code for Manhattan and **718** for the other boroughs. Caveat: these are the old standard area codes; the explosion of cell phones and faxes means overlay area codes **646** and **917** are used from time to time throughout the metropolitan area.

BIBLIOGRAPHY

Ｉt would be folly to try to list all the books about the Hudson Valley. There are more than a dozen biographies just of Franklin and Eleanor Roosevelt and dozens more editions of Washington Irving's legendary tales, so this list is just a reference point. Most of these books are on sale in the gift shops of the mansions and historic homes that are mentioned in Chapter Six, *Mansions of the Hudson Valley.* Two excellent resources are Hope Farm Press (800-883-5778; www.hopefarm.com) and Black Dome Press (518-734-6357; www.blackdome-press); both specialize in books about New York State and the Hudson Valley.

Books You Can Buy

CHILDREN'S BOOKS

Cooper, James Fenimore. *The Last of the Mohicans.* 1826. Many editions and publishers; this is the original.
————. *The Spy.* 1821. Many editions and publishers; this is the original.
Irving, Washington. *The Sketch Book.* 1819. Many editions and publishers; this is the original and contains "The Legend of Sleepy Hollow" and "Rip Van Winkle."
Seeger, Pete. *Pete Seeger's Storytelling Book: A Collection of Stories of America's Past.* Harcourt Brace, 2000.

FOOD & WINE

Malouf, Waldy. *Hudson River Valley Cookbook.* Harvard Common Press, 1998.
Thomas, Marguerite. *Touring East Coast Wine Country: A Guide to the Finest Wineries.* Berkshire House Publishers, 2002.

HISTORY, MEMOIR & LORE

Baxter, Raymond, and Arthur Adams. *Railroad Ferries of the Hudson.* Fordham University Press, 1999.
Clyne, Patricia Edwards. *Hudson Valley Tales and Trails.* Penguin USA, 1997.
Diamant, Lincoln. *Chaining the Hudson: The Fight for the River in the American Revolution.* Citadel Press, 1994.
Goodwin, Doris Kearnes. *No Ordinary Time: FDR and Eleanor on the Home Front in WWII.* Touchstone Press, 1995.
Grant, John, James Lynch, and Ronald Bailey. *West Point: The First 200 Years.* Globe Pequot Press, 2002.
Hamilton, Captain John. *Hudson River Pilot: From Steamboats to Super Tankers.* Black Dome Press, 2001.

Irving, Washington. *Knickerbocker's History of New York.* Gretna, LA: Firebird Press, 1809; re-issue 1998.

Klein, Aaron. *Men Who Built The Railroads.* Gallery Books, 1986.

Klein, Milton M. *The Empire State: A History of New York.* Ithaca: Cornell University. Press, 2001.

Letters about the Hudson River: 1835-1837. Hope Farm Press.

Livingston, Edwin Brockhorst. *The Livingstons of Livingston Manor.* Milwaukee: Curtis House Publishers.

Lossing, Benson Jack, and Pete Seeger. *The Hudson: From the Wilderness to the Sea.* Black Dome Press, 1995.

Mabee, Carleton. *American Leonardo: Life of Samuel F. B. Morse.* Fleischmanns, NY: Purple Mountain Press.

Philip, Leila. *A Family Place Hudson Valley Farm: Three Centuries, Five Wars, One Family.* NY: Viking, 2001.

Purcell, Sarah, and Edward Purcell. *Critical Lives: Eleanor Roosevelt.* Indianapolis: Alpha Books, 2002.

Roosevelt, David B. *Grandmere: A Personal History of Eleanor Roosevelt.* Warner Books, 2002.

Ruttenberger, Edward. *Indian Tribes of the Hudson.* vol. 1 to 1700, vol. 2 1700–1850. Hope Farm Press.

Spiegel, Ted. *New York's Hudson: America's Valley.* Kingston, NY: Involvement Press, 2000.

Vanderbilt II, Arthur. *Fortune's Children: The Fall of the House of Vanderbilt.* HarperCollins, 2001.

Williams-Myers, Albert James. *Long Hammering: Forging An African-American Presence in the Hudson River Valley to the Early 20th Century.* Africa World Press, 1994.

NATURAL & ENVIRONMENTAL HISTORY

Adams, Arthur. *Hudson River Guidebook.* Fordham University Press, 1996.

Cronin, John, and Robert F. Kennedy, Jr. *The Riverkeepers.* Touchstone Books, 1999.

Stanne, Stephen P., Roger G. Panetta, and Brian E. Forist. *The Hudson: An Illustrated Guide to the Living River.* Rutgers University Press, 1996.

Van Zandt, Roland. *Chronicles of the Hudson: Three Centuries of History and Adventure.* Black Dome Press, 1998.

PHOTOGRAPHY, ART & ARCHITECTURE

Driscoll, John. *All That is Glorious Around Us: Paintings from the Hudson River School.* Ithaca: Cornell University Press.

Dwyer, Michael Middleton, ed. *Great Houses of the Hudson River.* NY: Bullfinch Press/Little Brown & Co., 2001.

Fire & Ice: Treasures from the Photograhic Collection of Frederic Church at Olana. Ithaca: Cornell University Press.

Powell, Earl. *Thomas Cole.* Harry Abrams, 2000.

Randall, Monica. *Phantoms of the Hudson Valley: Glorious Estates of a Lost Era.* Overlook Press, 1995.

Ryan, James Anthony. *Frederic Church's Olana: Architecture and Landscape as Art.* Black Dome Press, 2000.

Yaeger, Bert. *The Hudson River School: American Landscape Artists.* NY: Todtri Publishers.

RECREATION & TRAVEL

Bennell, Paul. *Garden Lover's Guide to the Northeast.* Princeton Architectural Press, 1999.

Bern, Ron, and Manny Luftglass. *Gone Fishin': 100 Best Spots in New York.* Rutgers University Press, 2000.

Fagan, Jack. *Scenes and Walks in the Northern Shawangunks.* New York–New Jersey Trail Conference, 1999.

Ferris, Garry. *Presidential Places: Guide to Historical Sites of U.S. Presidents.* Winston-Salem, NC: John Blair Publishers, 1999.

Harrison, Marina, and Lucy Rosenfeld. *Walks in Welcoming Places.* NY: Michael Kesend Pubishing, 1995.

———. *Walks in the Northeast for Stollers of All Ages and the Disabled.* NY: Michael Kesend Publishing, 1995.

Green, Stella, and H. Neil Zimmerman. *50 Hikes in the Lower Hudson Valley.* Woodstock, VT: Backcountry Guides, 2002.

Perls, Jeffrey. *Paths Along the Hudson: Guide to Walking and Biking.* Rutgers University Press, 1999.

Travelog: The Tour Guide in Your Car. Lower Hudson Valley. Travelog Corp., 2000. CD, audio tape, maps.

———. Mid-Hudson Valley. Travelog Corp., 2000. CD, audio tape, maps.

———. Eastern Catskills. Travelog Corp., 2000. CD, audio tape, maps.

Books You Can Borrow

Dumwell, Frances. *Hudson River Highlands.* Columbia University Press, 1991.

Eastlake, Charles. *Hints on Household Taste: Classic Handbook of Victorian Interior Decoration.* Dover Publishing, 1969.

Eberlain, Harold Donaldson, and Cortland Van Dyke Hubbard. *Historic Houses of the Hudson Valley.* Dover Publishers, 1991.

Glunt, Ruth. *Lighthouses and Legends of the Hudson.* Monroe, NY: Library Research Associates, 1990.

Kovel, Ralph, and Terry Kovel. *Know Your Antiques: An Illustrated Guide to Victorian Treasures.* Crown Publishers, 1990.

Marranca, Bonnie, ed. *Hudson Valley Lives: Writings From 17th Century to Present.* Overlook Press, 1991.

Metropolitan Museum of Art. *American Paradise: World of the Hudson River School.* Harry Abrams, 1988.

Rajs, Jake. *The Hudson River: From Lake Tear of the Clouds to Manhattan.* Monacelli Publishers, 1996.

CLIMATE & SEASONS

The eight counties of the Hudson River Valley region covered in this book run north from New York City for 150 miles, thereby encompassing the full range of weather you might expect from the four seasons. As ever, it's colder and snowier longer the farther north you go, as it is when tucked back in the hills. Here are some average temperatures:

The climate ranges from average January temperatures of 23° (low) and 37° (high) Fahrenheit closer to NYC to 13° and 31° at Albany, and 7–16 inches of snow, respectively. In July, those temperatures reach 69°–84°. Note: April brings an average three inches of snow during its 36°–58° range in Albany, but only one inch and 44°–60° near NYC. Expect 39° and 62° for Albany's October average lows and highs, and 51° and 65° farther south. October and April precipitation averages near three inches in both locales. For information: www.weather.com; www.weatherunderground.com; and http:weather.lycos.com (where we obtained these temperature averages).

ENVIRONMENTAL ORGANIZATIONS

Hard work preserves the Hudson River, designated one of 14 American Heritage Rivers. If you're interested, here are good organizations to contact for more information.

Hudson River Sloop Clearwater, Inc. (914-454-7673; www.clearwater.org; 112 Market St. Poughkeepsie, NY 12601) Education and environmental advocacy organization founded by legendary folk singer Pete Seeger includes the sloop itself (see Chapter Five, *Arts & Pleasures,* under "Hudson Valley Fairs & Festivals" and Chapter Seven, *Recreation,* under "Cruises & Tours").

Riverkeeper Inc. (914-424-4149; 800-21-RIVER; www.riverkeeper.org; 25 Wing & Wing; PO Box 130, Garrison, NY 10524) A Hudson River advocacy group, which takes on such activities as patrolling the river, looking for polluters. The group is not afraid to file lawsuits on the river's behalf. Robert F. Kennedy, Jr., is one of the group's founders and its attorney.

Scenic Hudson River (845-473-4440; www.scenichudson.org; One Civic Center Pl., Ste. 200, Poughkeepsie, NY 12601) Environmental nonprofit organization is focused on land protection along the river, which includes a land trust (separately incorporated).

HANDICAPPED SERVICES

See the section "Tourist Information" for a listing of the region's travel offices to obtain information about disability services for travelers. The *New York State Citizen Guide* (www.nysegov.com) connects users to a range of useful state services, including fishing access and outdoor facilities with handicapped accessible facilities under its tourism resources.

Fabulous Facts

• In 1886, one of the country's first planned — and gated — communities opened in Orange County. Tuxedo Park contained 22 "cottages," two lakes, and a luxurious clubhouse, all ringed by a 24-mile stone fence eight feet high. The wealthy enclave was designed by resident architect Bruce Price, whose daughter Emily described it as "the most formal place in the world."

The special dinner jackets without tails, worn by the men of Tuxedo Park, became known as tuxedo jackets, and Emily Price became better known by her married name, Emily Post. Tuxedo Park is still a private, gated community, adjacent to Harriman State Park.

• The first section of the Appalachian Trail opened in 1923 at Bear Mountain. The trail now runs some 1,000 miles from Maine to Georgia.

• When it opened in 1924, the Bear Mountain Bridge was the longest suspension span in the world. It is 1,632 feet long and cost $4.5 million to build. The Appalachian Trail crosses the Hudson via this bridge.

• The first railroad in America ran between Albany, NY, and Schenectady, NY, a distance of 11 miles.

• The "black dirt" farming area of Orange County is one of the largest onion-producing areas in North America, with more than 14,000 acres of vegetable farms. The dirt was formed from a glacial lake 12,000 years ago, and the region once was known as "the drowned lands."

• Two U.S. Presidents, Franklin Delano Roosevelt and Martin Van Buren, were born in the Hudson Valley, spent most of their lives here, and are buried here. Also Vice-President Nelson Rockefeller and Thomas Jefferson's Vice-President, George Clinton, were lifelong valley residents and also are buried here. Clinton was New York State's first governor; Rockefeller was a four-term governor.

• Washington Irving was the first American writer to gain international reknown for his stories about the Hudson River Valley: "Rip Van Winkle" and

"The Legend of Sleepy Hollow." James Fenimore Cooper, whose *The Last of the Mohicans* and *The Spy*, similarly romanticized the valley and its residents.

• While headquartered in Newburgh, NY, for the last months of the Revolutionary War, General Washington instituted the Badge of Military Merit, the forerunner of the Purple Heart, the Congressional Medal of Honor, and the Legion of Merit. The Continental Army was headquartered nearby in New Windsor, which also was the birthplace of DeWitt Clinton, the New York State Governor who spearheaded construction of the Erie Canal in the early 1800s.

• The 1967 classic movie *Hello Dolly*, starring Barbra Streisand and Walter Matthau, was filmed in and around Garrison, NY. The town's gazebo is prominently featured in the movie.

• In 1896, the second automobile race in the U.S. was from New York City to Irvington-on-Hudson, south of Tarrytown, NY. It was sponsored by the publisher of *Cosmopolitan* magazine.

• Until it closed in 1996, the General Motors plant at Tarrytown, NY, was the company's oldest plant and produced more than 12 million Chevrolet, Pontiac, and Oldsmobile cars and trucks, as well as airplane bomber wings for the military in WWII. The factory was a descendent of a factory that opened there in 1900 to build the Stanley Steamer, a steam-powered "horseless carriage." The riverside factory site is now being converted into housing and open parkland.

• In 1801, two mastodon skeletons were discovered at digs at the Masten farm near Newburgh, NY. Since then, more mastodons have been uncovered in Orange County than anywhere else in the Northeast. It is believed that the rich "black dirt" deposits of the region helped to preserve the bones.

• The stallion Hambletonian, named for the horse-racing village in Yorkshire, England, was owned by an Orange County horseman, William Rysdyk. In his lifetime, from 1849 to 1876, Hambletonian sired more than 1,300 foals. More than 99 percent of today's trotters and pacers in North America trace their pedigrees to this horse.

• Two of the most venerable products in American supermarkets were from the Hudson Valley. The cereal H-O Oats was created at a gristmill in Craigville, NY. In 1917, Emil Frey, inventor of Liederkranz cheese, perfected the process for Velveeta cheese at a factory in Monroe, NY.

• Thomas Edison opened the first generating station of his Edison Electric Illuminating Company on Pearl Street, near Wall Street in Manhattan. In 1884, one of his first generating stations outside Manhattan was in Newburgh, NY.

• Potato chips were invented and first served at Moon's Lake House in Saratoga Springs, NY, in the late 1800s and were originally known as Saratoga chips.

• In 1776, the first Shaker community in America was settled in Albany, NY. The burial site of Ann Lee, founder of the Shaker Movement, is in the Shaker Cemetery there.

HOSPITALS & EMERGENCY MEDICAL SERVICE

WESTCHESTER COUNTY

Hudson Valley Hospital Center (914-737-9000; 914-737-9000 emergency room; www.hvhc.org; 1980 Crompond Rd., Cortlandt).

Phelps Memorial Hospital (914-366-3000; 914-366-3590 emergency room; www.phelpshospital.org; 701 N. Broadway, Sleepy Hollow) Also offers "prompt care" (914-366-3660) from 2pm-11pm, seven days a week, for immediate treatment needs, not life-threatening.

Westchester Medical Center (914-493-7000; 914-493-7307 emergency room; Valhalla) Major medical center includes major trauma center, burn center, and a children's hospital among four specialty facilities. Affiliated with New York Medical College.

DUTCHESS COUNTY

Northern Dutchess Hospital (877-729-2444; 845-876-3001; 845-871-3440 and 845-871-3441 emergency room; www.northerndutchesshospital.com/; 6511 Springbrook Ave., Rhinebeck).

St Francis Hospital (845-483-5000; 845-431-8220 emergency room; www.stfrancishospital.com; 214 North Rd., Poughkeepsie).

Vassar Brothers Medical Center (845-454-8500; 845-454-8500 emergency room; www.vassarbrothers.org; Reade Place, Poughkeepsie).

COLUMBIA COUNTY

Columbia Memorial Hospital (518-828-7601; 518-828-7601, ext. 8500 emergency room; 71 Prospect Ave., Hudson).

ROCKLAND COUNTY

Good Samaritan Hospital (845-368-5000; www.goodsamhosp.org; 255 Lafayette Ave., Suffern, NY) Area level II trauma center and chest pain diagnostic centers in emergency room. Call main number to reach ER.

Nyack Hospital (845-348-2000; 845-348-2345 emergency room; www.Nyackhospital.org; North Midland Ave., Nyack, NY).

ORANGE COUNTY

St Luke's Cornwall Hospital (845-561-4400; 845-561-4400, ext. 2305 emergency room; www.Stlukeshospital.org; 70 DuBois St., Newburgh) Hospital has additional campus (845-534-7711; 19 Laurel Ave., Cornwall).

ULSTER COUNTY

Benedictine Hospital (845-338-2500; 845-338-2500; 845-334-4902 emergency room; www.benedictine.org; 105 Mary's Ave., Kingston).
Emergency One Urgent Care Center (845-338-5600; 40 Hurley Ave., Kingston) Urgent care, but not for major medical emergencies.
Kingston Hospital (845-331-3131; 845-334-2890 emergency room; www.kingston regionalhealth.com; 396 Broadway, Kingston).

ALBANY COUNTY

Albany Memorial Hospital (518-471-3221; 518-471-3111 emergency room; www.nehealth.com; 600 Northern Blvd., Albany).
St. Peter's Hospital (518-525-1550; 518-525-1315 emergency room and cardiac center; www.stpetershealthcare.org; 315 S. Manning Blvd., Albany).

LATE-NIGHT FOOD & FUEL

A s you travel the region's roads, keep an eye out for a couple of chains, often replete with gas stations, which generally are open well into the evening: Cumberland Farms and Stewart's Shops, liberally represented throughout the valley on both sides of the Hudson. Also, there are 24-hour food and fuel facilities at rest stops and exits along the north-south NYS Thruway, I-87. (See the section "Road Service" below for 24-hour towing services.)

DUTCHESS COUNTY

The Eveready Diner (845-229-8100; Rte. 9N, Hyde Park) Located halfway between Poughkeepsie and Rhinebeck. Open Sun.-Thurs. until 2am, Fri., Sat. 24 hours. Visible from Rte. 9.
The Palace Diner (845-473-1576; 194 Washington St., Poughkeepsie) Located in the city's historic district, right off Rte. 9 via the Washington St. exit. Open "round the clock" every day.

ULSTER COUNTY

The College Diner (845-255-5040; 500 Main St., New Paltz) Open 24 hours.
The Plaza Diner (845-255-1030; New Paltz Plaza, Main St. (Rte. 299), New Paltz) Open 24 hours, seven days a week.
Sunoco Gas Station (Rte. 299 at South Putt Rd. (Rte. 299), New Paltz) Located right off NYS Thruway. Open 24 hours.

GREENE COUNTY

Fox Run Park Travel Plaza (518-731-2722; NYS Thruway exit 21B, Coxsackie) Includes gas, Texarado Steak House, Red Carpet Inn, TJ Sports Bar, and truck stop.

MEDIA

MAGAZINES

Hudson Valley Magazine (914-485-7844; www.hudsonvalleymagazine.com; 40 Garden St., Poughkeepsie) Regional monthly magazine.

NEWSPAPERS

Hudson Valley

Albany Times Union (518-454-5694; www.timesunion.com; 645 Albany Shaker Rd., Albany) Daily out of the state capital. Weekend arts and entertainment section called "Preview" is published on Thurs.
The Journal News (914-694-9300; www.nyjournalnews.com; One Gannett Dr., White Plains) Daily covering Westchester, Putnam, and Rockland Counties; the weekly entertainment/what's going on section called "The Line" comes out on Thurs.
The Poughkeepsie Journal (800-765-1120; www.poughkeepsiejournal.com; PO Box 1231, 85 Civic Center Plaza, Poughkeepsie) New York's oldest newspaper covers the Mid-Hudson Valley region. Travelers can check the "Enjoy" section, a pull-out tab published on Fri., to find out what's going on in arts and entertainment.
MidHudsonCentral.com A centralized spot to check out the area's local papers published by the Journal Register Co., including the *Daily Freeman* of Kingston, the *Hyde Park Townsman,* and the *Putnam County Courier.*
Times Herald-Record (845-341-1100; 40 Mulberry St.; PO Box 2046, Middletown) Coverage of the Hudson Valley and Catskills regions; includes a daily arts, lifestyle, and entertainment section called "The Buzz."

New York City

New York Daily News (212-210-2100; www.nydailynews.com; 450 W. 33rd St., New York) Includes weekend entertainment/arts section published on Fri.
New York Post (212-930-8000; www.nypost.com; 1211 Sixth Ave., New York) Includes weekend arts/entertainment section published on Fri.

The New York Times (212-556-1234; www.nytimes.com; 229 W. 43rd St., New York) Includes Fri. "Escapes" section and Sun. arts coverage.

RADIO

Rockland/Westchester:

WFAS-FM 1230, White Plains; News/talk.
WHUD-FM 100.7, Peekskill; Adult contemporary.

Orange/Dutchess/Ulster:

WGNY-AM 1220, Newburgh; News/talk.
WNJP-FM 88.5, National Public Radio.
WCZX-FM 97.3, Poughkeepsie; Oldies.
WRWL-FM 107.3, Poughkeepsie; Country.
WKIP-AM 1450, Poughkeepsie; Talk.
WDST-FM 100.1, Woodstock; Modern rock.

Columbia/Greene:

WCKL-AM 560, Catskill; Standards.
WHUC-AM 1230, Hudson; News.
WRIP-FM 97.9, Windham; Oldies.
WCTW-FM 98.5, Catskill; Light, adult contemporary.

New York City:

Several stations have strong enough signals to carry 100 miles north and more.
WCBS-AM 880; News.
WINS-AM 1010; News.
WFAN-AM 660; Sports talk.
WABC-AM 770; Talk.
ESPN-AM 1050; Sports talk.

TELEVISION

Most of New York City's TV stations reach well into the Hudson Valley.
WCBS-TV Channel 2, CBS
WNBC-TV Channel 4, NBC
WNYW-TV Channel 5, FOX
WABC-TV Channel 7, ABC
WWOR-TV Channel 9

WPIX-TV Channel 11, UPN
WNET-TV Channel 13, PBS

Albany's TV stations serve the northern half of the Hudson Valley.
WRGB-TV Channel 6, CBS
WTEN-TV Channel 10, ABC
WNYT-TV Channel 13, NBC

ROAD SERVICE

Courtesy Tarrytown Castle

Horses and fences are part of the landscape in parts of the Hudson Valley

To contact AAA: **800-AAA-HELP.**

WESTCHESTER COUNTY

Mill Road Service Station and Towing, Inc. (914-793-3355; 430 White Plains Rd., Eastchester) Complete repairs and 24-hour towing.

DUTCHESS COUNTY

Lake Service Station (845-221-2255; 831 Beekman Rd. (at Sylvan Lake Rd.), Beekman) Located two miles east of Taconic Pkwy. Snacks and fuel (fuel until 10pm). 24-hour towing.

Paino's Towing & Recovery Corp (845-297-8686; 1106 Rte. 9 and Smithtown Rd., Wappingers Falls) 24-hour towing.

ULSTER COUNTY

Tom's Repair Shop (845-255-1288; 101 S. Putt Corners Rd., New Paltz) 24-hour towing.

COLUMBIA/GREENE COUNTIES

Dave's Towing Inc. (518-943-5470; 421 Columbia St., Hudson; 518-943-5470; 280 Main St., Catskill) 24-hour towing and full automotive repair.

TOURIST INFORMATION

REGIONAL

Historic Hudson Valley (914-631-8200; www.hudsonvalley.org; 150 White Plains Rd., Tarrytown, NY 10591) Excellent web site for exploring the region from an historic preservation and education organization that operates several of the mansions included in this book.

Hudson Valley Network (www.Hvnet.com) and **Hudson Valley Guide** (www. hudsonvalleyguide.com) are both good places to look for regional information.

New York State (800-CALL-NYS or www.iloveny.com, for travel and lodging information). The **Department of Parks** web site: www.nysparks.state.ny.us.

WESTCHESTER COUNTY

Westchester County Office of Tourism (914-995-8500; 800-833-9282; www. westchesterny.com; 222 Mamaroneck Ave., Ste. 100, White Plains, NY 10605).

PUTNAM COUNTY

Putnam Visitors Bureau (845-225-0381; 800-470-4854; www.visitputnam.org; 110 Old Rte. 6, Bldg. 3, Carmel, NY 10512).

DUTCHESS COUNTY

Dutchess County Tourism Promotion Agency (845-463-4000; 800-445-3131; www.dutchesstourism.com; 3 Neptune Rd., Ste. M-17, Poughkeepsie, NY 12601).

COLUMBIA COUNTY

Columbia County Tourism (518-828-3375; 800-724-1846; www.columbiacounty ny.org; 401 State St., Hudson, NY 12534).

ROCKLAND COUNTY

Rockland County Office of Tourism (800-295-5723; 845-708-7300; www.rock land.org; 8 New Hempstead Rd., New City, NY 10956).

ORANGE COUNTY

Orange County Tourism (845-291-2136; 800-762-8687; www.orangetourism .org; 30 Matthews St., Ste. 111, Goshen, NY 10924).

ULSTER COUNTY

Ulster County Tourism (845-340-3566; 800-DIAL UCO; www.co.ulster.ny.us/ tourism; 244 Fair St., PO Box 1800, Kingston, NY 12402).

GREENE COUNTY

Greene County Tourism and Information Center (518-943-3223; 800-355-CATS; twww.greene-ny.com; PO Box 527, Catskill, NY 12414) Take NYS Thruway, exit 21; the center is to the right.

IF TIME IS SHORT

It's hard to select among the myriad choices awaiting visitors to the Hudson Valley, but here are some suggestions for day trips for those with limited time.

LOWER HUDSON VALLEY

Cold Spring

Wander the historic main street of this sleepy village, which starts at the river and continues on the other side of the MetroNorth-Amtrak train tracks. The four-block main street is lined with interesting shops, galleries, and several fine restaurants. You can walk from town to **Boscobel,** another historic riverfront mansion, or hike one of the trails outside town to a dramatic overlook of **Storm King Mountain.**

Tarrytown

Take NY Waterway on a scenic one-hour cruise from Manhattan to Tarrytown, where a waiting van whisks you to two historic Hudson River mansions: **Philipsburg Manor,** a 17th-century Dutch manor house and farm, demonstrating Colonial crafts and farming; **Kykuit,** the opulent, art-filled, impeccably landscaped estate of three generations of the Rockefeller family. Then prowl the **Sleepy Hollow Cemetery** for the graves of writer Washington Irving and industrialists Walter Chrysler and Andrew Carnegie.

West Point & Bear Mountain State Park

The museum at **West Point** contains one of the world's largest collections of military memorabilia, the grounds are rich with American history, and the view of the Hudson River north from **Trophy Point,** where additional historic weapons are displayed, is beyond beautiful. A few miles away, **Bear Mountain State Park** is one of New York State's most diverse, with pristine lakes, hiking trails, a carousel and demonstration zoo for kids, ice-skating in the winter, and a huge, dramatic log and stone reception building with restaurants and gigantic fireplaces guarded by life-sized, carved wooden bears.

MID-HUDSON VALLEY

Hyde Park

Within a few miles of one another are the presidential library and lifelong home of Franklin Delano Roosevelt, which he called the "summer White

House," **Val-Kill,** the cottage of the "First Lady of the World" Eleanor Roosevelt, and the opulent **Vanderbilt Mansion** — all National Historic Sites. Also in Hyde Park is the **Culinary Institute of America,** where the nation's best chefs are trained. In addition to four gourmet restaurants, the CIA has cooking demonstrations and a gift shop full of kitchen gadgets and cookbooks.

New Paltz

One block from the busy main street is a window to the past, the original **Stone Houses** built by French Huguenots in the 1670s. Outside town is the vast and pristine **Minnewaska State Park Preserve,** which borders the **Mohonk Preserve** and the fairy-tale splendor of the **Mohonk Mountain House,** perched atop a glacial lake. This is also the place to watch rock climbers defying gravity on the sheer granite cliff wall, known as "The Gunks."

Rhinebeck

Antique shops, a selection of fine restaurants, and historic inns, including the **Beekman Arms** — the oldest inn in New York State, built on the intersection of two stagecoach routes in the late 1600s — have made Rhinebeck a tourist mecca.

UPPER HUDSON VALLEY

Hudson

Several dozen antique shops line the main street of this picturesque town, offering a variety of collectibles ranging from baseball memorabilia to museum-quality Shaker furniture.

Hudson River School

The two most famous members of this group of landscape artists were Thomas Cole, its founder, and Frederic Church. Their art-filled homes — Cole's **Cedar Grove** in Catskill and Church's **Olana** south of Hudson — are on opposite sides of the Hudson River, within view of one another at the **Rip Van Winkle Bridge.** Both men had panoramic river views that inspired their romantic landscapes.

Index

LODGING BY PRICE CODE

Price Codes:

Inexpensive	Up to $65
Moderate	$65–$100
Expensive	$100–$175
Very Expensive	$175 and up

COLUMBIA COUNTY

Moderate
St. Charles Hotel, 48

Moderate–Expensive
Hudson City B&B, 47

DUTCHESS COUNTY

Inexpensive
Cottonwood Motel, 42
Porter House, 43

Moderate
Grand Dutchess, 43
Red Hook Inn, 44

Moderate–Expensive
Beekman Arms, 45
Delameter House, 46

Expensive
Bykenhulle House, 40
Inn at the Falls, 43

Le Chambord, 41

Expensive–Very Expensive
Old Drovers Inn, 40

Very Expensive
Bullis Hall, 39
Millbrook Country House, 42
Troutbeck Inn, 38

GREENE COUNTY

Inexpensive
Stewart House B&B, 60
Tumblin' Falls House, 62

RESTAURANTS BY PRICE CODE

RESTAURANTS BY CUISINE

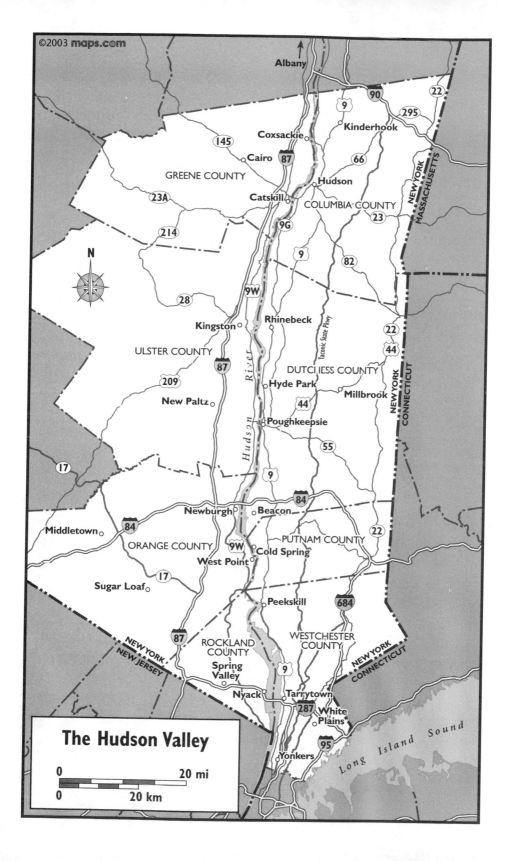

©2003 maps.com

The Hudson Valley

0   20 mi

0   20 km

Albany

90

9

295

22

Kinderhook

Coxsackie

145

66

Cairo

87

Hudson

Catskill

23A

Columbia County

23

9G

9

82

214

9W

28

Rhinebeck

Taconic State Pkwy

Kingston

22

44

Ulster County

87

Dutchess County

209

Hyde Park

Millbrook

New Paltz

44

Poughkeepsie

55

17

9

84

Newburgh

Beacon

Middletown

84

22

Orange County

Putnam County

9W

Cold Spring

West Point

17

Sugar Loaf

Peekskill

684

87

Rockland County

Westchester County

New York / Connecticut

Spring Valley

9

Nyack

Tarrytown

287

White Plains

Yonkers

95

Hudson River

New York / Massachusetts

New York / Connecticut

New York / New Jersey

Long Island Sound

N

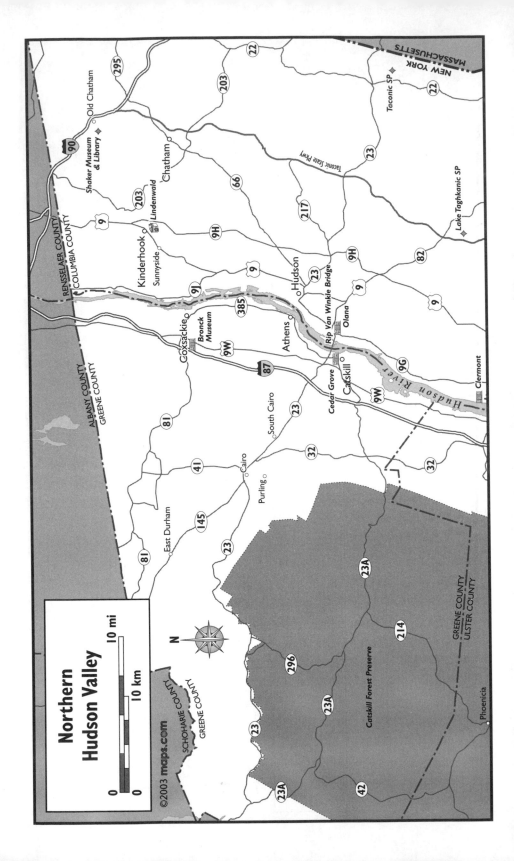

Northern
Hudson Valley

©2003 maps.com

10 mi

10 km

0   0

N

RENSSELAER COUNTY
COLUMBIA COUNTY

ALBANY COUNTY
GREENE COUNTY

SCHOHARIE COUNTY
GREENE COUNTY

GREENE COUNTY
ULSTER COUNTY

NEW YORK
MASSACHUSETTS

Taconic State Pkwy

Hudson River

Catskill Forest Preserve

295

22

203

90

203

9

66

217

22

23

82

9H

9H

9

9

9

9H

9

385

91

9W

87

81

23

32

32

81

41

23

145

23

23A

214

296

23A

23

42

23A

9G

9W

Old Chatham

Shaker Museum
& Library

Chatham

Lindenwald

Kinderhook

Sunnyside

Coxsackie

Bronck
Museum

Athens

Hudson

Rip Van Winkle Bridge

Olana

Cedar Grove

Catskill

Clermont

South Cairo

Cairo

Purling

East Durham

Phoenicia

Taconic SP

Lake Taghkanic SP

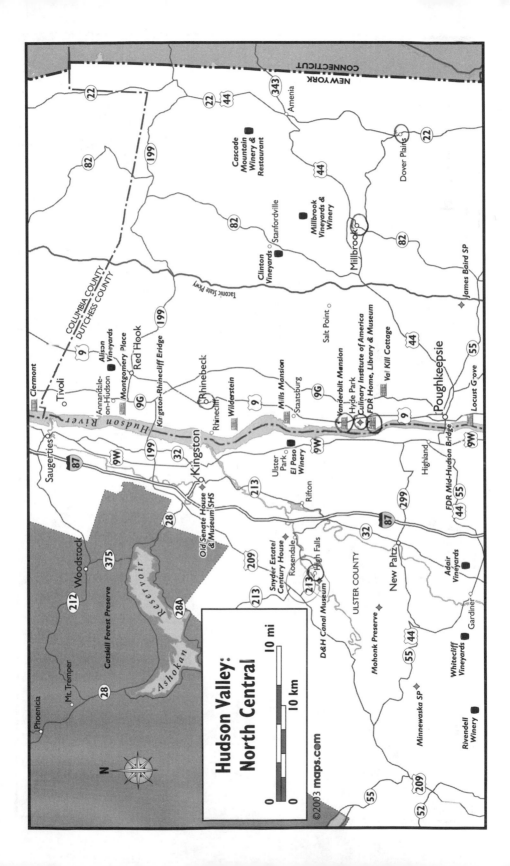

Hudson Valley:
North Central

©2003 maps.com

10 mi
10 km

N

CONNECTICUT
NEW YORK

22
44
22
Amenia
343

Cascade Mountain Winery & Restaurant

44

Dover Plains
22

82
Stanfordville
82

Millbrook Vineyards & Winery

Clinton Vineyards

Millbrook
82

199

82

COLUMBIA COUNTY
DUTCHESS COUNTY

Taconic State Pkwy

James Baird SP

Salt Point

Clermont
Tivoli

9
Alison Vineyards
Montgomery Place
Red Hook
199

Annandale-on-Hudson
9G
Rhinebeck

Kingston-Rhinecliff Bridge
Rhinecliff
Wilderstein
9
Mills Mansion
Staatsburg
9G

Vanderbilt Mansion
Hyde Park
Culinary Institute of America
FDR Home, Library & Museum
Val Kill Cottage
44

Poughkeepsie
55

Hudson River

Saugerties
9W
199
32
Kingston
9W
9
Locust Grove
9W

87

Old Senate House & Museum SHS

Ulster Park
El Paso Winery
213
Rifton

Highland
FDR Mid-Hudson Bridge
44 55

Woodstock
375
28

Reservoir

209
Rosendale
High Falls
213

Snyder Estate/ Century House

D&H Canal Museum

299
32
87

New Paltz

Adair Vineyards

Catskill Forest Preserve
212

28A

Ashokan

ULSTER COUNTY

Mohonk Preserve
55 44

Gardiner

Phoenicia
Mt. Tremper
28

Minnewaska SP

Whitecliff Vineyards

Rivendell Winery

55
209
52

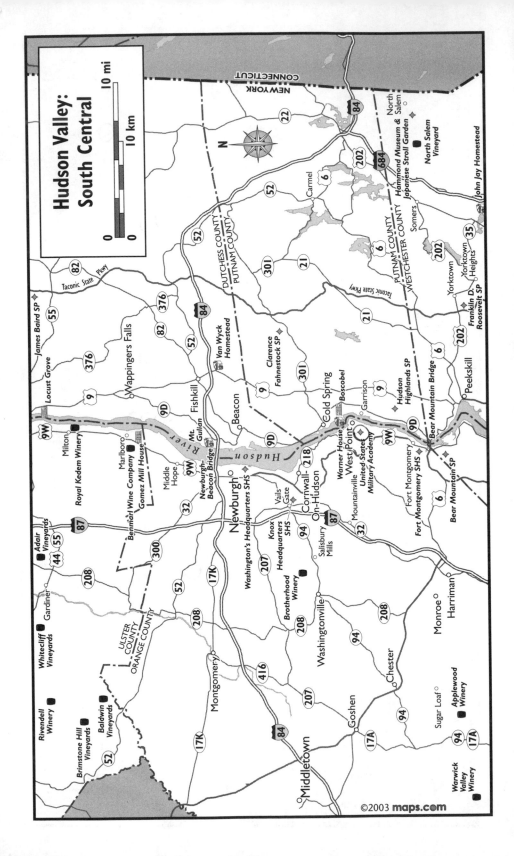

Hudson Valley: South Central

10 mi

10 km

CONNECTICUT

NEW YORK

84

North Salem

Hammond Museum & Japanese Stroll Garden

North Salem Vineyard

John Jay Homestead

202

684

22

N

Carmel

6

Somers

52

WESTCHESTER COUNTY

PUTNAM COUNTY

202

301

21

Yorktown

35

DUTCHESS COUNTY

PUTNAM COUNTY

Franklin D. Roosevelt SP

Yorktown Heights

82

Taconic State Pkwy

James Baird SP

55

376

84

52

Van Wyck Homestead

Clarence Fahnestock SP

Taconic State Pkwy

21

202

Locust Grove

376

82

52

301

6

Peekskill

Wappingers Falls

9

Fishkill

9

Cold Spring

Boscobel

9

Hudson Highlands SP

Bear Mountain Bridge

9W

Milton

9D

Beacon

9D

Garrison

202

Royal Kedem Winery

Mt. Gulian

Hudson River

9W

West Point

9W

9D

Marlboro

Benmarl Wine Company

Gomez Mill House

Newburgh-Beacon Bridge

218

Warner House

United States Military Academy

Fort Montgomery

Bear Mountain SP

Middle Hope

9W

Newburgh

Cornwall-On-Hudson

Mountainville

Fort Montgomery SHS

6

32

Washington's Headquarters SHS

Knox Headquarters SHS

Vails Gate

Adair Vineyards

87

300

Salisbury Mills

87

44

55

Gardiner

207

94

32

208

52

17K

Brotherhood Winery

208

Washingtonville

208

Monroe

Harriman

Whitecliff Vineyards

ULSTER COUNTY

ORANGE COUNTY

208

Montgomery

208

94

Chester

Rivendell Winery

Brimstone Hill Vineyards

Baldwin Vineyards

52

17K

416

207

Goshen

Sugar Loaf

Applewood Winery

84

17A

94

94

17A

Middletown

Warwick Valley Winery

©2003 maps.com

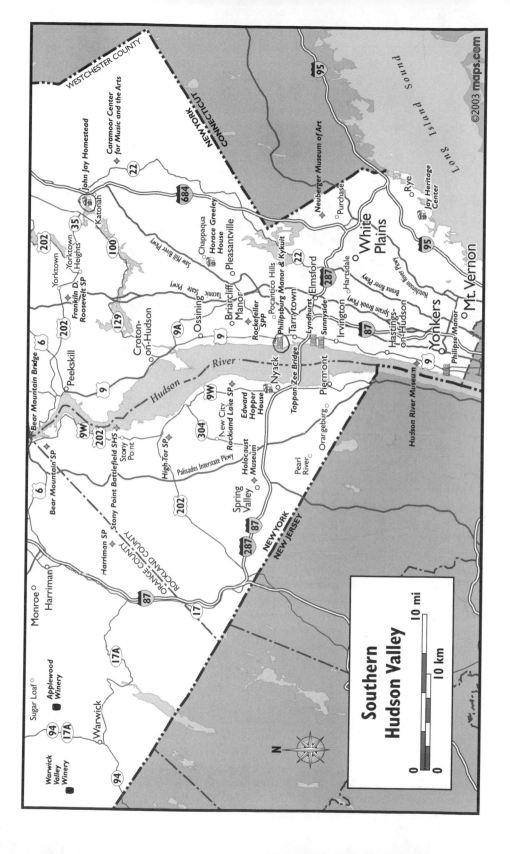

Southern Hudson Valley

©2003 maps.com

About the Author

Yorghos Kontaxis

Longtime journalist Evelyn Kanter has been a news writer, producer, and reporter for The Associated Press, NBC News, CBS Radio and ABC News in New York, including consumer reporter for WABC TV "Eyewitness News." She is a graduate of the University of Missouri School of Journalism, where she majored in broadcasting. Since leaving the world of microphones and video cameras, Evelyn has contributed to numerous travel guidebooks, and to such magazines as *Travel & Leisure, Budget Travel, Skiing, Brides,* and *New York Magazine.* Her articles and photographs have also appeared in the *New York Times, New York Post, New York Daily News,* and other newspapers. An international traveler and avid skier and outdoors enthusiast, she lives and works in New York City.